The Sixties in the News

ALSO BY WILLIAM J. RYCZEK
and from McFarland

Baseball on the Brink: The Crisis of 1968 (2017)

Blackguards and Red Stockings: A History of Baseball's National Association, 1871–1875, Revised Edition (2016)

Connecticut Gridiron: Football Minor Leaguers of the 1960s and 1970s (2014)

Crash of the Titans: The Early Years of the New York Jets and the AFL, rev. ed. (2009)

Baseball's First Inning: A History of the National Pastime Through the Civil War (2009)

The Yankees in the Early 1960s (2008)

The Amazin' Mets, 1962–1969 (2008)

When Johnny Came Sliding Home: The Post–Civil War Baseball Boom, 1865–1870 (1998; paperback 2006)

The Sixties in the News
*How an Era Unfolded
in American Newspapers,
1959–1973*

William J. Ryczek

McFarland & Company, Inc., Publishers
Jefferson, North Carolina

Library of Congress Cataloguing-in-Publication Data

Names: Ryczek, William J., 1953– author.
Title: The sixties in the news : how an era unfolded in American newspapers, 1959–1973 / William J. Ryczek.
Other titles: How an era unfolded in American newspapers, 1959–1973
Description: Jefferson, North Carolina : McFarland & Company, Inc., Publishers, 2021 | Includes bibliographical references and index.
Identifiers: LCCN 2020045393 | ISBN 9781476679860 (paperback : acid free paper) ∞
ISBN 9781476641263 (ebook)
Subjects: LCSH: United States—History—1961–1969. | United States—History—1969– | United States—Politics and government—1961–1963. | United States—Politics and government—1969–1974 | United States—Social conditions—1960–1980. | CYAC: Popular culture—History—20th century.
Classification: LCC E839 .R93 2020 | DDC 973.92—dc23
LC record available at https://lccn.loc.gov/2020045393

British Library cataloguing data are available

ISBN (print) 978-1-4766-7986-0
ISBN (ebook) 978-1-4766-4126-3

© 2021 William J. Ryczek. All rights reserved

No part of this book may be reproduced or transmitted in any form or by any means, electronic or mechanical, including photocopying or recording, or by any information storage and retrieval system, without permission in writing from the publisher.

On the cover: Young "hippie" in front of protest in Chicago 1968 (Library of Congress); young women at the Civil Rights March on Washington, D.C., circa 1963 (National Archives); Vietnam protest in front of the White House, 1971 (Library of Congress); Frank Sinatra, Jr., and Frank Sinatra at the Americana Hotel, 1963 (Photofest)

Printed in the United States of America

McFarland & Company, Inc., Publishers
Box 611, Jefferson, North Carolina 28640
www.mcfarlandpub.com

To Ann
For generations, comedians have had a field day with Mothers-in-Law
But *my* Mother-in-Law, who shares my love of books,
has been nothing but kind, generous, hospitable, and good company
for more than 40 years

Table of Contents

Introduction — 1

1. Thus Spoke Nostradamus: How Well Did Experts Predict the Future? — 5
   Tomorrow's World: 20-Hour Week, Factories Manned by Robots, *New York Herald-Tribune*, October 9, 1961 6 • A Forecast of Economic Growth in the United States, *New York Times*, September 8, 1963 7 • End of Hunger in U.S. in 3 Years Envisioned, *Bridgeport Post-Telegram*, January 1, 1970 9 • College Freshmen Travel in Time, *Hartford Courant*, September 19, 1971 12 • Young Entrepreneur Plans Data College, *Hartford Courant*, February 1, 1972 13

2. Where Are They Now? Figures from the Past — 16
   Reputed Last Civil War Veteran Dies in Texas After Long Illness, *New York Times*, December 20, 1959 16 • Edith Piaf Dead; Cocteau Hears It, Dies, *New York Daily News*, October 12, 1963 19 • Silent Film Star Found Penniless in St. Louis, *Hartford Courant*, February 22, 1964 21 • Alan Freed, Disk Jockey, Dead; Popularized Rock 'n' Roll Music, *New York Times*, January 21, 1965 23 • Father Divine, Cult Leader, Dies; May Have Been 100, *New York Daily News*, September 11, 1965 29 • "Playboy" Manville Dies; Wed 11 Times, *Hartford Courant*, October 9, 1967 33 • James Roosevelt Stabbed During Family Quarrel, *Bridgeport Post and Telegram*, May 16, 1969 39 • Willie Sutton Is Freed After 17 Years in Prison, *New York Times*, December 25, 1969 41 • Untitled, *Hartford Courant*, November 13, 1971 46 • FDR Son Accused of Murder Plot; Elliott Denies It, *Bridgeport Post-Telegram*, September 18, 1973 47

3. Where Were They Then? Those Who Later Became Famous — 52
   Prince's Nip in a Pub May Bring a Caning, *New York Times*, June 20, 1963 52 • Books of the Times; Young Bohemians—Canadian Style, *New York Times*, September 12, 1963 54 • New-Found Stardom Worries Dustin Hoffman, *New York Times*, December 30, 1967 56 • Mitt Romney Marries Ann Davies, *New York Times*, March 22, 1969 57 • Peanut Farmer Wins Democratic Runoff in Georgia, *Bridgeport Post-Telegram*, September 24, 1970 60

4. The Times They Are a Changin': Culture Shock of the 1960s — 63
   2 Professors Lose Bias Suit Appeal, *New York Times*, December 31, 1962 64 • Tough "Hoss" Manucy Has Solution for St. Augustine: Fire Negro Help, *Hartford Courant*, June 30, 1964 66 • Connecticut Boy Loses Appeal to Wear Beatle Bangs to School, *New York Times*, December 16, 1964 69 • "Georgie Porgie"

Sings, *Hartford Courant*, December 9, 1965 72 • 'Rebel Priest' Urges Fellows to Form Labor Union, *Hartford Courant*, February 23, 1966 75 • Meredith Injured While on March, *Hartford Courant*, June 6, 1966 78 • Curves Have Their Day in Park; 500 at a "Fat-in" Call for Obesity, *New York Times*, June 5, 1967 80 • Coed Disciplined by College Becomes Dropout at Barnard, *New York Times*, September 4, 1968 82 • Writer Changes Sex; Will Wed Negro Man, *Bridgeport Post-Telegram*, November 21, 1968 84 • The Name of Model Agency That They Work for Is Ugly, *New York Times*, March 7, 1969 89 • Bishop Pike: A Life Marked by Turmoil and Drama, *New York Times*, September 7, 1969 90 • Young Pair Take Lives as Protest Against the War, *New York Daily News*, October 17, 1969 94 • Sketches of 4 Seized as Bombing Suspects, *New York Times*, November 14, 1969 99 • Young Millionaire Brody's Checks Not Covered by Cash in Bank, *Bridgeport Post-Telegram*, January 19, 1970 106 • Hairy Youths Have Right to Jobless Pay, *Hartford Courant*, May 28, 1970 110 • Vatican Asking All Priests to Affirm Celibacy Yearly, *New York Times*, February 10, 1970 111 • Disappointed, *Hartford Courant*, January 19, 1971 113 • Long Hair is Sign of a Sissy, *Hartford Courant*, May 22, 1973 114

5. Social Issues: Sex and Drugs and Rock and Roll   116
Nudie Films—All the Time Volleyball, *New York Herald Tribune*, Early 1960s, Date Unknown 116 • Growth of Overt Homosexuality in City Provokes Wide Concern, *New York Times*, December 17, 1963 117 • Narcotics a Growing Problem of Affluent Youth, *New York Times*, January 4, 1965 120 • Folk Singer Loses; Shoots Self Dead, *Bridgeport Telegram*, January 28, 1967 122 • Nude Model Placed on Probation, *Bridgeport Post-Telegram*, February 15, 1967 124 • Nude Model Leaves College Voluntarily, *Bridgeport Post-Telegram*, March 23, 1967 125 • Screen: "The Trip" on View at 2 Houses, *New York Times*, August 24, 1967 127 • The See-Through Look, *New York Times*, April 24, 1968 129 • Nudity Moves into Center Stage, *New York Times*, April 25, 1968 130 • Topless Dancer Runs for Stanford Student Body President, *Hartford Courant*, May 1, 1968 131 • Miss Moorman in Football Togs Plays in "Mixed Media Opera," *New York Times*, June 11, 1968 134 • Actresses Talk About Onstage Nudity, *New York Times*, February 17, 1969 135 • Art Linkletter Says Daughter Died on LSD, *New York Daily News*, October 6, 1969 137 • Addict, 12, Found After 3-Day Spree, *New York Times*, January 29, 1970 139 • Ex-Staples Honor Student Nabbed in N.Y. Drug Haul, *Bridgeport Post-Telegram*, May 23, 1970 141 • Gay Liberation, *Hartford Courant*, October 22, 1970 143 • Drill for GI Junkies: A Nauseating Shoot-Up, *Hartford Courant*, November 14, 1970 144 • 73-Year-Old Pot User Asks Legalization of Marijuana, *Hartford Courant*, October 15, 1971 146

6. As Long as We Both Shall Love: The Evolution of Marriage   148
Reno Ranches: Divorce Havens for Rich, *New York Times*, October 28, 1963 149 • Nude Newswoman Covers Wedding in Nudist Camp, *Hartford Courant*, May 11, 1964 151 • Andy Williams Tells How to Stay Married, *Hartford Courant*, February 13, 1967 153 • Broker's Estranged Family Pickets Dad at Exchange, *New York Daily News*, March 30, 1967 155 • Five Women Protest the "Slavery" of Marriage, *New York Times*, September 24, 1969 158 • Fired for Living Out of Wedlock, Clerk Sues, *Middletown Press*, January 7, 1970 160 • Couples Share Rent, Chores (and Sex), *Hartford Courant*, August 2, 1970 161 • "Do Your Own Thing" Concept Starts Marriage "Vibrating," *Hartford Courant*, February 12, 1971 164 • $1 Million in Dispute in Bigamist's Estate, *Bridgeport Post-Telegram*, December 5, 1971 165 • Jane

Table of Contents ix

Fonda, Tom Hayden Wed in Free-Form Rite, *Bridgeport Telegram*, January 22, 1973 168

7. **You've Come a Long Way, Baby: Women in the 1960s**   171
   The Lonely Turn to Public Dances, *New York Times*, November 19, 1963 172 • Women Made to Help Men, *Hartford Courant*, February 16, 1965 174 • Teen Girls Ask Hints on How to Win Boys, *New York Daily News*, Early 1960s, Date Unknown 174 • Dean of Women Handles Male Students' Problems, *Hartford Courant*, June 15, 1965 175 • Meter Girls Have It Maid Again After New Shape-up, *New York Daily News*, September 9, 1965 177 • Most Beautiful By-Line, *Newsday*, September 25, 1965 178 • Bill Allowing Women at Bars Gets Favorable Report from House, *Hartford Courant*, May 23, 1967 180 • Miss Shape, *Hartford Courant*, October 16, 1967 181 • If She's a Doctor or a Lawyer, Men Seem Wary, *New York Times*, June 13, 1969 182 • Svelte Blonde Is a Commercial Pilot, *New York Times*, February 16, 1970 183 • Sophia Loren Kisses off WLM (Women's Liberation Movement), *The Bridgeport Post*, September 25, 1970 185 • Descendant of Grant Scoffs Lib, *Hartford Courant*, October 11, 1970 185 • Liberation Shunned by Women, *Hartford Courant*, February 11, 1971 187 • Gals—Here's Check List; How Do You Measure Up?, *Hartford Courant*, October 19, 1969 189

8. **Mad Dogs and Skyjackers: Crime Keeps Up with the Times**   190
   Blackmailed for Love & 56G by Father of 8 Babies She Slew, *New York Daily News*, October 9, 1962 190 • Had Night Job: Burglary, *New York Daily News*, December 31, 1962 192 • Slaying Ends a Happy Triangle, *New York Daily News*, October 1963 193 • Public Flogging Seems Near an End in Delaware, *New York Times*, February 2, 1964 195 • Sinatra Witness Tells of Plot Tip, *New York Times*, February 25, 1964 198 • Man Sets Up Guillotine to Kill Wife, *The Morning Record* (Meriden, CT), October 14, 1965 202 • 500G Bank Suspect Caught in Vegas, *New York Daily News*, April 1, 1967 203 • Warhol Gravely Wounded in Studio; Actress is Held, *New York Times*, June 4, 1968 205 • Italian Factions Back Minchiello; Extradition Proceedings Started to Gain Custody of Minichiello, *New York Times*, November 3, 1969 209 • Hijacker Tells of Cuban Imprisonment, *New York Times*, November 3, 1969 211 • Cockpit Gun Battle Climaxes $100 Million Skyjack Thriller, *Bridgeport Post-Telegram*, June 5, 1970 215 • Oldest Convict, *Hartford Courant*, October 30, 1970 217 • Police Kill TV Assailant in Toronto, *Hartford Courant*, December 15, 1970 218 • Hijacker Gives Up at Argentine Field, *Hartford Courant*, August 5, 1971 221 • Bingham's Mother Waiting for Word, *Hartford Courant*, August 24, 1971 224 • Texas Ranger Kills Gangster from Bonnie and Clyde Era, *Bridgeport Post-Telegram*, October 15, 1971 229 • Tax Agents Walk Nude in Memphis, *Bridgeport Post-Telegram*, June 16, 1972 230

9. **It's All About the War: Politics in the Vietnam Era**   233
   The Klansman, *Unknown New York Newspaper*, October 16, 1960 233 • Sen. Goldwater Asks: Must Public Subsidize Shirkers, Illegitimacy? *New York Herald Tribune*, Date Unknown 234 • Poverty Program Now Faces Big Test, *New York Times*, August 16, 1964 236 • The U.S. in Vietnam: Why It Is There, *New York Times*, February 12, 1965 240 • Agnew Says "Effete Snobs" Incited War Moratorium, *New York Times*, October 20, 1969 243 • President Proud to Have Agnew in Administration, *New York Times*, October 31, 1969 244 • Text of President Nixon's Address to Nation on U.S. Policy in the War in Vietnam, *New York Times*, November 4, 1969 246 • Agnew Says TV Networks Are Distorting

Table of Contents

the News, *New York Times*, November 14, 1969 251 • 3 Networks Reply to Agnew Attack, *New York Times*, November 14, 1969 252 • Agnew Becomes Duffer for a Day, *New York Times*, February 8, 1970 253 • Brother Takes Role in War, *Bridgeport Post-Telegram*, May 18, 1971 255 • President's Cousin Seeks Help, *Hartford Courant*, June 4, 1971 257

10. **From Panty Raids to Anti-War Protests: Student Unrest**   261
    Negro Students Killed in Riots, *Hartford Courant*, February 9, 1968 261 • Trinity Trustees Captive, *Hartford Courant*, April 23, 1968 263 • Trinity Strike Ends in Accord, *Hartford Courant*, April 25, 1968 265 • Student Anti-War Strike Urged, *Hartford Courant*, April 25, 1968 266 • Wesleyan Thinks Things Over, *Hartford Courant*, April 26, 1968 269 • The Negro Student at an Integrated College: His Problems, Attitudes and Goals, *New York Times*, June 3, 1968 270 • Student Protest Flares in Europe, *New York Times*, June 4, 1968 272 • Teen-Age Revolt: Is It Deeper Today Than in Past Generations?, *New York Times*, October 7, 1968 274 • Student Protest 1969: Less Concerned with War Than with Other Issues, *New York Times*, January 14, 1970 279

11. **It's All About Me**   282
    1,000 Antiwar Demonstrators Block Traffic; 6 Held in Sit-in, *Hartford Courant*, May 13, 1972 282 • Watkin's Glen: "The Ultimate Bummer," *Bridgeport Post-Telegram*, July 30, 1973 285

Bibliography   291

Index   295

Introduction

I've saved you a lot of time. It took me over 35 years to assemble the collection of newspaper clippings that comprise the basis for this book. Over those three and a half decades, I spent thousands of hours hunched over balky microfilm readers in New York City and various Connecticut libraries. Bulbs blew out, paper got jammed, but it was worth all the aggravation because I was able to learn about one of the most remarkable eras in American history.

That wasn't my purpose. I was researching baseball and football and came across these subjects by accident—something that may not happen when utilizing online search engines. Modern research techniques allow you to quickly find what you are looking for, but often with no context. When you scan leisurely through microfilm, you find a lot of things you aren't looking for and sometimes they provide insight to what you *are* looking for. In this case, I learned that the world of sports was greatly influenced by what was going on around it.

This book covers the years from 1959 through 1973—the 1960s, with a prelude and a tail. We are now looking back fifty years at that momentous decade. A nostalgic view may seem inappropriate for such a violent and divisive time, yet the era frames the coming of age of a generation of Baby Boomers, the shaping of their minds, attitudes, and ultimate destiny.

This is not a narrative history of the major event of the 1960s; this is what you would find if you perused the newspapers of the era. There are stories about people you have never heard of, people who belong to another era. The vibe of the 1960s was not created solely by Lyndon Johnson, Abbie Hoffman, and Jimi Hendrix. In order to recapture the feeling of the time, one must read what people were reading every day, information that shaped their view of the world and guided their actions. Much has been written about the Vietnam War and the civil rights movement, but that was not all people thought about. There were other things going on, some of them fascinating.

The United States underwent dramatic change during the 1960s; we were not the same country in 1973 that we were in 1959. The World War II generation was grudgingly yielding to the cresting wave of Baby Boomers, whose attitudes were molded by the escalating conflict in Vietnam, which was very different from their parents' war. There were no villains like Adolf Hitler and Benito Mussolini; and there weren't any Winston Churchills in South Vietnam. It was hard to tell the good guys from the bad guys, and many young Americans preferred Ho Chi Minh to the shady dependents the United States kept propping up in Saigon.

Life for black Americans and women changed significantly in the 1960s, but perhaps the most dramatic advances in civil rights and equality were made by the gay community. In the early 1960s, homosexuality was still considered a psychological disorder, to be treated like any other. The goal was to "correct" the behavior and turn the "sufferer" into a heterosexual. Television shows of the day—even those whose stars prided themselves on their liberal views—were filled with homophobic jokes. The Smothers Brothers, known for their progressive racial and antiwar attitudes, didn't hesitate to make fun of effeminate men or dress men in women's clothes for a gag.

By 1973, women were playing a much greater role in mainstream American life. They took small steps rather than giant leaps, and the presence of a woman in a previously male-dominated field always produced surprise and amusement. It would be a long time before reporters wrote about accomplished women without mentioning their appearance. Reading a 1965 article about Gloria Steinem, titled "Most Beautiful Byline," helps one understand why she became such an ardent feminist. The writer scarcely mentioned her literary attributes because he was so enthralled with her physical ones.

In the early 1960s, the goal of most American women was finding a husband and raising a family. There was a prevalent fear of either becoming an "old maid" or marrying and then getting divorced. Divorces were not easy to obtain, and one of the articles below focuses on a Reno ranch where women stayed to establish residency and obtain a Nevada divorce.

The institution of marriage underwent tremendous changes, beginning with the question of whether it was even necessary. By the late 1960s, respectable couples were living together without getting married. The more adventurous had group marriages, called polyfidelity. Polyfidelity never caught on, perhaps because many participants found that while keeping one partner happy wasn't always easy having multiple partners was not any easier.

Some of the changes to marriage, such as the loosening of defined gender roles, have remained, but most of the more revolutionary forms of matrimony proved short-lived. Jane Fonda married director Roger Vadim in a casino in 1965, radical Tom Hayden in a free-form hippie-dippy ritual in 1973, and billionaire Ted Turner in a lavish, over-the-top ceremony in 1991. The form of the nuptial didn't matter that much; all three unions ended in divorce.

Prominent people of earlier eras made reappearances during the 1960s, sometimes in obituaries. They include a silent film star, sons of a president, and a famous criminal. The adjective normally used to describe criminals is infamous, but Willie Sutton was a popular, well-liked felon. He was a link to the crime wave of the 1930s who re-invented himself as a lovable old man when he was released from prison in 1969. In 1959, a man claiming to be the oldest surviving Civil War veteran died in Texas, at the supposed age of 117. A little research revealed he was a fraud, as was almost everyone claiming to be a Civil War veteran during the 1950s.

Along with people from the past are people from the future. Dustin Hoffman was a young actor collecting unemployment compensation following his first major role and singer and songwriter Leonard Cohen had just published his first novel. Mitt Romney was getting married and Prince Charles was getting in trouble.

Some of the stories described here are more interesting than earth-shaking, but it is impossible to write a book about the 1960s without covering the twin and often related issues of Vietnam and student unrest. As the United States inched deeper and deeper into Vietnam and draft calls and casualty lists grew longer, students rose in anger on college campuses. There were other grievances, but Vietnam was perhaps the most visceral. The left wing wanted the United States out of Southeast Asia and it wasn't long before Lyndon Johnson and then Richard Nixon wanted nothing more than to get out of Vietnam, but it wasn't that easy. A series of articles from the *New York Times* explains how the U.S. wound up in Vietnam, and Nixon's 1969 speech laying out his plan for an eventual end to the war encapsulates his dilemma.

Retrospectively evaluating predictions is always entertaining. During the 1960s, a lot of people were sure they knew what life would be like in the future, and since their future is our past, we know that almost all of them were dead wrong. We have not been made irrelevant by robots, are not living in communes, and have not solved every social problem. The best prediction was that of a young man named Ward Warren, who said in 1972 he believed that someday all of the world's knowledge would be housed on computers we could access from our homes and offices. He also predicted on-line college courses. Despite his power to divine the future, however, Warren did not cash in on his prescience. For most of his career, he made his living producing canned term papers for college students.

Since I was alive during the time period covered by this book, it seemed appropriate to include a couple of incidents that I was personally involved in: a massive rock concert and an antiwar protest march. Looking back with the perspective of more than 45 years of life experience, I thought about why we did what we did and what I think of it decades later.

By simply reprinting the articles, I would have passed on what I learned from the microfilm. But a lot of time has passed since those events transpired, and a lot more information is available, just as Ward Warren predicted. I researched the incidents set forth in the articles and, where possible, provided background and epilogue. Some stories had rather amazing developments, with twists and turns unforeseen at the time.

For many this will be a trip down Memory Lane, for others a view of the 1960s zeitgeist, as reported in the daily paper—the news feed of its day. Time gives us perspective to determine what constituted lasting change and what was just downright silly. Fifty years from now, someone else will look back on the current era with the same sense of perspective, and I guarantee that what we think is happening now and how it will impact the future will appear differently to that generation.

Imagine yourself on the lower level of Wesleyan University's Olin Library on a Saturday afternoon in January. It's warm and cozy and the only things in the room are you, a microfilm reader, and several reels of the *Hartford Courant*. Enjoy your afternoon.

1

Thus Spoke Nostradamus
How Well Did Experts Predict the Future?

Baseball manager Casey Stengel once said, "Never make predictions, especially about the future." Jason Kuznicki of the Cato Institute explained why. "[W]henever anyone tries to predict the future," he wrote, "if they are not predicting the occurrence of a regular or pre-arranged event, the chances are they are probably dead wrong." One of the biggest problems, Kuznicki said, is that prognosticators usually imagine a central authority controlling all activity, whereas events are actually a function of a series of unconnected impulses.

Citing economist F.A Hayak, Kuznicki pointed out that one of the obstacles to accurate prediction is that we do not know how we or anyone else will think in the future. "[W]hat we will think five years hence," he said, "cannot be known to us unless we think it already, because the very act of predicting it means that we somehow have access to that knowledge already."

Guesses that come close are often the result of luck rather than brilliance. Many claim that the legend of the great Nostradamus was based primarily upon inaccurate translations or interpretations of his writings, or a somewhat tenuous connection to actual facts. If Nostradamus needed a little help, how could his descendants hope to do better?

Predicting the future is a perilous exercise. You are the only one who remembers when you were right, and everyone remembers when you were wrong, especially if you were *really* wrong. In the 1960s and early 1970s, there were a number of people who speculated on what life would be like in the 1970s and 1980s. Since it is now 2020, we can go back and see how accurate they were.

Other sources:
Cato's Letter, Fall 2018, Volume 16, Number 4

Tomorrow's World: 20-Hour Week, Factories Manned by Robots

New York Herald-Tribune, October 9, 1961

One of the most persistent beliefs of the early 1960s was that mechanization would almost completely displace humans from the workforce. The only question was whether this was a good thing, giving people more leisure time and a higher standard of living, or whether it would lead to mass unemployment and misery.

Gerald Piel, publisher of *Scientific American* and a member of the famous brewing family (his grandfather founded Piel Brothers Brewery in 1883) wrote a book called *Science in the Cause of Man*, in which he discussed the issue of worker displacement. "Could it be," he asked, "that technological progress has now reached the point where full employment is an unattainable goal?" The country was on the back side of a recession which had increased unemployment to about 7 percent and Piel wondered if this was not a cyclical trend but a permanent change.

Piel believed that measuring employment was an outmoded concept, that the work week would soon shrink to 20 hours, and that we might eventually have a "workless" society. "The subversion of work," he wrote, "which began with the rise of the machine, is now being completed through the disemployment of the human nervous system." The human nervous system was being replaced by robots, which could perform tasks that Piel believed humans could not. He claimed that, in 1961, robots out-numbered human workers and that one "robot" could do the work of many humans. The article was accompanied by a photo of a giant mechanized switchboard used by American Telephone and Telegraph. AT&T estimated that in order to replace the computerized equipment, it would need to employ 120 percent of the country's female labor force (switchboard operator was a female job in 1961).

Many workers who thought they were employed, Piel said, were not really working; they were merely distributing what others had made. "[M]ost Americans," he wrote, "are not engaged in work at all." He estimated that, in 1961, only 25 million people (out of a 70 million labor force) were actually "working." And once computers learned to type, he said, the number would be even fewer.

Unbeknownst to Piel, the greatest reduction in the work week had already taken place. Great Britain maintains statistics dating back to the early 19th century, and in 1833 the average Briton was working 67 hours per week. By 1961, the British work week had declined to 39 hours. By 2016, it had dropped further, but only to 32 hours, nowhere near the 20 hours or the "workless" society Piel envisioned.

Perhaps the difference lies in his definition of work, which Piel believed was limited to manufacturing or any process that produced goods. That had been the historic definition of direct labor, but not having a job that produced goods did not mean that one was unemployed. Many of the jobs that exist today, such as dog walker, personal shopper, and life coach, were unimaginable in 1961. So were most jobs related to computers. Automation has progressed beyond any point Piel could have conceived in 1961, yet many people complain of job-related stress and, thanks to ubiquitous technology, being tied to their jobs 24 hours a day. In some ways, technology has made us work longer, although not physically harder.

Gerald Piel lived until 2004 and was thus able to experience the technology boom firsthand. In 2001, he published a book titled "The Age of Science: What Scientists Learned in the 20th Century" in which he stuck to science and stayed clear of sociological predictions. Piel was better looking backward than forward, for in 2001, no one was talking about a 20-hour work week, and while the thought of robots still causes some people anxious moments, they are most aggravating when we are dealing with the them as consumers. Automation has replaced humans in many fields, but unemployment is lower than it was in 1961. Work, although in a different form, appears to be here to stay.

Other sources:
FRED Economic Data—Federal Reserve Bank of St. Louis
New York Times, September 7, 2004

A Forecast of Economic Growth in the United States

New York Times, September 8, 1963

In 1963, the *Times* printed a forecast, issued by the Center for Economic Projections, of a number of economic indicators for the next decade. Below are their predictions and the actual results.

	Actual 1962	Prediction for 1973	Actual 1973
Private Domestic Investment	$76.6 billion	$140.0 billion	$280.9 billion
Per Capita Personal Income	$2,052	$2,608	$5,372
Civilian Labor Force	71.8 million	87.7 million	90.5 million
Unemployment Rate	5.6%	4.0%	4.6%

	Actual 1962	Prediction for 1973	Actual 1973
Gross National Product	$553.9 billion	$904.9 billion	$1,441.4 billion
Population	186.6 million	226.6 million	211.9 million
Average Work Week	40.5 hours	37.4 hours	38.6 hours

As can be seen above, the economists weren't really close on most of their predictions. One reason was that they underestimated the rate and impact of inflation. From 1958 through 1965, inflation never reached 2 percent in any year. In 1966, it was 3.46 percent, and increased each year before hitting 6.2 percent in 1969. In 1973, it was 8.7 percent. That caused the nominal dollar results to outpace most of the projections.

Other changes likewise escaped the prognosticators. Although the population did not increase to the levels predicted in 1963, women began entering the workforce in greater numbers, causing the labor force to increase to a higher level than predicted and unemployment to likewise exceed the projection.

The common wisdom of the early and mid–1960s, as stated earlier, was that automation would significantly shorten the work week. Many thought it would be much shorter than the economists' projection of 37.4 hours, and that mankind's greatest challenge would be finding meaning in a life with little work and lots of leisure time. Today, technology has reached levels never imagined in 1963, yet the work week has not declined commensurately. If it had, we would hardly be working at all.

The fact that acknowledged experts can be so far off in their predictions provides insight to what F.A. Hayak told us about the difficulty of attempting to foresee the future, even by those who know more about their subject than anyone else. The one change all experts agreed on, the rapidly shrinking work week, did not occur. Predictions by anyone, even experts, are merely educated guesses, and material changes in the environment, whether demographic, economic, technological, or social, can cause results no one could have foreseen by extrapolating current trends. Thus, when we hear that all the experts are certain of what the future will bring, we should be skeptical. Predictions are not science, even when they are produced by scientists. Real life has a way of stubbornly finding its own path.

Other sources:
    ttps://www.bls.gov/opub/mlr/1986/11/art2full.pdf
    FRED Economic Data—Federal Reserve Bank of St. Louis
    http://www.inflation.eu/inflation-rates/united-states/historic-inflation/cpi-inflation-united-states.aspx

End of Hunger in U.S. in 3 Years Envisioned
Bridgeport Post-Telegram, January 1, 1970

What better way to start a new decade than with a 623-page report from The White House Conference on Food, Nutrition and Health setting forth a plan to end hunger in the United States? According to Dr. Jean Mayer, the director of the conference, solving the hunger problem would not be all that hard. "All of us are troubled," said Dr. Mayer, "by the fact that we pay $4 billion not to grow food and we have a hard time to find $5 billion to get rid of hunger."

The plan that emanated from the conference featured three major initiatives. The first was increased government subsidies in the forms of "a liberalized food stamp program, expanded school lunch programs, and a drive to get food stamps and commodity programs in more than 300 counties not participating in the federal assistance efforts."

A second objective was to better measure the results of the existing programs. It was noted that while many initiatives had been launched, there had been minimal effort expended in monitoring their effectiveness.

The third leg of the platform was education. Once people became more aware of nutrition, they would change their diets to include more fruits and vegetables and fewer fatty, non-nutritious foods. "Given the proper tools," Mayer said, "the poor would learn quickly to eat nutritionally but 'it will take a longer period to solve malnutrition among the affluent.'" It was not clear why the affluent were malnourished.

At the time of the report, it was estimated that there were somewhere between 15 and 25 million people who lacked adequate food supplies. One question that must always be asked when an expert says that solving a problem is relatively easy is why it hadn't been solved already. The reason, said President Richard Nixon, was that after the economic boom that followed World War II, people forgot about the problem of hunger. The fact that food shortages could exist in a county as prosperous as the United States, he said, was "embarrassing and intolerable" and he talked of establishing a federal agency to deal with hunger.

The first element of the plan laid out by the White House Conference was to expand the food stamp and school lunch programs. In 1970, when the report was issued, federal benefits paid under the SNAP (food stamp) program were less than one billion dollars. Had they increased at the rate of inflation, benefits would have totaled $6.7 billion in 2016. Instead, they were $67 billion, a ten-fold increase in real dollars. In 1976, approximately 8 percent of the U.S. population received SNAP benefits; five million had been added in 1971 alone. The number of SNAP recipients peaked at about 15 percent of the population in 2013. Administrative costs of the SNAP program have grown in tandem with the benefits, increasing from $400 million in 1976 to $4.4 billion in 2016. Dr. Mayer and her associates could not have hoped for more.

The school lunch program, which was initiated under President Harry Truman in 1946, has expanded to breakfast and in some cases dinner, and many school districts continue to run the programs throughout the summer. In most inner-city areas, the percentage of students who qualify for free lunches is so high that all students are included in the program.

Despite the massive increase in food subsidies, hunger did not disappear, as predicted, within three years. In 1974, one year after the projected end of hunger, *Time* magazine declared that the United States had a "food crisis."

In 2017, there are a plethora of non-profit organizations working to try to eliminate or alleviate hunger. They have differing approaches, but the one thing they agree on is that hunger is a big problem. According to feedamerica.org, 41 million people "struggle with hunger," far more than the 15 to 25 million estimated to be hungry in 1970.

One of the difficulties of measuring hunger is that it is a rather subjective standard, and most of the data consists of self-reporting. In addition to hunger, we now have "food insecurity," defined by the United States Department of Agriculture as "a household-level economic and social condition of limited or uncertain access to adequate food." Hunger, on the other hand, is "an individual-level physiological condition that may result from food insecurity."

Food advocates identify a number of reasons for the large number of hungry people. In *American Wasteland*, Jonathan Bloom claimed that 40 percent of all food produced in the United States is ultimately thrown away. Among other things, he blames unnecessary expiration dates. Robert Egger, the founder of the DC Central Kitchen Campus, blames hunger on the USDA for promoting non-nutritious foods produced by favored companies.

Most of the reasons given for hunger are economic. "Hunger isn't about food," said one advocate. "It's about jobs and wages." Margot Nitschke of the Alliance to End Hunger says, "Hunger is a racial equality issue."

One thing that is rarely mentioned is the third part of Dr. Mayer's strategy, nutrition education, for perhaps the most baffling trend of the 47 years since the White House Conference is an increase in hunger coupled with an even more pronounced rise in obesity. Even stranger is the fact that the highest obesity rates are present in the same demographic that has the highest percentage of hunger. Among African Americans, 48.4 percent are overweight or obese (compared to 36.4 percent of whites) while 21.5 percent of African Americans suffer from hunger (compared to 10 percent of whites). Thus, 70 percent of the black population is either overweight or malnourished. A sarcastic observer might say that if the obese population gave a portion of their food to the hungry, both groups would be in balance.

But it's also likely that some people are counted in both categories—obese and hungry. Common sense is not science, but when a group's two major problems are obesity and hunger, one must ask how that can be.

One of the reasons might be the way in which hunger or "food insecurity" is defined. Part of the Department of Agriculture's definition says that food security is "access by all members [of a family] at all times to enough food for an active, healthy lifestyle." This is a very inclusive definition that may include people who have more than enough to eat most of the time.

A major factor contributing to growing food insecurity is the increase in single parent families. "Once limited to poor women and minorities," said singlemotherguide.com, "single motherhood is now becoming the new 'norm.'" From 1970 to 2016, the number of children living in single parent households increased dramatically from 12 percent to 27 percent.

Among families headed by single mothers, poverty and hunger are also the new norm. The 2016 poverty rate for single mothers was 35.6 percent, compared to a poverty rate of 6.6 percent for married couples. In addition, 31.6 percent of all families headed by a single mother are "food insecure." The large increase in single parent families has undoubtedly hindered efforts to reduce hunger.

Dr. Mayer's 1970 prediction—or perhaps it was a wish—that hunger would be ended in three years didn't come to fruition, despite that fact that the federal government provided even more resources than Mayer ever dreamed was possible. Far more money is spent on food programs today than in 1970, yet the problem is supposedly getting worse. Most proposed solutions are financial although some, like Jonathan Bloom's call to decrease needless waste, would increase the supply of food at virtually no cost. The astronomical growth in the administrative costs of the SNAP program does the opposite, increasing costs without impacting the supply or availability of food. A bloated bureaucracy also provides incentive to make certain the problem is never solved.

Today, few are predicting the end of hunger in the United States. Many are angry about it, many have suggestions to improve the situation, but everyone, even organizations that have ambitious slogans, seems to think that hunger will be with us for a long time. The optimism of the Nixon administration is as long gone as the Nixon administration itself and the non-profits that fight hunger don't anticipate going out of business anytime soon. Chalk up Dr. Mayer as another prognosticator who missed by the proverbial mile.

Other sources:

https://www.theatlantic.com/politics/archive/2016/01/5-things-you-didnt-know-about-hunger-in-america/458757/

http://www.feedingamerica.org/hunger-in-america/hunger-and-poverty-facts.html

https://www.ers.usda.gov/topics/food-nutrition-assistance/food-security-in-the-us/definitions-of-food-security.aspx#ranges
http://time.com/4477157/hunger-america-history/
http://www.trivisonno.com/food-stamps-charts
https://www.niddk.nih.gov/health-information/health-statistics/overweight-obesity
http://alliancetoendhunger.org/hunger-poverty-race-and-the-alliances-racial-equity-project/
https://singlemotherguide.com/single-mother-statistics/
https://www.ojjdp.gov/ojstatbb/population/qa01201.asp?qaDate=2016

College Freshmen Travel in Time
Hartford Courant, September 19, 1971

On Saturday, September 18, 1971, I was in the fourth day of my freshman year at the University of Connecticut, but I was not one of the sixteen incoming students selected to board an imaginary time machine and transport themselves to 1981.

I wish I had been asked to participate, for in those days, freshman orientation consisted of bringing students to campus and leaving them to entertain themselves for five days before classes started. By Saturday, we were immensely bored, and would have settled for a time machine just to take us to Monday morning and our first class.

This survey was very subjective; the students were simply asked to imagine what the world would be like in 1981. They saw it as follows:

"The students thought the powerful institutions would be manufacturing [wrong] and computer [right], the television networks [cable television was coming of age by 1981 and networks were declining in importance] and the federal government [as always], but that the important professions would be social work and education [chalk that up to youthful idealism]."

Curiously, opinion was divided as to whether future governments would be liberal or conservative [this was during the Nixon presidency] and Spiro Agnew and William Buckley were named as the most likely future presidents. Within two years, Agnew would resign the vice presidency in disgrace and Buckley, whose only political race was for mayor of New York City in 1965, never ran for any office again.

As incoming college students, it was perhaps with more hope than prescience that they saw the university of the future as "more humanized" with "meaningless tests and exams abolished." Families would be smaller, with two or three children, but in addition to traditional families, communes would flourish. Life in the communes would be based more on "friendship and convenience" than sex. "Sex will be more personal," said one female student.

Like everyone of that era, the students thought that the typical work week would decline to four days or possibly three. They believed people would have more respect for jobs like street sweeping [not that they wanted to do them] and that traditionally prestigious jobs like law and medicine would be held in less esteem.

Eighteen-year-olds tend to be idealistic, and the UConn Class of 1975 was no exception. "One coed said she would admire 'real' people leading 'real lives.'" On the other hand, when asked about where they expected to be personally in 1981, six of seven in one group saw themselves "living in a suburban or rural setting, married and working in a job they liked." There was no mention of communes, which apparently were for other people.

Since the identities of the students were not revealed, we don't know how many were happily married, employed in compatible jobs, and living in suburbia by 1981. By then, some of them were probably divorced, employed in dead end jobs, or living in their parents' basement. But if one knew what the future held, life would be pretty boring. Do any of us want to know our death date? By 1981, I was married to someone I didn't know in 1971—she was just 14 years old then—and we were living in a city I had never been to in 1971. Predicting the future is a tricky business.

Young Entrepreneur Plans Data College
Hartford Courant, **February 1, 1972**

After presenting so many inaccurate predictions of the future, we'll end with one that was right on the mark. Many of the prior prognosticators were experts in their fields, but perhaps the most accurate prediction I came across was made by 23-year-old Ward Warren, who wasn't acknowledged to be an expert in anything other than the somewhat shady business of providing college students with ghost-written term papers.

"Imagine a college," the article began, "with no books, no papers, no professors. The student sits at the keyboard of a giant computer which is hooked up to a mammoth memory bank containing all the world's knowledge." If you could imagine that, you would have imagined the internet and on-line education, something that seemed fantastic in 1972, when computers were huge mainframe monstrosities operated by stacks of punch cards.

"Eventually," said Warren's associate Jim Crawford, "we want to computerize everything. All the written materials in the biggest libraries in the country will be put into a computer." "Tuition would be cut in half," Warren said of his prospective university, "so members of minority groups, anyone can get knowledge. And I consider knowledge the key to the future of mankind." He also noted that, since no one would have to spend time going to libraries to look things up "People will have more time for other creative activities." Like texting cute pictures of their cats.

"Very soon," Warren said, "anyone can pick up any documents in any city in the nation by means of a giant network of Xerox telecopiers. The document can be transmitted in five minutes from anywhere to anywhere."

Warren, a recent graduate of Babson College and the son of a professor, was a tall, solidly built, good-looking young man with longish but neat hair and a dark mustache. His speaking delivery was as logical as his mind, his words pouring forth in a series of numbered points laced with clear logic.

Warren said he expected to have his computerized school in operation by 1975 or 1976. He didn't, and I could find no record of his ever starting an on-line university; his energy was primarily devoted to Termpapers Unlimited, which he founded in 1970 with his older brother Kenneth. For a fee as low as $2.50 per page, TPU supplied students with scholarly term papers that it billed as research aids. The price of masters or doctoral theses was negotiated on an individual basis. Warren claimed to have earned $1.8 million selling papers in 1971 and called himself "probably the youngest self-made millionaire in the country."

Selling papers or dissertations as finished products would be aiding and abetting cheating, which Warren insisted he was not doing. The papers were sent as photocopies, he said, and students had to re-type them. Perhaps, while doing so, they might add some of their own ideas. Or, freed from the drudgery of producing term papers, they might engage in some real learning. "Look," Warren said, "all these companies do is sell students term papers. It's up to the student to decide what to do with a paper, and we can't police every student." Of course, why would a student purchase a paper other than to submit it? And if everything was so above-board, why was it necessary to keep the customer lists confidential?

The papers were written by moonlighting graduate students, teachers, and other educated, underemployed scholars. All were college grads, and most held master's degrees or doctorates. They earned $2–4 per page and most were happy to have the work. An ambitious researcher and writer could earn $3–400 a week, at a time when college graduates with a business degree might hope for a starting weekly salary of $200.

Termpapers Unlimited was well-organized and tracked the papers it sold to make certain that duplicates were not submitted to the same professor. On one occasion, however, a student lied about the identity of his school, and a Harvard history professor received two identical papers on Benjamin Disraeli. Apparently, contrary to Ward's supposition, nothing had been changed in the re-typing.

On another occasion, the same paper was submitted to three different professors at the same school. Two gave it an A and one gave it a C, branding it "too polysyllabic." One student brazenly submitted a purchased paper titled "Why I Wouldn't Use a Professional Term Paper Writing Service."

Warren was under constant scrutiny and eventually legislation was introduced in a number of states that prohibited the sale of academic papers. Still, there were enough non-regulated states to allow Warren to maintain a thriving business. His success encouraged competition, including the cleverly named Planned Paperhood and Quality Bull.

Although legislators attempted to rein in the paper-for-hire companies, they continued to operate, eventually moving onto the internet. In 2001, there was a company called 1st Term Paper, operating under a domain name registered to a gentleman named Ward Warren. It was not the university he'd prophesied, but much of what he'd foreseen in 1972, as fantastic as it had seemed, had come to fruition without his help. Although he was a high profile, self-proclaimed millionaire in 1972, Warren has cruised below the radar ever since, and very little can be found about his recent activity. Still, of all the prophecies set forth above, Ward Warren must be recognized as the closest to the Nostradamus of legend.

Other sources:
Oakland Tribune, January 24, 1972
The Argus, February 29, 1972
The Harvard Crimson, May 20, 1971

2

Where Are They Now?

Figures from the Past

"Where are they now?" is often asked about former celebrities. If you were reading the newspapers during the 1960s, you would have learned, often through an obituary, about a number of people who'd been out of the public eye for some time. There were aging criminals from the lawless 1930s like Willie Sutton, silent film stars like Mae Murray, and a man who claimed to be the last living Civil War veteran. Some people, like the Roosevelt brothers, didn't just reappear; they created fresh news. Below are stories of people familiar to Baby Boomers' parents, not so familiar to the Boomers, and almost completely forgotten today. We bring them back one more time.

Reputed Last Civil War Veteran Dies in Texas After Long Illness

New York Times, December 20, 1959

The fighting part of the Civil War ended in 1865, but for many Union and Confederate veterans, the war never ended. For decades afterward, they held reunions, talked about old times, argued about strategy, and maintained friendships forged in the heat of battle. For most of them, it was the defining experience of their lives. People weren't very mobile in the 19th century, and many soldiers saw more of the country during their few years of military service than they saw during the rest of their lives.

In 1866, Union veterans formed the Grand Army of the Republic, which at its peak boasted more than 400,000 members. In 1889, veterans of the Confederate Army established the United Confederate Veterans, which maintained a robust membership into the early 20th century, when the old soldiers began to die off. The UCV published a regular magazine, *Confederate Veteran*, and held annual rallies; the final UCV rally took place in 1951 in Norfolk, Virginia, and was attended by three veterans. That was down from the four men (whose average age was 100.5) who attended two years earlier in Little Rock.

One of the 1949 attendees, Thomas E. Riddle of Wichita Falls, Texas, was unmasked as an imposter who was born in 1862 and would thus have been only three years old when the war ended. Two others were potential frauds, leaving James W. Moore as the only one of the four "veterans" whose service record could be verified.

As the distance from Appomattox increased and the number of witnesses declined, the claims of many alleged veterans became more difficult to prove. But people were loath to cast aspersions on the valor of those who said they'd fought in the conflict, and when Walter Washington Williams died on December 19, 1959, claiming to be the last surviving Confederate veteran, his passing was accompanied by considerable pomp and circumstance.

Williams, who said he was 117 years old on his last birthday, died at his Houston home after a fourth attack of pneumonia. Lyndon Johnson, then Majority Leader of the Senate, said that Williams' death "seals the door on a great but tragic era." Texas Governor Price Daniel, using the words of Stonewall Jackson, said, "General Williams (In 1954, Williams had been made an honorary colonel in the United States Army and the Governor of Texas had gone one better, naming him an honorary brigadier general) has 'passed over the river to rest in the shade of the trees' with the hundreds of thousands of soldiers in blue and gray who went before him."

Ulysses Grant III, chairman of the Civil War Centennial, called for a national day of mourning in honor of Williams' death. Soldiers from the Fourth Army at nearby Fort Hood escorted Williams' body to the South Main Baptist Church and he was buried with full military honors in Mount Pleasant Cemetery. A large plaque was erected on the site that described Williams as "reputed to have been the last surviving soldier of the Civil War."

Walter Williams, by the time he died, was a wisp of a man who weighed just about 100 pounds. His sight and hearing were nearly gone, his mind was cloudy, and he was extremely frail. Yet seven months before his death, Williams had taken part in Houston's Armed Forces Day parade, riding in an ambulance and managing a feeble salute for the crowd.

There wasn't a lot of independent documentation of Williams' early life and reporters relied on him to provide the details. He said he'd been born in Mississippi in 1842, enlisted in the Confederate Fifth Cavalry in 1864, and served as a foragemaster under General John Hood until the end of the conflict. "That meant I got the grub for the others," he said, adding that the only thing he shot during his service was cattle.

Williams said that after the war he moved to Texas, where he was a cattle rancher and hunter, claiming to be a prolific deer hunter who didn't give up the sport until he was 107. His grandchildren said he was one of the last cattle drivers along the old Chisholm Trail.

Much of what Williams and his family said, however, had to be taken with several grains of salt. The National Archives, which maintains the most comprehensive catalogue of Civil War veterans, had no record of his service, but that was not definitive, for in 1959 there were many gaps in the Archive records. The Confederate Army was particularly negligent in its record-keeping during the final year of the war, when soldiers were deserting frequently and the army was in total disarray. Not having a record in the National Archives did not make Walter Williams a liar. In fact, an archive in Jackson, Mississippi did contain a record of Private Walter Williams of the Fifth Cavalry.

More than three months before Williams' death, Lowell K. Bridwell wrote a syndicated article casting serious doubt that Williams had fought in the Civil War. His birth record from Itawamba County, Mississippi, had long since been destroyed, so Bridwell used census records to track Williams. He found an 1860 census that listed Walter Williams as five years old, and a Texas census record from 1870 that showed him to be 15. That was consistent with Williams' claim that he had moved to Texas after the war. But if that was the correct Walter Williams, he had been ten years old when the war ended. Bridwell concluded that Williams was "a Confederate veteran only in his memory clouded mind."

If Walter Williams hadn't fought—or foraged—in the Civil War, who was the true last survivor? John Salling, who'd died in March 1959, had for years been hailed as Virginia's last surviving Confederate.

In 1933, Salling applied for a pension, stating on his application that he had been born in 1846, had been a member of Company B of the 25th Virginia Regiment, and had been assigned to work in the saltpeter factories of Richmond during most of his war service. The pension office checked the Virginia State Library, the primary source for military records, but was unable to find any record of Salling's service. By 1933, the state wasn't getting a lot of applications for Civil War pensions and decided to approve Salling's application based upon his sworn statement that he had served. Two years after Salling died, at the reported age of 112, a memorial plaque was placed at his gravesite indicating that he was "Virginia's Last Confederate Veteran."

In 1991, historian William Marvel wrote an article in *Blue and Gray* magazine called *The Great Imposters*. He found records indicating that Salling was born in 1858 rather than 1846, which would have made him too young to serve in the war, and a mere 100 when he died. Perhaps someone should have checked on what the Confederate Army fed its soldiers, for if the "last survivors" were to be believed, they seemed to have remarkable longevity. Williams said he was 117 and Salling claimed to be 112, at a time when the life expectancy for American males was 67.

Marvel also de-bunked the claims of many other long-lived "veterans," most of whom lied about their service to claim veterans' pensions when they fell on hard times during the Great Depression. His research showed that the last legitimate surviving Union veteran was Albert Woolson, who died August 2, 1956. Woolson, however, was a drummer who saw no combat. The last combat veteran to die on the Union side was James Albert Hard, who died March 12, 1953.

The oldest surviving Confederate soldier whose record could be verified by Marvel was Pleasant Riggs Crump, who died December 31, 1951, at the age of 104. Later research showed that there may have been veterans who survived Crump, but the records are inconclusive.

Marvel's research came more than three decades after Walter Williams died thinking that people believed his claim to be the last living Confederate veteran. While he was not the oldest surviving veteran, he was the last person *claiming* to be a Civil War veteran. Lyndon Johnson said that Williams' death sealed the door on an era, and it did, the era of falsely claiming to be a Confederate veteran. The next war was the Spanish-American War, and by that time military record-keeping had become much more precise. When the end of the 20th century came along, there were no men claiming to be 120-year-olds who had ridden up San Juan Hill with Teddy Roosevelt. Walter Williams was indeed the last of an era.

Other sources:
http://www.civilwarhome.com/grandarmyofrepublic.html
https://en.wikipedia.org/wiki/United_Confederate_Veterans
https://news.google.com/newspapers?id=Z1crAAAAIBAJ&sjid=8JwFAAAAIBAJ&pg=6005,512182&dq=walter+williams+last+civil+war+veteran+national+archives&hl=en
http://www.encyclopediaofarkansas.net/encyclopedia/entry-detail.aspx?entryID=7916
http://www.virginiamemory.com/blogs/out_of_the_box/2010/10/06/generaljohn-salling-virginias-last-confederate-veteran/

Edith Piaf Dead; Cocteau Hears It, Dies

New York Daily News, October 12, 1963

Edith Piaf and Jean Cocteau were both French. They were both renowned for their artistic talent and by the end of the day on October 11, 1963, they were both dead. Piaf was the first to go, and when Cocteau was informed of her death the previous day, he said, "I have had a temperature since early this morning, and I must say that the death of Edith Piaf has given me new breathing pains." Soon afterward, he died.

Piaf was not just a great singer; she had a story. The daughter of an acrobat and a singer, Piaf was supposedly named after Edith Cavell, the

British nurse who was executed for aiding the escape of French soldiers in World War I. She was brought up by her grandmother in a brothel and lost her sight as a young girl. After four years of blindness, the prostitutes from her grandmother's establishment financed a pilgrimage to the Cathedral of St. Therese of Misieux, after which Piaf miraculously regained her sight.

Blessed with her sight as well as a magnificent voice, Piaf, known as "The Little Sparrow," went from singing on the streets with her father to international stardom. But her personal life was filled with tragedy. She had a daughter at 17, but showed little interest in parenting. After the girl's father took custody of her, she died at the age of two. A theater owner who first "discovered" the young singer was murdered in a gangland killing in which Edith was initially suspected of being an accomplice. It was at that time she changed her name to Piaf to avoid the scandalous implications of the murder.

In 1947, her lover, former middleweight boxing champion Marcel Cerdan, was killed in a plane crash. At the time of her death, Piaf was married to 27-year-old Theo Sharpe, her former hairdresser who had aspirations of becoming a singer. It was common in those days for older men to marry younger women, but for a 47-year-old woman to marry a man 20 years her junior was scandalous.

Following a serious auto accident, Piaf became dependent on morphine and alcohol, addictions from which she never really recovered, and which contributed to her early death. She had been in poor health for several years and a series of further automobile accidents accelerated her decline. By 1962, she was down to 66 pounds. Although she could barely function, Piaf continued to sing, but her last performances were sad caricatures of her earlier work. When she died on October 10, 1963, from liver cancer, her last words were, "Every damn thing you do in this life, you have to pay for." Piaf's talent and sad life provided the inspiration for a 2007 Academy Award winning film called *La Vie en rose*, after one of her most famous songs.

Jean Cocteau had to become a successful artist without the benefit of an impoverished youth. His father was a wealthy attorney, allowing Cocteau the freedom to become an *avant-garde* poet without worrying about the necessity of earning a living. Although his father committed suicide when Cocteau was nine, his mother was able to maintain the family's upper-class lifestyle.

Cocteau began writing while still in his teens and soon became an admired poet, playwright, and author. During World War I he served as an ambulance driver in the French Army and after the war ended, he resumed his writing career and developed a serious addition to opium.

As a young man, Cocteau carried on an affair with a Russian princess, but soon he began having relationships with older, well-connected men. For the rest of his life, his physical relationships were almost exclusively homosexual. As the years went on, he stopped seeing older men and began romancing young, attractive ones. The love of his life was an actor named Jean Marais, a magnificently handsome and well-built physical specimen who was 24 years younger than Cocteau.

When he began his affair with Marais, Cocteau beat his opium habit. In 1929, the same year he was cured, he produced perhaps his most famous work, *Les Enfants Terrible*. Cocteau began writing movie roles for Marais and, according to one source, "Cocteau and Marais soon became the most notorious couple in Paris."

During the German occupation of France during the Second World War, it was very dangerous to be an open homosexual in Paris. Cocteau had protectors, but Marais got into a dispute with a critic, who denounced him to the Nazis. One of Cocteau's friends was German sculptor Arno Breker, who was close to Hitler. He'd told Cocteau to come to him if he needed help, and the writer used his connection to see that Marais was spared.

After the war, Cocteau worked extensively in film, often with Marais. Like Piaf, he was in a sense, famous just for being Jean Cocteau. Also like Piaf, his health had become fragile by 1963. The breathing pains he felt after hearing of Piaf's death were the onset of a heart attack, to which Cocteau succumbed at the age of 74.

Jean Marais continued to act, appearing in his final film in 1996. He died two years later at the age of 84. Although he had other relationships, he remained close to Cocteau until the latter's death and later wrote a memoir of him.

Piaf and Cocteau were part of the same artistic community and she appeared in his one act play *Le Bel Indifferent* in 1940. Twenty-three years later, they were linked once more when the two legends of the French world of arts and letters died within hours of each other.

Other sources:
   https://en.wikipedia.org/wiki/%C3%89dith_Piaf
   New York Times, January 29, 2004.
   https://en.wikipedia.org/wiki/Jean_Cocteau
   https://www.britannica.com/biography/Jean-Cocteau
   http://www.homohistory.com/2012/09/jean-cocteau-and-jean-marais-first.html
   The Independent, November 10, 1998

Silent Film Star Found Penniless in St. Louis
Hartford Courant, February 22, 1964

Marie Adrienne Koenig was born in New York City in 1885 and by the time she was 21, she was dancing on the Broadway stage under the name

Mae Murray. Mae joined the famous Ziegfeld chorus line two years later; by 1915 she was one of its top attractions.

Shortly afterward, Murray began acting in motion pictures and soon became a star. In 1919, she played opposite Rudolph Valentino in *The Delicious Little Devil* and eventually she married producer Robert Z. Leonard and formed her own production company. Her most famous role was in Erich Von Stroheim's *The Merry Widow* in 1925. Murray and Leonard lived in a flashy Italian Revival style mansion in Hollywood Hills and she spent money with little thought that it wouldn't keep rolling in forever.

Mae wasn't a great actress; she relied on her good looks (she was known as "the girl with the bee sting lips"), her costumes, and a very emotional persona. She was supposedly the model for Norma Desmond (played by Gloria Swanson) in the Billy Wilder movie *Sunset Boulevard*. Mae had a sultry look; her sensuous lips (which almost looked as though they'd been surgically enhanced) were always accentuated by bright red lipstick. It was the early days of the movies, and theatergoers were so thrilled by the sight of moving images on the screen that they were very forgiving of a lack of acting technique.

Talking films were Murray's undoing. She made her first talkie in 1931 (*Peacock Alley*) and it was a bomb. Her lack of acting ability was highlighted when she had to recite dialogue and her career went rapidly downhill. She might have survived but for the bad advice of her fourth husband, David Mdivani. David was one of three handsome Russian brothers who invented titles for themselves and came to America looking to make their fortune through marriage. His brothers Serge and Alexis married famous actress Pola Negri and heiress Barbara Hutton, respectively, while David wed the fading Mae Murray in 1926.

On David's advice, Mae walked out on her MGM contract, incurring the powerful ire of Louis B. Mayer, who was a bad person to antagonize. He made sure that Murray found little work in Hollywood and her career essentially ended. Her last film appearance was in 1931 and by 1934 she was bankrupt and divorced, as David went in search of a more promising meal ticket.

In 1936, Murray was arrested for vagrancy when she was found sleeping (wrapped in one of her old fur coats) on a park bench in New York City. Friends helped her get back on her feet, and the remainder of Murray's career consisted of appearing in nostalgic reviews, lying about her age and wearing layers of makeup and outfits that made her appear even older. By the 1960s, she was not working at all, and appeared in the news for the first time in many years when she was found on the streets of St. Louis in a somewhat disoriented state.

St. Louis police brought Murray to the Salvation Army shelter. She gave her age as 65, although she was actually 79. Murray told the police she thought she was in New York, where she had intended to go to interest someone in publishing her biography. Since a biography had already been written in 1955, that was an unlikely prospect.

The *Hartford Courant* article about Murray was illustrated with two photos, one from 1930 and the second the day she was found in St. Louis. In the 1964 photo, she was as heavily made up as ever and was wearing a black dress, coat, gloves, stockings, and what appears to be a blond wig under a large hat. "She is the picture of a perfect lady," said Salvation Army Captain Fred Major. "She looks very dignified." Captain Major paid her $13.20 hotel bill and tried to figure out what to do with her.

The Motion Pictures Relief Fund in Hollywood said they would have friends meet her and bring her back to her apartment at the Motion Picture House in Woodland Hills, California. Her son, Daniel Cunning, the offspring of Murray and Mdivani who ran a shoe business in Troy, New York, said he would provide his mother with whatever help she needed.

Murray was returned to Woodland Hills, where she died about a year later, on March 23, 1965. In 2016, her Hollywood Hills mansion was placed on the market for $1,749,000. The front walk still consisted of a trail of heart-shaped stones supposedly given to Murray by one of her lovers.

Other sources:
https://en.wikipedia.org/wiki/Mae_Murray
http://www.imdb.com/name/nm0615141/bio?ref_=nm_ov_bio_sm
http://www.queensofvintage.com/the-rise-and-fall-of-mae-murray/
Los Angeles Times, September 22, 2016

Alan Freed, Disk Jockey, Dead; Popularized Rock 'n' Roll Music

New York Times, January 21, 1965

In the late 1950s, Dick Clark and Alan Freed hosted rock and roll dance shows on television. Clark, an up and comer who took over *American Bandstand* as a 26-year-old in 1956, was trying to make a name for himself, while Freed was already the most famous disk jockey of his era. By 1965, Freed was dead, and the ageless Clark was in the midst of a career that would make him a show business legend. Each flirted with scandal and Freed, a brash iconoclastic pioneer, was ruined while Clark, a non-controversial, business-savvy follower, survived and prospered.

Freed was just 43 when he died and like an athlete who peaked at a young age, his downfall was tragic, and his final years were pathetic. At the time of his death he was broke, sick, alcoholic, on his third marriage, and the fans who had worshipped him a decade earlier had abandoned him.

Rock and roll is still with us, but the man who claimed he gave the genre its name, and who was the catalyst in its rise to popularity, was gone.

A native of Johnstown, Pennsylvania, Freed grew up in Salem, Ohio, son of a clothing store clerk who was also a musician. In high school, Alan played trombone in the school band and fronted a group called the Sultans of Swing, named after the famous Harlem ensemble. After studying mechanical engineering at Ohio State University, he joined the Army in September 1940 but was discharged just eight months later due to sinusitis and problems with his legs and feet.

Freed had taken some speech courses at Ohio State, and after he left the Army, he found a job at WKST, a classical music station in New Castle, Pennsylvania, earning $17 a week. He was at the station only four months, but one evening he was pressed into duty as a disk jockey, discovered he liked it, and found he had an aptitude for the job. Over the next few years, like most young men starting out in radio, Freed did a little of everything. He handled some World War II news broadcasts, did a little high school basketball, and acquired a reputation as a nervous, often irritable man who could be difficult to get along with.

By 1946, the 25-year-old Freed was doing a studio show on WAKR in Akron, Ohio, called Request Review. He took requests, ad-libbed, and established a rapport with the studio audience. When that show was canceled, he got an evening spot called Wax Works. By 1948, reporters were calling him "hip" and said he appealed to young audiences. On the air, Freed read poems, told stories, and initiated his trademark habit of beating rhythm to the music with his palm.

Two years later, Freed was at WJW in Cleveland, where he became a national figure. He championed a form of rhythm and blues he called rock and roll, which had African American origins and was unfamiliar to most white Americans. The new music form was controversial, and Freed claimed that many of the people opposed to it were racist. The White Citizens Council of Birmingham, Alabama, denounced rock music and urged that it be banned. "Not a word was raised against it," Freed said, "until I drew 80,000 persons—almost all Negroes—to the Cleveland Arena [for a rock and roll stage show]."

The crowd at the Cleveland Arena for the Moon Dog Ball on March 21, 1952, was probably closer to 25,000 or 30,000, but the capacity of the arena was only 10,000 and there were so many erstwhile gate crashers that the dance had to be stopped. There was no room for dancing and a cacophony of crowd noise drowned out the music. When the dancers left the arena, the floor was littered with broken whisky bottles, there was a least one stabbing, and Freed admitted that the idea had been a mistake. Some called it the first rock and roll concert, but if so, it was a bad example. Afterwards, Freed was sued for $50,000 by a group called the Orioles, who said he used their name to promote the event when they had never been contracted to appear.

Although many disliked rock and roll due to its racial origins, Freed also drew fire from the other side of the political spectrum, as he was accused of what is now referred to as "cultural appropriation," trying to exploit a musical form that many blacks thought belonged to them.

In 1954, Freed went to New York, the country's largest radio market. At WINS, he called himself "King of the Moon Doggers," but even that enmeshed him in controversy. First, WJW claimed it held the rights to the Moon Dog appellation. Freed therefore changed from *The Moondog Show* to *The Alan Freed Show* and began to refer to himself as "King of the Rock and Rollers."

His troubles weren't over, however. A blind New York poet/songwriter named Louis Hardin, who frequented the Times Square area, claimed that he had been known as Moondog for many years. Hardin eventually sued Freed and won a $6,000 judgment for his illegal use of his name.

Despite his tribulations, or perhaps because of the notoriety they brought, Freed established a sizable, loyal following. He was playing music few others were playing and he was a formidable personality, challenging authority and becoming a hero to many rebellious youths. It was estimated that he had more than 2,000 fan clubs and received 10,000–15,000 letters per week. Most rock and roll fans were high school students and Freed cultivated the teen age market, creating an "us against the world" mentality. Teenagers were treated unfairly, he told them, and they were more than willing to believe him. After discussing a public comment regarding troublesome teens, Freed told his listeners, in an outraged tone, "Since when is it a crime to be a teenager?"

It is difficult in retrospect to realize just how controversial music that now seems so tame was in the mid–'50s. Most songs were about innocent love, and Freed's shows contained dedications for birthdays, to loved ones, and featured messages like, "To Carol, I'll always love you" and "Marcie, please give me another chance." It was all quite innocent, and while many claimed rock and roll led to juvenile delinquency, song titles like *To Know Him is to Love Him*, *True Love, True Love*, and *Come Into My Heart* don't compare to current rap titles like *Slob on My Knob*, *Big Pimpin'* and others whose names are represented in mainstream media as a stream of asterisks and hashtags, like *F*** tha Police* and *Break a B**** Neck*. Freed's show was more reminiscent of the Mouseketeers than the Black Panthers.

Still, the music was considered obscene and sinful by some and 25-year-old Little Richard, when leaving music for a career in the ministry, disavowed rock and roll because he said, "God doesn't like it." God had never gone on record to that effect, although it was always assumed that His taste leaned toward hymns and Gregorian chants, but such was the odium of rock and roll that everyone accepted Little Richard's explanation. Station KWK of St. Louis smashed all of its rock and roll records and vowed never to play it again.

In 1957, Freed added television to his repertoire, appearing on the ABC show *The Big Beat*. "I intend to show everyone in the family," he said, "that this is a healthy, normal music." The show didn't last long; ABC canceled it after an episode during which Frankie Lymon, black lead singer of The Teenagers, danced with a white girl. Mixing races, especially when broadcasting into the South, and particularly when it involved touching or romance, was a dangerous undertaking. Rock and roll mixed races like few other activities during the 1950s, which is why many considered it subversive.

Freed also appeared in a number of movies, always playing himself in films that were primarily a medley of rock and roll songs worked around an unimaginative plot of high school romance. The first, released in 1954, was *Rock Around the Clock*, starring Bill Haley and the Comets. Two years later, there was *Rock, Rock, Rock*, which introduced Tuesday Weld as a lovestruck teenager whose vocals were performed by Connie Francis. In 1957, Freed appeared in *Don't Knock the Rock* and *Mister Rock and Roll* and two years later he was in *Go, Johnny, Go*. He usually received top billing and as the classic song tells us, all he had to do was Act Naturally.

Freed found himself enmeshed in controversy again after a riotous 1958 concert in Boston. Joe Smith, a Boston DJ who worked with him on the Boston show, said, "There was a little to-do afterwards, and Alan made a mistake. Boston was a very jumpy town; very strict and Catholic and church-managed. And him just bringing the show pissed off a lot of people anyhow. We hired extra cops, and at some point the cops said, 'You gotta turn the lights on, they're getting crazy here,' and so they turned the lights on, and Alan said, 'It looks like the police don't want you to have a good time here. Come on, let's have a party.' And kids started coming out of the seats and surged toward the stage. It was a kind of a messy evening."

After the show ended, several youths went on a rampage. There was vandalism, there were several stabbings, and Freed was arrested. As always, there was a racial tint to the accusations, as papers reported that at least six victims were attacked by Negro men or women. Editorial comment was almost exclusively negative. Boston Mayor John Hynes called the concerts a "disgrace" and banned all future rock and roll events. New Haven, Connecticut; Troy, New York; Newark, New Jersey; and other cities banned rock concerts, and a Massachusetts state legislator proposed a law banning rock concerts at any state-owned facility.

"Alan Freed should be banned," said the *Woburn Times*, "from ever conducting a youth entertainment session in Boston or anywhere else." After a New York concert in 1957, a paper reported, "teenagers danced on the seats, necked in the aisles and screamed and shouted, as wide-eyed

2. Where Are They Now?

Freed gazed in ecstatic joy and wondered why the kids were so inhibited and backward in expressing themselves."

Freed was eventually acquitted of the Boston charges, but the incident led to his departure from WINS. In his letter of resignation, he wrote, "I feel that you have failed to stand behind my policies and principles." On the other hand, WINS was upset about the negative publicity and Freed's many outside interests, which they believed detracted from his duties at the station. Despite his popularity, they were happy to see him go.

Soon Freed had problems that were far more serious than a rock and roll riot. By the late 1950s, it was generally known that some disc jockeys were accepting money from record companies in return for playing their records on the air; the concept was known as "payola." In 1959, after a number of quiz show scandals highlighted the corruption of television and radio, law enforcement authorities began to investigate record company payola.

Freed denied taking any illegal payments, but said he was employed as a "consultant" by record companies to determine whether their product was good. This was a very fine distinction, especially if Freed invariably thought the records were good and played them on the air. He also admitted he received a number of Christmas gifts from record companies but claimed that was a common business practice.

After leaving WINS, Freed went to work for WABC, which fired him when he refused to sign a statement denying he had been paid by the record companies. He said that to sign the statement would have been an insult to his integrity and that payola "may stink but it's here and I didn't start it."

Freed went from WABC to WNEW television to do a show similar to *American Bandstand*, but left after two weeks, after signing a statement that he hadn't taken any improper payments "as an employee," a somewhat empty gesture since he'd just gotten there.

In 1960, Freed was indicted and accused of taking more than $30,000 in bribes from record companies. The practice was not illegal everywhere, but it was prohibited in New York, the situs of the lawsuit. Subpoenas uncovered some incriminating evidence. Conant Distributing Company paid Freed $2,000 in 1959 and issued him a 1099 tax voucher. A record distributor said he had loaned Freed $11,000 and forgiven the interest.

Freed pleaded guilty and received a suspended sentence and a $300 fine. A further ramification was that Freed owed almost $38,000 in back taxes.

Dick Clark was also suspected of taking payola, and Clark had numerous outside interests that represented potential conflicts. But Dick Clark was in many ways the polar opposite of the man he competed against for the teenage audience. Freed was reckless and unafraid to venture to the edge of a cliff, while Clark was much more cautious and dissembling in his response to the payola accusations. While Freed admitted to some things and insisted that payola was common practice, Clark denied everything. Authorities were unable to pin anything on him and he escaped unscathed.

By the time he was convicted on the tax charge, Freed's life was in shambles. He'd always had an unstable personal life and it wouldn't have taken much to send him into a tailspin. He'd had three marriages, the first to Betty Lou Bean in 1943, which produced two children. They separated in 1948 and divorced in 1949, with Betty Lou citing neglect of duty and extreme cruelty.

Although he'd been a bad husband, Freed was devastated by the divorce. At 3:00 a.m. on June 29, 1950, he sat down and wrote Betty Lou a long, pathetic, self-pitying letter. Given Freed's problems with alcohol and the time of day, it is likely he was drunk. The letter was several pages long, consisting of a series of thoughts connected by dashes. "I have never loved you as deeply as now," Freed wrote. "We ought to be together—you and I." He admitted that the breakup was his fault, largely because he wanted to be, as he put it "a big shot." "I was so blind—so much a big shot." At the end, he told Betty Lou he was turning to religion. "…the great big shot—Alan Freed—is turning to prayer and God."

Apparently, God wasn't the answer, for about six weeks after he wrote the beseeching letter, he looked to more earthly pleasures for solace, and married his second wife, Marjorie. Freed had never been a good manager of money and between alimony, child support, and a new wife, he was strapped, resulting in a bankruptcy filing in May 1951.

In 1953, Freed fell asleep at the wheel while driving home after a show and had a serious, near-fatal accident. He spent almost four months in the hospital and three more months recuperating at home, doing his show from a chair next to his bed.

In July 1958, Marjorie Freed went to Mexico to obtain a divorce, on the grounds that she and Alan had incompatible temperaments. On August 14, 1959, Freed took his third wife, Inga Boling, who had been his secretary. She was 24 and he was 38.

By the time he was arrested, Freed was in Los Angeles working for KDAY, but he left the station after pleading guilty. Alan Freed had gone from the top of the Moondog world to the bottom of the barrel, and it wasn't easy for him to accept. On the stationary of New York's Park Sheraton Hotel, he scribbled, "To be humble in the face of success, is, at most, the <u>least</u> difficult. But to be arrogant when you have fallen—one must be a real man."

By the end of 1964, Freed was approaching the end of the road. His drinking had seriously affected his health, he was unemployed, and he was broke. At the height of his fame, he'd spent money carelessly, and on a salary of around $15,000 per year, probably needed payola money to cover expenses. At one point during the 1950s, his Lord and Taylor charge card had a balance of nearly $11,000, which would be about $100,000 in today's currency.

In December 1964, Freed wrote a letter to a man identified only as "Morris" asking for a loan so he could relocate to Long Island to take a job. His house had been foreclosed upon and he asked Morris to respond in writing because he did not have a phone. He said that, although his wife Inga was working at the Riviera Hotel, they sometimes had difficulty finding money to buy food. "I hate to beg," he said, but he did. Freed told Morris he was having problems with kidney stones but was getting better.

He wasn't. On New Year's Day 1965, Freed was admitted to the hospital with gastrointestinal bleeding, caused by cirrhosis of the liver. By the 20th of January, he was dead. His death certificate said his last job was with station KNOB.

Freed left quite a legacy to rock and roll, but what he left Inga wasn't pretty. In July 1965, she received a letter from the IRS looking for $21,450 in back taxes. But her late husband's reputation soared once the grimy details of the recent past were forgotten and the music world focused on the glory of the Moondog days and the birth of rock and roll. Two movies were made about Freed's life and he got a star on the Hollywood Walk of Fame. In 1986, he was elected a member of the first class of inductees to the new Rock and Roll Hall of Fame. When cities bid for the right to build the museum, one of the claims in support of Cleveland was the fact that Freed had first popularized rock and roll on WJW. In death, Alan Freed was truly a "big shot," one of the most influential figures in 20th century music and possibly the most important of anyone who neither sang nor played a note. Freed is long gone, but rock and roll is here to stay.

Other sources:

> Freed's tribute website, alanfreed.com, is a treasure trove for researchers. It contains news clippings and numerous original items, including high school yearbooks, legal documents, accounting invoices, and countless other source documents. All of the supplementary material for this section came from information found on that website, including original documents and the thorough biography written by Ben-Fong Torres.

Father Divine, Cult Leader, Dies; May Have Been 100

New York Daily News, **September 11, 1965**

One of the most bizarre and tragic incidents in American history is the mass suicide orchestrated by cult leader Jim Jones in 1978 at his Jonestown community in northwest Guyana. The strange series of events began when Jones ordered the murder of Congressman Leo Ryan, who was conducting an investigation of his activities. Ryan and four others, including two members of an NBC news crew, were gunned down November 18, 1978, as they were boarding a plane.

Later that day, Jones told the inhabitants of Jonestown that the cult was in dire straits. His great hope, an attempt to negotiate asylum in the Soviet Union, was doomed after Ryan's murder and he believed the United States was about to attack the compound in retaliation. The only way out, Jones told them, was mass suicide, which he proposed to accomplish by having them all drink cyanide-laced Flavor-Aid (not Kool-Aid as commonly reported). A total of 912 Jonestown residents, more than a quarter of whom were children, followed orders and perished.

In 1972, six years before the mass suicide, Jones had unsuccessfully attempted to take over the International Peace Mission, a group formed by the late Father Divine. He claimed to be the re-incarnation of Divine, even though he was 32 years old when Divine died. Jones explained the contradiction by stating that Father Divine's spirit had entered Jones' body after death.

The relationship between Jones and Divine was portrayed in the 1980 film, *The Guyana Tragedy: The Story of Jim Jones*, with James Earl Jones playing the role of Father Divine. By that time, Father Divine was pretty much a forgotten figure. Few knew who he was and why was it important for Jim Jones to make people believe that Father Divine's soul was within him.

There are many individuals who are famous in their own time but forgotten soon afterward. In the 1930s Father Divine was known throughout the United States, but by the time he died in 1965, Divine was just an odd figure from the past. He was an evangelist without the staying power of Billy Graham and a civil rights leader without the legacy of Martin Luther King.

Father Divine, whose real name may have been George Baker, was not 100 when he died in 1965. He was believed to have been born around 1876 and was therefore closer to 90. Father Divine's early history is very vague; he intentionally obscured many facts, the better to portray himself as a deity from a mysterious place. He may have been born in Maryland, or possibly the Deep South. He was bald (his portrayal by James Earl Jones, who sported a full head of hair, was not accurate), short (approximately 5'2") and in later life he was chubby. Most of his followers believed that Father Divine was the personification of the Second Coming, and he himself hinted as much without saying it directly. "I don't have to say I'm God," was his standard response.

In the early 1910s, Divine preached in the south in partnership with Samuel Morris and John Hickerson, but they parted company in 1912. Divine had developed a complex philosophy, partly based on the concept of positive thinking; he was sort of an earlier, African American version of Dr. Norman Vincent Peale. Divine's principal message was peace—he believed the greeting "Peace" should replace "Hello"—but one of the major tenets of his teaching was celibacy, which so enraged the husbands of his early female followers that they had him arrested for lunacy. Divine refused to give his name when he was arrested and was tried as John Doe (alias God). He was acquitted, and the episode gained him widespread publicity.

In 1919, the minister, apparently dissatisfied with John Doe, gave himself the name Major Jealous Divine, but his followers generally referred to him simply as Father Divine. That same year, he married a woman named Penninah, who was several decades older than him. Divine claimed that, due to his belief in celibacy, the marriage was never consummated. Also, in 1919, Divine moved to Sayville, located on the southern shore of Long Island. He was the first black to own a home in Sayville, which he was able to purchase because the German seller of the property was angry with his neighbor and retaliated by selling his property to a black man.

As expected, Divine had a number of problems with his white neighbors. Not only was he the first black man in town, he sponsored communal living at his home. He was accused of operating a harem, for apparently the Sayville neighbors were unaware of the celibacy plank of Divine's platform. By the time Divine had been in Sayville for a few years, he had built up a vast following, estimated as high as two million, including a large number of whites.

In May 1932 Divine was convicted of disturbing the peace. Judge Lewis Smith sentenced him to a year in prison and sternly lectured him from the bench. A few days later, a seemingly healthy Judge Smith died of a heart attack, giving rise to the rumor that his death was the direct result of having sentenced Divine. More likely, it was the result of Smith's pre-existing heart condition, but the possibility that Divine had somehow used his divinity to strike down the judge made a much better story.

After he left prison, Divine moved to Harlem, where he had many followers, and became active in the civil rights movement. He was a great proponent of integration and the elimination of racial labels, claiming that he was not black. Due to his unique beliefs and lifestyle, however, Divine never became part of the mainstream civil rights movement.

The 1930s were a time of great success and serious setbacks for Divine. By the end of the decade, one of the most economically dismal in U.S. history, his group had accumulated assets valued at an estimated $15 million, including six Harlem hotels. Divine's followers operated a number of successful businesses and donated the lion's share of their profits to the movement. The preacher took no direct compensation, saying, "I am a free gift to the world, gratis to mankind." Somehow, however, he managed to live a very lavish lifestyle, being driven in limousines and dressing in expensive clothing. Divine's enemies always accused him of lining his own pockets from church funds.

The movement was threatened during the 1930s when one of Divine's followers, a man named John Hunt, who called himself John the Redeemer, kidnapped a 17-year-old girl, called her the Virgin Mary and said that he would produce with her, by means of an Immaculate Conception, a messiah. When it turned out that Hunt was using the tried and true method of conceiving a child, the girl's parents contacted the media and the publicity was extremely harmful to Divine.

A second follower, Faithful Mary, did not live up to her name, split from Divine, and attempted to form a competing congregation. Faithful Mary eventually returned to the fold, but more trouble developed when Divine was sued by a couple that wanted to leave the flock but said Divine would not return money he had taken from them. In order to escape the ensuing judgment, Divine fled to Pennsylvania, returning to preach in Harlem only on Sundays, when warrants could not be executed.

Penninah died in 1943, although Divine never announced or acknowledged it. Death was a strange thing in Divine's world, tinged with claims of reincarnation and souls moving to other bodies. He was strongly against life insurance, which might be hard to collect if one insisted that the dead person had been reincarnated.

In April 1946, Divine secretly married Edna Rose Ritchings, a 21-year-old blond, blue-eyed white woman. Like his first wife, Ritchings was known as Mother Divine, and as he had done when marrying Penninah, Divine announced that the marriage would be celibate. He said Ritchings, who had first become enamored of Divine's teachings when she was 15, was the reincarnation of his first wife. As with the case of Jim Jones, the problem was that Ritchings was alive when Penninah died, but like Jones, Divine claimed that his widow's spirit had moved into Ritchings' body.

There are several extant videos of Divine speaking, and his style was typical of the evangelist preacher. He was emotional, he was repetitive, he rambled, and he was vague, sounding a bit like Casey Stengel as he ranged from one topic to another. "The individual is the personification of that which expresses personification," he once said. "Therefore he comes to be personally the expression of that which was impersonal, and he is the personal expression of it and the personification of the pre-personification of God Almighty! Peace, it's wonderful!" And his listeners roared.

One of Divine's followers gave him a 72-acre estate in Gladwyne, Pennsylvania, complete with a castle-like residence, where the preacher lived for the rest of his life. By the 1950s, he had become more of a curiosity than a powerful force, and the number of followers dwindled. Old age took away many of the old flock, and practicing celibacy is not a good long-term formula for building a congregation.

After Divine died in 1965, his followers continued to speak of him in the present tense, insisting that he was still with them. Mother Divine carried on the movement for many years, until her death in 2017 at the age of 91.

Other sources:
  https://en.wikipedia.org/wiki/Father_Divine
  https://www.youtube.com/watch?v=1vzEMT35Iyg
  Father Divine visits Hope Farm, 1938, Part 2—https://www.youtube.com/watch?v=hG-09gRuBVhE
  Father Divine: A Study in Charisma, a Film by Leo Levy—https://www.youtube.com/watch?v=izA20-vUEW0
  http://www.pbs.org/thisfarbyfaith/journey_3/p_10.html
  https://www.thoughtco.com/the-jonestown-massacre-1779385

"Playboy" Manville Dies; Wed 11 Times
Hartford Courant, October 9, 1967

In the 21st century, living together without the benefit of a marriage license is common, and if one isn't particularly good at matrimony, there's no need to keep trying to get it right. But during the first half of the 20th century, and well into the 1960s, it was a social taboo for unmarried men and women to live together; respectable couples who wanted to co-habit generally made a trip to the altar. Romance led to marriage, and there were a few hopeless romantics who kept getting married again and again, either trying to find the right partner or perhaps just enjoying the variety.

Multiple marriages were generally reserved for the rich and famous, since divorce was an expensive proposition. Actress Elizabeth Taylor was married eight times, including twice to Richard Burton. For a family act, it was difficult to match the Gabor sisters. Zsa Zsa was married nine times. One of her marriages lasted only two days while the most enduring of the first eight endured for just seven years. Finally, in 1986, Zsa Zsa got it right. She wed Frederic Prince von Anhalt and remained married to him until her death in 2016 at age 99.

Frederic, who was Mr. Gabor for 30 years, was not really a prince; he was a German businessman who bought the title by getting himself adopted, at the age of 37, by the ex-wife of a son of Kaiser Wilhelm II. Maybe, marrying for the ninth time at age 69, Zsa Zsa finally found the secret to lasting happiness. Or perhaps she'd simply run out of steam and lacked the energy to get divorced and look for #10. Frederic was also experienced at matrimony and had been around the block a time or two; this was his eighth marriage and while he was married to Zsa Zsa, he admitted to a 10-year affair with Playboy Playmate Anna Nicole Smith.

Magda Gabor was married six times. She was widowed twice, three marriages ended in divorce, and one was annulled. The latter union lasted just a month, and two other marriages were terminated within a year. For the last 22 years of her life, Magda was single. The third Gabor sister, Eva, was married five times.

In total, the Gabor sisters were married 20 times, perhaps establishing a record for three sisters, at least three famous sisters. But on an individual basis, none of the Gabors equaled the record of Tommy Manville, who married eleven times. "When I meet a beautiful girl," he once said, "the first thing I say is 'Will you marry me?' The second thing I say is 'How do you do?'" Douglas Keister called Manville the Paris Hilton of the 20th century—someone who was famous merely for being famous.

Manville preferred blondes. "I have no prejudice against brunettes," he said. "But they always seem to have such an inferiority complex because they're not blond." Most of his wives were about 5'6" tall and had two other things in common. All but two were showgirls or actresses, and none were wealthy until after they divorced him.

Manville didn't marry for money because he already had a lot of it, although after each divorce, he had a little less. "She cried," he said at the termination of one of his marriages, "and the judge wiped her tears with my checkbook."

Born April 9, 1894, Manville acquired his alimony capital as heir to the Johns-Manville fortune. In 1901, his father, Thomas Manville, Sr., merged his Manville Covering Company, founded in 1886 by Tommy's grandfather, C.B. Manville, with a company founded in 1858 by H.W. Johns that produced asbestos-based fire retardant roofing material.

Tommy was a rebellious youngster and had run away from eight schools, according to his count, by the time he was 12. He also said he hopped freight trains and lived as a hobo for a time, unusual activities for the offspring of an industrial tycoon. Like so many sons of wealthy, successful men, young Tommy had a strained relationship with his father. "A son can never be his father," he said much later. "I couldn't compete with my father. When he died I had nothing but money. The only field of competition open to me was love."

In 1911, when he was just 17, Manville embarked on the career that would make him famous; he got married for the first time. His first wife was a Ziegfeld showgirl named Florence Huber, who he married five days after they met. In order to make the marriage legal, Manville lied and said he was 21. His father, who was in Europe when he heard the news, was furious and vowed to have the marriage annulled when he returned to the United States.

Manville's father cut him off from the family money, so he took a $15 a week job in a Johns-Manville plant. In subsequent years, Tommy worked as an elevator operator and bellboy and the newlyweds lived in a furnished room that cost $6 a week. The marriage didn't last, but although no one

2. Where Are They Now?

knew it at the time, it was one of Manville's more enduring relationships. The couple separated in 1917 after six years of marriage, but they were not divorced until 1922. Florence thought she had married a rich man and living in a $6 a week room was not what she had in mind. She missed the glamour of show business and didn't take to being the wife of an heir playing a blue-collar worker.

Three years after his divorce from Huber, 31-year-old Manville married his father's 22-year-old stenographer, Lois McCoin. His father liked McCoin and approved of the match. The senior Manville died of a heart attack a month after the wedding and, despite their testy relationship, left his son a significant amount of money. There were conflicting stories about the size of the inheritance. Some reports said it was $10 million, while others said it was $10 million plus a large amount of Johns-Manville stock. In a 1933 article, former fiancée Neva Lynn said she believed he was worth $40 million. Manville once said that his father left him "only" $50 million and he made the rest of his fortune through investments. That would indicate that he had a great deal of money, but when he divorced his ninth wife in the late 1950s, he said he was down to his last $2 million and had to sell his mansion.

A year after his father died, Manville deserted Lois, who collected alimony of $19,000 per year until she died in 1929. Single once more, Tommy Manville became an enthusiastic participant in the lively Manhattan social scene of the late 1920s. Lynne called him "the idol of Broadway's night life" who wanted to be "Broadway's perfect playboy." "He's just a generous overgrown kid at heart," she said, "who resembled a youngster playing cowboy."

Once he had his inheritance, Manville gave up his menial jobs. Although he was only in his 30s, he described himself as a retired businessman who spent his time looking after his investments. One of his former girlfriends claimed he was a very astute investor who had gotten out of the stock market without losing very much in the Crash of 1929.

Manville wasn't single for long. In 1931, he married actress Avonne Taylor, who'd appeared in *My Best Girl* in 1927 and *Honor Among Lovers* in 1931. He proposed to her after an evening in the Grand Central Casino and they were married the next day. Two days later, the marriage was in trouble and within 34 days it was over. Manville said Taylor liked to put on airs, which made him uncomfortable. She departed with a reported $150,000, which would allow her to put on airs for several years.

Manville's fourth wife was another actress, Marcelle Edwards, who appeared in *Show Boat*, *Bandwagon*, and *The Vanities* and was once named Miss Broadway. She and Manville wed in 1933 and Manville said he was done marrying; Marcelle had everything he wanted. They were divorced in 1937, and it turned out that Manville had everything she wanted. Four years of marriage got her a $200,000 settlement. Manville claimed that Edwards was the only one of his wives who was physically abusive. Once, the police were summoned and, when they arrived on the scene, found the couple chasing each other around the mansion.

In 1941, the 47-year-old Manville took 22-year-old Bonita Edwards as Wife #5, but the marriage (which took place after a 17-day courtship) was dissolved just two months later. Wife #6 was Wilhelmina (Billie) Boze, married in 1942 and divorced in 1943. By that time, it seemed that Manville was either striving to set a record or he wasn't trying very hard to make a good match. His first marriage, even though he had been very young, lasted 11 years, but by the 1940s, Manville's marriages were lasting a year or less, and the courtships were getting shorter and shorter.

The seventh marriage was the shortest of all. Less than eight hours after Manville wed Macie Marie Ainsworth in 1943, they announced that they were headed for divorce court. Some guests were probably still at the reception.

Number eight was Georgina Campbell in 1945. Campbell, one of the two wives not in show business (the other was Lois McCoin) was a reporter. She was assigned to do a story on Manville and ended up with a diamond in addition to a scoop. The liaison lasted longer than his marriage to Ainsworth, but it was over soon enough. For $1,000 a month, Campbell became another ex–Mrs. Manville. She was killed in an auto accident in 1952 while driving to meet Manville for breakfast.

Anita Roddy-Eden, a blond dancer, was wife number nine, and after just ten days of marriage, Manville placed full-page newspaper advertisements announcing that he was no longer responsible for her bills. Apparently, Anita reformed, at least temporarily, and the two got back together. But soon there was another ad: "My wife Anita Eden Manville having AGAIN left my bed and board, I am no longer responsible for any debts she may have incurred." Needless to say, the two were soon divorced. Anita eventually wrote a book titled *Lives and Wives of Tommy Manville.*

Number 10 was Patricia Gaston, a 27-year-old showgirl whose marriage to Manville lasted two months. Manville said that newspaper columnists had the two of them married before they even met. "I read about it in the column," he said, "so I went backstage to meet her and we had a chemical reaction and were married the next day."

In addition to the wives there were many, many girlfriends and a few fiancées who never made it to the altar. One of them was showgirl Neva Lynne, who was in a production called *Hot-Cha.* Ms. Lynne shared her experiences with *The Albuquerque Journal* in 1933, shortly after their engagement ended, describing her relationship with Manville and giving readers an insight into the personality of the serial groom.

Manville had proposed to Lynne earlier that year. "Well," he told her, "I guess we'll get tied up." They were supposed to be married during the summer of 1933, but three days before the scheduled date, Manville said he had to leave on business and postponed the wedding until October. While Manville was away, Neva went to visit her ill sister. When she returned, she learned that her fiancée had married Marcelle Edwards.

When she heard the news, Lynne called Manville, who was polite and apologetic—but married. Like the others left behind, Neva wasn't bitter—or surprised. Manville was, she admitted, impulsive. The two remained on good terms and double dated on at least one occasion after their engagement ended.

Manville had also been engaged to Marian Carewe, Colette Francis, and Nina Pierson; he called off the latter engagement when he met movie star Claire Windsor. He was dating Windsor when he met Neva Lynne. Then he left Lynne to marry Edwards. As one can see, Manville's love life was very complicated. He said he received many letters proposing marriage, most of which contained photos. Showgirl Anne Bernie proposed to him for the publicity value, and he encouraged things like that. "It's Leap Year," he once said. "Come on, girls. This is your chance."

Even Manville's non-marital romances cost him money. When his affair with Elinor Troy ended, he told her to see his lawyer, who gave her a generous settlement. He said Troy was not the right girl for him because she couldn't cook and expressed shock that most beautiful showgirls were not skilled in the culinary arts.

Manville was not a man without vices, but alcohol was not one of them. He rarely drank, often going months without touching liquor, which made his impetuous proposals even more puzzling. His vice was matrimony. "Marriage is a beautiful institution," he once said. "If I hadn't thought so, I wouldn't have tried it so often." "His one real hobby in life," Lynne said, "is women. They take most of his time."

Another vice was seeking attention, which Manville did not only by marrying frequently, but by spending lavish amounts of money. During the Depression, he believed that his spending was patriotic. Manville generally carried at least $5,000 in cash, in an era when $5,000 was a couple of years' salary for the average American. He once spent $3,000 to fly Elinor Troy from Hollywood to New York to have lunch with him.

In addition to his cash, Manville carried a revolver, tear gas, and a blackjack, always fearing that he would be robbed. Once when he was dating Neva Lynne, a car blocked his path and, thinking they were about to be abducted, Manville chased the pursuers off by firing a shot at them.

Like many egotists, Manville often referred to himself in the third person. As 1941 began, he made a New Year's Resolution not to marry again.

"Still," he said, "I might meet some lovely creature who can cook and, well, nobody knows what Manville might do next."

In 1958, when he was between wives ten and eleven, Manville had a date with a reporter named Norma Lee Browning, who wrote about the evening for the *Chicago Tribune*. Although Manville didn't marry Miss Browning, he was more than willing to tell her about his numerous ex-wives. "I was very much in love with all of them when I married them, or at least soon after," he said. He claimed that one of the problems with most of his wives was that they didn't like the publicity that came with marriage to the famous Tommy Manville. "But I think my main trouble," he confided, "was that I spoil them." He was an excellent cook, and liked doing the housework, an unusual trait for a man born in the 19th century. Then Manville hit on a more plausible reason that his marriages hadn't lasted. "That's the trouble with some of these girls I married," he told Miss Browning. "They're too damned young and too impressed with money." He said he didn't think he'd marry again.

One of the things that most impressed his date was the fact that he remembered each of his ex-wives' names and always referred to them in chronological order. He remained on good terms with all of them (perhaps because he'd been very generous in his settlements—it was estimated that they totaled between one and two million dollars) and had eight-foot portraits of each, which he hung in *Bon Repos*, his 28-room Mamaroneck estate. Neva Lynne said he also had a nine by fifteen portrait of her, but he kept all the paintings off the walls if his current wife objected.

Despite his statement to Browning, Manville had one more marriage left in him. The eleventh and final wife was Christiana Erdlen, who was 19 (Manville was 66) when they married in 1960. Although his previous ten wives had produced no children, he came close with Christiana, who suffered a miscarriage in 1961. Apparently, by that time Manville, like Zsa Zsa Gabor, had gotten the hang of marriage, for the couple lived a relatively quiet existence in Chappaqua, New York, until Manville's death in 1967. He'd been suffering from a heart ailment (an appropriate end for a man of such prodigious romantic feats) for six years become he succumbed at the age of 73.

Other sources:
Chicago Tribune, October 9, 1967.
web.archive.org/web/20070213054347/http://news.yahoo.com/s/ap/20070209/ap_on_en_tv/anna_nicole_smith_125
www.mausoleums.com/portfolio/manville-mausoleum/
The Albuquerque Journal, November 19, 1933
Salt Lake Tribune, December 29, 1940
San Antonio Light, March 2, 1941
Ogden Standard Examiner, August 11, 1935

James Roosevelt Stabbed During Family Quarrel

**Bridgeport Post and Telegram,
May 16, 1969**

Only two sons of U.S. Presidents (John Quincy Adams and George W. Bush) became presidents. Several presidents had no sons, others had sons that lived productive, reputable lives, but there were many presidential offspring who were unable to handle the pressure and temptations of being the son of the most powerful man in the United States. The Roosevelt boys fell into the latter category.

Franklin and Eleanor Roosevelt had six children, one of whom, Franklin D. Roosevelt, Jr., died as an infant in 1909. Daughter Anna and four sons lived to adulthood. James Roosevelt, our subject, was the oldest, born in 1907. Elliott, the second Franklin Delano Roosevelt, Jr., and John were born in 1910, 1914, and 1916, respectively.

The lives of the younger Roosevelts were tumultuous. Anna was married three times. Elliott was married five times and dogged by scandal his entire life (see below). Franklin Jr. was also married five times. John, the loyal family man among the siblings, was married just twice.

James Roosevelt made his father's career his own. Like Franklin Sr., James attended the exclusive Groton prep school and Harvard College (Class of 1930). Following his graduation, he had a brief but profitable career in insurance before going to work in the White House in 1937. James was always at his father's side, helping him maneuver on his braces and serving as a key aide.

Controversy followed James throughout his career. He was a business partner in several ventures with Joseph Kennedy, Sr., who was probably not a bootlegger, as often rumored, but was almost certainly a stock manipulator. Like Kennedy, James was involved in the Hollywood movie industry, and virtually everything he did was based upon being the well-connected son of the President of the United States. When Roosevelt, who had no military experience, was made a lieutenant colonel in the Marine Corps during World War II, there was a storm of protest.

Although his appointment was heavily criticized, James, to his credit, saw active duty during the war. When it ended, he took up the family business—politics, serving as a congressman from California from 1955 through 1965. He resigned his office in 1965 to run, unsuccessfully, for mayor of Los Angeles.

By 1969, Franklin, Sr., was 24 years in the grave, James's active political career was over, and he was on his third marriage. He divorced his first wife, Betsey Cushing, daughter of a prominent Boston brain surgeon, in 1940. One of the reasons for the split was that James, while hospitalized for an ulcer at the Mayo Clinic in 1938, met an attractive nurse named Romelle Schneider. They married in 1941 and had three children (he had two children with his first wife). James and Romelle divorced in 1955 and James married his third wife, Gladys Irene Owens, in 1956.

James and Gladys lived in Geneva, where he served as director of three mutual funds sponsored by Investors Overseas Service and as president of I.O.S. Management Company. Since it involved James Roosevelt, of course, there was a certain shadiness to the affair; shortly before he assumed his duties with I.O.S, the company had been under investigation by the Securities and Exchange Commission.

At about 11:00 p.m. on May 15, 1969, at their vacation villa in the Vienna suburb of Vésenaz, the Roosevelts had an altercation, during which Gladys picked up a dagger Roosevelt had kept as a souvenir of World War II and plunged it into her husband's back. James managed to stagger to a neighbor's house and was taken to a local hospital. After surgery, he was reported to be in good condition and was expected to be discharged in a few days. His wife was taken to the Bel-Air Clinic.

Although initial reports indicated that he had been attacked by a "mentally unstable woman" Roosevelt confirmed that the woman was his wife and that she had recently been depressed. Perhaps the cause of the depression was that he had begun divorce proceedings. The timing of Roosevelt's divorces and re-marriages suggests that there was extra-curricular activity during each marriage, which would have provided plenty of incentive for Gladys to bury a dagger in James' back.

Roosevelt was released from the hospital in less than two weeks. Gladys was freed on bail (paid by James) but remained in the clinic. In October, with his divorce final, James married Mary Winskill, a 32-year-old British woman who had been the teacher of James' and Gladys' ten-year-old son.

Gladys was never charged in the stabbing and when she was released from Bel-Air she returned to the United States. She died in 1987 at the age of 70 in a fire at her Rancho Mirage home that was started by a cigarette.

James resigned his position at I.O.S after rogue financier Robert Vesco absconded with $200 million from the fund. He moved back to California, became a lecturer at the University of California at Irvine and Chapman College and served as a business consultant. Roosevelt also formed a lobbying organization called the National Committee to Preserve Social Security and Medicare, key components of his father's legacy.

In 1986, his son, James Roosevelt, Jr., ran against Joseph P. Kennedy II, son of Robert Kennedy, for the office of U.S. Representative from Massachusetts. In the contest between two great Democratic families, Joseph emerged the winner. James, Sr., died in 1991 from complications of Parkinson's disease at the age of 83. He was survived by his wife Mary, who is still alive as of the date of this writing.

Other sources:
  Chicago Tribune, May 17, 1969
  Los Angeles Times, August 14, 1991

Willie Sutton Is Freed After 17 Years in Prison

New York Times, December 25, 1969

Some people, like Tommy Manville and Father Divine, had been out of the news for years because their time had passed. Willie Sutton was out of the limelight because one does not generally create news during 17 years in prison. The only way a prisoner could make news is if he escaped, which Sutton did on two notable occasions, but that was when he was a younger man. He'd been securely lodged in Sing Sing since 1952.

There were many renowned criminals during the lawless 1930s, but only a few achieved lasting fame. There were Clyde Barrow and Bonnie Parker, famous mostly because they were a male and female team. There were criminals with catchy nicknames, like Pretty Boy Floyd, Machine Gun Kelly, and Baby Face Nelson. Willie Sutton never had a female partner, and while he acquired some nicknames during his long career, he earned his fame with his talent and personality. "[H]e captured the public's imagination," Ira Berkow wrote of Sutton, "like no criminal perhaps since Jesse James." "It's ridiculous," Sutton replied. "I can't even ride a horse."

Willie Sutton became famous because of the magnitude of his crimes (he held up nearly 100 banks for an estimated $2 million), his mild manner (he never killed anyone), and because of his numerous attempts to escape from prison. Sutton, like so many criminals of the 1930s, was a sharp dresser who, when he wasn't wearing one of his many disguises, wore expensive suits. Unlike today's hoodlums, who favor hoodies and baggy pants, Sutton, Clyde Barrow, and their contemporaries were protective of their image and preferred to be photographed in expensive tailored suits.

Born in Brooklyn in 1901, Sutton began committing crimes when he was just ten years old and left school after the eighth grade. His mother tried to raise him as a good Catholic but Sutton, although always obeying the commandment "thou shalt not kill," completely ignored the one that read, "thou shalt not steal." His mentor was veteran lock-picker Doc Tate, a fashion plate in his own right, who taught Sutton to dress well and plan his jobs carefully. "I think I can say," Sutton told an interviewer in 1971, "that I was the most careful thief that ever operated." Before he held up Manufacturer's Trust in 1950, he cased the bank for a month, noting the movements of all bank employees. On the day of the robbery, Sutton followed the first employee into the building, held him at gunpoint, and waited until the rest of the staff arrived and the vault was scheduled to open. When the mailman came in, Sutton said politely, "Won't you please join the rest of the party?" He and his accomplices cleaned out the vault and left quietly.

Sutton is best known for a famous quote. When he was asked why he robbed banks, he supposedly said, "Because that's where the money is." It was a great line, but Sutton, like Yogi Berra, never said most of the things he said. He always denied uttering the line, and when asked why he really robbed banks, said, "Because I enjoyed it. I loved it. I was more alive when I was inside a bank, robbing it, than at any other time in my life.... Me looking at a bank was like some other guy looking at a beautiful woman. Irresistible.... You have to be totally committed. I can assure you that I was totally committed to robbing banks." "Once," he said, "even though I had $30,000 in my pocket, I went by a bank, and I just had to meet its challenge. I took that bank all right, even though I didn't need the money."

In 1953, while in prison, Sutton worked with Quentin Reynolds to produce an autobiography, *I, Willie Sutton*. With the proceeds from his book and the subsequent television rights, Sutton established the Willie Sutton Helping Hand Fund. The original intent of the fund was to help rehabilitate criminals, but in 1960, Sutton petitioned to change the trust so that his daughter would receive the proceeds.

Although he often used accomplices, Sutton preferred working alone. He was a quiet, solitary man by nature, and also believed that partners were ultimately unreliable. Sooner or later, one of them would tell a wife or friend and the whole scheme would come unraveled. He used a number of disguises, posing as guards, delivery men, etc., to gain entrance to banks before they opened. He used wigs and false mustaches and played his roles brilliantly, acquiring the nickname "Willie the Actor."

Although Sutton disliked violence, he always carried a gun for, as he explained, you couldn't rob a bank on charm. His primary weapon, however, was a disarming personality. Most bank robbers wound up killing someone when they panicked, but Sutton had a calming influence. "Relax, folks," he'd say to the tellers, "it's only money and it's not your money."

Sutton went to jail for the first time in 1919. He achieved nationwide notoriety in 1930 when he lifted $130,000 worth of gems from a Broadway jewelry store while disguised as a Western Union messenger. He was quickly captured and sent to Sing Sing under a lengthy sentence but broke out in November 1932. Sutton remained at large until February 1934, when police found him living in Philadelphia with a woman named Irene (or Ida) Sarvary; they were using the names Mr. and Mrs. Richard Courtney. This time Sutton was sentenced to 25 to 50 years.

Some of Sutton's escape attempts were unsuccessful. In 1941, he spent a year and a half crafting a very realistic plaster mask, complete with his own hair taken from the prison barber, and a plaster hand that he planned to leave in his bed while he escaped. It was a work of art, but unfortunately, the mask was discovered before he could make the attempt. In April 1945, on his fifth attempt (he made 10 overall) Sutton spent six months digging a tunnel, but when he emerged at the other end, he found himself face to face with two policemen.

Two years later, Sutton successfully broke out of Pennsylvania's Holmesburg Prison along with four other inmates. Three were quickly recaptured but Sutton and Frederick (The Angel) Tenuto got away. For Tenuto, a 30-year-old hood serving time for armed robbery, it was his third escape. Sutton made it back to New York, where in March 1950 he pulled off a $64,000 heist of a Manufacturers Trust office. He was also suspected of numerous other crimes, some of which he committed, others which merely matched his technique. Whenever a robber used a clever disguise and didn't harm anyone, the famous Willie Sutton was a prime suspect.

Sutton had a number of odd jobs during his years of freedom, including a stretch on the government payroll. Under the name Edward Lynch, he earned $1,200 per year as a porter on the city "poor farm" on Staten Island. He was able to avoid notice because, unlike so many criminals of the 1930s, he lived unobtrusively. Sutton was an average sized man at 5'8" and 155 pounds, and he did not drink, smoke, or have an active night life. When Pretty Boy Floyd pulled his first big job, he rolled ostentatiously back into town in an expensive car and flashy clothes that no one believed he had acquired honestly. Sutton blended easily into New York, Philadelphia, and other places he called home after his escapes.

On February 18, 1952, Willie's luck ran out. A 24-year-old subway passenger named Arnold Schuster, who worked in his father's dry-cleaning shop, recognized Sutton from a wanted poster and notified police, who arrested him. Although the police didn't tell the public about Schuster, the young man, seeking publicity and a reputed $70,000 reward, told his story to the press. Two weeks later, after receiving a number of threatening calls and letters, Schuster was murdered. Although the killing remained unsolved, mobster Joe Valachi later testified that the hit had been ordered by Mafia boss Albert Anastasia, who simply disliked snitches. Sutton always regretted the fact that Schuster had been killed for informing on him.

After he was back in custody, Sutton received a sentence of life plus

105 years, with an additional 30 years for his escape. He was sent back to Sing Sing, from which he had escaped in 1932, and given the same number (84599) that he had before. At 51, Sutton was becoming a little old for the arduous task of escaping, and after his prior escapades, he wasn't about to take his jailers by surprise. They kept a close eye on him, and he remained in prison until Christmas Eve 1969. By that time, he was 68 and in very poor health. His biggest problem was hardening of the arteries and it appeared that he might require major surgery.

Throughout his latest sentence, Sutton had been a model prisoner, working in the laundry, reading, and studying. Despite the fact that he had tried to escape so often, Sutton adapted to prison life relatively well. Still, he told his attorney in 1958, "If I stop thinking of breaking out of jail, you'll know I'm dead."

His 1969 release was somewhat of a surprise, since he had recently been denied parole, but some complex computations and the herculean efforts of Attorney Katherine Bitsis made him a free man. "I couldn't believe it," he told reporters as he left prison, "but here I am, and it's a wonderful feeling."

Bitsis had known Sutton for more than a decade, meeting him while representing his alleged accomplice Thomas (Scup) Kling. Sutton said she was the only person he knew who had more guts than he did.

After his release, Sutton stayed out of trouble, living quietly in Sarasota with his sister, Helen Motolla. He was famous by that time, and in 1970 Sutton did an advertisement for Connecticut Bank and Trust and its new photo ID credit card. "Now when I say I'm Willie Sutton," he said, "people believe me." At the end of the spot, the announcer urged viewers to come to CBT and tell them, "Willie Sutton sent me." He became somewhat of an elder statesman and often spoke at banking seminars on the subject of security.

In 1977, Sutton was interviewed by television critic Dick Ryan for his opinions on current police and detective shows. He dismissed *Starsky and Hutch* and *Baretta* as unrealistic, assuring Ryan that Robert Blake was too small to do the things he was supposed to be doing. James Garner was too silly for his taste, but he liked *Kojak* who, Sutton said, was "the only one who talks and acts like the officers I encountered in my lifetime." "I like Charley's Angels," he added. "You can never get into trouble watching pretty girls." Sutton ventured into movies, and said he didn't like *Bonnie and Clyde* because it didn't emphasize the planning that was necessary for a successful bank robbery.

In 1976, Sutton released his second book, *Where the Money Was*. Though he denied saying it, Sutton wasn't above using his most famous quote to promote his book. During his book tour Sutton gave a lengthy interview to Ira Berkow, telling him that he commenced his life of crime because he wanted to give nice things to his mother. Once, when he sent her $5,000, Mrs. Sutton, correctly suspecting that the money had come from criminal activity, donated it to the church. "That really hit me," Sutton said, "that I couldn't please my mother." The thing he most regretted about his career was the pain it brought to his loved ones. His wife had divorced him when he was in prison.

Many criminals have been portrayed as sympathetic, but upon closer scrutiny, most were not. At best, they exhibited the occasional acts of kindness or humanity that every human being, over the course of several decades, inevitably does from time to time. At heart, they are cruel people, which is what permits them to commit the acts for which they become notorious.

Willie Sutton, however, appears to have been an exception. Some aberration in his personality, the love of bank robbery and his desire to excel at it, seems to have driven him to commit crimes, and he tried to carry out his dream in as innocent and kind a fashion as possible. On the one occasion where he was indirectly responsible for a killing, he regretted it for the rest of his life, even though he had nothing directly to do with it.

Sutton had charm; he was a self-effacing, likeable man with a sense of humor. Although he had virtually no formal education, he was well-spoken and articulate. Dick Ryan said Sutton "studied more literature, history and philosophy during his 36 years in prison than most self-respecting Phi Beta Kappas do in a lifetime." He had also become an expert court stenographer, and his knowledge of the law allowed him to assist other prisoners to prepare appeals. He was so respected by the prison community that he was able to use his influence to act as a peacemaker during a potential riot at Attica in 1967. Had he still been incarcerated four years later, when the deadly riot erupted at the New York prison, perhaps things would have been different, but perhaps not, for Sutton was a criminal from the old school, while the 1971 Attica inmates were a revolutionary breed.

When he was in prison, Sutton received numerous letters that could be classified as fan mail. As an old man, he became part of the establishment, writing books, filming commercials, and giving speeches. Willie Sutton became famous because he was one of the most unique criminals of all time. He lived to a ripe old age, passing away at 79 on November 2, 1980, having been a free man for nearly 11 years.

Sutton's death was as secretive as his life on the lam. There was no formal announcement and the undertakers and cemetery workers who buried him in his native Brooklyn refused to comment. He had wanted to spare his family the publicity. "We've had enough of it all our lives," his sister said. But Sutton could not control his final destiny; he told his sister he wanted to be cremated, but she ignored his wishes and had him buried instead.

Other sources:
https://www.fbi.gov/history/famous-cases/willie-sutton
https://www.snopes.com/quotes/sutton.asp
New York Daily News, July 17, 2011
High Point Enterprise, August 7, 1971
Doylestown Intelligencer, September 13, 1976
Nashua Telegram, November 19, 1980
Independent Press Telegram, September 4, 1977
Charleston Gazette, February 13, 1955
Danville Bee, August 4, 1960
Bridgeport Telegram, February 27, 1958
Portland Press Herald, April 9, 1950
Kingston Daily Freeman, May 3, 1952
Lima News, September 2, 1934
San Antonio Light, October 5, 1941
Dunkirk Evening Observer, July 24, 1947

Untitled

Hartford Courant, November 13, 1971

The hostilities of the First World War came to an end on November 11, 1918. Exactly seventeen years later, on November 11, 1935, 66 veterans of the war chipped in ten cents each to buy a bottle of champagne. They called themselves The Last Man Club and vowed to meet each November 11th thereafter, with the last survivor among them to receive the champagne.

On the 53rd anniversary of the armistice, four members of the Last Man Club met in Indianapolis. They were not the only survivors, but they all lived near the Indiana city and were among the few members who were healthy enough to travel. Seventy-nine-year-old Charles Peevler, secretary and treasurer of the club, said that he had verified that at least 40 of the original members had passed away. Seventeen were known to be alive and the remaining nine had dropped out of sight.

In addition to Peevler, Thurman Marshall, William Schenmeker, and Victor Rigot came to the Indianapolis meeting. "It's not the party it used to be," said Marshall. "But we still shoot the breeze, have a nip or two, talk about old times. And the odds of getting that champagne get better all the time."

The Indianapolis group was one of a number of Last Man Clubs. On Armistice Day 1988, 96-year-old Albert Furrer drank a toast from a bottle of champagne at his nursing home in San Pablo, California. But it was not the bottle of 1921 French vintage champagne the 31 members of his club had purchased in 1932; that had long since soured.

Furrer's Last Man Club had been a true band of brothers. "We made friends," he said, "got together, did a lot of golfing, went to the same resorts.... This went on for 50 years." One thing they never did was talk about the war and there were no tall tales about heroic deeds. Furrer readily admitted that he was no hero. "I tried my darndest to get out," he said.

A year earlier, Furrer and Victor Parachini were the only attendees at the group's 55th annual banquet. Three months later, Parachini was dead and Furrer was the last man standing—or at least sitting in his wheelchair. He made one toast—to his friend Victor.

More than 22 years later, the true last man, 110-year-old Frank Buckles, died. Buckles had an advantage in the war of attrition; he was just 16 when he enlisted in 1917. He was rejected by the Marines and the Navy, but the Army took his word that he was of age, and the last survivor was permitted to enlist on August 14, 1917.

Buckles went to France in 1918 but never got close to the action. It wasn't until the Second World War, when he was a civilian caught in Manila during the Japanese attack in December 1941, that he found himself in peril. He was interned and spent the next 3½ years in confinement before being liberated in February 1945.

In addition to having enlisted at a very young age, Buckles had good longevity in his bloodline; his father lived to 97 and a sister to 104. As the 21st century dawned, the old soldier became a celebrity. His home state of West Virginia dedicated a section of highway to him. In 2008, Buckles was invited to the White House by President George W. Bush. On the 90th anniversary of the Armistice, he was recognized as the last living veteran of the great conflict. Unlike the alleged Civil War veterans described earlier, Buckles was legitimate.

Although none of the four members of the Last Man Club that met in Indianapolis in 1971 lasted as long as Buckles, they had some life left in them. Victor Rigot was the first to pass, in 1974 at the age of 76. He was followed the next year by "Red" Marshall, who passed away at 78.

Charles Peevler and William Schenmeker staged a spirited battle for the champagne. On May 22, 1988, Schenmeker died at the age of 94, leaving Peevler as the Last Man. He survived until September 12 before passing away at 96.

FDR Son Accused of Murder Plot; Elliott Denies It

Bridgeport Post-Telegram, **September 18, 1973**

James was not the only problematic Roosevelt. All of his siblings attempted to make a career of being Franklin Roosevelt's son; they tended to eschew hard work, preferring to chase easy money in ways that were not always legal or ethical. Although the Roosevelt sons displayed a lifelong penchant for getting in trouble, none was suspected of murder until September 18, 1973, when Elliott was accused of paying for the assassination of the Prime Minister of the Bahamas, Lynden O. Pindling.

In fairness, Roosevelt's accuser, Louis Pasquale (The Doctor) Mastriana, was an abominable character. He was a con artist and convicted stock swindler who was, at the time of his testimony before the Permanent Senate Subcommittee on Investigations, a prisoner at the federal penitentiary in Texarkana, Texas. It was not Mastriana's first time in jail; he'd spent a good part of his adult life there.

Mastriana, who'd been granted immunity in return for his testimony, said that in 1968, Roosevelt and Michael McLaney, a gambling impresario and reputed associate of mobster Meyer Lansky, offered him $100,000 to kill Pindling because the prime minister, after accepting a significant amount of campaign contributions from McLaney, failed to issue him a gambling license. The Bahamas had allowed casino gambling for many years, but in 1958 the business was opened up to foreign operators, which brought a host of organized crime figures to the islands.

The heavy-set, balding, 51-year-old Mastriana told Illinois Senator Charles Percy that he received a down payment of $10,000, of which $7,500 was a check from Roosevelt dated May 17, 1968, drawn on the Bank of Nova Scotia and $2,500 was a check from McLaney to Roosevelt endorsed to Mastriani. "They came to me," Mastriana said, "and offered me $100,000 to kill, to whack [Pindling]." Who are "they?" Percy asked. "Roosevelt and McLaney." He said he had recorded conversations with Roosevelt on equipment furnished to him by the U.S. Postal Service, for which he was an informer.

After taking the money, Mastriana chickened out. He was afraid he wouldn't be able to escape from the island and that Pindling's popularity (he was the first black man elected to rule over the former British colony) would make it impossible for him to avoid capture.

Evidence submitted to the subcommittee included a copy of the check from Roosevelt, a letter from Roosevelt to Mastriana offering him a job as an account executive for a company called Directions, Inc. for $10,000 per year and a photograph of Elliott inscribed "To My Friend and Associate, Louis Mastriana."

The subcommittee tried to get Roosevelt's side of the story, but by the time they reached Miami, where he had a public relations business, he had left for Portugal. On October 2, Roosevelt returned to the United States and appeared before the subcommittee. The senators paid homage to Roosevelt's family and then asked him to respond to the allegations. Elliott said,

2. Where Are They Now?   49

"I completely and categorically deny each and every charge made before the subcommittee." Earlier, he told a reporter, "It is an utter and complete fabrication and outright lie made by a man who is know (sic) con-artist who has been convicted, who has been put in jail, who has been adjudged by the courts of New Jersey as a mental incompetent, and who conned me and my associates out of $10,000 in Miami."

A number of troubling facts, unrelated to any assassination attempt, surfaced concerning Elliott Roosevelt. Mastriana was in jail for dealing in stolen securities and claimed that Roosevelt had been involved. On the day Roosevelt testified in the Senate, a man named Patsy Lepera, who had extensive Mob connections, said that Roosevelt stole securities in 1969 and 1970. Roosevelt said both men were lying.

There was no denying the fact that Roosevelt knew Mastriana, Lepera, and other members of the underworld. "A tremendous number of fiends and strange characters came through my office," he said. He didn't explain why he gave them large checks and autographed photos of himself and offered them jobs, or why a significant number of those fiends and strange characters had a common interest in stolen securities. McLaney, Roosevelt's alleged accomplice in the murder for hire plot, was also a convicted stock stealer.

Mastriana was potential political dynamite, for he had a connection with Miami banker Charles "Bebe" Rebozo, a close confidant of then-President Richard Nixon. A few years earlier, Mastriana had $115,000 in checks representing proceeds from the sale of stolen securities that he needed to cash. A mutual acquaintance introduced him to Rebozo, who allowed Mastriana to cash the checks at his bank. Unfortunately for Mastriana, he had been unable to hold onto the proceeds of his criminal activity. "Between the broads and gambling," he said, "I went broke."

Elliott Roosevelt's background wasn't as sordid as that of Mastriani, Lepera, or McLaney, but he had been involved in some highly questionable activities. In the late 1930s, he was said to have agreed to use his Texas radio stations, in collaboration with Nazi sympathizer James Rhodes Davis, to support a revolt led by defeated Mexican presidential candidate Juan Andreu Almazan.

In 1943, General Elliott Roosevelt was sent to California to learn about airplanes. He was immediately taken in hand by John Mayer, publicist for the Hughes Aircraft organization. Mayer's role was to convince Roosevelt to recommend to the U.S. Government that they purchase his company's XP-11 plane. He knew his mark well, for Mayer's main weapon was entertainment rather than technical detail. Over the next few days, he spent nearly $6,000 on Elliott Roosevelt, mainly on the engagement and provisioning of attractive young actresses. He later testified that he paid the women from $100 to $400 per day. One of the actresses was Faye Emerson, who did quite a sales job on the married Roosevelt. The next year, he obtained a divorce and made Emerson his third wife.

Not surprisingly, despite the objections of Chief of the Army Air Force Henry (Hap) Arnold, Roosevelt recommended that the U.S. order the Hughes plane. Elliott complained to his father that Arnold was giving him a hard time, and the general reluctantly signed off. Hughes had a $43 million order and Lockheed, which had a better plane but no actresses on retainer, came up empty. In 1947, Roosevelt was asked to testify about the matter before a Senate Subcommittee but was never charged or censured.

McLaney, Roosevelt's alleged accomplice in the murder-for-hire plot, had previously been linked to the CIA's efforts to depose or kill Fidel Castro. After Pindling refused to grant him a gambling license, he realized he could not do business in the Bahamas and moved his operation to Haiti, where he was able to establish a casino business under the protection of dictator "Papa Doc" Duvalier.

No charges were ever brought against Roosevelt for his alleged role in the attempted murder of Pindling. He had denied the accusation and the U.S. Senate wasn't eager to dig too deeply into the affairs of the son of a revered former president. After all, Pindling was still alive and no one had been harmed. Democrats wanted to preserve the legacy of Franklin Roosevelt and Republicans wanted to avoid any testimony that might implicate Bebe Rebozo. They let the matter drop.

What was abundantly clear, however, was that Elliott Roosevelt associated with some shady characters, and while he may not have been guilty of hiring hit men or stealing stock, he knew men who did. And it's hard to believe he didn't know what they were doing. But fortunately for the Roosevelt family, the 1973 incident was Elliott's last major peccadillo. He managed to stay out of trouble until his death in 1990 at the age of 80.

It wasn't in Mastriana's nature to stay out of trouble. He continued to involve himself in shady enterprises, including the Bank of Sark, a shadow operation with a phony façade, no staff, and no money behind it. Its main purpose was to launder the proceeds of stolen securities. Mastriana died in 1983 at the age of 61 and if there was any truth to his accusations about Roosevelt, it died with him.

Other sources:
New York Times, October 4, 1973
Jet Magazine, October 4, 1973
http://jfk.hood.edu/Collection/White%20Materials/Watergate/Watergate%20Items%2006520%20to%2006702/Watergate%2006577.pdf
Interference: How Organized Crime Influences Professional Football by Dan E. Moldea, Open Road Media, 2014

2. Where Are They Now? 51

Mystery Man, William Rhodes Davis: American Nazi Agent of Influence, Dale Harrington, Brassey's, Washington, D.C., 1999
https://en.wikipedia.org/wiki/Elliottt_Roosevelt
https://bahamianology.com/Elliottt-roosevelt-son-of-former-american-president-franklin-d-roosevelt-implicated-in-plot-to-kill-bahamian-prime-minister-lynden-pindling-1973/

3

Where Were They Then?
Those Who Later Became Famous

Occasionally, one comes across an article that is unremarkable save for the fact that the subject later became famous. A young college student named Mitt Romney got married in 1969. Whatever became of him? A fledgling actor named Dustin Hoffman, just off his first big role, was collecting unemployment compensation. A teenaged Prince Charles was getting into teenage trouble. An obscure peanut farmer from Georgia won a gubernatorial primary. Below is a chronicle of the soon-to-be-famous.

Prince's Nip in a Pub May Bring a Caning
New York Times, June 20, 1963

It's hard to remember that Prince Charles was ever young. He seems to have been perpetually middle-aged, even when he was marrying Diana at the age of 32. But like all of us, Charles was once an adolescent, prone to the trouble that teenagers, even royal ones, inevitably wind up in.

Charles had a difficult childhood. His father was a forceful figure and often overbearing and his mother, her days filled with ceremonial duties, was frequently absent. Neither parent was demonstrative, and the children were as likely to be greeted with a handshake as a kiss. One of Prince Phillip's main concerns was that Charles toughen up, and he frequently criticized the young heir, whose diffident personality caused him to shrink inward rather than fight back. Philip had been a star athlete in his youth and wanted Charles to follow in his footsteps, but the son proved inept on the playing field and uninterested in athletic games.

Charles's education began with his governess, Catherine Peebles, who home-schooled him as a child. In 1957, when he was eight, his parents decided that Charles would be the first heir to the throne to attend a regular school. He began classes at the Hill House School in Knightsbridge, but had difficulty fitting in with the other children. After six months his parents sent him to board at the Cheam School in Hampshire, which Philip had attended as a boy.

Charles didn't have a particularly happy experience at Cheam; the other boys didn't get close to him for fear of being accused of trying to curry favor. His protruding ears made him the butt of jokes and his lack of athletic skill inhibited his ability to blend in. At age nine, Charles was named Prince of Wales, which did little to make him one of the guys.

At Cheam, however, Charles finally acquired some interests of his own. He was not a highly skilled rider like his sister Anne, but he took an interest in polo. Polo ponies didn't have to jump, something Charles had always feared in the steeplechase. He also liked the theater, and played a passable Richard III in a school production. Overall, however, school was not a happy time for Charles. He spent many weekends with family friends, who say he was often teary.

From Cheam, the Queen Mother wanted to send Charles to Eton, but Philip preferred Gordonstoun, a private school in Scotland that he had attended. Therefore, in May 1962, Charles began his tenure at his father's alma mater, a strict institution that required the wearing of shorts in all weather and insisted that windows be left open year round, to facilitate the toughness that Philip wanted to see in his son. The Crown Prince viewed his time at the school as a "prison sentence." He was often bullied, but he never fought back.

In June 1963, 14-year-old Charles was sailing with his schoolmates on the Gordonstoun ketch, the *Pinta*, in the Outer Hebrides. Afterwards, the group planned to see a movie at the Stornaway Playhouse, but first Charles, his bodyguard David Green, and four other boys went to a bar at Stornaway's Crown Hotel. When they walked in, Charles ordered a cherry brandy and put down his two shillings and six pence. "I said the first drink that came into my head," he said later, "because I'd drank it before, when it was cold, out shooting." Ordering an alcoholic drink, however, was something a British subject, even a prince, was not allowed to do legally until they were 18. But Charles got his brandy, for "a royal command for a drink hardly could be refused."

Unfortunately, there was a tabloid reporter on the scene, and the incident was reported around the world. At first, Buckingham Palace denied that it had taken place. A day later, they changed their story, with the explanation that the Queen had been misled and Scotland Yard was investigating.

In the aftermath of the affair, David Green, who was one of Charles's few friends, was fired, which greatly upset the Prince. "I have never been able to forgive them for doing that," he said much later. As for the caning mentioned in the headline, that was a stretch. The Gordonstoun headmaster, F.R.G. Chew, said he might take disciplinary action against Charles after reviewing the incident and admitted he had a cane that he used to administer punishment in severe cases. He would not say whether the cane would be used on the Crown Prince, and it is almost certain that it did not strike the Royal Bottom.

The scene of Charles's indiscretion, the Crown Hotel, closed in 2014. Many years earlier, the lounge had been renamed the Prince of Wales Bar in honor of Charles and his historic brandy. In 2003, while having a couple of drinks with his father, Prince William said, "Look, Pops, they've got cherry brandy." Charles rolled his eyes. "Don't believe everything they tell you," he replied.

Other sources:
Vanity Fair, March 2017. http://www.vanityfair.com/style/2017/03/the-isolating-boarding-school-days-of-prince-charles
http://www.telegraph.co.uk/news/uknews/1433549/Look-Pops-Theyve-Got-Cherry-Brandy.html
http://www.heraldscotland.com/news/13141389.Hotel_where_prince_sought_brandy_to_close/

Books of the Times
Young Bohemians—Canadian Style

New York Times, September 12, 1963

Leonard Cohen was one of the most talented songwriters ever to come out of Canada and one of the best lyricists of his generation. The haunting *Hallelujah* is perhaps his most memorable composition, and songs like *Bird on a Wire*, *Light as the Breeze*, and *Joan of Arc* were covered by such diverse artists as Judy Collins, Johnny Cash, Billy Joel, and Joe Cocker. Richard Gehr wrote in *Rolling Stone*, "[Cohen's] rumbling voice, Spanish-y guitar lines and deeply poetic lyrics transubstantiated the sacred into the profane and vice versa."

But songwriting was not the skill that Cohen initially believed would make him famous. Long before he began to make his living writing songs, he was a novelist and a poet. As Gehr said, "Poetry, fiction and songwriting were more or less equal forms of expression to Leonard Cohen—although one paid a hell of a lot better than the others."

Cohen was a secondary folk figure of the 1960s, never as famous as icons like Bob Dylan and Joan Baez, strumming simple chords on his guitar and singing his rich, soulful ballads. By the 21st century, when Dylan and Baez were seen as legendary figures from the distant past, Cohen was writing original music and had become an octogenarian sex symbol, appealing to a new generation with his suits, his hats, and his craggy, oddly handsome looks. We go through different stages of attractiveness as we age, Cohen once said, progressing from irresistible, to resistible, to invisible, to repulsive, and then to cute. He, Cohen said, had reached the final stage.

With fresh, evolving ensembles, Cohen continued to tour, putting on three-hour shows even when he was past 80. One reason for his longevity was a passion for his work and another was the fact that he had fallen victim to an unscrupulous manager who lost all his money. Cohen took to the road out of necessity at a time when he might have preferred a quiet retirement.

In his seventies and eighties, Cohen achieved his own unique look. Old rockers like Steven Tyler, Mick Jagger, and Neil Young look like 70-year-old men wearing rock star Halloween costumes, their teenaged hair encircling a grandfather's face. Cohen never looked like most musicians of the 1960s; he could have passed for a Jewish professor. Although he occasionally sported a beard or longish hair, he generally looked as though he should be teaching sociology at NYU. In his old age, Cohen appeared on stage in a suit and fedora, the latter accessory becoming his most recognizable trademark; many fans wore fedoras to his concerts in tribute.

But the young Leonard Cohen didn't wear hats and he was not a singer. He didn't begin performing until 1967, when he was 32 years old. Thirty-two was a very advanced age for a generation that professed not to trust anyone over 30, and what made the transition even more difficult for Cohen was the fact that he was terrified of appearing on stage.

On February 22, 1967, Cohen made his first appearance as a singer, as part of a benefit concert for radical radio station WBAI. The bill included Pete Seeger, Tom Paxton, and Judy Collins, all experienced performers who had sizable followings. "I can't sing and I certainly can't perform," Cohen told Collins, but she insisted that he play.

Cohen's first attempt seemed to prove him correct. He couldn't get his guitar tuned, his voice broke as he tried to sing *Suzanne* and, embarrassed and frustrated, he abruptly left the stage. Later in the set, he asked to try again, and Collins agreed to sing the song with him as a duet. This time, he got through it, and although it was a long time before he was comfortable on stage, Leonard Cohen was a singer.

In 1963, however, Cohen was a poet and writer who had just produced his first novel, *The Favorite Game*. Like nearly all first novels, *The Favorite Game* was autobiographical, following Lawrence Breavman through a Jewish, mostly Canadian journey, with many of its best scenes taking place in Cohen's hometown of Montreal. There was alienation, a search for meaning, and a lot of sex, so much sex that one prospective publisher found it excessive.

It was a coup to have one's first novel reviewed in *The New York Times*, and somewhat of a surprise given the difficulty Cohen had in getting it published. After receiving a $2,000 grant, he spent time in London and the Greek island of Hydra writing the book that was first called *Beauty at Close Quarters*. His initial publisher rejected it and he finally convinced Secker and Warburg to take it after cutting the original draft in half. It was three years after his original submission before *The Favorite Game* finally appeared in print.

"The Favorite Game," reviewer Charles Poore wrote in the *Times*, "...is a sort of miniature convention against all the conventions." Whatever that means. "[It]," Poore continued, "will be read on a thousand North American campuses this fall—while older readers will wait for some judge to tell them whether it's daring enough to warrant a capital outlay."

Despite the favorable review, *The Favorite Game* sold only about 1,000 copies. It quickly faded into obscurity, reappearing in 2003 when a movie based upon the novel was produced by Bernar Hebert. The movie had no more success than the book.

Cohen wrote just one more novel, *Beautiful Losers*, which appeared in 1966. He also issued two collections of poetry, *Flowers for Hitler* (1964) and *Parasites of Heaven* (1966). His first novel was the more popular of the two, and the second did not receive critical acclaim nor did it sell particularly well. Disappointed with his lack of commercial success, Cohen decided to use his poetic talent to pursue the more mainstream field of songwriting. The rest, as they say, is history.

Other sources:
"Leonard Cohen: 20 Essential Songs" by Richard Gehr, *Rolling Stone*, November 16, 2016
I'm Your Man: The Life of Leonard Cohen, Sylvie Simmons, Harper Collins, New York, 2012
http://www.leonardcohenfiles.com/rigelhof2.html
http://www.imdb.com/title/tt0299868/

New-Found Stardom Worries Dustin Hoffman
New York Times, December 30, 1967

"While people are lining up for half a block outside the Lincoln Art Theater to see a new star named Dustin Hoffman in a new $3-million movie called 'The Graduate,' the new star is lining up downtown for a $55-a-week unemployment check." Thus began the article describing how Hoffman, after a decade of limited success, finally hit it big in the role of Benjamin Braddock.

Hoffman grew up in Los Angeles and dropped out of college in 1956 to pursue an acting career. He was not conventionally handsome and not old enough for character roles, so he struggled for many years. "I lived below the official American poverty line until I was 31," he said.

Hoffman was 30 when director Mike Nichols chose him to play Braddock. Robert Redford had been one of the candidates for the role, but Nichols thought he was too good-looking; no one would believe he had trouble finding women. Burt Ward, who played Robin, the Boy Wonder in the *Batman* series, was another possibility, but his managers wanted to maintain his image as Robin and turned the part down.

That left Hoffman, who was scheduled to play German playwright Franz Leibkind in Mel Brooks' *The Producers* but went to test for *The Graduate* anyway. In his words, the screen test was a "disaster." "But Nichols," he said, "clever guy that he is, saw something in me that he could use. Panic? Maybe. Anyway, I got the role and I was acutely depressed." Brooks agreed to let him out of *The Producers*; after all, Brooks' wife Anne Bancroft was to play Mrs. Robinson. Kenneth Mars wound up playing Leibkind.

The film, of course, was a spectacular success and Hoffman was paid $20,000, much more than he had earned for any previous role. But when it was over he was out of work, which was the reason he was collecting unemployment compensation.

In 1968, the year after *The Graduate* appeared, producer Sidney Pink released *Madigan's Millions*, an Italian-Spanish comic crime movie that had been filmed two years earlier. Hoffman played Jason Fistor, supporting Cesar Romero and Elsa Martinelli. The following year, Hoffman starred in *Midnight Cowboy* with Jon Voigt and his days of collecting unemployment compensation came to an end.

Notes: The stockinged leg in the iconic advertisement for *The Graduate* did not belong to Anne Bancroft. It was the leg of Linda Gray, then an unknown actress who later starred in the television series *Dallas*. One of the main themes of the film was the inter-generational romance between the naïve Benjamin Braddock (Hoffman) and the mature, seductive Mrs. Robinson (Bancroft). At the time the film was released, Hoffman was 30 and Bancroft was 36.

Other sources:
  http://mentalfloss.com/article/72639/12-seductive-facts-about-graduate
  https://www.biography.com/people/dustin-hoffman-9341124

Mitt Romney Marries Ann Davies
New York Times, **March 22, 1969**

The 22-year-old Mitt Romney who got married in 1969 was not that much different from the 65-year-old who ran for President in 2012. George Bush was an irresponsible party animal at Yale and Bill Clinton and Barack

Obama were busy sowing wild oats during their college days, but young Mitt Romney didn't seem to have a lot of wild oats to sow. He was that rarest of birds during the 1960s—a young conservative.

Willard Mitt Romney came from a privileged background; his father was George Romney, Secretary of Housing and Urban Development in the Nixon administration and formerly CEO of American Motors, governor of Michigan, and Republican presidential candidate. Mitt was named after George's business associate J. Willard Marriott and George's cousin Milton "Mitt" Romney, who spent six years in the National Football League in the 1920s with the Chicago Bears and Racine Legion. The youngster was initially called Billy, but out of admiration for his uncle he told everyone he preferred to be known as Mitt.

When Mitt was in the seventh grade, he entered the prestigious Cranbrook School in Bloomfield Hills, Michigan. He was not a stellar student, nor was he very athletic. "He was in many ways the antithesis of what he's portrayed as today," said classmate Jim Bailey. "He was tall, skinny, gawky, had a bad complexion." Mitt was less interested in academics, sports, or social life than he was in his father's career. He helped out in George's gubernatorial campaign, worked in his office as an intern, and talked with him about the cars they were building at American Motors.

When Mitt was a senior, he began dating Ann Davies, who attended Kingswood, the sister school of Cranbrook. They met at a birthday party when Mitt was 18 and Ann was 15, and their first date was the movie *The Sound of Music*. At his senior prom, Mitt proposed and Ann accepted.

Mitt began his college career at Stanford University, where his conservative Mormonism, with its prohibitions against drinking and smoking, was in stark contrast to the revolution that was sweeping American campuses. Mitt wore sports coats and ties while his classmates walked around in jeans, sandals, and beads. One of the resident assistants in his dorm was a junior named David Harris, a leader of Stanford anti-war activity. Harris later became a national figure in the draft resistance movement and eventually served time in prison. From 1968 through 1973, he was married to folk singer Joan Baez, whose mention of her husband's incarceration wound up on the Woodstock live album.

At Stanford, Harris had numerous ideological discussions with Romney and attempted to shake his conservative views, but Mitt was not buying. Despite their differences, however, the two were friendly and their discussions were always civil and respectful. Once, on a visit to the uber-liberal University of California at Berkeley, Mitt borrowed Harris's faded jeans, work jacket, and moccasins so he wouldn't stand out.

He may have worn Harris's clothes, but he never did adopt his principles. At a campus anti-draft rally, a newspaper photographer snapped a picture, which appeared on the front page, of Mitt protesting against the protesters, wearing a blazer and holding a sign that read, "Speak Out, Don't Sit In."

At the end of his freshman year, Mitt withdrew from school and spent the next two and a half years on a Mormon mission. Had he stayed at Stanford, would his political views have changed? Harris thought they might have. "There were plenty of people," he said, "who started to the right of Mitt Romney who ended up as full-scale hippies." When Mitt's mission ended, however, he elected to enroll at the Mormon Brigham Young University rather than return to Stanford.

Mitt and Ann were ready to marry, but religion posed a potential problem. Ann's parents, Mr. and Mrs. Edward Davies, were nominal Episcopalians. Edward had no use for religion, however, and had convinced his wife to stop attending church regularly. The Romneys, of course, were devout Mormons; George had been born in a Mormon colony in Chihuahua, Mexico. In those days, the wedding of two people of different faiths was referred to as a "mixed marriage," and while they were becoming more common, they were still cause for raised eyebrows.

When Mitt began talking to Ann about the Mormon faith, she was receptive, and while he was away on his mission, Ann approached George Romney and said she was interested in converting. After speaking with Mr. and Mrs. Davies to be certain they had no objection, George guided Ann through the conversion process, and she became a Mormon.

Even with both bride and groom professing the Mormon faith, the logistics of the wedding were a bit dicey. On March 21, 1969, there was a ceremony at Bloomfield Hills, Michigan (where Mitt was raised) performed by Elder Edwin Jones of the Church of Jesus Christ of Latter Days Saints, followed by a reception for about 300 guests. On the 22nd, the couple flew to Salt Lake City for a second ceremony at the Mormon Temple. As non–Mormons, Mr. and Mrs. Davies were not allowed inside the temple.

The Bloomfield Hills ceremony was the main event. The bride wore a "demure ivory organza gown with Venetian lace at the yoke and hem and on the train." Just three months earlier, Julie Nixon, daughter of the president-elect, had married David Eisenhower, and many thought Ann Romney's dress was very similar to Julie's. "Ann was so busy on a school project sending Christmas cards to servicemen in Vietnam," said her mother, "that she didn't pay any attention to Julie's wedding."

The guest list was impressive, as might be expected when the groom's father was a cabinet member and the father of the bride was president of Jered Industries. George Romney had made his reputation as CEO of American Motors, and the auto industry was well-represented by Semon E. Knudson, president of the Ford Motor Company, James M. Roche, chairman of the board of General Motors, George Russell, vice chairman of General Motors, and Edward Cole, president of General Motors.

Following the Salt Lake City ceremony, the couple left for a honeymoon at an undisclosed location. Unlike the marriages of Tommy Manville (see Chapter 2) that of Mitt and Ann Romney endured. When delivering the commencement address at Southern Virginia University in 2013, Romney urged the graduates to marry young. "I'm so glad I found Ann when I was still so young," he told them. Mitt quoted the Bible for support, but the main reason for his statement was the happiness of his own marriage, an adventure that began on March 21, 1969.

Other sources:
   http://archive.boston.com/news/nation/articles/2007/06/24/privilege_tragedy_and_a_young_leader/?page=4
   The Atlantic, April 2013

Peanut Farmer Wins Democratic Runoff in Georgia

Bridgeport Post-Telegram, September 24, 1970

When Jimmy Carter ran for President in 1976, he positioned himself as an "outsider," which was a very good thing to be in the post–Watergate era. It was not the first time Carter had been an "outsider"; he'd played that hand in his native state of Georgia during the 1970 gubernatorial race.

Carter's first elected office, which he held from 1963 to 1967, was State Senator for his hometown of Plains. He had his sights set on becoming governor, but in 1966 he placed third in the Democratic primary, behind former governor James Arnall and infamous segregationist Lester Maddox. Maddox won the runoff, but in the general election, Republican Bo Calloway beat Maddox by the narrow margin of 3,000 votes.

Arnall ran as an Independent, however, preventing Calloway from receiving a majority. Under Georgia law, if no candidate polled more than 50 percent of the vote, the legislature chose the governor. The Democrat-dominated Georgia legislature chose Maddox.

A Georgia governor could not succeed themselves, and therefore Maddox was ineligible to run in 1970. Times were changing, even in Georgia, and none of the leading contenders for governor was an avowed segregationist. J.B. Stoner, a KKK leader who had been active in the Florida race riots (see Chapter 4) received less than 3 percent of the vote in the Democratic primary.

3. Where Were They Then?

The two principal candidates for the nomination were Carter and former Governor Carl Sanders, who'd preceded Maddox and was eligible to run again. Sanders was a racial moderate and progressive by Georgia standards; he had been cooperative when the federal government intervened to end segregation. Sanders was also relatively young at 45, a year younger than Carter. A major blemish on his record was his endorsement of Maddox in the 1966 election, which Sanders attributed to party loyalty.

Carter projected the image of a casual, informal man of the people. In an era when most politicians, including Sanders, wore a suit and tie on all occasions, Carter campaigned in open-necked shirts and rolled up his sleeves. Soon, Sanders was doing the same and said that Carter was not what he pretended to be—a poor, simple, hard-working farmer. When Carter took over the family peanut business, he struggled for several years, living in subsidized public housing for a time. But Jimmy Carter was a Naval Academy graduate who understood the scientific principles involved in growing peanuts. By 1970, he was a hard working but very prosperous farmer.

Jimmy Carter was not a segregationist. In the 1950s, he had been the only white man in Plains who refused to join the White Citizens' Council. He was the new style of Southern politician, neither a Dixiecrat nor a liberal. Carter defied categorization and was therefore called a moderate. While Sanders had a progressive record on race while he was in office, he carried the stigma of having endorsed Maddox, who'd first come to prominence by refusing to serve blacks in his Atlanta restaurant at a time when the law required him to do so.

The 1970 runoff campaign was bitter. Sanders, who had initially tried to ignore Carter, went after him with a vengeance once he realized that the peanut farmer presented a serious threat. He challenged Carter to a debate, which the latter refused. Carter's supporters criticized Sanders' immaculate appearance and the fact that he flew to campaign stops in a private jet. He was too "slick," they said.

Carter beat Sanders by 87,000 votes but missed achieving a majority by less than 2 percent of the vote. The two men were paired in a runoff election, in which Carter, who'd started the race as a relative unknown, was suddenly the favorite. He defeated Sanders decisively with 59 percent of the vote.

Georgia did not have a Republican governor from 1872 until 2003, so the winner of the Democratic primary was pretty much assured of winning the general election. Sure enough, Carter defeated Republican Hal Suit, a television newscaster and first-time candidate, by almost the same margin by which he'd beaten Sanders in the runoff. The lieutenant governor's race was separate from the gubernatorial election, and Lester Maddox was elected, although he was not Carter's running mate. In his inaugural address, with Maddox on the podium, Carter said, "The time for racial discrimination is over."

It had been a long quest for Jimmy Carter, presaging his marathon run for the Presidency. He'd begun campaigning as soon as he lost the 1966 primary and estimated that he'd shaken 700,000 hands and made 1,500 speeches over four years.

In 1976, of course, Carter defeated incumbent Gerald Ford and became the 39th president of the United States, the first peanut farmer elected to the position. The candidate for the American Independent Party, which was established by George Wallace in 1968, was Lester Maddox. Maddox received 170,000 votes.

Other sources:
>https://en.wikipedia.org/wiki/Carl_Sanders
>https://en.wikipedia.org/wiki/Georgia_gubernatorial_election,_1970
>https://en.wikipedia.org/wiki/Georgia_gubernatorial_election,_1966
>https://millercenter.org/president/carter/life-before-the-presidency
>https://en.wikipedia.org/wiki/Lester_Maddox
>*Charlotte Herald News*, November 4, 1970.
>*Ames Daily Tribune*, September 23, 1970.
>*Medicine Hat News*, January 19, 1971.

4

The Times They Are a Changin'

Culture Shock of the 1960s

Bob Dylan was not the best guitarist of his generation, and he certainly didn't have the most melodious voice. Songwriters like Leonard Cohen wrote more beautiful and touching lyrics. But Dylan seemed to catch the wave of what was happening in the 1960s and became the voice of his generation, much as Jack Kerouac was the voice of the beat generation a decade earlier. Kerouac was not a great writer (Truman Capote contemptuously referred to his work as "typing") but, like Dylan, he captured the spirit of his time.

When Dylan sang "The times they are a changin,'" he hit the nail right on the head, for the 1960s were a decade of revolutionary change—changes in sexual relationships, dress, morals, race relations, and just about everything else. After only a few years, the America of 1960 was scarcely recognizable.

Men's fashion drew more attention during the late 1960s than it had since the colonial era of powdered wigs, knee breeches, silk stockings, and buckled shoes. What men wore wasn't as important as the fact that for the first time in many years they cared about what they wore.

The most controversial fashion issue for men of the 1960s was their hair. Nineteenth century pioneers wore long hair and beards, but mainly because they didn't have regular access to barbers. During the 1960s, long hair was a symbol rather than a matter of convenience. Students and employees fought for the right to wear their hair as they chose and many a family was torn by disputes between father and son over the length of sonny's hair.

Another issue that separated the young people of the 1960s from their parents was their use of mind-altering drugs. Drug use was not new to America; there were opium dens in the 19th century. But prior to the 1960s, drug use was generally confined to lower class and criminal elements. By the mid-1960s (see Chapter 5) the boys and girls next door were smoking marijuana and the more adventurous were experimenting with LSD.

The Civil Rights Act of 1964 put an end to legal racial segregation in America. While the Act was not a magic elixir that eliminated racism, anyone who tried to enforce segregation no longer had the law on their side. But Americans' respect for the law was at a low point during the 1960s. Thirty years earlier, the country experienced a massive crime wave, with gangsters like John Dillinger and Bonnie and Clyde becoming anti-heroes to a generation embittered by a deep economic depression. The bank robbers of the '30s were economically motivated, but those who wantonly ignored the law during the 1960s generally did so for moral rather than economic reasons. Segregationists defied federal troops to maintain their archaic social structure, while young revolutionaries bombed buildings to protest the war in Vietnam and social injustice.

Change is stressful and sometimes, particularly in 1968, it seemed as though America was coming apart at the seams. But the United States is a resilient nation. We survived the 1960s. Later, we survived Watergate, the resignation of a president, and the disco era. But it wasn't easy.

2 Professors Lose Bias Suit Appeal

New York Times, December 31, 1962

Art professor Josef V. Lombardo and philosophy professor Joseph Mullally (the *Times* misspelled his name as Mulally) felt they were being denied promotion by New York's Queens College because of illegal bias. Lombardo and Mullally were not black, Hispanic, or Asian. They were not gay or disabled. They claimed they were discriminated against because they were Roman Catholics.

Both men had impressive credentials. Mullally, who was 49 years old in 1962, was born in Ireland and after immigrating to the United States earned a doctorate from Columbia in 1944. His first teaching assignment was at Notre Dame University, which he left in 1950 to accept a job at Queens College.

Lombardo, five years older than Mullally, also received his doctorate from Columbia. In the 1930s, he spent time at the University of Florence and then went to Queens for the first time in 1938 as chairman of the art department. After teaching at NYU and Columbia, he later returned to Queens.

The allegations that led to the lawsuit were first made in 1958, when the two professors appealed to the Board of Higher Education, which found no evidence of discrimination. Although Lombardo was Italian, he chose to base his claim on religion, though he had intimated as early as 1942 that the college discriminated against him due to his ethnicity.

After the Board denied their claim, Lombardo and Mullally filed a lawsuit, which they lost. They appealed and lost again, when the Court of Appeals in Albany voted 5–2 to uphold the original decision. The majority opinion stated that the two men had failed to prove that the decision not to promote them was based primarily on their religion and that their claim was founded only on "a few instances of alleged bigotry many years ago."

Lombardo and Mullally had one more chance, however, for the New York State Division on Human Rights had begun its own investigation. That raised the hackles of the Board of Higher Education, which tried to stop the new probe, claiming that the Human Rights Division did not have authority to hear the case. After a spirited skirmish, it was ruled that the investigation could continue.

In 1960, the Commission found "there had been a policy of resistance to the employment and promotion of Catholics in teaching positions at Queens College." President Harold Stoke issued a strong response:

"The agitation about anti–Catholic discrimination at Queens College," Stoke said, "has been fostered, if not originated, almost entirely by a few members of the college's own staff. These persons, unable to convince colleagues of their qualifications for advancement, have over a period of years, deliberately charged religious discrimination to explain their lack of academic success and to obtain promotion."

Lombardo sued Stoke for libel. The complaint was dismissed and Lombardo's appeal was denied. But in 1966, the Division on Human Rights ruled that the college had discriminated against three Catholic assistant professors, Lombardo, Mullally, and David Guy Powers.

By the time the decision came down, Joseph McMurray had replaced Stoke as President. McMurray, as his name might indicate, was an Irish Catholic and, ironically, it had been suggested that his religion had been one of the reasons he'd been named President. McMurray promoted Dr. Lombardo to full professor; Powers had been promoted while the inquiry was underway.

In 1970, the Division on Human Rights ruled that the college had denied tenure to Dr. Lawrence Castiglione because he was Catholic and Italian-American. It was a sorry legacy for Queen's College, but today the institution has come full circle. One doesn't need to look very far on its website to find enthusiastic commitments to diversity and inclusion. Queens, it was noted, is America's most ethnically diverse county, the college's students come from more than 150 different countries, and one of the school's activities is "celebrating the borough's many ethnic communities." Even Catholics.

Other sources:
https://www.leagle.com/decision/196641218ny2d3941365
Observation Post, March 17, 1966
https://www.leagle.com/decision/196247337misc2d4361318

When *Affirmative Action is White: Italian-Americans in the City University of New York, 1976–Present*, Liana Kirillova, Southern Illinois University at Carbondale, 2016
http://www.qc.cuny.edu/about/Pages/default.aspx
New York Times, September 11, 1964, and March 24, 1999
Prabook.com

Tough "Hoss" Manucy Has Solution for St. Augustine: Fire Negro Help
Hartford Courant, June 30, 1964

In 1963 and 1964, St. Augustine, Florida, the oldest European settlement in the United States, was the scene of some of the country's most violent racial strife. One doesn't generally think of Florida as the Deep South, although no state is farther south. But when people speak of the Deep South they are usually referring to states like Alabama, Mississippi, and Georgia. The southern part of Florida, which by the early 1960s was home to a large number of transplanted northerners, was relatively racially tolerant. So was western Florida. Unlike many southern police forces, Tampa's law enforcement community cracked down hard on white vigilante groups. But the northern section of Florida, particularly Jacksonville and St. Augustine, was as virulently racist as Mississippi or Alabama. During the Jacksonville riots of 1960, police stood by and watched as blacks were brutally beaten by whites.

After the 1954 Brown v. Board of Education ruling, race became the dominant issue in Florida politics. Governor Farris Bryant pledged to maintain the legal separation of races even if it meant fighting the federal government, and he had plenty of help. By 1957, Florida had the second highest number of Klansmen of any state in the Union, and most of them were concentrated in the northeast part of the state. As the ranks of the Klan increased, the FBI mobilized against them, infiltrating a number of Klaverns and trying to stir up dissension in the ranks.

St. Augustine was home to 4,000 blacks, whose activities were restricted by the segregationist Florida laws and by the determination of the city's 11,000 whites to keep them in subjugation. There were two types of white supremacists in St. Augustine. The first was the "respectable" kind, which consisted of many of the city's leading businessmen and politicians. Mayor Joseph Shelley, the police chief, and Sheriff L.O. Davis were staunch segregationists, while the business community was led by H.E. Wolfe, a contractor and banker, and Dr. Haygood Norris.

There was also a less respectable contingent in the segregationist camp, led by Hoss Manucy, a man John Herbers of the *New York Times* described as "220 pounds of brawn and belly. He wears a T-shirt, jeans and a battered black cowboy hat that hides his bald spot. Black hair curls around his ears and he usually is in need of a shave."

Halstead "Hoss" Manucy (the *Courant* misspelled his first name as "Halsted") was the leader of an organization called the Ancient City Hunting Club, which Manucy claimed had 1,476 members. It was unclear exactly what the Ancient City Hunting Club was hunting but it appeared that blacks were its primary quarry.

Manucy was generally believed to be an Exalted Cyclops of the Ku Klux Klan, although he denied it. "I'm not a member of the Klan—I'm Catholic," he said, "but I'm not knocking it either. I think the Klan is a very good organization." More than a decade later, in 1976, when Manucy was interviewed by Edward Kallal, Jr., he said, "I met some fine people in the Klan. It's just as legal as the NAACP." He described attorney Jess "J.B." Stoner, a Klan leader and head of the National States Rights Party as "a hell of a nice guy." That was an interesting characterization of a man who, while running for governor of Georgia in 1970, stated that Adolf Hitler had been too moderate.

But Stoner was not *that* nice a guy. He defended James Earl Ray for the murder of Martin Luther King and in 1980 was convicted of the 1958 bombing of Birmingham's Bethel Baptist Church. (In the 1970 gubernatorial race, Stoner proved Leo Durocher's theory that nice guys finish last, losing badly to Jimmy Carter and his Republican opponent.)

Manucy's family supposedly came to the St. Augustine area in 1769. ("That's why we like to fight for it," he said.) Hoss played tackle at St. Joseph's Academy, and beginning in 1955 he delivered cars for an area body shop. He had a minor criminal history he dismissed as "a whisky record. I never stole anything." Manucy said his goal was "to keep our kids white kids for the next 100 generations," and launched a campaign to have all employers fire their black employees. "A Negro can't make a living without a white man," he said. "He will have to go north, where the welfare checks are bigger."

In June 1963, after unsuccessfully attempting to get city leaders to discuss the racial issue, St. Augustine's blacks began demonstrating, which brought the full force of the police and the Ancient City Hunting Club down upon them. Gunfire was exchanged in the streets. Sheriff Davis, who was Manucy's high school football coach, deputized over 100 men, including Manucy. The vigilantes were never hindered by the police, and they were highly organized, communicating by citizens band radio in order to learn where the blacks were marching.

When the blacks demonstrated, Manucy's men marched against them, always, he noted, with legal permits. "Every time they'd march," he said, "we'd march." "There's no white man scared of a Negro," he boasted. "That's a proven fact in St. John's County." There wasn't a lot to be scared of, since whites had the police on their side.

Finally, the white leaders agreed to meet with the black protestors to discuss their grievances. It didn't go well. One of the whites read from a pamphlet, and every time the word Negro appeared in the text, he substituted "nigger." Another white suggested that, to lower the tension level, the reader use the proper word. He did, and afterwards Dr. Robert Hayling, a black dentist and one of the leaders of the integrationist movement, said, "at least we accomplished one thing—one of us has learned a new word." That was about the only thing that was accomplished, and the violence continued. Hayling's life was threatened and shots were fired at his house.

In September, the Klan held a mass cross-burning ceremony, and when Hayling and some of his followers got too close, they were beaten with chains. Four white men were arrested, but they claimed Hayling had pulled a gun on them, and the latter was convicted and fined $100. His home was attacked a second time a few months later.

When a white man was killed by gunfire—it was not certain who fired the shot—four blacks were indicted, included one of the leaders of the integrationist forces. Meanwhile, the violence continued, and St. Augustine became a virtually lawless city. Civil rights activists from around the country rallied to the cause and in April, 71-year-old Mary Peabody, mother of the Massachusetts governor, was jailed for taking part in a protest. Martin Luther King, Jr., arrived in town on May 27 and the following day led a massive night march.

With national attention focused on the Florida city, St. Augustine became an embarrassment and its tourist trade was decimated. When the complicity of the police with Manucy's group became evident, Federal Judge Bryan Simpson ordered St. Augustine's police force to "engage in real enforcement."

After that, the police began acting like legitimate officers of the law. They had plenty of opportunity, for Manucy's gang was in full swing, assaulting newsmen and attacking blacks who were attempting to integrate the city's beaches. State police went down to the beaches, clubbing and arresting white counter demonstrators. Now the war was between the white supremacists and the police, which is what it should have been from the start.

The final blow was the passage of the Civil Rights Act. While the law had previously been a weapon of the segregationists, it was now on the other side. Manucy was furious. "There was nothing in the Civil Rights Act of 1964 for white people," he said in his 1976 interview. "It was all for the coloreds—the niggers.... Lower white class people can't get the same breaks they get. Chinese and Japanese can't come over and get the same breaks they get."

In 1964, Manucy, seeking to be paid for the information, told the FBI that William Rosencrans, a white supremacist, was involved in a bombing incident. It turned out that Rosencrans was not complicit in that incident, but he was convicted of unrelated charges and sentenced to seven years in prison. Manucy's actions created a deep rift in the segregationist ranks, even though Hoss redeemed himself by being imprisoned briefly for refusing to provide a list of Klan members.

After 1964, membership in the Ancient City Gun Club declined. The FBI was successful in breaking down the Klan by spreading rumors that its leaders were informers, bringing them in for questioning to build suspicion that they were cooperating. The FBI was good at dirty tricks, and many of them worked, turning the segregationists against each other.

Jimmy Brock, manager of Monson's Motor Lodge, was the toast of the segregationists when he was photographed pouring an unidentified liquid into the lodge's swimming pool when blacks and white sympathizers attempted to integrate it. After the Civil Rights Act was passed, Brock served blacks at the Lodge restaurant, and his property was bombed.

Shortly after the Civil Rights Act became law, James Jackson, one of the integrationists, encountered Manucy as he was leaving a hardware store. The two were old adversaries, but apparently Manucy didn't recognize Jackson as they accidentally bumped into each other. "Now I'm not a tall man," Jackson said, "but he was shorter than me, and he looked up at me and said, 'Excuse me sir.'" Jackson burst out laughing. "Excuse me sir! The biggest smile came over my face."

Manucy died in 1995 at the age of 76.

Other sources:

1976 Interview with Halstead Manucy by Edward Kallal, Jr., February 21, 1976
http://cdm16000.contentdm.oclc.org/cdm/ref/collection/p15415coll1/id/1042
New York Times, June 20, 1964
Anarchy in St. Augustine, by Larry Goodwyn, *Harper's Magazine*, January 1965
https://en.wikipedia.org/wiki/J._B._Stoner
The FBI, COINTELPRO-WHITE HATE and the Ku Klux Klan in Florida 1964–1971

Connecticut Boy Loses Appeal to Wear Beatle Bangs to School

New York Times, December 16, 1964

On February 9, 1964, the Beatles appeared on the *Ed Sullivan Show*, the first time they had been on American television. American girls loved them, and many American boys thought that perhaps if they looked like the Beatles, girls would love *them*. But 15-year-old Edward Kores, Jr., a freshman at Connecticut's Westbrook High School, learned that while looking like a Beatle on the *Ed Sullivan Show* was acceptable, showing up at Westbrook High School looking like a Beatle was not.

Kores wore bangs, but otherwise his hair was relatively short, not reaching either his ears or his collar. "He has little bitty bangs in the front," said his mother Beatrice. "They end about one and a half inches above his eyebrows. If his haircut were extreme, I would have something to say." Edward's father, a carpenter, also had no problem with his son's hairstyle. "I don't believe my son is offending good taste," he said, "and besides, no one has ever called him a Beatle. He isn't even a Beatle fan. He just likes to wear his hair in bangs."

The principal of Westbrook High had a major problem with Edward's bangs, claiming they were a distraction to the other students. He was determined that no student at his school would look like a Beatle, and like another son of a carpenter, Edward Kores was about to become a martyr.

During class one day, one of Edward's teachers told him that if he didn't comb his hair to the side, he would be suspended. When he refused, the school made good on its threat, suspending him on November 13 and telling him he could not return to class without an acceptable hairstyle. "Since when is there a law in Connecticut," Edward's father asked, "that can compel a boy to comb his hair a certain way."

On three occasions, Edward attempted to return to school with his bangs but was turned away. By that time, the issue had been reported in newspapers around the country, and Westbrook High came under the national microscope. Apparently, there weren't a lot of pressing educational issues in Westbrook in December 1964, for it wasn't long before the entire school system became involved in the case of Edward Kores's bangs. Superintendent of Schools Arnold Oliver backed up his principal, the Westbrook Board of Education voted to support Oliver, and the suspension remained in place. Kores's parents appealed to the State Commission on Civil Rights, which refused to hear the case.

The Kores family hired attorney Vincent Vishno of New Haven to represent them. Vishno met with Oliver, but Dr. William J. Sanders, the State Education Commissioner, ordered the superintendent to use the state's compulsory education law to force Kores to return to school. If he did not, his parents could be fined five dollars a week.

On December 18, Kores was told that if he did not return to school with an acceptable hairstyle by December 21, the matter would be referred for criminal prosecution. Kores went to Westbrook High on the 21st, with his bangs, and was turned away for the fourth time. A couple of days later, Kores's parents announced that he would transfer to a private school after the Christmas holidays and the controversy came to an end.

It was twenty years before Edward Kores appeared in the news again. On Friday evening, August 24, 1984, he was at Frankie's, a popular shoreline restaurant owned by the ex-husband of his sister Jeanne. By that time,

Kores was a self-employed logger living in nearby Lyme, unmarried but with two daughters.

A band called Linda and the Loveletters was playing at Frankie's that evening, but Kores and 43-year-old William Cole of Essex were not interested in music. For several months, the two men had been arguing over a woman, and that evening the dispute escalated. Kores and Cole went out to the parking lot to settle the matter, and shortly afterward patrons heard a single gunshot. Kores fell to the ground, mortally wounded in the abdomen, while Linda and the Loveletters, oblivious to what was happening outside, played on. Kores was rushed by ambulance to the Shoreline Clinic, but died within the hour. Cole was taken into custody in the restaurant parking lot and charged with first degree manslaughter. He was released the following day when bail was posted by his attorney, Haiman Long Clein.

The story doesn't end there. Clein, Cole's attorney, was involved in another killing ten years later, as a principal rather than as an attorney. By that time, Clein's life was in shambles. His practice was in serious financial trouble, he had become a heavy user of cocaine, and he was having an affair with Beth Carpenter, a young lawyer he'd hired as an associate. One of the reason Clein's firm was in trouble was that he was diverting money to support Carpenter's lifestyle.

Carpenter also had a serious problem. She was trying to obtain custody of her 3-year-old niece for her parents on the grounds that her sister's new husband, Anson "Buzz" Clinton, III, was an unfit parent. Clein decided that the best solution was to get rid of Buzz Clinton, and he paid used car dealer Mark Depres, a former client, approximately $10,000 to kill him. Depres, accompanied by his 15-year-old son Christopher, lured Clinton to Rocky Neck State Park, discharged five shots into his body, and left him dying on the beach.

Depres initially admitted killing Clinton, but later changed his story and said that his son pulled the trigger. Christopher denied firing the shots, saying that his father asked him if he wanted to do the shooting, but he declined. The jury believed Christopher and sentenced Mark to 45 years.

After the murder, Carpenter fled to Europe. In late 1995, when a warrant was issued for Clein's arrest, he also disappeared. After two months on the run, police apprehended him in Sunset Beach, California, while he was talking with Carpenter on a pay phone.

In 1997, Clein pleaded guilty to a reduced murder charge, was sentenced to 35 years in prison, and agreed to testify against Carpenter. In 2002, Carpenter returned to the United States and was put on trial for murder. She was convicted and sentenced to life without parole.

It started with a Beatle haircut and ended with two murders. Perhaps Albert Oliver had been correct. Let teenage boys wear their hair over their forehead and there was no telling where it would lead.

Other sources:
Middletown Press, August 25 and 26, 1984
Hartford Courant, November 7, 1997, February 4, 2002, February 14, 2002, and March 18, 2003
Glens Falls Post Star, December 22, 1964
Syracuse Post Standard, December 17, 1964
Dover Daily Reporter, December 24, 1964

"Georgie Porgie" Sings
Hartford Courant, December 9, 1965

Like Edward Kores, George Leonard, Jr., liked to wear his hair in a way that irritated school administrators. George had a reason for his hairstyle, however; he was a rock and roll singer who performed under the name Georgie Porgie.

Leonard, born in Pawtucket, Rhode Island, in 1947, began taking music lessons in grammar school and was soon pursuing advanced studies at the Berklee School of Music in Boston. While still a teenager, he began sitting in on jazz sessions in Providence clubs. The proprietor of the "*Tete a Tete*" gave Leonard the nickname Georgie Porgie because of his youth, and he carried it throughout his music career.

Shortly after the Beatles appeared on the *Ed Sullivan Show*, George decided to adopt the Beatle cut and change the name of his band, which consisted of him and his two sisters, from the Georgie Porgie Trio to Georgie Porgie and the Cry Babies. They switched from jazz to rock and roll and began playing at amusement parks, school dances, and church halls.

In the meantime, Leonard's family had moved from Pawtucket to Attleboro, Massachusetts. On September 11, 1964, the second day of his senior year at Attleboro High School, George was told by Principal Joseph E. Joyce, Jr., that he would have to cut his hair before he would be allowed back in school. George refused and his parents sued the school system.

The lawsuit was based on three principal claims. First, George's hairstyle was an integral part of his role as a musician. Second, since he was a minor, his appearance was the responsibility of his parents, and the school's interference was an invasion of privacy. Finally, the Leonards argued that George's hairdo was a form of freedom of expression that was protected by the Constitution.

The court initially ruled against the Leonards, based upon the theory that George's hair could "disrupt and impede" school decorum. Although George lost, the case had dragged on for a year and the national attention it attracted caused his music career to blossom. Afterwards, when people asked him about his first hit, he always said, "The lawsuit was my hit record." It became an even bigger hit when in December 1965 the Massachusetts Supreme Court reversed the lower court and ruled in his favor.

Georgie Porgie didn't become as famous as the Beatles, but he had a pretty good career. When the Rolling Stones came to Rhode Island, the Cry Babies were the opening act. With two new members, the band recorded its first single, *Love You Girl Always*.

For the rest of the 1960s, George played in New York, cut a song about the lawsuit, titled *No More School*, and signed a contract with Jubilee Records that resulted in the release of the group's first national single. Despite some successes, The Cry Babies never really made it big; they were always on the fringes, playing some choice venues but never quite getting that big break.

In 1970, George's sister Judy and her husband Danny left the band and returned to Rhode Island to start a company that provided outfits for rock musicians. The business was successful and their clients eventually included The Temptations, Doc Severinson, and Mott the Hoople.

Meanwhile, George composed a rock opera called *Bozo—An Evolutionary Rock Musical*. *Bozo* never became as popular as *Tommy*, but Leonard performed the opera for several years throughout New York and New England on college campuses and clubs.

By the late '70s, cable television had taken hold, and George produced and starred in his own public access show, *Commander Video: Spaceman Cable TV*. By that time, however, Leonard had a young son and needed to earn a living; he went to work for his family's cleaning business.

The final chapter of George Leonard's musical career was an act in which he played a caricatured 1950s crooner he called Elvis Sinatra. For five years, Elvis Sinatra played at an East Village, New York, jazz club and released an album. One of the tracks was featured in the movie *Shallow Hal*.

In 2015, Georgie Porgie and the Cry Babies were inducted into the Rhode Island Music Hall of Fame, but long before that, George Leonard had become a hero to a rebellious generation of American youth. As Rick Bellaire wrote, "Every kid who sports long hair, pink hair or a shaved head, or wears a nose ring, a tattoo, or makeup, owes his right to do so to the musician who became known to the world-at-large as Georgie Porgie."

Postscript: At the end of the decade, a case involving long hair nearly reached the United States Supreme Court. The tale began in the fall of 1970 when Chesley Karr of Coronado High School in El Paso, Texas, was told that he and 21 other boys would need to cut their hair before they would be allowed to return to school. Karr was the only one who refused. He appealed to the school board, and when they backed Coronado High, Karr sued. His father, an insurance agent, supported him and got some lawyers from the American Civil Liberties Union to assist with the case.

The suit claimed a violation of Karr's first, ninth, and fourteenth amendment rights. Despite the constitutional gravity of the case, there was a lot of silly testimony at the trial. When Carr's lawyers asserted that girls' long hair wasn't disruptive, the defense claimed "[G]irls are by tradition the long-haired of the human species." The football coach at Austin High School testified that he didn't think long hair was "manly." The mayor of El Paso claimed that most long-haired boys were troublemakers. School officials worried that long-haired boys might try to sneak into the girls' bathrooms or locker rooms. Finally, the school claimed that boys didn't know how to care for long hair and were therefore unclean.

It was a pretty flimsy defense, but the school system was relying on the premise that they had the authority to make rules and those rules did not have to be logical or constitutional. In this case, they were wrong, for on November 19, 1970, the court ruled that Karr's right to wear his hair as he chose was indeed protected by the constitution. The school could only make rules that infringed on students' constitutional rights if they had a compelling reason, and apparently the court didn't think that the possibility of boys sneaking into the girls' room, smelling rank, or appearing unmanly were sufficient.

The School Board appealed, and the Fifth Circuit Court of Appeals agreed to hear the case, also granting the school a stay of execution for the order to eliminate its ban on long hair. That meant Karr could not attend school with his long hair, and after being turned away, he flipped a one-finger salute to Coronado High as he walked through the parking lot.

In April 1972, the Court of Appeals reversed the lower court and ruled that the school had the right to ban long hair. They found nothing in the constitution about haircuts and did not think hairstyles were a form of free speech.

The appeals court decision had been an 8–7 vote, indicative of the division in the legal system on the subject of hair regulations. Karr therefore felt that if he could get the U.S. Supreme Court to hear his case, he had a chance of prevailing. Unfortunately, the Court was not willing to listen to Chesley Karr. There were a lot of important matters before the court in 1972, involving the death penalty, high finance, and other weighty issues. Long hair was not a matter of life or death, and Karr had not been severely harmed by his expulsion, since he had since earned his high school diploma outside the school system and started college.

When the Supreme Court declined to hear the case, with liberal Justice William O. Douglas dissenting, Chesley Karr's battle was over. But the war would eventually be won. Today students can wear their hair in just about any style and color they choose, including many ways the students in Karr's class never dreamed of. Another barrier had come down.

Other sources:
http://www.ripopmusic.org/musical-artists/musicians/georgie-porgie/
Flaunting the Freak Flag: Karr v. Schmidt and the Great Hair Debate in American High Schools, 1965–1975, Gael Graham, *Journal of American History*, 91 (September 2004)

"Rebel Priest" Urges Fellows to Form Labor Union

Hartford Courant, **February 23, 1966**

Whose side would God be on if the priests' union went on strike against the Catholic Church? Thirty-one-year-old Reverend William DuBay wanted to find out, for it was his goal to organize the 58,000 Catholic priests in the United States. "We need an American Federation of Priests," he said, "because priest, like teachers, are employees." "The business concerns of church administrators," DuBay claimed, "have all but stifled the effectiveness of priests and have created widespread dissatisfaction."

The California clergyman, who entered the seminary at age 13 and was ordained in 1960, had never been a typical priest. In 1964, as pastor of a primarily black congregation, he became interested in the civil rights movement and accused 78-year-old James Francis Cardinal McIntyre of the Diocese of Los Angeles of "failing to give white Catholics moral leadership on racial discrimination." He said McIntyre was guilty of "gross malfeasance in office," wrote to Pope Paul VI asking for his removal, and released a copy of the letter to the press.

When the Diocese built schools for Mexicans and blacks, McIntyre inflamed DuBay by stating, "What is wrong, what is immoral, that they should live among their own kind—Irish with Irish, Poles with Poles, Mexicans with Mexicans, and Negroes with Negroes?" McIntyre believed that integration was a political issue and had no place in church policy.

The church supported its cardinal, pointing out a number of instances in which McIntyre and the church had come out in favor of equal rights for blacks. DuBay did not back down and, from that point, his relationship with the church was headed for an inevitable end.

The young priest was called to McIntyre's office for a 35-minute hearing to discuss his demands. The result was that McIntyre relieved DuBay of his administrative duties but allowed him to remain in the priesthood. When he emerged from the meeting, DuBay was asked if he was still a priest. "My collar's still on," he replied.

DuBay was transferred to a white parish in Anaheim and then a second time to become chaplain of St. John's Hospital in Los Angeles, where he was forbidden to discuss racial issues. He called the moves "retaliation."

After his second transfer, DuBay made his appeal for a union, listing ten essential demands:

1. Grievance machinery
2. Fair hearing by peers before suspension
3. Protection from arbitrary and oppressive transfers
4. Freedom to preach
5. Uniform leave policy
6. Open personnel files
7. Freedom of residence
8. Promotions without chancery favoritism
9. Professional salary schedule which makes priests independent of the wealthy
10. No mandatory fulfillment of such non-professional chores as money counting, rectory watching, bookkeeping, fund raising and janitorial tasks.

The list was challenging and provocative for an organization founded on unquestioning obedience, and Requirement #10 might make it difficult to operate a church. On the other hand, the Second Vatican Council, which concluded in December 1965, had called for a liberalization of church policy and an emphasis on individual conscience. DuBay's demands, however, contemplated a bit more freedom of expression than the Vatican had in mind.

DuBay's call for a union was set forth in his book *The Human Church*, a highly controversial work that espoused radical ideas such as the popular election of bishops for two-year terms, the elimination of parochial education, and giving local congregations the right to establish their own liturgy.

The publication of *The Human Church* was the last straw for McIntyre, who suspended DuBay from the priesthood. Although DuBay and his supporters called for an open trial, he had burned too many bridges and his continuing insubordination made the Catholic Church simply want to be rid of him.

DuBay served as a consultant for a while and then went to work at Syanon, a rehabilitation center for recovering narcotics addicts. In 1967, he performed the marriage ceremony of LSD guru Timothy Leary and his third wife, Rosemary Woodruff, a former actress and stewardess. It was quite a ceremony, for reportedly a number of guests were tripping on acid.

On August 10, 1968, two years after the publication of *The Human Church*, DuBay married 29-year-old Mary Ellen Wall, the divorced wife of a former Army major with four children ranging in age from 6 to 11. Initially, the ceremony was to have been performed by a rabbi, but he backed out when the situation became too controversial for his taste. Presbyterian

Minister Mason C. Harvey stepped in and officiated. Mary Ellen wore a pink mini-dress and DuBay wore slacks, a forest green Nehru jacket, and a peace medallion. For a priest, even a suspended one, marrying was bad enough, but marrying a divorcee was a double whammy. DuBay was excommunicated.

After his expulsion, DuBay lived with his attractive wife in the San Jacinto Mountains, managed a theater, and continued to work for social and religious change. He opened a union office for priests, but only a handful signed up and he abandoned the effort. DuBay traveled to Los Angeles once a week to visit a psychiatrist who was helping him deal with the changes in his life. He grew a beard and put the priesthood and the Catholic Church behind him. "Call me Bill," he told a reporter who came to interview him. In October 1969, he and Mary Ellen had a son.

In September 1971, DuBay, during an interview with *McCall's* magazine, admitted that he and Mary Ellen were having marital problems. The DuBays fought a lot and finally Mary Ellen told Bill that if he didn't seek additional psychological help, she was going to divorce him. She said he was not attentive and didn't listen to her. Bill admitted that he was not good with relationships and blamed his training as a priest. "The church has successfully implanted in its priests," he said, "an almost crippling inability to carry out a healthy relationship. We're still not sure our marriage will survive." In fairness, the Catholic Church was not training its seminarians to be good husbands.

Before the end of 1971, DuBay moved to Seattle and published a book on homosexuality, titled *Gay Identity: The Self Under Ban*. He then announced that he was gay and established a counseling group for gays with drug addictions, which he named the Stonewall Group. In April 1972, Mary Ellen filed for divorce, citing irreconcilable differences.

From that point, DuBay became a wanderer, moving and changing careers with great frequency. He worked in a residential treatment center, managed a health food store in Alaska, worked for the mayor of North Slope Borough, and published newsletters about the resource conflicts between oil companies and the Inupiat Eskimos.

In 1987, DuBay moved to California and became a technical writer and in 2001 he became a "plain language" consultant. He has written three books on plain language and currently lives on Whidbey Island, near Seattle. DuBay does not practice any religion, and said, "I'm more of an atheist than anything else right now. Or at least an agnostic."

It had been quite a journey for a man who entered the seminary at 13. He'd gone from celibate priest to renegade priest to married man and excommunicated priest to gay man. There was a liberal thread to his career choices, but his path was remarkably eclectic. There is no priests' union today, and while there has been change in the Catholic Church, it was primarily generated from without as a result of sex scandals rather than by any internal revolt. William DuBay, who wanted to be a change agent, appears to have been a committed but confused man who had difficulty discovering who he really was. What began in the mid–1960s as a quest for religious change became a lifelong journey with an indefinite end.

Other sources:
> https://en.wikipedia.org/wiki/William_DuBay
> https://www.americamagazine.org/content/all-things/what-ever-happened-father-william-dubay
> https://www.revolvy.com/main/index.php?s=William%20DuBay&item_type=topic
> *Ogdensburg Journal,* July 14, 1969
> *Gay Seattle, Stories of Exile and Belonging,* Gary Atkins
> https://www.instagram.com/p/BY14Mn9gBXL/
> *Billings Gazette,* June 17, 1964
> *Lawrence Daily Journal-World,* September 18, 1970
> *Dover Times Reporter,* April 26, 1972

Meredith Injured While on March
Hartford Courant, June 6, 1966

In September 1962, James Meredith became the first African American to enroll at the University of Mississippi. Segregationists were not about to allow him to break the color line without putting up a fight, and Meredith's initial appearance on campus instigated riots in which two were killed and 200 injured. It took twenty thousand Army troops to finally quell the disturbances. When quiet was restored, Meredith registered under the protection of federal marshals and spent the entire year under their watch. Many of his fellow students shunned him, and some openly harassed him, but he persevered and graduated in the spring. He'd completed three years at the predominately-black Jackson State College and needed only a year at Ole Miss to finish.

Nearly three years after his graduation, Meredith, along with three companions, undertook a 225-mile march from Memphis, Tennessee, to Jackson, Mississippi, to encourage Mississippi blacks to register to vote. He said that by marching openly he would "show Mississippi Negroes they had nothing to fear."

He wound up showing them they had quite a bit to fear. At one point during the second day of the march, Meredith and his small entourage were roughly three miles from Hernando, Mississippi. As had become routine, they were passed by several cars with Confederate flags waving from the windows and occupants who shouted obscenities at them.

4. The Times They Are a Changin'

Forty-one-year-old Memphis native Aubry James Norvell, a hardware store clerk and a member of the Ku Klux Klan, planned to do more than just scream obscenities. He was crouched in a culvert beside the road, cradling a 16-gauge shotgun loaded with #6 bird shot. As the caravan passed him, Norvell rose up and shouted "James Meredith—I only want James Meredith."

"Hit the dirt," someone yelled, but Meredith didn't hear him. Norvell fired three shots, striking Meredith in the back and the legs, covering his green sports shirt with blood. "Oh, my god," Meredith screamed as he fell to the pavement.

A doctor soon arrived and determined that Meredith's wounds were not life-threatening. FBI agents and state troopers, who were keeping a close watch on the marchers, chased Norvell into the woods and apprehended him easily. Although he readily admitted firing the shots, that was not necessarily an open and shut case in 1966 in Mississippi. Therefore President Johnson ordered Attorney General Nicholas Katzenbach to "spare no effort in bringing the gunman to justice."

Klansmen were not known for deep thinking, and Norvell had not anticipated the reaction to his shooting of Meredith. Rather than frighten the marchers, it strengthened their resolve. Many newcomers, including Martin Luther King, Marlon Brando, Sammy Davis, Jr., and Dick Gregory, joined the march. Meredith, whose wounds turned out to be minor, soon re-joined the group, and when the marchers entered Memphis, they were greeted by a crowd of 15,000. Although the white residents of Tennessee weren't any happier to see them than the people of Mississippi had been, they knew enough to leave them alone; shooting Marlon Brando or Sammy Davis wouldn't help the cause. In the meantime, thousands of black voters had been registered.

Norvell pleaded guilty and therefore there was no testimony and no explanation of his motive. He was sentenced to five years in prison but served just 18 months. Norvell died in 2016 at the age of 91, and by that time hardly anyone remembered what he had done in 1966. There were a couple of brief comments of condolence in response to his on-line obituary, the longest of which read, "My condolences to the Norvell family. I have been a neighbor of Mr. Norvell for approximately 50 years, and used to see him often as I walked my dogs in the neighborhood. He will be missed."

James Meredith is still alive as of this writing, and his political philosophy is a very unusual and puzzling one for a civil rights pioneer. Recipient of a law degree from Columbia, Meredith is a lifelong Republican who ran for office in New York and Mississippi. Later in his life, he was employed by North Carolina Republican senator Jesse Helms, viewed by many as a right wing racist. He also supported the campaigns of segregationist Ross

Barnett and former Klansman David Duke. James Meredith, one of the leading symbols of the southern civil rights movement, said that he was not a civil rights advocate; he only wanted for himself the rights to which any American was entitled.

Other sources:
https://www.americanheritage.com/node/132692
https://en.wikipedia.org/wiki/James_Meredith
New York Times, August 18, 1963

Curves Have Their Day in Park; 500 at a "Fat-in" Call for Obesity

New York Times, June 5, 1967

The 1960s was a decade of protest. There were rallies and demonstrations against the war in Vietnam and against racism. On June 4, 1967, in one of the more unusual rallies of the decade, 500 people gathered in the Sheep Meadow section of New York's Central Park to "celebrate human obesity." The event was organized by Steve Post of radical radio station WBAI-FM because he felt that fat people were the objects of discrimination. Post was not fat, although he had once weighed 250 pounds and said, "I wish I did again."

Post was a counterculture radio personality who hosted a call-in show called *The Outside*. He was satirical, irreverent, and a fervid supporter of left-wing causes. One of his heroes was comedian Lenny Bruce, who he served briefly as an assistant. Post flunked out (or dropped out—sources differ) of junior college and took a job as a bookkeeper at WBAI but soon became an on-air personality. As a talk show host, he did some bizarre things. For about a year, he conversed with a regular caller known as "The Enema Lady," who described her activities to Post in great detail.

Post saw an article in *The New York Times Magazine* about the stigma faced by obese youngsters and how it affected their adult lives. As a former fat child, he identified with them and noted that the article was located between ads for chocolate layer cake and a weight loss device. Madison Avenue created a need, Post said, by establishing an ideal body type and then catered to that need with weight loss products. "The advertising campaigns of Madison Avenue," he said, "have attempted to make us feel guilty about our size. People should be proud of being fat."

Post jokingly talked about doing a "Fat-In" and spoke of the indignity fat people face in trying to squeeze into subway seats and through turnstiles. He and his colleagues wrote satirical poems and songs about being fat and performed them on the air. When listeners started asking for details of the Fat-In, he decided to turn his joke into an actual event.

Post was surprised at the number of people who showed up. Not all were fat, but those who were dressed to accentuate their size, sporting horizontal stripes, using tape measures as belts, and wearing tight-fitting stretch pants. Nearly all of them brought food and shared it with each other. Signs and banners were an integral part of any protest and in Sheep Meadow there were signs that read "Fat Power," "Think Fat," and "Help Cure Emaciation—Take a Fat Girl to Dinner."

Susan Goldman, a student at Sarah Lawrence College, whose friend said she was 5 foot 2 and weighed 150 pounds, carried a bag with candy and thickly buttered slices of pumpernickel bread. A life saver was taped to her forehead. A trim 17-year-old said he wasn't fat but was trying to be. A history teacher named Jerry Friedman said that obesity could bring about world peace. "If everyone was fat," he reasoned, "there'd be no war. No one could pass the physical."

The highlight of the protest came when Post burned a diet book and a picture of emaciated English model Leslie Hornsby, known as Twiggy, who epitomized fashion's obsession with thinness. As with any respectable protest, there was an anti-protest. A trim karate instructor named Ron Rosen burned one sign and smashed another with a bamboo pole because he said it insulted his fat friends.

The Fat-In was a one-time event, but its effects were lasting. Dr. Charlotte Cooper, who wrote a book called *Fat Activism: A Radical Social Movement*, said it was the beginning of the "Fat Feminism" campaign. A few months after the event, Lew Louderback wrote an article in *The Saturday Evening Post* called *More People Should be Fat*. Louderback was a fat man with a fat wife and he encouraged the American Civil Liberties Union to recognize fat people as an oppressed minority. Apparently, someone was listening, and obese people are now protected under the Americans with Disabilities Act. When Post died in 2015, a Fat-In placard was exhibited at his memorial service. What had begun as a joke had turned into a social landmark and the beginning of a crusade.

Other sources:

    http://obesitytimebomb.blogspot.com/2016/02/100-fat-activists-2-steve-posts-fat-in.html
    https://www.wbai.org/articles.php?article=2167
    Playing in the FM Band, Steve Post, Viking Press, New York, 1974
    Reducing Bodies: Mass Culture and the Female Figure in Postwar America, Routledge, a division of Taylor and Francis, New York and London, 2017
    Independent Record, June 5, 1967

Coed Disciplined by College Becomes Dropout at Barnard

New York Times, September 4, 1968

Barnard College, the sister school of Columbia University, was beginning to loosen up in the 1960s. Early in the decade, Barnard women obtained the right to wear pants or shorts (as long as they weren't going near the Columbia campus) but by 1968, they weren't satisfied with wearing pants.

Rebellion was in the air but compared to the violence taking place at nearby Columbia, what passed for rebellion at Barnard was relatively tame. In the fall of 1968, a 20-year-old sophomore named Linda LeClair made national news by living with her boyfriend in an off-campus apartment. Sharing buildings wasn't as bad as occupying them, but it was against Barnard College regulations. Any student whose hometown was more than 50 miles from campus was required to live in a school dormitory.

Ms. LeClair had lived in a dormitory during her freshman year, before an illness required her to take a leave of absence. She returned in January 1967 and shortly thereafter met a Columbia sophomore named Peter Behr at a dormitory dinner party. Using a fake employment ad placed by a friend, LeClair told the school she had a job as a live-in caretaker and would therefore not be living in campus housing. Instead, she moved into a four-room apartment with Behr.

On March 14, 1968, the *New York Times* ran a story about unmarried student couples living together. LeClair agreed to be interviewed but requested anonymity, since she was in violation of her school's housing policy. She was identified in the article as "Susan" but gave enough details about herself to allow Barnard officials to learn "Susan's" true identity. LeClair became known as "Barnard's Kiss and Tell Girl."

As Barnard prepared to bring LeClair before a disciplinary board, she and Behr mounted a publicity campaign. "The media coverage," LeClair said many years later, "made it into a story about sex ... but really it was about power and equality."

LeClair asked that students be allowed to choose their own living arrangements and not be treated like children. She pointed out that while males at Columbia could live pretty much wherever they liked, Barnard women were confined to campus and could not leave their dorms after 9:30 p.m. on weeknights. If there was a boy in the room, the door had to remain open at least the width of a book. Of course, some books were very thin, and the Barnard girls joked about using matchbooks.

Barnard's policies were paternalistic and out of step with the times, but President Martha Peterson was in a difficult position. While students wanted more freedom, alumnae and donors believed in the old methods and let Peterson know they would not be happy—and might not donate—if the school allowed Barnard girls to live with men without the benefit of marriage.

Trying to satisfy everyone, the school took a "middle-of-the-road" position that satisfied no one. Peterson dodged the question of co-habitation and punished LeClair for lying about her housing situation. She banned her from campus dining facilities and dormitory social events. Barnard's rules were changed to allow students to live off campus if they had their parents' permission.

That didn't help LeClair, whose parents strongly disapproved of her living with Behr and cut off her financial assistance when they found out about it. That got the attention of conservative columnist William F. Buckley, Jr.

"Miss LeClair's parents," Buckley wrote in the *National Review*, "were finally consulted, and it transpires that they, being of the older generation of course, disapprove their daughter's habits, and have gone so far as to cease to send her money. Mr. Behr, who is a draft evader, is apparently unable to take up the slack; so that perhaps the indomitable Miss LeClair will list herself as an unemployed concubine and apply for relief from the City, which has never been known to deny relief to anyone who applies for it: and that should settle the economic exigencies of the matter."

Less prominent folks also had strong opinions. A letter to the editor of *Time* magazine read: "I don't know what kind of student Linda LeClair is or what kind of a mistress she makes, but judging from the picture of her apartment, she makes one lousy housekeeper. Doesn't Barnard College have a Home Economics department?"

LeClair and Behr were not mere sybarites; they were dedicated radicals who wanted to change society. Behr, as Buckley indicated, was a draft evader. When he received his draft card in 1966, he sent it back in protest. When he received a questionnaire from the Selective Service, he wrote them a long letter about "the uselessness of violence." When Behr got an induction notice, he went to the Fort Hamilton Induction Center in Brooklyn and burned it in front of about 50 students even though, had he gone inside, he would have been rejected due to a recent illness and a felonious assault charge related to a Columbia protest.

In July 1968, following the uproar over their living arrangements, Behr and LeClair spent a month at a communal farm in southern Vermont, before quarrelling with the leaders and leaving to hitchhike to the West Coast. Although the commune was a bad experience, the couple hoped to try it again with a more compatible group of farmers.

When the 1968–69 school year began, President Peterson said LeClair would be allowed to attend school if she agreed to abide by the rules. Instead, LeClair announced that she was withdrawing from college, while Behr said he was not certain whether he would return to Columbia for his senior year.

The couple's future plans were indefinite, but although neither believed in marriage, they said they wanted to settle down and have children. Whatever they did, however, they didn't want to do it in New York City. "The city is a dying thing," LeClair said. "We're killing ourselves off slowly here with smoke, noise, anger, guns, everything."

Other sources:
Columbia Spectator, March 14, 1968, April 19, 1968, and March 27, 2013
https://barnardarchives.wordpress.com/2013/02/14/barnard-in-a-time-of-love-and-war/
http://althouse3.blogspot.com/2008/05/linda-leclair-is-not-hip-shes-housewife.html

Writer Changes Sex; Will Wed Negro Man

Bridgeport Post-Telegram, November 21, 1968

One of the more revolutionary developments of the 1960s was inter-racial marriage. While it wasn't universally applauded, marriage between whites and blacks was becoming much more common and by 1968, it wasn't even newsworthy.

But sex changes were still front-page news. The word "transgender" was first used by Dr. Harry Benjamin, who began working with people who wanted to change their gender in the 1940s. Benjamin's most famous patient was Christine Jorgenson. Christine began life as George, served in the Army at the end of World War II, had gender re-assignment surgery in Denmark, and emerged from the operating room as an attractive 26-year-old blond woman.

Jorgenson sold her exclusive story to the *American Weekly* for $20,000 and became an advocate for transsexuals. In 1970, *The Christine Jorgenson Story*, a movie loosely based on her memoir, made Jorgenson part of pop culture. According to Wikipedia, Nation of Islam leader Louis Farrakhan, during his earlier career as a calypso singer, recorded a song about Jorgensen, called "Is She Is or Is She Ain't?"

Another man who made the transition to woman was writer Gordon Langley Hall. Hall had been a newspaper society editor and wrote 20 books, including biographies of Princess Margaret, Jackie Kennedy, Lady Bird Johnson, and Mary Todd Lincoln. (Note: I will refer to Hall as "he" during the time he lived as a man and "she" during the time she was a woman.)

After her surgery, Hall wrote quite a bit about herself and claimed that, unlike Christine Jorgenson, she had been born with ambiguous sexual equipment. Her female genitalia, she said, resembled a male's, and she was therefore raised as a boy, although she always believed she was female.

Hall said he was the illegitimate child of Jack Copper, the chauffeur of author Vita Sackville-West, and was born on Sackville-West's estate. He was later adopted by a man named Stringer Davis and his wife, Dame Margaret Rutherford, a British actress perhaps best known for playing Miss Marple in the movies based upon Agatha Christie's novels.

After being raised in England, Hall lived briefly in Canada, returned to England, and finally settled in the United States. He became close friends with painter Isabel Whitney, who reportedly left Hall $2 million when she died in 1962. After Whitney's death, Hall moved to Charleston, South Carolina, and lived in an historic home in an area that had a large gay population.

That brings us to the period of the *Post-Telegram* article. Nineteen sixty-eight was a very eventful year for Gordon Langley Hall. First, he had a sex change operation at Johns Hopkins University and took the name Dawn Langley Hall. Soon afterwards, Dawn announced that she was going to marry a 22-year-old black man named John Paul Simmons. Hall said it was the first inter-racial marriage in the history of Charleston; it was also the city's first inter-racial marriage involving a transgender person. To make things even more controversial, there was a significant age difference between the bride and groom. Dawn said she was 31, but London sources claimed she was 39 and, according to her obituary, she was actually 45.

Everyone found something in the marriage to offend their sensibilities. Dame Rutherford was reported to have said, "I am delighted that Gordon has become a woman, and I am delighted that Dawn is to marry a man of another race, and I am delighted that Dawn is to marry a man of a lower station, but I understand the man is a Baptist!"

In 1971, Dawn announced that she was pregnant, which seemed to be a miracle for a transsexual and only remotely possible even if one believed her claim that she was incorrectly classified at birth. She walked around Charleston with her large belly and went to Philadelphia to deliver the child in order, she said, to avoid the circus atmosphere in Charleston. Dawn returned with a daughter named Natasha Simmons and a birth certificate for the skeptics.

For the rest of her life, Dawn Simmons lived a marginal existence, always short of money and coping with a mentally ill husband. She wrote three autobiographies: *Dawn: A Charleston Legend, Man into Woman,* and *All for Love* before she died in Charleston in 2000 at the age of 77, leaving her husband, daughter, and three grandchildren.

In 2004, historian Edward Ball published *Peninsula of Lies: A True Story of Mysterious Birth and Taboo Love*. Ball had heard the remarkable story of Dawn Simmons and was determined to uncover the truth. He traveled to Duke University to examine Dawn's voluminous papers. He went to England to interview people who had known her as a young man. He visited Charleston to meet the many people who'd known Dawn as both a man and a woman. He established a relationship with Dawn's daughter Natasha. He spent a great deal of time investigating the issue of "inter-sex individuals," those who fall somewhere between male and female classification. What Ball learned during his prodigious investigation was remarkable and quite different than what Dawn Simmons had written about herself in her three autobiographies.

Ball found that Gordon Hall was born in 1922 to a 16-year-old unmarried girl of modest means named Marjorie Hall Ticehurst. He was raised by his grandmother, another woman of modest means, who Gordon claimed was a newspaper reporter, although that wasn't true. Throughout his youth, Gordon was surrounded by strong women and preferred playing with dolls to sports.

Marjorie Ticehurst later married a man named Jack Copper, who agreed to pose as Gordon's father, although he was not. Marjorie and Jack were servants at Sissinghurst Castle, owned by Vita Sackville-West. Gordon visited often, and became close to West, who lived an eventful life even by the standards of the British artistic class. She was bi-sexual and had affairs with the writer Virginia Woolf and the daughter of Alice Keppell, mistress of Edward VII.

Hall had some charm and managed to convince people that he was more like Vita Sackville-West than Marjorie Ticehurst and Jack Copper. He became a society writer, covering weddings and social events for local newspapers. In 1946, Hall went to Canada for a year to teach the children of an Indian tribe, and wrote a book about his experiences called *Me, Papoose Sitter*.

After returning to England to teach art and theater for a spell, Hall immigrated to the United States, carrying with him an invented background of nobility and culture. He arrived in New York in 1952 and took a job at Altman's Department Store. As had been the case with Vita Sackville-West in England, the course of his life in America was changed by a wealthy woman, Isabel Whitney. Isabel, an elderly, unmarried artist of some renown, was a member of the wealthy and famous Whitney family. She was a diminutive 4'11" tall and got around on crutches, due to an injury suffered in a fall.

Hall and Whitney lived together in Whitney's home on West 10th Street and had a strange, undefined relationship. It was romantic in an asexual way; Whitney was sincerely fond of Hall, who catered to her needs and assuaged her loneliness.

Hall lived well in New York, thanks to Whitney's money. He returned to England to buy an expensive home and flaunt his newfound wealth, letting all his old acquaintances know that the son of servants had made good in America. Soon after he returned to New York, he learned that Isabel had leukemia. She wanted to move to a warmer climate, and Hall went to Charleston to buy a home for the two of them. Just two weeks after the purchase, however, Isabel died without having left New York.

Gordon moved to Charleston and again created his own image—a wealthy author living in a restored old home he called the Dr. Joseph Johnson House after the original owner. Hall continued to write biographies of famous women, once interviewing Lady Bird Johnson personally. Although the books did reasonably well, they were not works of art, and some of Hall's facts were questionable. James Reston of the *New York Times* said in his review, "Mr. Gordon Hall has written a book about Princess Margaret. He has written a book about Jacqueline Kennedy. He has now written a book about Lady Bird Johnson. He must be stopped before he strikes again."

While Gordon Hall's public life revolved around respectable Charleston society, he had a second identity in the discreet, underground world of Charleston's homosexual community. Ball interviewed gay men who'd had trysts with Hall, and he was still a man when he met John Paul Simmons.

Hall eagerly pursued Simmons, who was heterosexual and had no interest in a physical relationship with Gordon Hall. Hall then began dressing in women's clothing, which Simmons found strange rather than alluring. When Simmons continued to rebuff his advances, Hall told him he was going to the Johns Hopkins University Gender Identity Clinic.

Hall was not, he insisted, going to have surgery to transition from male to female. He was simply going to have surgery to free the female sex organs he claimed had been in him from birth. The assertion that he was "inter-sex" became a key part of the Gordon Hall/Dawn Simmons story that was portrayed in the three autobiographies.

Was Gordon Hall, as he claimed, a biological woman who had been assigned the wrong gender at birth? Ball was determined to find out and delved deeply into the gender identity and inter-sex world. He spoke with several experts on the subject and with the cosmetic surgeon who performed the operation on Hall. They told him that Dawn's story was a total fabrication.

Most people who want to change their gender, the surgeon told him, claim to be inter-sex, and it is almost always a case of wishful thinking. Some of the people believed by doctors to have naturally transitioned their sex as adults were found to be frauds who were using hormones rather than experiencing spontaneous bodily change. Hall's claim that he began menstruating while he was still a man was almost certainly false. True inter-gender people (or hermaphrodites, as they were commonly known) are extremely rare, and Gordon Hall was not one of them.

After Hall emerged from Johns Hopkins as Dawn Pepita Langley Hall, she married John-Paul Simmons in a ceremony that scandalized Charleston society. The social darling became a pariah whose social life after her wedding was mostly confined to the city's black community.

One of the most remarkable aspects of Dawn's situation, and one of the key pillars upon which the inter-sex claim was based, was the birth of Natasha. Someone who was merely transgender or transsexual could not bear a child, since they would have neither ovaries nor a uterus. Ball therefore set out to find the truth about Natasha's birth. Although he had established a good relationship with Dawn's daughter, she of course could not provide details. John-Paul could, if Ball could find him and if his mental illness would allow him to communicate coherently.

The marriage of Dawn and John-Paul had not gone well. John-Paul ran through Dawn's money, rarely worked, began drinking and philandering, and became physically abusive. He was diagnosed as schizophrenic and spent many years in hospitals and halfway houses. It would not be easy to find him, get him to talk, or evaluate the veracity of what he might say.

After heroic efforts, Ball located Simmons and managed to overcome privacy laws, the protectiveness of his medical providers, and Simmons' difficulty with communication. When Ball interviewed him, Simmons talked incessantly, and while much of his speech was rambling, Ball believed that he spoke the truth on critical matters. Simmons told Ball that Natasha was indeed his child, but the mother was one of his girlfriends. Dawn had paid the girl's father $1,000 for the baby.

What about the birth certificate, which appeared to legitimize Dawn's story? It turned out that there were two birth certificates. The first was the real one, which gave Natasha's last name as Simmons, and listed the real mother. Dawn Simmons had used that to obtain a second document in Philadelphia which identified her as Mrs. Simmons, the mother. She had gone to Philadelphia not for privacy, but in order to obtain documentation she could not get in Charleston.

Ball's book is called *Peninsula of Lies* and the story of Natasha's birth was the culmination of a life built almost entirely on untruths. Jack Copper was not Gordon's real father. Her grandmother was not a journalist who passed on her talent to Gordon. The story of the English life she told in America was greatly exaggerated, as was that of the American life she related to her English relatives. She was not an inter-sex person, but just another homosexual male who wanted to become female. She did not become a biological mother. Even the great quote from Dame Rutherford about being upset that Dawn married a Baptist was Dawn's creation. Virtually everything the public knew about Gordon Hall/Dawn Simmons simply wasn't true. But they were great stories, ones that Dawn was capable of telling convincingly and stories that people wanted to believe, because they were so riveting. Dawn Simmons yearned to be famous, and perhaps her foremost talent is that she was one of the world's greatest con artists.

Other sources:
New York Times, September 24, 2000
Peninsula of Lies: A True Story of Mysterious Birth and Taboo Love by Edward Ball, Simon & Schuster Paperbacks, New York, London, Toronto, Sydney, 2004

The Name of Model Agency That They Work for Is Ugly

New York Times, **March 7, 1969**

"I'm dating a model," is a line designed to impress one's acquaintances. But not if the model came from the agency called "Ugly," run by young Englishmen Robin Wright, Max Forsythe, Timothy Miller, and John Claridge. All except Claridge had experience in advertising, and had come to believe that consumers couldn't identify with the unrealistically beautiful or handsome models that normally appeared in print and television ads. "In the advertisements for second-hand cars," Forsythe said, "we want the salesman to be believable as a second-hand car salesman ... it used to be really hard to find real people—genuine looking ones."

The agency's first call for talent was blunt. "Are you ugly?" it read. Far too many people thought they were ugly, and after being overwhelmed with applicants, the agency ran a second ad: "Are you really ugly?" Of the roughly 1,000 who answered the second ad, Wright and his colleagues determined that about 150 were sufficiently ugly. "They are neither dull faces nor stupid ones," Wright explained. A crooked jaw and an imperfect nose graced the faces of most Ugly models, who were part-timers and told not to expect to make a living simply by being ugly. Average income was about $14.40 per hour, and virtually all models had other employment.

Wright believed that standards were changing in the late 1960s and pointed to musicians like Ringo Starr and models like Twiggy and Veruschka, who had unconventional features that might have been unacceptable a decade earlier. The initial success of the Ugly Agency led the partners to develop a plan to open a United States office within a year. They wouldn't take Ronald Reagan or any of the astronauts, Wright said. "But we would love Hubert Humphrey."

It turned out that ugliness was not a passing fad. The agency, operated by Marc French, is still in existence today. It represents over a thousand models, ranging in age from 18–100. The theme is not so much ugly as unusual. "We like our women fat and our men geeky," said French. Among Ugly's clients are 8'1" Sultan Kosen, the world's tallest man, and a woman with more than 2,500 piercings. Ugly's models have appeared in innumerable ads and films, including the Harry Potter series and nearly all of the James Bond movies that were filmed after the agency was formed. In 2010 England's Channel 5 produced a documentary on the Ugly Agency.

The current trend toward diversity has made French's firm more relevant than ever. He speaks of "celebrating diversity" and features disabled and ethnic models. French, who also runs a traditional modeling agency known as Rage, is poised to celebrate Ugly's 50th anniversary in 2019—a half century of providing the world with ugliness.

Other sources:
http://www.ugly.org/2016/
Daily Mail, August 26, 2010, and February 16, 2018

Bishop Pike: A Life Marked by Turmoil and Drama
New York Times, September 7, 1969

Bishop James A. Pike, like Father William DuBay, was a clergyman who wanted to transform organized religion. Like DuBay, Pike more frequently transformed himself, and like DuBay, he had little impact upon his intractable church.

Pike was a very famous man in his day. Ian Hunter wrote in 2004, "Episcopal Bishop James Pike may be a forgotten man today, but four decades ago he made a big splash in the ecclesiastical pond, albeit usually because of self-aggrandizing, sometimes heretical remarks." "During his peak in the Fifties and Sixties," wrote Michael Maudlin, "Pike was one of the most recognized Christians of his time, on par with Bishop Fulton Sheen and Bill Graham.... Bishop Pike was the public face of Christianity for many in America."

James Pike was born into the Catholic religion and as a youth intended to become a Jesuit priest. But by the time he got to college, Pike considered himself to be an atheist. He abandoned the idea of the priesthood for law, graduating from Yale Law School and practicing in Washington, D.C., with the Securities and Exchange Commission. During World War II, Pike served in Naval Intelligence.

In 1946, Pike reconciled with religion and was ordained an Episcopal priest. By that time, his marriage to his first wife, the former Jane Alves, had been annulled and in 1942 he had married a Jewish woman, the former

Esther Yanovsky. Since Pike had been married to his first wife for several years, the annulment, which enabled him to have the second marriage recognized by the church, was highly controversial.

Pike began his religious career in Poughkeepsie, New York, but his fiery speaking style soon earned him the position of chaplain at Columbia University. In 1953, he began preaching at St. John the Divine Cathedral in Manhattan. Pike was a politically active priest, espousing a number of liberal causes, and soon began to attract national attention. St. John the Divine was a huge church and Pike spoke before three to four thousand people each Sunday. He invited Martin Luther King, Jr., to speak at St. John's in 1956, at a time when the 27-year-old civil rights leader was little known outside the South. From 1955 through 1961, Pike hosted a Sunday afternoon talk show on ABC and appeared on the cover of *Time* magazine.

In 1958, Pike was appointed a bishop, and with his media savvy and charismatic personality, gained a substantial following. He rejected a number of accepted beliefs, such as the virgin birth of Jesus, the concept of a Trinity, and the idea of Hell. In 1960, Pike wrote an article in *The Christian Century* in which he claimed that Joseph was the biological father of Jesus. During the next four years, he published three books: *A Time for Christian Candor* (1964), *What Is This Treasure* (1966), and *If This Be Heresy* (1967).

"Dr. Pike wrote poor theology," Edward Fiske said in *The New York Times*, "that could easily be picked apart by trained scholars, and his sermons were rambling and self-centered. But he asked a lot of the right questions." "Everything I'm saying has a question mark at the end," Pike once said.

By 1966, the Episcopalian hierarchy was tired of Pike's questions, and decided it was time to wreak him asunder. Several bishops tried to have him convicted of heresy, but the church, worried about the impact of a heresy conviction on their reputation, settled on a motion of censure.

Pike was clearly diverging from Episcopalian orthodoxy. He explored new phenomena like the use of psychedelic drugs (he supposedly experimented with them himself) and the ability to communicate with the dead. He supported the ordination of women, racial desegregation, and the inclusion of the LGBT population in the church.

"He reflected the modern tendency," said Fiske, "to suspect orthodox systems almost by definition and to hold everything up to radical questioning, the characteristic admired in scholars, tolerated in youths, but generally unacceptable in Bishops."

Late in 1966, following his censure, Pike resigned as a bishop because he said he could no longer support established Christian doctrine. He became Theologian-in-Residence at the Center for the Study of Democratic Institutions in Santa Barbara, California.

Pike's fascination with communicating with the dead began early in

1966, following the death of his 20-year-old son, James, Jr. Young Pike committed suicide in a five-dollar-a-night New York hotel room, blowing half his head off with a shotgun. A long farewell note did not disclose a motive, but although James was known to have used hallucinogenic drugs, it was believed he killed himself because he couldn't cope with his homosexuality.

After his son's death, Pike claimed that strange things were happening around him, such as objects moving without apparent cause. He became almost obsessed with the occult and attempting to make contact with his son.

On September 3, 1967, Pike held a televised séance with the psychic the Reverend Arthur A. Ford and believed Ford put him in contact with his son. Ford had a well-honed knack for making people believe they were communicating with the dead. Although the Reverend apparently did have some psychic gifts, he supplemented them by doing extensive research on residents of the hereafter. From his research, Ford uncovered obscure tidbits that his audience believed he could only know if he was in contact with the dead person. His excellent memory enabled him to call up a dazzling bit of data at the right moment. Without modern search engines, it wasn't easy to be a credible medium, but Ford was a dogged researcher with a great memory.

Pike's obsession with contacting the dead did serious harm to his reputation and credibility, as did his chaotic personal life. In 1964, Pike admitted to a drinking problem and joined Alcoholics Anonymous. Prior to his son's death, he had separated from his second wife, and in 1966 he met Diane Kennedy, a 29-year-old student who was taking a summer course with the 55-year-old Pike. Kennedy wrote a book after Pike's death, in which she described him at the time of their meeting as a separated man in the process of obtaining a divorce. What she did not mention was that he also had a 43-year-old mistress named Maren Bergrud.

Bergrud was a troubled parishioner who came to Pike for help and wound up as his secretary and lover. On June 4, 1967, she called Pike and told him she was in his apartment and had taken 55 sleeping pills. Pike rushed over and tried to revive her but was unsuccessful. When he realized that Berglund was dead, he removed the body from his apartment and tore off part of her suicide note.

In 1968, Pike and Kennedy were married, after Pike received a second controversial annulment. On September 2, 1969, Pike and his new wife were in Israel gathering information for a book he was writing about the origins of Christianity. They rented a car and left Jerusalem to explore the wilderness where Jesus had supposedly been tempted by the devil. Soon they were lost, and the car became stuck fast in mud. A person more familiar with the operation of a jack probably could have salvaged the situation, but James Pike was more conversant with scripture than auto mechanics, and he and Diane found themselves stranded in the desert.

Abandoning the car, the Pikes walked for about two hours before James became exhausted and said he could go no further. The couple managed to find some shelter from the blistering desert sun, but Diane realized that if they stayed there much longer, they would die. She decided to leave her husband and try to get help.

Wandering in unfamiliar country without the aid of a map, Diane soon found herself deep in a canyon. She managed to climb the steep walls and find a dirt trail, which eventually led to a paved road, where Diane was discovered by a security guard—cut, bruised, and exhausted.

She was brought to Bethlehem and told the police, "We tried to follow Jesus' footsteps. We wanted to see the conditions Jesus knew. Jim had been here six times before and I had been here once. It was our first time in the desert. We didn't take a guide. We were very stupid about that."

Pike's disappearance was big news. Hundreds of volunteers joined police to form a search party, and while they found the abandoned car, there was no sign of the former bishop. It was more than 100 degrees in the desert, and after three fruitless days, the searchers realized that the chances were slim that Pike, who had no provisions, was still alive.

The redoubtable Dr. Ford appeared on the scene and said he had a vision of Pike alive but very sick and sheltered in a cave. Other mediums got into the act, but none was able locate Pike. On September 7th, without supernatural assistance, searchers found the body. Pike had attempted to follow Diane's path and scattered various items in his wake to aid search parties. It appeared that he had been attempting to scale a canyon wall when he slipped and fell to his death.

Diane said, "There could have been no more appropriate place for Jim to die, if he had to die. He died in the country he loved as though it were his own, in the wilderness where Jesus, according to the Gospels, went to pray and meditate."

If anyone remembers James Pike today, it is probably either as the man who had a televised séance or the one who died on a bizarre desert journey. He was a famous man in his time, and much of his fame was due to his being one of the few religious authority figures who was in tune with his times. Like so many charismatic people, however, Pike was a deeply flawed individual, leaving a trail of discarded wives and dead bodies behind him. He was more media savvy than brilliant, and in the end the bad judgment that had troubled him throughout his life brought that life to an end.

Other sources:

https://www.episcopalchurch.org/library/glossary/pike-james-albert
https://en.wikipedia.org/wiki/James_Pike
http://www.itsgila.com/headlinersbishoppike.htm. Diane Kennedy Pike's quotes regarding her husband's final moments are from this source

http://www.touchstonemag.com/archives/article.php?id=19-02-045-b
New York Times, March 11, 1973
New York Times, August 1, 1976
Sticky Fingers: The Life and Times of Jann Wenner and Rolling Stone, Joe Hagan, Knopf and Doubleday Publishing Group, New York, 2017
Desert Sun, June 15, 1967
http://www.christianitytoday.com/ct/2004/augustweb-only/8-30-12.0.html

Young Pair Take Lives as Protest Against the War
New York Daily News, October 17, 1969

On October 15, 1969, the New York Mets beat the Baltimore Orioles 2–1 in the fourth game of the World Series. It had been an amazing year for the Mets and for their 24-year-old pitcher, Tom Seaver, who pitched the entire 10 innings. Seaver and the Mets were the big story that day, but they competed for attention with about 200 people who stood outside Shea Stadium handing out leaflets protesting American involvement in Vietnam, for October 15th was Moratorium Day throughout the United States.

Met fans had a long history of banners and signs and on this day there were banners that read: "Met fans for Peace." They featured a picture of Seaver and a reprint of an article in which he said that if his team won the World Series, he would pay for an ad saying that if it was possible for the downtrodden Mets to be World Champions, it was possible to end the Vietnam War.

There was controversy before the game when Mayor John Lindsay, a liberal Democrat, ordered all flags in New York City, including the one at Shea Stadium, to be flown at half-staff in honor of the moratorium. Baseball Commissioner Bowie Kuhn overruled Lindsay and insisted that the Shea Stadium flag be hoisted to the top of the pole.

Moratorium Day was the brainchild of anti-war activists David Hawk (an ironic name for an anti-war activist) and Sam Brown, both of whom had worked in the presidential campaign of Eugene McCarthy the previous year. People all across the country were doing what the protestors at Shea Stadium were doing, handing out anti-war materials and urging that the United States withdraw from Vietnam.

It was estimated that somewhere between one and two million people took part in moratorium events and the largest crowd, estimated at 250,000, gathered in Washington, D.C., where Doctor Benjamin Spock, the famous pediatrician and staunch antiwar activist, gave a speech.

There were counter demonstrations and many Americans drove with their headlights on during the day to express their support of the war effort. General Earle Wheeler, Chairman of the Joint Chiefs of Staff, dismissed the protestors as "interminably vocal youngsters, strangers alike to soap and reason."

Prior to the moratorium, some people had done more than march and pray to stop the war. In Vietnam, a number of Buddhist monks lit themselves aflame in protest. In October 1967, Florence Beaumont, a 55-year-old member of the Peace and Freedom Party and a married mother of two grown daughters, drove her pickup truck, filled with anti-war literature, to the Los Angeles Federal Building. Before she left, she told her husband, "It's not worth living when you have no redress from your representatives. All you receive from them is form letters." Mrs. Beaumont doused herself with gasoline, lit a match, screamed, ran about forty feet, and collapsed in a mass of flame.

Sixteen-year-old high school student Ronald Brazee drove to Syracuse and lit himself on fire in front of a church. He left a note that read, "I'm giving my life, not in war, but to help end it. If giving my life will shorten the war by even one day, it will not have been in vain." He died in a hospital five weeks later. A 27-year-old Zen Buddhist student gave his life in 1967 and musician Steve Sexton burned himself to death in protest in 1968.

Joan Fox and Craig Badiali were among the roughly one thousand people who attended a Moratorium Day rally at Glassboro State College in Glassboro, New Jersey. She was 16, he was 17, and both were seniors at Highland Regional High School in Blackwood, New Jersey. Craig was born and raised in Blackwood, except for a year that he lived in Hawaii, while Joan was born in nearby Philadelphia. The Foxes moved to Blackwood when she was three, one of many families who'd left the deteriorating inner city of Philadelphia for the suburbs.

Blackwood was a blue-collar town filled with people who were generally optimistic about their future. The postwar years had been good ones for skilled workers and most owned homes and had hopes that their children would go to college and have better lives than they'd had.

The Badiali family was headed by Bernard Badiali, Sr., who spent 22 years in the Air Force and in 1969 was employed as a construction supervisor. His older son, Bernard, Jr., was a 21-year-old college student who'd recently moved back home with his wife and small child. The senior Badiali was a tough disciplinarian, but that was not unusual for the era; the family was close and well-functioning. The Fox family was also typical of those found in Blackwood. One of Joan's older brothers was serving in Vietnam and another was a Vietnam veteran and a Blackwood police officer.

Joan and Craig had been dating since ninth grade. They shared an interest in intellectual topics; both were voracious readers of serious books. Both were outwardly conventional; Joan was a varsity cheerleader who loved sports and Craig was president of Artisan Club, the school drama association. They had a number of friends, however, who were more radical.

Craig was serious about many things. He wrote poetry, loved music and playing the guitar, and wanted very much for people to care about each other and get along. Between 1968 and 1969, the attitudes of both Craig and Joan toward the Vietnam War changed. In the fall of 1968, they had attended a rally to support the troops in Southeast Asia, but by 1969 they were adamantly against the war. The return of Craig's brother Bernie, who was vehemently anti-war, may have contributed to the change in attitude.

When the 1969–70 school year began, Craig seemed much more serious than he had been the previous year. He joked around less and began to spend more time either alone or with Joan. He and Joan didn't go out with friends as often as they had in the past. Craig became profoundly depressed, and his poetry grew increasingly morbid.

> Oh please come the day
> When I can believe
> That we must feel sorrow
> To appreciate love and beauty
> Right now, it seems not worth it
> I'm so sorry, so sorry

Craig also fell in love with a song written by Peter Yarrow of Peter, Paul and Mary, called *The Great Mandala*, which told of a martyr who died in prison after going on a hunger strike to protest war and killing. Craig told friends he had become an agnostic.

On Monday, October 13, two days before the Moratorium, Craig went to a friend's house in the evening to watch *Rowan and Martin's Laugh-In*. On Tuesday, he sat at his desk writing 12 farewell letters, averaging about a page and a half each, to family and friends. Joan sat in her own home and did the same. After he finished writing his letters, Craig burned most of his other writing. He wanted to world to remember him only by what he wrote that evening.

When they returned from the Glassboro rally, Craig was upset. He told his brother that people treated the outing as a "lark" and that they were not serious enough about ending the war. Many students had skipped school and didn't even go to the rally. Some who did go seemed more interested in following the Mets score.

The two teens told their parents they were going back to Glassboro for a candlelight evening vigil. But they didn't. Craig picked up Joan at seven o'clock and drove Craig's 1962 Ford Falcon to a dirt road called Bee's Lane in a section of town known as Chews Landing. They pulled over to the side of the road, attached a vacuum cleaner hose to the exhaust pipe and ran it through a hole in the floorboards. Craig started the engine and by about 7:30, both were dead.

All night, both families tried to find out why their children hadn't returned from Glassboro. It wasn't until morning that a passerby saw the car, which he thought was abandoned. A short while later, however, he ran into Officer Joseph Reichert and told him what he'd seen. Reichert, knowing that two teenagers were missing, drove to Bee's Lane and came upon a horrible scene.

Exposure to carbon monoxide not only kills, it disfigures, and when Officer Reichert opened the unlocked door, he found two bodies covered with soot and residue, their faces distorted and lifeless. Two dozen letters were on the dashboard and two guitars were propped in the back seat.

People in the town of Blackwood were stunned. Joan's neighbor, Mrs. Barbara Walter, said, "She was no hippie, not by any means. That's what makes it seem so impossible." Principal Virginia Foreron said she didn't know the two were anti-war. She thought most students at Highland Regional supported the war and pointed out that the school had sent packages to the troops during the past year.

Foreron said that Fox and Badiali were "average youngsters with average grades." Generally, when young people die tragically, they are given almost superhuman qualities, but those who died protesting the war were apparently not going to be exalted. Virtually no mention was made of the deaths at Highland Regional High School and flags continued to fly at full staff in the days after the dual suicide. Craig and Joan had made it clear that they wanted to be martyrs and the Town of Blackwood made it just as clear that they were not going to allow that to happen.

The families were devastated, and Bernie, Jr., wondered if his mother would survive the shock. He went to the family doctor and got tranquilizers for everyone. Death in an automobile accident would have been almost unbearable. Suicide was worse, and suicide for a cause like ending the Vietnam War was nearly impossible for the people of conservative Blackwood to understand. The question heard most often in the coming weeks was, "Why?" There was speculation that either Craig or Joan was on drugs or that Joan was pregnant. The consensus was that the suicide had been Craig's idea and Joan had followed along.

The police took custody of the letters. One of them was in an envelope that read simply "Why?" It read, "Why? Because we love our fellow men enough to sacrifice our lives so that they will try to find the ecstasy in just being alive." It was signed, "Love—Peace, Craig B." Another letter read, "If just one person is touched enough to do something constructive and peaceful with his life then maybe our deaths were worth it."

Camden County medical examiner Thomas R. Daley, summarizing the letters for the press, said, "They were very unhappy that people don't love each other ... the kids were disenchanted with the way things were in the world." It would have been better, perhaps, since Fox and Badiali had written many long letters, to let them speak for themselves, but it was cleaner to dismiss them with a couple of phrases. The only letters that were delivered, already opened, were the ones written to the two sets of parents. The police retained custody of the others, on the grounds that they would be too upsetting to the recipients. Friends were left wondering if Craig or Joan had written to them and, if so, what they had said.

A story as tinged with drama and emotion as that of Craig Badiali and Joan Fox was certain to gain media attention and sure enough, newspaper reporters, television crews, and magazine writers descended on Blackwood. The Fox and Badiali families didn't want to talk, although brother Bernard made a brief statement on behalf of his family, saying, "My brother died for his convictions. They were antiwar."

Although Craig, in his letter to his parents, had asked to be cremated privately, father and son felt that Mrs. Badiali needed the finality of seeing the body one last time and decided to hold a funeral limited to immediate family. Although the funeral director did his best to keep the press at bay, they gathered across the street and aimed their cameras at anyone coming or going, trying to get pictures through the windows. Fox and Badiali were laid to rest beside each other in the Church Street cemetery while the parents tried to cope with the loss and get on with their lives.

Bernard Badiali, Sr., died in 1992 and his wife Frances died in 2017 at the age of 93. Craig's brother, Bernard J. Badiali, Jr., began teaching high school English in 1970. In 1979, he obtained a master's degree from Glassboro State College and in 1985 a Ph.D. in Curriculum and Instruction from Penn State. He was a professor at Penn State until 1992, when he left to teach at Miami University in Ohio and serve as chair of the Department of Education Leadership. Badiali returned to Penn State in 2004 and is still teaching there. He co-authored a book titled *Teacher Leader* in 2001.

Author Eliot Asinof had gone to Blackwood in 1969 to write an article on the suicides for *Seventeen* and two years later, Bernie, Jr. asked him to write a book about Craig and Joan. *Craig & Joan: Two Lives for Peace*, appeared in 1971. The Badialis and many of Craig and Joan's friends were interviewed but the Fox family did not cooperate. Asinof sold the film rights and a screenplay was commissioned, but it does not appear that a movie was ever made.

Asinof, who is most famous for *Eight Men Out*, the story of baseball's 1919 Black Sox, was very much against the Vietnam War. He was also very critical of Blackwood, painting it as a stagnant, closed-minded blue-collar community with a backward way of thinking. Liberal thinkers have always been frustrated when members of the working class aren't interested in overthrowing the system, only wanting to better their families within the system. Asinof was no exception.

Many of Blackwood's newer residents had come from the deteriorating city of Philadelphia and felt lucky to live in a town like Blackwood. They liked the system that had allowed them upward mobility, and they tended to be patriotic and suspicious of those who were critical of America, especially those who had long hair and smoked pot.

Asinof came down hard on Highland Regional High School as close-minded and lacking critical and open-minded thinking, but much of his strident criticism seemed like the typical complaints of high school students. There wasn't enough time between classes; teachers were stuck in their ways and discouraged original thought. Blackwood was typical of most small towns in the 1960s and Highland was like most high schools.

Craig Badiali and Joan Fox wanted to help end the Vietnam War by their deaths. But the war ran its normal course before ending in 1975. Monks and a few Americans lit themselves on fire and two high school students died in a parked car, ending lives that might have been much more productive than their deaths. But teenagers in distress don't think that way. The president of the drama club chose drama, but the only results were two devastated families and two promising young lives snuffed out. The Vietnam War killed over 50,000 Americans, and foreign wars continue to take the lives of Americans today. The future that the two young idealists dreamed of on Bee's Lane in 1969 remained just a dream.

Other sources:

    https://jtonzelli.com/2015/10/16/reading-craig-joan-two-lives-for-peace/
    http://thespeaker.co/wp-content/uploads/2013/06/The-Self-Immolators.pdf
    http://news.bbc.co.uk/onthisday/hi/dates/stories/october/15/newsid_2533000/2533131.stm
    The Amazin' Mets, 1962–1969, William J. Ryczek, McFarland and Company, Publishers, Jefferson, NC, and London, 2006
    Desert Sun, October 17, 1969
    The Daily Register, October 17, 1969
    Bakersfield Californian, October 17, 1969
    Newark Advocate, October 29, 1969
    Tyrone Daily Herald, October 20, 1969
    https://ed.psu.edu/directory/bxb8
    http://www.units.miamioh.edu/eduleadership/faculty/badiali/badiali_eval/badiali_vita.pdf
    https://en.wikipedia.org/wiki/Eliot_Asinof
    New York Times, November 6, 2008
    Asinof, Eliot, *Craig & Joan: Two Lives for Peace*, Dell Publishing Company, New York, 1971

Sketches of 4 Seized as Bombing Suspects

New York Times, November 14, 1969

Jane Alpert came from a nice Jewish family from Forest Hills, New York. Her father, John, was vice president of a dental equipment firm and her mother was a junior high school math teacher. Jane graduated from Forest Hills High School in 1963 with a stellar academic record; she was a semi-finalist for a National Merit Scholarship (not one of 34 New York winners, as the *New York Times* reported). A classmate said, "She was just like everyone else. We were excited, bright, intellectual kids. We all knew we'd make good. We were not political at all.... I don't think my generation really got involved in being interested in politics until after the [Kennedy] assassination."

In September 1963, Alpert matriculated to Swarthmore College as an English major. The *Times* reported that she graduated with honors in 1967 and took a job as an editorial secretary at Cambridge University Press in New York City, where she quickly rose to a junior editor position.

Jane Alpert's background was not as squeaky clean as the *Times* indicated. The All-American girl gone radical was an appealing story, but it was not exactly true in Alpert's case, for she had experienced a few bumps along her road to Cambridge Press. She had a very difficult relationship with her mother, was insecure about her looks, and at one point was under the care of a psychiatrist. Alpert was always haunted by the feeling that she didn't quite fit in with any group.

Alpert did, as the *Times* reported, graduate from Swarthmore, but not without incident. At the end of her freshman year, she had begun dating a young man to whom she became engaged. They spent a night in the university's guest housing together, which was against the rules, and to escape discovery, Jane attempted to climb out a window and jump to the ground. She slipped, fell awkwardly, crashed into a pine tree, broke three vertebrae, and ended up in a body cast. One of the deans figured out what had happened and forced her to take a one-year leave of absence for the crime of co-habitation.

After spending a year at Barnard, Alpert returned and finished her studies at Swarthmore, where she became involved in the protest movement. She was arrested at one protest, but was released to her parents and never charged.

Back at Swarthmore, Alpert ended her engagement and became pregnant by another man, getting an abortion in Philadelphia. She had a series of friendships with outlandish characters and was constantly conflicted between the prospect of having a successful, conventional career or fulfilling her romantic notions of saving the world. She read Ayn Rand's *Fountainhead*, and while she was turned off by Rand's libertarian, individualist philosophy, Alpert was fascinated when the heroine helped the hero destroy an ugly building by exploding it.

While working at Cambridge Press, Alpert began pursuing a master's degree in Greek at Columbia University. Nineteen sixty-eight was the year of activism on college campuses and no campus was as violent as Columbia. Alpert began to gradually slide away from the conventional world, attending her first anti-war demonstration in April of 1967. Still, no one thought of her as a violent radical. She was vocal and opinionated but didn't appear to be dangerous.

Then Alpert met Samuel Melville, a 34-year-old drifter who worked for a radical newspaper called *The Guardian*. Melville's real surname was Grossman; he'd taken the name Melville in honor of author Herman Melville. His father, with whom he had a very troubled relationship, was an avowed Communist. Sam was married and had a child, although he had long since separated from his wife.

It was love at first sight when Alpert met Melville in the fall of 1968 at a Community Action Coalition demonstration. "The combination of sexual love," she wrote later, "and radical ideology was more than irresistible.... For me, the difference between being a liberal and a radical activist was Sam Melville."

Alpert and Melville had a passionate but tempestuous relationship. The sex was great, according to Alpert, but Melville also liked to sleep with other women, and called her possessive when she protested. They played games with each other. He left her briefly but returned. She dated others to make him jealous. In addition to his desire for variety, Melville had a disturbing penchant for sexual dominance, asking Alpert to call him Master and insisting she read *The Story of O*, a pornographic tale of sadism and masochism.

Alpert became jealous when Melville began sleeping with fellow radical Pat Swinton and retaliated by commencing a lesbian affair with Swinton. Eventually, the combination expanded to a threesome and then a foursome, and it seemed a minor miracle the group found time for their revolutionary activity amidst all the sexual couplings. "Did all of us feel interested in bombing buildings," Alpert wondered, "only when the men we slept with were urging us on?"

In November 1968, Alpert dropped out of Columbia. Five months later, she quit her job at Cambridge Press, telling her boss she had decided to work to better society. Alpert and Melville moved to a small East Village apartment that rented for $69.40 per month, priced cheaply because it was dilapidated and in a very bad area. The former junior editor of Cambridge Press joined the staff of an underground publication called *The Rat*.

One of Melville's associates was Swinton's boyfriend, John D. Hughey, III who, like Alpert, came from a respectable middle-class background. (Note: In her autobiography, Alpert changed some names to protect people, and referred to Hughey as Nate Yarrow.) His father, Dr. John David Hughey, was Secretary of the Europe and Middle East Division of the Baptist Foreign Mission Board in Richmond, Virginia. Young Hughey spent twelve years in Sweden with his family, then returned to the United States, achieved high honors in a Richmond high school, and attended Duke University. Like Alpert, Hughey had an epiphany and dropped out of Duke in 1966. When he announced his plan to leave, his father tried to dissuade him, but Hughey told his father he felt closed in and Duke was too artificial for him. He stopped communicating with his family and went to New York, where he worked for Greyhound Bus Lines and *The Guardian*, where he met Sam Melville.

George Demmerle was a 39-year-old unemployed die maker and enigmatic figure whose relatives described him in very contradictory terms. One called him a reclusive loner, another an outgoing apolitical person, a third a "brilliant but hopeless case" who was involved in radical causes, and a fourth believed that he was a supporter of right wing politics and possibly George Wallace.

Demmerle had a difficult childhood. He was one of 13 children in a family that was deserted by his father; he lived for a time in a charitable institution. Demmerle's passion was art, but he was never able to convert that passion into a career. By 1968, he was very involved in the counterculture, even serving as Abby Hoffman's bodyguard. In April 1969, Demmerle was arrested while trying to crash a Commodore Hotel luncheon featuring Hubert Humphrey. Four months later, he met Melville at Woodstock.

Demmerle went by the name Prince Crazy and led a group called the Crazies. He infiltrated the Yippies and tried to get Jerry Rubin to blow up the Brooklyn Bridge. At the end of a rally, Demmerle would shout, "Who wants to go out and get arrested?" A number of idealistic youngsters would wreak havoc and get arrested, but no one seemed to notice that Demmerle rarely got arrested.

The reason Demmerle was rarely arrested was that he was an informer, although he later claimed he had been converted by the people he had been paid to inform upon. He professed to be committed to the Yippie agenda, and after Rubin died one of his followers spotted Demmerle at a memorial service, weeping profusely.

By 1969, the radical left had turned to violence and was looking to destroy the government by any means. That summer was the season for bombing, especially in New York City. In addition to actual explosions, there were more than 100 hoaxes. The *New York Times* Building, the Manhattan Criminal Courts Building, a Penn Central train, the Pan Am Building, and many other sites were evacuated after threats were made. In Washington, D.C., a bomb exploded in the Madison Hotel just hours after former Ambassador Averill Harriman had spoken there. None of the bombings resulted in serious injuries, but it was a frightening time, for no one knew where the radicals would strike next. A message sent to the Associated Press read, "The establishment is in for some big surprises if it thinks that kangaroo courts and death sentences can arrest a revolution."

Melville was the first of Alpert's group to become interested in bombing. He learned how to build a bomb, but although he had the most technical knowledge of the group, he was often reckless and rarely planned his actions carefully. The others felt he continually put them in danger with his carelessness. The scholarly Alpert, on the other hand, was a meticulous researcher and planner. When two Canadian fugitive radicals came to New York, Alpert went to the library and learned how to hijack a plane. She told the Canadians exactly what to do and they pulled it off.

Melville and his associates stole a cache of dynamite, which they initially stored in Melville and Alpert's refrigerator. Melville planted one of the bombs, in what Alpert later referred to as an impulsive, poorly planned attack, in an office of Marine Midland Bank. She claimed that Melville bombed Marine Midland because he was angry that she had threatened to leave him. When Alpert learned what he had done, she was furious. Alpert wanted to destroy property and terrorize the establishment, but she didn't want to injure innocent people. She insisted on calling Marine Midland to warn them, but the bank didn't take the call seriously. The explosion injured 20 employees.

The strains in the Melville-Alpert relationship resulted in more explosions in New York City. Melville had said that women shouldn't be involved in bombings, because they weren't tough enough, and Alpert wanted to prove to him that she could bomb as well as a man. On September 18, 1969, she planted a bomb on the 40th floor of the Federal Building at Foley Square. "I felt as I imagined I would on my wedding day," she wrote later. "Weighed in the balance against the fear of arrest was the anticipated thrill that we would soon be openly celebrated as heroes." When they saw the explosion from their rooftop, the group was jubilant.

Eventually, dissension permeated the ranks of the radicals. Some were getting cold feet, while others had no fear and wanted to escalate the violence. In addition to the risk of blowing themselves up or being killed while attempting to plant a bomb, it was almost inevitable that they would eventually be caught, for they were amateurs playing a dangerous game.

In November, their luck ran out. Demmerle and Melville were arrested when they were caught placing explosives in National Guard trucks outside the 69th Regiment Armory and Alpert and Hughey were picked up shortly thereafter. Demmerle, the informer, was released, and later collected a $25,000 reward from Marine Midland. Alpert, Melville, and Hughey were charged with six bombings in New York between July 27 and November 12: three government buildings, the RCA Building, Marine Midland, and a United Fruit Company Pier.

Melville and Demmerle were drifters, and while Hughey came from a privileged background, Jane Alpert was the main story. The media was enthralled with the idea of an educated upper middle class young woman becoming a violent radical, and wrote headlines like "'Loveliest Girl' Among Alienated, Typical of Many," and "From Honors to Handcuffs."

Alpert was released on $20,000 bail posted by her parents, but Melville remained in prison. While free on bail, Alpert appeared at demonstrations in New York, where she was hailed as a hero. She regretted that she could not go to a protest in New Haven, Connecticut, since under the terms of her release, Alpert could not leave Manhattan.

Alpert and Hughey pleaded guilty to conspiracy, but before she could be sentenced, Alpert jumped bail and took up life underground. By fleeing, she scuttled a plea bargain for Melville, who was sentenced to 13 years in prison for his role in eight different bombings. Ironically, he was sentenced in the Criminal Courts Building he had attempted to blow up.

Melville had no remorse, and his time in prison was turbulent. When Alpert went to visit him, he would put his hand up her dress and pull her onto his lap until they were separated by the guards. During a conference with his attorney, he overpowered a marshal and tried to escape, only to be captured within minutes. The next year, Melville was transferred to Attica State Prison, where he was believed to be one of the organizers of the deadly riot that September. He was killed during the uprising and Alpert came back in disguise to view his body.

A book of Melville's writings, titled *Letters from Attica*, was published in 1973, and included an introduction by Alpert, which ignited controversy in the radical world, for she had some harsh words for Melville and the radical Weathermen.

For more than four years, Alpert lived under six different aliases and took menial jobs such as secretary at a Jewish school and waitress at a New England ski lodge. She gradually came under the influence of Robin Morgan and became an ardent feminist. Morgan replaced Melville as the dominant influence in Alpert's life, and while the two women did not have a sexual relationship, there was a close emotional bond and Alpert was as desperate to earn Morgan's approval as she had been with Melville. As a feminist, Alpert rejected the Weathermen and the radical movement as blatantly sexist.

Life in hiding was not glamorous. At one point, Alpert met up with Weatherman Mark Rudd, who was also underground. Their encounter, of course, included sex. There were a few fleeting romances during Alpert's years on the run, but for the most part, she led a life of constant motion, changing identities, and personal relationships that were limited by the need to conceal her identity. That greatly troubled Alpert. She ached to tell people that she was not just a lowly waitress or secretary, but a famous wanted criminal. On many occasions, she was indiscrete and disclosed information that put her and her associates in danger.

In 1973, Alpert wrote a feminist manifesto called *Mother Right* that was published in *Ms. Magazine*. After the article appeared, Alpert waited to be apprehended, but apparently no one was interested. As time went by, people forgot about her and only those in her very small circle even knew that she was wanted.

By 1974, Alpert felt that the Watergate scandal had changed American attitudes and that the radicals of the 1960s were no longer viewed as dangerous monsters. She was also tired of running and longed to resume a professional life under her own identity. On November 19, 1974, she turned herself in and surrendered to the authorities.

Alpert's attorney asked for a sentence of alternative service, noting that she had surrendered voluntarily and lived an exemplary life since jumping bail. The judge disagreed and in January 1975 sentenced her to 27 months in prison (18 for conspiracy and 9 for jumping bail). An additional four months was later added for contempt of court when she refused to testify against her former friend and fellow bomber Pat Swinton.

After she heard her sentence, Alpert embraced her parents in the courtroom and talked with them for several minutes. They had supported her unfailingly, despite her often callous treatment of them. The bail money they forfeited when she vanished had created a severe financial hardship. Still, they continued to give her money when she was on the run and visited her when they could, using assumed names. Alpert dedicated her memoir to them.

Alpert had a difficult time in prison, for she had been branded as an informant. When she was released in 1977, she took an apartment in Greenwich Village and directed her efforts toward feminism and a number of liberal causes.

In 1981, Alpert released her memoir, *Growing Up Underground*, which infuriated many in the radical movement who hadn't already been offended by *Mother Right*. *Growing Up Underground* is a remarkable book. What most people found interesting was that Alpert blamed her bombing activity on her sexual attraction to Melville. As Eden Ross Lipson said in *The New York Times Review of Books*, "a one-time heroine was just an old-fashioned slave of desire." He called the book a "girlish diary ... untroubled by perspective, reflection or insight." *People Magazine*, which at that time covered more substantive topics than it does today, called it a "bomb and tell memoir."

Any memoir of the type that Jane Alpert wrote involves self-examination, but she seemed to equivocate about her past life. "I'm not that person anymore," she wrote. "I don't reject her. I feel very compassionate for her.... I'm not entirely happy about the way in which I did it, but I'm glad that I did something."

John Hughey, who participated in the bombing of the Whitehall Induction Center, served his sentence and was released from prison in 1972, but his tribulations were not over. In 1975, when Swinton was finally apprehended, Hughey was called as a witness at her trial.

Despite the fact that he had been granted immunity, Hughey refused to testify against his former lover. Ironically, Swinton was acquitted, while Hughey was found guilty of civil contempt and returned to prison. Alpert and Hughey met in 1980, at which time the latter had forsaken politics and was living a respectable middle-class life with a partner, a respectable job, and a dedication to religion rather than radicalism.

By the time they were in their 30s, the revolutionaries of the '60s were no longer blowing up buildings. Many were working for the same causes, but employing different means. Perhaps Alpert said it best. "[T]he charged political atmosphere of the late 1960s," she wrote, "drove many of my generation over the edge."

Other sources:
https://en.wikipedia.org/wiki/Jane_Alpert
https://en.wikipedia.org/wiki/Sam_Melville
New York Times, January 14, 1975
http://sammelville.org/historical-inaccuracies/
People Magazine, November 9, 1981
New York Times, October 25, 1981
Growing Up Underground, Jane Alpert, William Morrow and Company, New York, 1981
https://law.justia.com/cases/federal/appellate-courts/F2/571/111/323038/
http://www.conspiracy-cafe.com/apps/blog/show/44175873-1969-a-year-of-bombings
http://www.ep.tc/realist/130/12.html
Altoona Mirror, June 20, 1970
Alamogordo Daily News, May 4, 1970
Hutchinson News, December 10, 1969
European Stars and Stripes, December 15, 1969

Young Millionaire Brody's Checks Not Covered by Cash in Bank

Bridgeport Post-Telegram, January 19, 1970

Many people celebrate when they turn 21 because they are old enough to drink legally. Michael James Brody, Jr., had a better reason to celebrate his 21st birthday because on that day he was eligible to receive a share of his late grandfather's $7 million estate. John J. Jelke, who made his fortune in oleomargarine, died in 1965, leaving a will that gave Brody his inheritance (estimated by his father at about $3 million) when he reached the age of maturity in October 1969.

The reason for the delay, presumably, was to allow Brody to acquire mature judgment and reason, but as Michael would demonstrate, it didn't come to him at 21. On January 3, 1970, less than three months after his inheritance, he married a beautiful woman named Renee who he met,

4. The Times They Are a Changin'

according to the *New York Times*, three weeks earlier when Renee sold him hashish. Returning from a Jamaican honeymoon on a 140-seat jet Brody chartered for the two of them at a cost of $7,340, he announced that he intended to make the world a better place by giving his money away.

Although Brody's father said the inheritance was about $3 million, Michael announced that it was $25 million and would soon grow to $50 million although, as in most things he said, he was vague about how the fortune would double.

On the grand side, Brody announced on a San Juan radio show that he planned to offer the North Vietnamese $10 billion to withdraw from South Vietnam, at which time he would pledge $20 billion to rebuild North Vietnam. Again, Brody did not mention how his fortune had ballooned to $30 billion. "Peace is what I want," he said, indicating that he was attempting to set up a meeting with President Nixon to discuss his plans to bring peace to the world and solve the nation's narcotics problem.

On the smaller side, Brody gave $2,500 to a man who was behind on his mortgage, $1,000 to a taxi driver, $500 to a heroin addict, $100 to a barber who opened a door for him, and $100 to a boy who delivered his newspaper. He gave out his address and phone number in Scarsdale, New York, where he was renting a $400,000 home, so that anyone who felt they needed money could get in touch with him. "I've never seen them before in my life," he said of the beneficiaries, "But if they think they need the money bad enough to come here and ask for it, they must need it." Western Union delivered 300 telegrams and had a backlog of 200 more, while the Scarsdale switchboard operator was just as overwhelmed.

By the morning after Brody made his announcement, people were standing in his front yard and crowding the office he'd established in New York City. He handed out about $60,000 worth of checks in 36 hours. Unfortunately, there was not nearly that much money in Brody's checking account. The checks "were not good at this time," announced J. Henry Neale, chairman of Scarsdale National Bank and Trust Company.

The rush finally became too much for the young man. "I want everybody out of this house right now," he shouted. "You've got to leave me three checks. I can't write my last three checks." Apparently, Brody subscribed to the theory that if he still had checks, there must be money in the account. "I need a system," he added.

Brody borrowed a private jet to fly to Puerto Rico with his new wife in order to get some rest. "When everyone is as rich as I am," he announced, "I'll go to a desert island and leave the world alone and make love to my wife.... Money hasn't made me satisfied. I wasn't satisfied until I met Renee. Now I have everything I want—love, fresh air, food. So why shouldn't I give my money away?" "Michael has always had Cadillacs and Corvettes," Renee said. "He thinks everyone should drive them. All he wants is a chicken farm and 13 children."

In addition to making love to his wife, Brody had another personal goal; he wanted to be a singer. The notoriety he created with his giveaways earned him a January 18th appearance on the *Ed Sullivan Show*, where he was paid $3,500 to sing Bob Dylan's "You Ain't Going Nowhere." He also got a record contract with RCA, but a single featuring "You Ain't Going Nowhere" and Brody's own composition, "The War is Over," received poor reviews. He cut a demo of his song, "I Love the World as It Falls on My Veins," but like the Dylan song he covered, it went nowhere.

Brody chartered a helicopter and flew to Washington, seeking a meeting with Nixon, but was told the President was unavailable. Then, as suddenly as it began, Brody announced that the giveaway program was over, not to be resumed until the Vietnam War ended. Ending the war became the consuming passion of Michael Brody's existence, and for a while he disappeared from public life.

By this time, Brody had established a reputation as a strange eccentric. He said he was a stock market whiz, was going to fund the construction of a spaceship, and had backing for a "Harlem project." Brody claimed to be working with President Nixon, Billy Graham, and Soviet leader Leonid Brezhnev to achieve world peace. He said he had the cure for many diseases, including cancer. At various times, he referred to his wealth as $25 million, $100 billion, and a trillion dollars. No one knows how much he actually gave away; estimates range from $100,000 to $300,000.

In October, Renee gave birth to a baby boy the couple named Michael James Brody, III, although they called him Jaime. Meanwhile, Jaime's father, who'd previously attended Butler University, enrolled at the University of Colorado. He was still obsessed with the war in Vietnam, however, and withdrew from school the day after the U.S. invaded Laos.

By that time, Brody, who'd been using drugs for some time—many of his outrageous statements had been made while he was on LSD—was having problems with Renee. On their way from Colorado to New York, they took a detour in order to obtain a quick divorce in Juarez, Mexico. When they arrived in New York State, Renee went to live with her parents in Ashokan while Brody rented a house in nearby Woodstock.

Brody visited Renee and Jaime frequently and soon they were living together. A relationship with Michael Brody was bound to be difficult, however, and Renee left him again. Brody had been diagnosed as a paranoid schizophrenic and he sometimes neglected to take his medication. His illness wasn't helped by his continuing use of LSD and his increasing consumption of alcohol.

Meanwhile, Brody resumed his one-sided correspondence with world leaders. He called the White House and said he was going to light himself on fire in front of the presidential mansion as an anti-war protest. After a couple of similarly strange calls, the Secret Service was dispatched to Connecticut to question Brody, who was living there with his family. Brody was rambling and almost incoherent during the interview, but to that point had done nothing that constituted a crime.

That changed on December 23, 1971, when he called the White House again. "This is Michael James Brody," he said. "I'm going to kill President Nixon tonight." When asked where he lived, he replied, "Don't bother to come and get me, because I'll be gone."

That was a crime, and Brody was taken into custody and sent to a psychiatric hospital. After extensive interviews, doctors determined that he was mentally ill, although probably not to the extent that he would be acquitted. Brody was released on bail posted by his father and went to live with his twice-divorced sister in a house she rented in Norwalk, Connecticut. Brody didn't have a job and just sat around his sister's house taking drugs and drinking. One night, when his sister and her daughter were away, he burned down the house.

Michael Brody was big news again, bigger than at any time since his giveaway spree in 1970. Geraldo Rivera came to interview him for ABC. CBS reported the story on its national news broadcast. Brody was in Fairfield Hills, a mental health facility, ranting at the staff and claiming he was Jesus Christ. In January 1972 he called the White House twice from a hospital pay phone. Eventually, Brody was transferred to Silver Hills in New Canaan, Connecticut.

The arson and related charges were dropped on the basis that Brody was mentally incompetent. He was released and resumed living with Renee, who probably should have had *her* mental competence questioned. Her ex-husband was deeply troubled, still indulging heavily in alcohol and drugs, and had no money. His inheritance was given away, spent, or tied up in trust. Brody worked briefly as a hospital orderly, but the job didn't last long. He and Renee lived on monthly distributions from Michael's trust.

Brody tried to write his autobiography and stay away from drugs, but he was drinking up to a case of beer a day. Gradually, he stopped taking his medicinal drugs and resumed the use of recreational drugs. Many days he simply stayed in bed.

Meanwhile, the Vietnam War, which Brody had tried so hard to bring to an end, was finally over. The day before the peace accord was to be signed, Brody drove to the home of Renee's parents in Ashokan. No one was home. Brody went to the closet where Robert Dubois kept his hunting rifle, loaded it, and sat down in a chair. Propping the gun between his knees, he reached down, pulled the trigger, and sent a bullet into his skull. He died instantly, just 24 years old. Although no one could explain why Michael

Brody did anything, many speculated that with the end of the war he felt he had no further purpose.

For the third time, Brody was big news. Walter Cronkite reported his death on the evening news. Dan Enright wrote a screenplay for a movie called "Kiss Away," based upon Brody's life, and gave it to John Travolta in 1977. Travolta wasn't interested and the project died.

Years later, Renee reflected on her life with Brody. "It's so hard to believe that we all lived through that," she said. "My attraction to Michael was almost supernatural. I really felt as if it were destiny—that we were meant to live through these things. ... It was a very idealistic time for America. It seemed like a great idea to give away all his money. At least in theory."

Other sources:
New York Times, January 27, 1973
https://gracedobush.com/2013/01/26/michael-james-brody-oct-31-1948-jan-26-1973/
http://www.michaeljbrodyjr.org/Michael-J-Brody-Jr/Welcome.html
New York Daily News, June 15, 2001
oleoheir.com

Hairy Youths Have Right to Jobless Pay
Hartford Courant, May 28, 1970

Youngsters like Edward Kores and George Leonard would eventually become adults and move from school to the workplace, where employers replaced principals as authority figures. Did employers have the right to dictate their employees' hair length? Or was the right to have long hair a basic human right, protected from discrimination?

The manager of the state unemployment office in Monterey, California, thought it wasn't. He'd been withholding unemployment compensation payments from young men who had long hair, sideburns, or beards, based on the rationale that they were purposely making themselves unappealing to prospective employers and thus voluntarily removing themselves from the labor market.

A 25-year-old car salesman from Monterey who was denied compensation decided to challenge the ruling. He had a mustache and a small, neatly trimmed Van Dyke beard and when he refused to shave them, he had been fired.

Harold Strauch, chairman of the California Unemployment Commission, ruled in the employee's favor. The "aesthetic pleasure" of an employer, Strauch said, "doesn't necessarily have to be satisfied by an employee." He admitted that a beard might induce a "queasy feeling" in an employer, but that was not grounds to deny a claim for unemployment compensation.

Since the beard was neatly trimmed and the employee was otherwise well-groomed, Strauch said, there was no intentional misconduct and the discharged employee was entitled to compensation.

Vatican Asking All Priests to Affirm Celibacy Yearly

New York Times, February 10, 1970

At the time of their ordination, Catholic priests are required to take vows of poverty, chastity and obedience. The vow of poverty is largely symbolic, as priests typically live quite comfortably. Obedience is expected in many professions, but promising to abstain from sexual activity is fairly unique to the Catholic vocation. As sexual mores evolved during the 1960s, and with rebels like William DuBay roaming Catholic rectories, the vow of chastity became very controversial.

By 1970, it had become an impediment to the recruitment of new seminarians. Still, the Vatican clung to tradition despite at least tacit knowledge that the vow was being ignored by an increasing number of prelates. Pope Paul VI asserted "celibacy, presented with ardor as part of total dedication to God, could do more to attract young men to priestly vocations than 'a formula humanly more natural and apparently easier.'"

Using the word "ardor" to describe something one doesn't do seemed odd, and in the world of 1970 the rule was anachronistic; most young men preferred "a formula humanly more natural." An annual requirement to have each priest affirmatively state they were celibate hinted that they weren't and put the men who were not chaste in a position where they had to lie, compounding their sin.

The history of priestly celibacy is somewhat vague. Prior to the time of Christ some holy figures, such as ancient Druid priests and Aztec temple priests, were believed to have maintained a state of celibacy as a way of elevating them above common men. Jesus was unmarried, and many of his close disciples were believed to be celibate, but Peter, his closest associate, was married. For the first thousand years of Christianity, there was no requirement that Catholic priests be celibate or even unmarried.

While there was no ironclad celibacy requirement, the first millennium saw a movement in that direction. In 304 C.E., Canon 33 of the Council of Elvira declared that any priest who slept with his wife the night before mass would be discharged, and in 325 the Council of Nicea promulgated what came to be known as the Nicene Creed, which stated that priests could not marry.

The Nicene Creed was roundly ignored, and a number of popes were married, the last being Felix V, who reigned from 1439 to 1449. Eleven popes were the sons of priests or other popes, and during the 15th century roughly half of all priests were married.

When Martin Luther broke from the Catholic Church, one of his assertions was that celibacy was unnatural and led to acts the church considered perverse, such as masturbation, homosexuality, and illicit affairs. "Nature never lets up," he said. "We are all driven to the secret sin."

In addition to the moral aspects of chastity, there were practical concerns. The families of married priests would need to be supported, and that would require diverting assets of the church. Marriage would also mean that wealth that would otherwise revert to the church would be left to the children of its priests.

The turning point in the battle over mandatory celibacy is often identified as the Council of Trent in 1563, which issued a proclamation that Catholic priests were required to abstain from all sexual activity, on the basis that having a wife and family would detract from priests' dedication to their vocation. As St. Paul had said, "the married man must please his wife, but the celibate man can please the Lord only." After the Council of Trent, those who lived a non-celibate life did so in private.

It is no longer 1563, and the world has changed, but the position of the Catholic Church on celibacy has not changed. There is a severe shortage of priests, as the number of Catholics worldwide increased 64 percent from 1975 through 2008, while the number of priests increased by just 1 percent. More than 20 percent of parishes did not have a priest, and those who remain in the priesthood are aging. The crisis has led to exceptions to the rule, such as allowing widowers and divorced men to serve. After they are ordained, however, they are expected to be celibate, and there has been no movement toward the ordination of women, which might also alleviate the shortage.

The biggest crisis in the church in recent years has been horrific sex scandals, primarily involving young boys, that have borne out the doleful predictions of Martin Luther. There is pressure on Pope Francis to abolish the celibacy requirement, but there is significant resistance from traditionalists within the church. One concern is that many priests, like William DuBay, are not prepared for marriage, and that being married to a priest is not an easy life. But other religions, which allow marriage, have managed to function. Continuing shortages of priests will perhaps move the needle, but it will not be an easy transition.

Other sources:

> *When Did the Catholic Church Decide Priests Should be Celibate?* By Helen L. Owen, October 2001, https://historynewsnetwork.org/article/696
> https://www.futurechurch.org/brief-history-of-celibacy-in-catholic-church

https://www.thestar.com/news/insight/2018/04/17/catholic-priests-take-a-vow-of-celibacy-when-theyre-ordained-but-when-they-break-that-vow-their-children-are-left-to-live-a-lie.html

https.www.futurechurch.org

Disappointed

Hartford Courant, **January 19, 1971**

"Disappointed" is the caption under a photo of 18-year-old Craig Brown, a conservative-looking psychology student at Cosumnes River Junior College in Sacramento, California. As part of a class experiment, Brown visited local business establishments, first in his normal attire, and then in an old army shirt, a bright serape vest, blue jeans held up by a rope, sandals, and a fake beard. For good measure, he wore a couple of buttons supporting the lettuce boycott of Cesar Chavez.

Conservative Brown went to a jewelry store and asked about getting credit to buy a diamond ring, and was told it would be no problem. The next day, in his hippie attire, he was ignored, and then subjected to a lecture about people who don't pay their bills.

Hippie Brown then went to a bank to apply for a loan to start a business. He told the banker he owned a $20,000 home free of debt and had a trust fund that paid him $800 per month. The man told him to start the business first and then come back to apply. The next day he went to another bank in his conservative dress with the same story and was told that there would be no problem arranging the loan.

Brown the Hippie was refused service in a restaurant because, he was informed by a waitress, of "certain laws on sanitation." Another waiter told him he probably couldn't afford the food.

Lest one think that prejudice was an exclusive province of the Establishment, each version of Brown purchased copies of the radical *Berkeley Barb* and *Berkeley Tribe*. As a hippie, he was charged 25 cents and asked if he wanted to buy some pot, while as a conservative, he was charged 50 cents, with no offer of drugs.

Craig Brown learned more about human behavior from his exercise than he would have gleaned from a dozen psychology textbooks. When it was over, he said he was disappointed in his fellow humans. He may have been disappointed, but he shouldn't have been surprised. It was a good lesson in human nature.

Other sources:

Star-News, January 19, 1971

Long Hair is Sign of a Sissy

Hartford Courant, May 22, 1973

By 1973, long hair on males was commonplace, and most high school principals had learned to accept it, but not everyone was ready to concede, particularly in Texas. Tony Simpson, football coach at Northshore Junior High School in Galena Park was one of those who didn't fancy the idea of men wearing their hair long and he wasn't bashful about expressing his opinion.

Simpson wrote the lead article in the monthly magazine of the Texas High School Coaches Association, in which he equated long hair with feminine qualities unbecoming of a football player. "It is time that American coaches," Simpson wrote, "stopped allowing themselves to be personally represented by male athletic teams and individuals that look like females.... Only in the animal world is the male designed to be the most attractive or the prettiest.... However, the male with long hair *is* cute, he *is* pretty and he *is* sweet." Simpson suggested that if the coaches grew their hair like the players, they might "scare the Russian and Chinese Communists to death with our lack of masculinity."

The country wasn't on the brink of extinction because of long hair, Simpson assured the coaches, "But it does indicate that the condition of the soul is not only abnormal, but reversed.... A woman who wants a feminine-appearing male is not a real woman in her soul." Simpson was a strong believer that hair length defined the relationship between the sexes. "A man's short hair," he wrote, "is a sign of authority over the woman."

Simpson worried about the long-term implications of hirsute athletes. "A good hair code," he advised, "will get the abnormals out of athletics before they become coaches and bring their 'losers' standard into the coaching profession."

Whenever anyone criticized long hair, someone else was certain to point out that Jesus had long hair and a beard, and he seemed to be an OK guy. Simpson covered that base by translating the Book of Revelations 1:14 from the original Greek and claiming that it proved that Jesus had short hair. Any artistic representation to the contrary, he said, "showing him to be a skinny, weak, long-haired hippie is wrong, anti–Christian, anti–Biblical."

Simpson was not alone in his beliefs, for a couple of weeks earlier the Coaches Association had instituted a ban on long-haired athletes (including bushy Afros) in high school all star games. Many scholastic athletes were threatening to boycott the events rather than cut their hair.

Simpson's article received nationwide publicity. It was summarized in the February 1974 issue of *Texas Monthly*, under the headline, "At

Quarterback, Number 24, Emory the Terrible, Wearing the Housedress and Bejeweled Kneepads." Apparently, someone at *Texas Monthly* had a puckish sense of humor, for on the same page there was a brief piece titled, "Do You, Billy Bob, Take Thee, Bernard?," about a former football player who was married to a female impersonator by a Dallas judge.

Today, Tony Simpson is an author of Christian books, including *The Power Zone*, touted as "The only Christian book that tells you HOW to live the Christian life, and details the 3 zones of carnality you will live in if you don't. The book that simplifies, clarifies, documents, and illustrates with 41 teaching diagrams."

It's not clear what is depicted in the diagrams, whether it's the dreaded carnality or the steps to effective genuflecting, but I wasn't moved to buy the book to find out. As seen in Simpson's photo that accompanies the book advertisement, he has kept the faith in the matter of hairstyle. His head is completely shaved, and the dog pictured with him is neatly groomed.

Other sources:
Texas Monthly, February 1974
Linkedin.com
New York Sports: Glamour and Grit in the Empire City, Stephen Norwood, editor, University of Arkansas Press, 2018.

5

Social Issues

Sex and Drugs and Rock and Roll

Sex and drugs and rock and roll were all part of the youth culture of the 1960s. Sex outside of marriage became increasingly acceptable, although sex between members of the same gender was still proscribed. Mind-altering drugs were used by young people as never before; they were easily obtainable and supplanted alcohol as the drug of choice. The innocent rock and roll of the 1950s morphed into the acid rock and hard rock of the '60s, much of it glorifying the drug culture. Some of the music could be better appreciated under the influence of drugs and some could only be appreciated under the influence of drugs.

The 1960s was also the decade during which Americans began taking their clothes off in places they had never taken them off before. Men and women appeared *sans habiliment* on the stage, at the beach, at rock concerts, and in films. As always, naked women were more welcome than naked men, but there were more of both genders than in any previous decade.

Nudie Films—All the Time Volleyball

New York Herald Tribune, Early 1960s, Date Unknown

Although the 1960s are remembered as a tumultuous and transitory decade, they began tamely, and sex was no exception. In the early 1960s, nudity was generally confined to what were known as "nudist colonies" and its artistic representation to crudely-made films that featured unclothed people photographed at discreet angles in "natural" surroundings. Joseph Morgenstern of the *Herald Tribune*, in the interest of art, visited a few Times Square movie houses to sample some nudist fare and was heartily unimpressed. "This crowded planet's population problems," he wrote, "would be at an end if sex were as dull as it is shown to be in the nudist film houses of Times Square."

Morgenstern became an esteemed film reviewer and, beginning in 1995, wrote reviews for the *Wall Street Journal*, but at the time of the subject article, he was just a young reporter dispatched to sample soft core Times Square pornography on a slow news day. Settling into his seat amidst a motley crew he described as "lonely men, timid men, disturbed men, or curious men," Morgenstern saw "cheerless views of bare-breasted specimens playing interminable games of volleyball in which no one keeps score and the team facing the camera is always equipped with bikini pants."

He was not impressed by *Blaze Starr Goes Back to Nature* and said the primary sins of *Paris Sins* were "bad dubbing, bad acting, bad direction and scratched film." What most impressed Morgenstern was the fact that most of the films were produced for approximately $30,000 and some had grossed as much as $1,000,000. Apparently, someone was watching.

It wouldn't be long before men didn't have to go to Times Square to see bare-breasted women. But Times Square kept pace with the times and by then, the women on their movie screens were doing a lot more than playing volleyball. But that's another story altogether.

Growth of Overt Homosexuality in City Provokes Wide Concern

New York Times, December 17, 1963

During the lifetime of baby boomers, there have been fewer changes more dramatic that the attitude toward homosexuality. Today, there are openly gay men and women in show business and politics, and professional athletes have begun to come out. Gays in the workplace are almost a non-issue. Such things would have been unfathomable in 1963, when New York Police Commissioner Michael J. Murphy told the *New York Times*, "Homosexuality is another one of the many problems confronting law enforcement in this city." He added that it was his belief that homosexuality was not really a criminal problem, but a medical and psychological issue.

Analytical psychologists, supposedly experts on human behavior, were asked for their opinions. "They have," said the *Times*, "what they consider to be overwhelming evidence that homosexuals are created—generally by ill-adjusted parents—not born. They assert that homosexuality can be cured by sophisticated analytical and therapeutic techniques." Which, for a fee, the psychologists were willing to provide.

The primary cause of homosexuality, according to the psychologists, was ill-adjusted parenting, defined as a "close-binding, intimate" mother and/or "a hostile, detached or unrespected father." Given the reprobation attached to homosexuality, fathers may have become hostile or detached simply because they saw their son exhibiting feminine behavior, rather than being the cause of that behavior.

Dr. Irving Bieber, an associate clinical professor of psychiatry at New York Medical College, conducted a nine-year study titled *Homosexuality—a Psychoanalytic Study of Male Homosexuals*, which was highly acclaimed and primarily responsible for the assertion that parents were responsible for their homosexual sons. "We have come to the conclusion," Bieber wrote, "[that] a constructive, supportive, warmly related father precludes the possibility of a homosexual son."

The reason for Commissioner Murphy's concern and for the feature article was the fact that New York was home to more homosexuals (frequently called "inverts") than any other area of the country. Even accounting for the fact that it was the largest city in the United States, the number of homosexuals in New York (estimated at 100,000 to 600,000) was proportionately much greater than that of any other metropolis. The exact number of homosexuals was difficult to obtain, since sex between members of the same sex was illegal, and those who practiced it generally did so surreptitiously.

The greatest concentrations of gay activity in the city were in Greenwich Village, the East Side from the upper 40s through the 70s, and the west 70s. In the area around Eighth Avenue and 42nd Street "there congregate those who are universally regarded as the dregs of the invert world—the male prostitutes—the painted, grossly effeminate 'queens' and those who prey on them." During the summer months, many gays vacationed at Fire Island and a section of beach at Jacob Riis Park.

New York attracted homosexuals because of the anonymity of the big city and because officials there were more tolerant. It was much easier to be gay in New York than in rural towns, and there was a much greater selection of potential partners. "The city's homosexual community," said the *Times*, "acts as a lodestar, attracting others from all over the country."

Although sex between two men was classified as sodomy (in 1963 that was the case in every state except Illinois), it was a misdemeanor and rarely prosecuted when it took place in private between consenting adults. Police raided gay bars and clubs but generally didn't peer into bedrooms. From 1960 through 1963, approximately 1,000 to 1,200 men per year were arrested for "overt homosexual activity."

There were a number of gay bars in New York, including a lesbian nightclub in Greenwich Village called The Swing Rendezvous, where women danced with each other to the music of gay icons like Edith Piaf and Judy Garland. The Seven Steps catered to homosexuals, but a number of famous heterosexuals like Errol Flynn, Audrey Hepburn, and John and Jackie Kennedy visited there on occasion. Other establishments included The Gold Bug, Bonnie and Clyde's, and The Ace of Clubs.

Several of the gay bars were operated by organized crime. Mafia bosses were remarkably tolerant of sexual deviants when they could charge exorbitant cover charges and drink prices. With limited alternatives, gays had no choice but to frequent the Mafia establishments if they wanted an active social life.

While psychologists viewed homosexuality as an illness, they were beginning to realize that it was not dangerous to heterosexuals, particularly young boys. "[T]ruly psychotic inverts who prey upon pre-adolescent boys are no more common than molesters of girl juveniles," said one. Most offenses involving minors were with consenting boys in their late teens.

The primary advocacy group for homosexuals was the Mattachine Society, which had absorbed the New York League of Homosexuals. The Daughters of Bilitis, a smaller organization, advocated for lesbians. Spokesmen for the Mattachine Society, who would not allow their names to be used in the *Times* article, claimed that homosexuals were born that way and could not, contrary to the psychologists' claims, be "cured."

The Mattachine Society was formed in 1948, when a man named Harry Hay, who was a supporter of Progressive Party presidential candidate Henry Wallace, established a group he called "Bachelors for Wallace." After the election, Hay decided to maintain the group, which he initially planned to call Bachelors Anonymous, in imitation of Alcoholics Anonymous. Instead, he settled on Society of Fools. Most of the founders were Communists. In 1951, the name was changed to the Mattachine Society, after a secret organization in Medieval France. Designer Rudi Gernreich was an early member, although he did not use his real name in any dealings with the group.

When the organization began to purge Communists from their ranks, many of the original members left. The group's main activity was opposing entrapment by police decoys, and by the early 1960s, the Society became a leader in the fight for gay rights. By the late '60s, the gay rights movement had become more radical and the Mattachines were dismissed as too conservative.

Homosexuality remained a dark secret throughout the 1960s, and it wasn't until the riots following a police raid on the Stonewall Bar in June 1969 that gays became openly assertive about their rights. In 1973, in a very controversial action, the American Psychiatric Association removed homosexuality from its list of mental disorders.

In 1980, the Association classified certain types of homosexuality as "ego-dystonic homosexuality," a condition in which homosexual arousal is unwanted and a lack of heterosexual arousal hindered the ability to achieve relationships.

That definition was eliminated in 1986, and a recent study at the University of California at Davis provided a very different assessment. "Some psychologists and psychiatrists still hold negative personal attitudes toward homosexuality," it stated. "However, empirical evidence and professional norms do not support the idea that homosexuality is a form of mental illness or is inherently linked to psychopathology." It was a long road from December 1963.

Other sources:
https://en.wikipedia.org/wiki/Mattachine_Society
http://psychology.ucdavis.edu/rainbow/html/facts_mental_health.html
Kitty Genovese: The Murder, the Bystanders, the Crime that Changed America, Kevin Cook, W.W. Norton and Company, New York and London, 2014. Cook's work paints a good picture of the gay scene in New York in the 1960s, especially in Greenwich Village. Kitty Genovese, whose murder spurred outrage over the alleged apathy of city dwellers, was a lesbian who socialized in the Village.

Narcotics a Growing Problem of Affluent Youth

New York Times, January 4, 1965

"It's the big thing," said a student at the Julliard School of Music identified only as David, "the hip thing to do." The hip thing was smoking marijuana, which David told reporter Martin Arnold was an integral part of his life, although he insisted he was not addicted. According to the *Times*, "David," "Betty," a recent graduate of Hunter College, and "Joan," daughter of a Westchester industrialist, typified a new phenomenon, the increasing use of drugs by middle class and upper class young people.

The New York Police Department said that drug use was its number one problem, and the biggest change in recent years had been the migration of narcotics from poverty-stricken areas to college and high school campuses and to Greenwich Village, which was home to many young hipsters. "He does it not to flee the misery of the slums," reporter Martin Arnold said of the new user, "but because he wants kicks, because experimenting with narcotics is 'in' is 'hip,' is considered even more challenging than the sex and liquor parties of a generation ago." Those who declined to smoke pot were seen as "square," and those who did saw themselves as hip.

David bought pot with the weekly allowance his mother gave him, but police files were replete with instances of prostitution and theft committed by relatively affluent youths in order to get money to buy drugs. Joan stole silverware, her mother's jewelry, and other items from her parents' home

5. Social Issues 121

to support her drug habit. She had been in and out of the hospital six times and had borne a child out of wedlock.

In addition to stimulating crime, police worried that drug use among the young would lead to addiction and a life of dependency. "The connection between marijuana and heroin," Arnold wrote, "is often as straight as a railroad track." Police predicted that approximately 35 percent of marijuana smokers would become addicted to narcotics of some kind and estimated that the number of addicts in New York ranged from 23,000 to 100,000.

The police admitted that marijuana itself was not addictive, but said that since as heroin could usually be obtained from the same sources, addiction to heroin was a real risk. Since most readers of the *Times* had probably not sampled pot, Arnold described the experience. "It distorts time and space, and the user often has a slight floating sensation. At the same time, he feels that he is functioning in slow motion. Marijuana generally releases inhibition and makes one susceptible to suggestion. Some people say it is a sex stimulant, but others find it has the opposite effect, deadening all sexual desire."

Betty said that, unlike alcohol, which dulled the senses, she had a greatly heightened sense of awareness when she smoked pot. She also said she was less likely to end up in bed with a man if she smoked marijuana rather than drinking alcohol.

The New York police believed that half of the drug addicts in the United States lived in their city, which was apparently as attractive to heroin addicts as to homosexuals. The Narcotics Bureau, with 200 officers, was the largest anti-drug police force in the world. New York Governor Nelson Rockefeller did what politicians always do when confronted with a problem, calling for "massive federal and state programs." Other New Yorkers, such as poet Allen Ginsberg, were moving in the opposite direction. Ginsberg was a leading member of an organization called Lemar, short for Legalize Marijuana.

Dr. Graham D. Blaine, Jr., thought that drug use among affluent youngsters was in part due to the fact that, not having had to struggle for basic necessities, they were looking for adventure and danger. "We give young people a lot," he said. "When a young man can raise his finger and mama gives him a Jaguar, things are too easy. He has never been tested in real danger."

"Ann," 25, had a particularly sad story. The daughter of a contractor, she came to New York after attending college for two years and got a job as a secretary-bookkeeper. She began dating a drug addict and after she came home drunk from a party one night, woke up to find her boyfriend pulling a needle out her arm.

Ann got high from the shot and then she got sick, so the boyfriend gave her another shot. She found that she liked being high and continued to shoot up. Eventually, Ann broke up with her boyfriend, but she kept hooking up with other addicts. She married two of them, had two children, and began committing crimes to pay for what had become a $35-dollar-a-day habit. When she was arrested for prostitution, Ann finally checked into a hospital for detoxification. At the time Arnold spoke with her, she was clean, but the only people who would associate with her were junkies and she was afraid she'd slip back into her old life.

The marijuana problem turned out not to be as severe as Arnold had feared. Most pot smokers of 50 years ago did not become heroin addicts, and many of them are today's business and political leaders, including those who didn't inhale. Since the youths profiled in Arnold's article used pseudonyms, we don't know what happened to them. It's likely that serious addicts like Jane and Ann had troubled lives, but that David, the music student, and Betty, the Hunter College grad, probably stopped smoking pot and grew up, like most of their peers. America had survived homosexuals and it would survive marijuana.

Folk Singer Loses; Shoots Self Dead

Bridgeport Telegram, January 28, 1967

"A moody young Italian folk singer," the article began, "used the crack of a pistol for his protest swansong." Reality television was decades in the future, but twenty-seven-year-old Luigi Tenco provided an ending to a San Remo song festival competition that the producers of *The Voice* or *American Idol* can only dream of.

Tenco, whose heritage was cloudy—his father either died or disappeared when he was an infant—lived in a number of Italian cities before he and his mother finally settled in Genoa. He showed an early love for music and began performing in high school, playing the clarinet in a group called the Jelly Roll Morton Boys Jazz Band, named after the American jazz pianist. Tenco also played in a group called I Cavalieri under the name Gigi Mai. In 1961, under his real name, he released his first single, "Quando? (When?)" and the following year, he made his first album, "Ballate e Canzoni."

Tenco's work was based on themes such as "social protest, racial brotherhood, peace and hopeless love." His music was deep, dark, and controversial and he was censored on numerous occasions, once for writing a song that was critical of the Catholic Church. Like many song writers, Tenco was often troubled and subject to dark moods; several of his songs contained hints of suicide.

Although Tenco was one of Italy's top folk singers, he suffered from severe stage fright. Before performing at San Remo, he downed a bottle of peach brandy and took some tranquilizers. Finally, after some coaxing, he went on stage and sang his own composition, "Ciao Amore, Ciao" (Goodbye Love, Goodbye) with French singer Dalida, to whom he had become engaged just days earlier.

Tenco was eliminated from the competition after the first round. When he discovered he had lost, Tenco was devastated. He got into his car and drove very fast and recklessly to the Hotel Savoy, where he was staying. After dinner, he said he was going to take a nap and went to his room. Tenco decided to take a permanent nap and put a bullet from a 7.65 caliber pistol into his head. Dalida found his lifeless body in the morning, along with a note that read, "I do this not because I am tired of life (on the contrary) but as a protest against a public that sends roses to the final and a jury that selects 'La Rivoluzione' (a competing song)."

Tenco was little-known to English speaking audiences, although an English version of his "Un Giorno Dapo L'Altro (One Day After the Other)" was recorded by Perry Como. But after his death, he became a legendary, heroic figure in Europe. Several performers said they had been influenced by him, and beginning in 1974, the Tenco Award was presented each October at San Remo. In 1999, there was a play titled "Solitudini—Tenco e Dalida" and the singer was also portrayed in a French television production about the relationship between him and Dalida. Tenco lost the battle but won the war.

Dalida was much more than a historical footnote to Tenco's suicide. Born Yolanda Cristina Gigliotti in Egypt in 1933, she won the Miss Ondine beauty pageant in 1950 and was crowned Miss Egypt in 1954. After doing a little modeling and acting, Dalida embarked on a remarkable career in music. She spoke and sang in several languages, and also sang in languages in which she was not fluent. During her long career, Dalida had 19 Number One hits in four different languages. In 1976, she recorded what was believed to be the first French disco song.

Dalida's love life was not as successful as her musical career. In 1956, she married Lucien Morisse, but the couple was divorced in 1961. At some point after that, she began her affair with Tenco. A month after Tenco's death, she attempted suicide by means of a drug overdose, but after spending five days in a coma, she recovered.

In 1970, Morisse, her ex-husband, committed suicide by shooting himself in the head. From 1972 through 1981, Dalida was romantically involved with Richard Chanfray, who committed suicide in 1983 by inhaling exhaust fumes from his car.

On May 2, 1987, Dalida attempted suicide a second time, again taking an overdose of barbiturates, and this time she was successful. The singer was found dead in her room at the Prince of Wales Hotel in Paris the following morning, along with a note that read, "Life has become unbearable for me.... Forgive me."

Like Tenco, Dalida became a legend after her suicide. She is the subject of numerous biographies and her fan club still maintains a website. A number of television documentaries and movies commemorated her eventful life. Dalida is an icon of the French gay community, and in 2002 a French postage stamp was issued to commemorate the 15th anniversary of her death.

Other sources:
https://www.theguardian.com/music/musicblog/2008/jan/24/unsungheroesno4luigitenco
https://en.wikipedia.org/wiki/Luigi_Tenco
https://en.wikipedia.org/wiki/Dalida

Nude Model Placed on Probation
Bridgeport Post-Telegram, February 15, 1967

Pinup pictures of the 1960s, even the famous *Playboy* centerfolds, are tame by today's standards. The women were strategically posed to hide the really naughty areas, and hands and stray bits of clothing were employed to give the photos more tease than sex. But nice college girls were not even supposed to pose for those types of photos, as eighteen-year-old University of Florida sophomore Pamme Brewer learned after displaying her "38–25–38 naked charms" in a publication called *Charlatan*.

Charlatan was an alternative magazine published by students at Florida State University and the University of Florida. It was an irreverent journal that specialized in topics that weren't allowed in official college publications, like sex, humor, and advice columns about sex. About the only advice college students received about sex from campus newspapers was not to have it, and therefore *Charlatan* was very popular, being voted the best college newspaper in America on at least one occasion. The editor in 1967 was a student named Bill Killeen, who decided to push the envelope by publishing a topless photo of Ms. Brewer, the first time *Charlatan* had gone that far.

Both Brewer and the editors of *Charlatan* knew the photo's publication would be controversial, but they wanted to challenge the administration. They had the audacity to take the photo in the University library, and the issue included an editorial essentially daring the school to take action.

The University of Florida administration couldn't ignore the challenge. If they let this pass, what might *Charlatan* do next? There was precedent for disciplining coeds for similar transgressions, going back to 1937, when a female music student at the University of Wisconsin, who was also a New York model, was expelled for posing nude for a drawing class. Posing in an art classroom was not nearly as shocking as posing for a picture in a widely-distributed magazine.

Brewer's coy photo was not crass pornography. "It's not a suggestive picture," said one member of the Board of Regents. "She's covered in all the appropriate spots." Yet, the school decided to take action, not against the newspaper or its editor, but against Pamme Brewer, whose presence on campus, they said, could be unsettling to other students. "When you go through classes with a girl after she has done something like this," said a university spokesman, "it's going to be a disturbing factor for everybody concerned, young men and women."

The American Civil Liberties Union got involved and hired young attorney Selig Goldin, who'd been active in civil rights litigation, to represent Brewer. Goldin insisted the Board hold an open hearing, which was packed with Brewer's student supporters. Goldin was a skilled litigator and succeeded in turning the proceeding from a trial of Pamme Brewer into an interrogation of the dean of women and her conduct in the matter.

Apparently, Goldin softened up the Board, or perhaps scared them, for while they found Brewer guilty of "inappropriate and indiscriminate conduct," they only placed her on probation, a rather innocuous sanction. They noted that it was Ms. Brewer's first disciplinary offense and that she might have been subjected to "undue pressure and influence." If she stayed out of further trouble, nothing more would happen to her.

The school had done something, but it hadn't done much, and one has the impression they would have been very happy to see the whole incident go away and for Pamme Brewer to keep her 38–25–38 charms under a sweater.

But Brewer was unrepentant. "I'd do it again," she said after judgment was rendered. "We have a right to be a citizen and to have the same rights as other citizens." "And," she added, "I'm nothing like the 38–26–38 (sic) either, like they said." It was apparent that The University of Florida regents had not seen the last of Pamme Brewer.

Nude Model Leaves College Voluntarily

Bridgeport Post-Telegram, March 23, 1967

Even though Attorney Goldin admitted that Brewer's punishment was more lenient than he expected, about 200 students staged an overnight protest outside Tigert Hall. If the university hoped that the entire incident would fade away, they were disappointed, for in less than a month a second photo of Ms. Brewer appeared in *Charlatan*. It was from the same session as the first one, and although her back was turned and her hands were strategically placed over the top 38 of her charms, it led to the end of Brewer's college career. Her parents, both conservative government workers based in Washington, thought she would be expelled and urged her to withdraw, which she did. The University denied that they were planning to expel Brewer and said they were surprised (but undoubtedly relieved) when she withdrew.

Pamme returned to her parents' home in Springfield, Virginia, and the elder Brewers tried to shield the family from the media. They supported their daughter and loved her, her mother said, but, "I'd like to paddle her backside." If she did, one can be certain that *Charlatan* would have been there to record the moment.

In January of 1969, another University of Florida coed appeared naked in a magazine, which caused a similar ruckus. Although it was troubling, an anonymous university spokesman said, "She hasn't got the physical equipment that Pam had." Nearly every article about Brewer noted her measurements, referred to her as a "bosomy coed" or something similar, and described her outfits.

After she left the university, Brewer and *Charlatan* editor Bill Killeen opened a store called the Subterranean Circus, which catered to hippie tastes, selling bell bottoms, Nehru shirts, Cossack shirts, underground newspapers, and incense. Part of the startup capital came from a loan from Pam's parents, who had apparently forgiven her. In January of 1968, Brewer was charged with selling obscene literature, but the charges were dropped. She was described in the news report as "the young nude model turned psychedelic businesswoman."

Twelve years after Pamme Brewer left the University of Florida, a coed named Louanne Fernald was a centerfold for *Playboy* magazine. Ms. Fernald's pictures showed a lot more flesh than Brewer had displayed in 1967, but no one threatened to expel her. A group of businessmen from Gainesville, pitching bond sales in Chicago and showing a little local pride, slipped a few photos of their University's star centerfold into their presentation to liven it up a little.

When Fernald posed for *Playboy*, Hugh Cunningham, assistant to the President of the University, was asked about the Brewer incident. "It's a wound," he said. "It's something in history. The University of Florida would like to forget it." Phyllis Meekly, the assistant dean of women, said that Brewer's case had caused the university to re-examine its way of thinking, and it now granted more rights to its students. Former President J. Wayne Reitz was unrepentant however, stating that "the faculty acted in its day." Things had changed since then, he said—for the worse.

Killeen and Brewer dated for a while, but in 1970 Pamme married a man named Tom Fristoe and moved to California. Many years later, Killeen heard that she was suffering from uterine cancer and called her on the phone. Although she was very weak, the two were able to have a brief conversation. "We showed 'em, Bill," she said, before she faded and told him she had to sleep. Pamme died shortly thereafter.

Other sources:
  http://billkilleen.blogspot.com/2011/12/send-in-clowns-weve-been-trying-to.html
  Interview of Phyllis Meekly by Lisa Heard, April 13, 1992. http://ufdc.ufl.edu/UF0000 6126/00001/16j
  Bradford Era, October 31, 1967
  Cedar Rapids Gazette, February 12, 1967
  The Arizona Republic, February 16, 1967
  Uniontown Morning Herald, February 10, 1967
  Pasadena Independent, January 4, 1968
  News Herald, Panama City, Florida, November 25, 1979
  Provo Daily Herald, January 28, 1969

Screen: "The Trip" on View at 2 Houses

New York Times, August 24, 1967

"[Bonnie and Clyde] was also the most controversial film during a very good year for the movies, and that may be as important as its greatness. People are not only going to movies in greater numbers than at any time since TV, but they seem to be taking movies more seriously and talking about them more."

That was critic Roger Ebert's commentary on the 1967 movie scene, a year in which film took a sharp turn from corny romances and John Wayne westerns to more serious fare. There were exceptions, like *Dr. Doolittle* and the James Bond film *Casino Royale*, but there were a number of serious films like *Guess Who's Coming to Dinner*, a tale of inter-racial romance, and *The Graduate*, a story of coming of age and inter-generational romance.

Sex and drugs were portrayed more often in mainstream movies, with Russ Meyers' *Valley of the Dolls* straddling the chasm between pornography and serious drama. The drug scene was big in 1967 and the film that most typified the drug culture was *The Trip*, a movie about drugs and only about drugs.

The people involved in the making of *The Trip* were more noteworthy than the film itself. The director was Roger Corman, who to that point was primarily known as the creator of numerous horror films. In 1958, he'd directed *The Cry Baby Killer*, which gave a young actor named Jack Nicholson his first prominent role. As part of his research for *The Trip*, Corman took LSD to see what it was like.

Nicholson wrote the screenplay for *The Trip*, which starred Peter Fonda, Bruce Dern, Dennis Hopper, Susan Strasberg, and Salli Sachse. The basic premise of the film is that Fonda, playing Paul Groves, a producer of television commercials who is in the midst of a divorce, decides to take LSD in order to find the true meaning of life.

The movie began with a disclaimer warning of the dangers of illegal drugs and then proceeded to spend an evening with Fonda while he experienced his trip. Once he took the drug, mixed with apple juice, we see an array of colorful, kaleidoscopic images whirling around the screen (the special effects were provided by Charlatan Productions). Dern was Fonda's mentor, guardian, and coach.

The film is a dual representation of Fonda's imagination, which consisted of swirling colors and images, complete with dwarfs in medieval costume and frantic lovemaking, and Fonda's experience in the real world during his trip.

My own observations of LSD use were not as dramatic. I remember coming back to my apartment one day in the mid-'70s to find a roommate tripping on acid. Unlike Fonda's exciting experiences, my friend was sitting in our living room staring at a revolving fan, which he said he'd been doing for several hours. If he was seeing fantastic images and believed he was making love to Susan Strasberg, he didn't mention it.

In *The Trip*, there was continuous drug talk and everything was "groovy" or "far out." The conversation was classic 1960s hippie jargon, such as "Don't make any demands on my head, man. I know your scene." The word "man" is continuously used as punctuation, as in "Relax, man," "Look at me, man," and "Come on, man." The version of the film that I watched on YouTube had Italian subtitles, and "man" was translated as "amico." "It's cool" was translated as "e freddo" or "it's cold." There may therefore have been many wannabe Italian hippies who greeted each other by saying, "It's cold, friend."

At one point, Fonda thinks he is dying and pleads with Dern for the Thorazine antidote, which Dern refuses to give him, telling him everything will be fine. Fonda then believes he's killed Dern and takes to the streets of Los Angeles, thinking the police are pursuing him. He has a number of adventures and strange encounters with people who aren't high.

By the end of the trip, Fonda is a different man. He acknowledges the shallowness of his life, pleading guilty to Dern in a scene that takes place with a carousel and calliope music in the background. "I can see right into my brain," he said at one point. Fonda bonds emotionally with Sachse, and says, "I love you and I love everybody else." The new genre of drug film had an ending as sappy as that of a Doris Day romance, except Rock Hudson wasn't tripping on LSD.

The Trip wasn't a great movie, but any experimental film is valuable for what it says about the time it portrays, and in that sense *The Trip* was successful. Further, it grossed more than $6 million after costing just $100,000 to produce and was the American entry in the 1967 Cannes Film Festival.

But Fonda wasn't completely happy with the movie, believing that they had not been true to Nicholson's script. At the end of the year, he sat down and conceived the idea for *Easy Rider*, which appeared two years later and became the classic film that *The Trip* was not.

Other sources:
http://www.rogerebert.com/rogers-journal/the-best-10-movies-of-1967
ttps://en.wikipedia.org/wiki/Roger_Corman

The See-Through Look
New York Times, April 24, 1968

The point of Marilyn Bender's article about sheer clothing was that fashion was becoming more daring and that, within a couple of years fashionable women would be wearing less and more provocative clothing. "A rash of see-through blouses and dresses," she wrote, "have been stridently promoted and advertised by magazines and stores and sold to countless women whose intentions about underpinnings cannot be immediately ascertained." It wouldn't be long, perhaps, before Aunt Trudy showed up at her nephew's birthday party in a see-through blouse.

Designer Yves St. Laurent was at the forefront of the see-through craze. The daring women who donned his clothes wore nothing over or under them, while the more discreet covered themselves with a jacket. One design featured strategically placed cloth pockets.

Yet, the women Bender described as pioneers of the see-through look invariably seemed to be actresses and models. They included women such as French model Monique Dutto, who attended a party thrown by dress designer Bob Bugnand. "She removed the jacket of her violet velvet pants," reported Bender, "and sat there in her black organdy [see-through] blouse." "The women were a little shocked," Dutto said, "but the men rather enjoyed it."

Other wearers of see-through blouses included actress Monique Van Vooren, who planned to wear one to the opening of *Hair*, where she apparently intended to compete for attention with the cast. Despite the efforts of some people in the fashion industry, however, it did not appear that the see-through craze was about to sweep the nation. "It's just plain vulgar," said Mildred Custin, president of Bonwit Teller. "It's a form of exhibitionism." "Fortunately," said Rosalind Starkman, Bloomingdale's corset and bra buyer, "very few women have the bosom of a Botticelli."

Short skirts were fine for most women, but they drew the line when it came to see-through fashion, which remained the province of actresses and models. As Mildred Custin said, wearing such items was a form of exhibitionism, and who is better at that than models and actresses.

Nudity Moves into Center Stage

New York Times, **April 25, 1968**

By 1968, nudity had moved from slimy Times Square theaters to Broadway, where *The Prime of Miss Jean Brodie* featured a topless scene. Off-Broadway, Phyllis Craig walked around the stage minus the top half of her bikini in *Scuba Duba*. "[T]he stage," said the *Times*, "is starting to claim a right to the extreme frankness now permitted its prime public competitor, the cinema."

Sex debuted on Broadway in 1926 in a play appropriately titled *Sex*, written by and starring Mae West. Ms. West did not remove her clothes, but the play was racy enough to get it raided by police at the instigation of "Holy Joe" McKee, president of the New York Board of Aldermen. Her performance cost West eight days in prison. Two years later, she appeared in another of her own plays, called *Pleasure Man*, about an actor who seduced showgirls. That show was also raided.

By 1968, New York laws had changed. Article 245 of the Code prohibited obscenity, which was defined as meeting all three of the following conditions: first, "if the predominate appeal is to 'prurient, shameful or morbid interest' in sex"; second, "if the material goes beyond 'customary limits of candor,'" and; third, "if the material is 'utterly without redeeming social value.'" That was a low standard, as it was difficult to prove that something had absolutely no redeeming value whatsoever. Therefore, actresses and, to a much lesser extent, actors, began to remove their clothes on stage.

Perhaps the most renowned Broadway play of the unclothed genre was the musical *Hair*, a celebration of the hippie culture billed as an American Tribal Love—Rock Musical. During one of the musical numbers, whatever cast members were in the mood removed their clothes. The intent of *Hair* was to shock, and there were numerous references to drugs, homosexuality, the Vietnam War, promiscuity, and miscegenation. But it was the nude scenes that everyone remembered. The actors had remained fully clothed in the off-Broadway version of the play, but when it moved to the big stage, director Tom O'Horgan decided that he needed to generate some publicity and off went the clothes.

Actresses in other New York shows were required to shed their clothes whether or not they were in the mood, and it wasn't easy for most. "I guess I was a little up-tight about it at first," said Ms. Craig, "but now I'm really enjoying it. I've never done anything like this before. It's really unlocked something within me as an actress."

Theater is art, art is supposed to have social meaning, and nudity was sometimes used to deliver that meaning. In *Christmas Turkey*, Bonnie Finberg, representing White Idealism, sat naked on a platter for the entire performance before being devoured by Angry Black Nationalism (played by Patrick Whitaker).

Broadway audiences responded with typical aplomb, for they were a much different group than the men Joseph Morgenstern observed in Times Square theaters. One man who tried to enter with a pair of binoculars was turned away. "Certainly we attracted some creeps and heavy breathers," said playwright Florence B. Hunt, whose *Tennis, Anyone?* featured a nude tennis player murdering an insane man who raped her, "but most of the people who came found it merely a good play." But the theater made sure, in its advertising, to let it be known that the audience would see a naked body. "You have to have something to attract the public," Ms. Hunt said.

Other sources:

//www.theguardian.com/theguardian/2013/sep/12/hair-musical-nudity-west-end
//broadway.showtickets.com/articles/10-most-controversial-shows-on-and-off-broadway/

Topless Dancer Runs for Stanford Student Body President
Hartford Courant, May 1, 1968

In the spring of 1968, a young woman named Victoria Bowles, who used the name Vicky Drake when she danced at The Morgue in Palo Alto, announced that she wanted to be president of the Stanford University student body. There was no question she had the body, but when her candidacy made national news, Stanford dean of students Joel Smith claimed that Drake was not a student. He puckishly described her as a "young woman of conspicuous talent," but said she was not eligible to run for office.

Drake, 21, said that she was registered as a Spanish major, was taking two courses, and had more than two years' worth of credits. In addition to her academic achievements, she noted that her measurements were 38–22–36, and it was soon discovered that, in addition to her topless dancing at The Morgue, she had recently posed nude for a campus magazine called the *Stanford Chaparral*.

None of that had anything to do with Drake's eligibility to run for president, but after lengthy debate, the leaders of the student government ruled that she would be allowed on the ballot. After the decision was announced, Dean Smith clarified his earlier remark. "For those who lack a sense of humor," he said, "I am eager to explain that my statement was intended as a joke."

The organization that governed Stanford students was called the Associated Students of Stanford University (ASSU), and soon there appeared on campus posters of a nude Vicky at the Stanford Mausoleum, with her knee raised in the time-honored pose used to obscure the goodies, accompanied by the slogan "Vicky for ASSU Pres."

"I am proposing nothing useful," she said. "Nothing more than a little distraction for a lot of book-weary students." Her biggest campaign issue was making the campus's Lake Lagunita a nudist facility for swimming and boating. In fact, "Nudity for Lake Lag" was her entire platform. When the *Stanford Daily* asked each candidate for their biography and platform, she provided neither, which didn't stop the paper from printing her photo.

Vicky campaigned enthusiastically, dancing topless at frat houses and dormitories and appearing more publicly in a bikini or a crocheted see-through dress. Her husband, Joe Reich, usually accompanied her. The poster of Vicky at the Mausoleum was in great demand, as was another of a naked Vicky holding a sign in front of her that had a picture of a beckoning Uncle Sam and the slogan, "If You're Good Enough, I Want You." A campaign button read, "Take another look at the 'o' in student body."

Although her campaign was not based on any serious issues, Drake had a highly qualified campaign manager, Frank Forrester "Forrest" Church, IV, son of long-time Idaho Senator Frank Church. Church didn't have a lot to do; one of his main tasks was operating the tape player for the music that accompanied Vicky's frat house dances.

In the initial balloting, Drake garnered more votes than any of the five other announced candidates and numerous write-ins. She had 1,575 votes and Denis Hayes, who finished second, had 1,232. Since she had not achieved a majority, however, she was required to take part in a two-person runoff with Hayes, a history major who eventually became national coordinator of Earth Day. Drake indicated that she would probably not debate Hayes, but would continue with her unique form of campaigning.

The *Stanford Daily* said "[Drake] now claims to be a serious candidate though she has shown no ability to speak coherently about student problems." After reviewing the qualifications of the two runoff candidates, the editor urged students not to vote for either of them, but that didn't dissuade them from electing Hayes. "My enemies will stop at nothing," Drake said. "They must have stuffed the ballot box."

A few months later, Hayes said, "[T]he more than two thousand people who voted for a topless dancer for ASSU President all shared at least one belief. Student participation doesn't amount to a tinker's damn at Stanford." He pledged to make the office more relevant.

After the election, Drake was far more relevant than Hayes. She was interviewed in the *Chaparral*. Her picture, fully clothed, appeared in *Time* magazine. In September, *Playboy* ran a feature on Drake's campaign titled *Student Body*. *Playboy* was several cuts above the *Chaparral*, and the September issue featured an interview with Stanley Kubrick, a playlet by Kurt Vonnegut, Jr., and letters to the editor responding to an article by Supreme Court Justice William O. Douglas about pollution and to a previous interview with economist John Kenneth Galbraith.

The theme of the September issue was the beginning of the college year, with articles like the *Playboy Pigskin Preview: A Swinger's Guide to Academe*, and a *Back to Campus Fashion Guide*. *Student Body* fit right in, and featured a reproduction of the famous poster at the Mausoleum and the one with the Uncle Sam sign. The show of skin was modest compared to what would appear in *Playboy* just a few years later, but readers saw everything that patrons of The Morgue could see.

The 1968 election was the high point of Vicky Drake's political career. She worked as a stripper from 1970 through 1974, touring the United States and Japan. In 1977, she obtained her teaching credentials from the University of California at Fullerton and worked as a teacher until 2005. Drake has been married four times, the first three times to an attorney, a publisher, and an English professor. She is now married to musician John Mitchell, uses the name Vicky Braga-Mitchell, and is a noted fractal artist. If you don't know what fractal art is, you are not alone, and therefore I supply a definition from Wikipedia:

"Fractal art is a form of algorithmic art created by calculating fractal objects and representing the calculation results as still images, animations, and media. Fractal art developed from the mid–1980s onwards. It is a genre of computer art and digital art which are part of new media art."

In 2003, Drake promoted a film called *The Beauty of Touch*, which featured naked dancers accompanied by her husband's music. She had not forgotten her roots.

Drake's campaign manager, Forrest Church, was called to the provost's office after the election and given a tongue-lashing for making a farce of it. As the son of a senator, Church was told that he should have known better. He did, and went on to a distinguished career as a prominent Unitarian Universalist minister and author. Church became a spokesperson for liberal religious views and in addition to writing numerous books, he often appeared on television. Although he has written much and much has been written about him, I was unable to find a single contemporary reference to his having served as Vicky Drake's campaign manager.

From topless dancer to teacher to fractal artist was quite a career path, and it would have been even more remarkable if Vicky Drake's resume had included ASSU President. She came close, closer than anyone like her probably could have expected to come at any time other than the late 1960s, when topless dancers who ran for office were taken seriously. In two 1968 elections, George Wallace made a credible run for the presidency and Vicky Drake was nearly elected president of the Stanford student body. Her candidacy was a great diversion for the students, provided titillating copy for the wire services and a few racy photos for readers of *Playboy* magazine. It was not a typical college election, but as Joel Smith said, Vicky Drake was "a young woman with conspicuous talent."

Other sources:

www.daysatknight.com/vicky-drake-topless-dancer-runs-stanford-student-body-president/
https://en.wikipedia.org/wiki/Vicky_Brago-Mitchell
https://en.wikipedia.org/wiki/Fractal_art
Playboy Magazine, September 1968
The Stanford Daily, May 1, 3, 9, 14, and 16, 1968
https://en.wikipedia.org/wiki/Forrest_Church
Being Alive and Having to Die: The Spiritual Odyssey of Forrest Church, by Dan Cryer, St. Martin's Press
http://filmthreat.com/news/live-nude-dancers/
http://www.abm-enterprises.net/webmistress.html

Miss Moorman in Football Togs Plays in "Mixed Media Opera"

New York Times, June 11, 1968

Who would imagine that a cellist would be one of the leaders of the clothes-less revolt? Not many, but Charlotte Moorman was no ordinary cellist. In the 1960s, she became perhaps the most famous practitioner of the art other than the legendary Pablo Casals, for Miss Moorman liked to play the cello topless at a time when most women who took off their tops were strippers, not classical musicians.

Moorman was born in 1933, and in 1952 she was named Little Rock's Miss City Beautiful. She had been playing the cello since the age of 10 and earned a bachelor's degree in music from Centenary College in Shreveport, Louisiana. After graduate study at the University of Texas, Moorman moved to New York in 1957 and enrolled in the Julliard School of Music. While working for a booking agent, she arranged Yoko Ono's American solo debut at Carnegie Hall, and later shared an apartment with Ono. In 1963, she founded the New York Avant Garde Festival.

Moorman was best known as a performer, however, and her signature piece was John Cage's *26'1.1499" for a String Player*. She added bizarre touches like drinking a Coke while playing, reading instructions from a Tampax box, and playing an Army practice bomb as if it were a cello. In February 1967, Moorman became famous when she played the cello (in a piece she called *Opera Sextronique*) wearing only a floor length black skirt. At one point, she played by means of mini-propellers attached to her breasts. For her efforts, Moorman was arrested and convicted of public indecency. She spent a night in jail, but received only a suspended sentence.

Although she was dismissed from the American Symphony Orchestra, Moorman became renowned as the "Topless Cellist" and appeared on numerous talk shows. Composer Edgard Varese called her the "Jeanne d'Arc of New Music." Moorman continued to shock her audience, and in one performance she sat nude behind a carved ice Cello.

Although Moorman's antics made her famous, she was not universally acclaimed. Her conservative family members wanted her to return to conventional cello playing and many feminists condemned her as narcissistic. During the 1970s Moorman, who'd achieved notoriety due to her bare breasts, was diagnosed with breast cancer. She had a mastectomy, but continued to perform during the 1980s. The cancer returned and she died on November 8, 1991, at the age of 57.

Other sources:
New York Times, September 9, 2016
https://www.artsy.net/article/artsy-editorial-the-topless-cellist-charlotte-moorman-finally-finds-her-place-in-art-history
https://en.wikipedia.org/wiki/Charlotte_Moorman
https://mitpress.mit.edu/books/topless-cellist
New York Times. November 9, 1991
https://www.huffingtonpost.com/entry/the-avant-garde-pioneer-and-proto-fourth-wave-feminist-that-art-history-forgot_us_56c62c04e4b041136f165928

Actresses Talk About Onstage Nudity

New York Times, **February 17, 1969**

Some women were OK with the idea of taking their clothes off on stage, but many were not, including Monica Evans. The British Evans was an accomplished actress, having played Cecily Pigeon in the stage version of *The Odd Couple*, which starred Art Carney and Walter Matthau, as well as appearing in the movie and the first season of the television show. She asked to be released from an $800 per week contract in *The Mother Lover* because it required some brief nudity. "I hadn't worked for a while," she said shortly afterward, "and that $800 looked like a million." But she left the ensemble rather than disrobe on stage.

"I'm not a prude," Evans insisted. "I love wearing the briefest sort of bikini. But I kept thinking of how I'd feel standing up there on the stage with all my clothes off. I kept thinking, that wouldn't be me the actress—that would be me ... nudity invades the rights of a human being. My body belongs to me—that's my private life, my personal territory." It wasn't long before all of Evans' life was private; her acting career ended in 1973 at the age of 33. "Nowadays," said German actress Sibylla Kay, who starred in *Monique*, "at one point or another you have to take off your clothes in a movie or you don't work."

In the *Times* article, Lewis Funke noted that few actresses were hesitant about appearing in their underwear, and most accepted nude appearances if they were seen from behind, but frontal views were another matter. "I will not face forward," said Valerie French, who took the role that Evans declined. "The scene is a gag and if it draws a laugh, all right. But facing front would be obvious, obscene and out of place."

Sweet Eros, a play about a disturbed man who kidnaps, rapes and tortures a woman, involved frontal nudity—about 45 minutes of it. Producer Michael Ellis and director Larry Arrick interviewed two dozen actresses before finding three who were willing to audition. Two of the three called to cancel before the reading. Sally Kirkland, who took the part, claimed proudly to have been the first nude performer on Broadway, but she was about seven months behind *Hair*.

The composition of the audience also made a difference in the amount of skin an actress was willing to display. Heather MacRae, part of the *Hair* cast, decided to remain clothed on the evening her parents, Gordon and Sheila, came to see her.

By the 1970s, doffing one's clothes on stage had become old hat, even when there was no hat. *Oh, Calcutta* was more sexual and less political than *Hair*, but nudity no longer guaranteed an audience. Several plays that featured unclad women did poorly. While Mae West had enraged the censors of the 1920s with tight dresses and some double entendres, the commonplace nature of full nudity by the 1970s made it unworthy of comment. If the play wasn't good, it didn't matter what the actors and actresses weren't wearing.

Other sources:
Middletown Press, April 15, 1970

Art Linkletter Says Daughter Died on LSD
New York Daily News, October 6, 1969

For many, Art Linkletter was the personification of wholesome Americana. For 25 years on radio and television he was the host of Art Linkletter's *House Party* and for 19 years he starred in a series called *People Are Funny*. His specialty was interviewing children and getting them to display their cuteness.

The real Art Linkletter was a genuine American success story. He was born Arthur Gordon Kelly but abandoned by his parents as an infant and adopted by the Linkletter family. After graduating from San Diego State College with a teaching degree, he got into the radio business and became a major success. A lifelong Republican, he campaigned for his friend Ronald Reagan when he ran for President.

Linkletter was a pragmatic man with good financial sense, and perhaps the only bad decision of his life was when his friend Walt Disney asked him to invest in his new California theme park. Linkletter wasn't sure it would be successful and turned Disney down.

Linkletter was married in 1935 and when he died in 2010 at the age of 97, he was survived by his wife Lois. A 75-year marriage is a formidable accomplishment for anyone, but even more impressive in the world of show business.

They say that bad things happen to good people, and in 1969 two *very* bad things happened to Art Linkletter. In July, his son-in-law, 33-year-old John Zweger, committed suicide, supposedly because he was despondent over the state of his insurance business.

The great tragedy of Linkletter's life occurred three months later and involved his 20-year-old daughter Diane. Diane, an aspiring singer, was depressed about her career prospects and worried that, as the daughter of a famous man, she would never be able to forge her own identity.

At three o'clock in the morning of October 4, Diane called Edward Durston in a state of great agitation (some accounts refer to the 27-year-old Durston as her boyfriend, others as simply a friend). Durston became very alarmed and rushed over to her West Hollywood Shoreham Towers apartment. The two talked until the sun came up, a deep and painful conversation.

At about 9:00 a.m., Diane went into the kitchen, and when she didn't reappear, Durston went to check on her. He walked in to see her climbing onto the sill of her sixth-floor window. She started to jump and Durston tried to grab her but she slipped from his grasp and plummeted to the sidewalk. Rushed to the hospital, she was pronounced dead at 10:30.

Linkletter was devastated, and the next day he announced that Diane's death was due to her use of LSD. Diane told her father six months earlier that she had taken the drug, but Linkletter wasn't certain if she'd taken it on the day she died or if she was suffering from a flashback. Diane's death wasn't suicide, he said, "It was murder. She was murdered by the people who manufacture and sell LSD."

An autopsy disclosed that there were no drugs in Diane's system when she died, but her father continued to insist that LSD was the cause of his daughter's death. For the rest of his life, Art Linkletter was a passionate anti-drug warrior. He was invited to tell his story in the White House by President Nixon and traveled around the country delivering speeches warning of the dangers of drug use.

In 1980, Linkletter had a dramatic confrontation with the high priest of LSD, Dr. Timothy Leary, when Leary was a guest on Stanley Siegel's WABC talk show. Siegel, whose show premiered in 1975, was a forerunner to reality television provocateurs like Jerry Springer. Siegel brought a severely inebriated Truman Capote on the set for an interview, grilled pioneer transsexual Renee Richards about her sex life, and enraged actress Marlo Thomas by insinuating that her Lebanese heritage made her an anti–Semite.

Siegel set Leary up by arranging to have Linkletter call in to confront him. Once Leary realized what was happening, he started to walk off the set, but Siegel grabbed him and pulled him back. Leary began laughing and mocking Linkletter, insulting him in a manner that foreshadowed the antics of Donald Trump. Linkletter accused him of being responsible for his daughter's death and Leary laughed at him. It was a bizarre scene, about as far removed from Linkletter's *House Party* as can be imagined.

Art Linkletter was the personification of the transition from the sanitized 1950s to the harsh realities that permeated American life by the end of the '60s. Those cute kids he interviewed in 1957 were, like his daughter, experimenting with drugs by the end of the next decade. The America that made Art Linkletter was gone forever. He and the country would never be the same.

Postscript: Edward Durston, who was present when Diane died, was involved in another mysterious show business death 16 years later. He was vacationing in Mexico with his girlfriend, buxom actress-model Carol Wayne, when the two had an argument. She stormed out of their hotel room and was later found dead, sprawled among the rocks near the ocean. Durston was never suspected of foul play and Wayne's death was ruled accidental.

Other sources:
https://en.wikipedia.org/wiki/Art_Linkletter
https://www.snopes.com/fact-check/the-scarlet-linkletter/
https://yesteryeargallery.wordpress.com/2013/02/25/what-really-happened-to-diane-linkletter/
http://afflictor.com/tag/stanley-siegel/

Addict, 12, Found After 3-Day Spree
New York Times, January 29, 1970

Prior to the 1960s, heroin addiction was generally confined to people on the fringes of society, such as prostitutes, homosexuals, and their like. But as drugs infiltrated American society, addicts became more—to use a current term—"diverse" and drug addiction became everyone's problem.

In 1960, 15 New York City teens died from the effects of heroin use. In 1964 the number of fatalities increased to 38, and in 1969 224 teenagers (55 of them 16 or under) were killed by the effects of heroin, more than ten times the number that died in 1960. Overall deaths from heroin in New York increased from 465 in the five-year period from 1950 to 1954 to 2,935 from 1965 to 1969. Perhaps the most shocking victim of 1969 was Walter Vandermeer of Harlem, who, two weeks after his 12th birthday, became the youngest known heroin fatality in the city's history.

Vandermeer's death became a rallying cry for action. Shortly afterward, Dr. Judianne Densen-Gerber, convinced that drug-addicted teens needed different treatment than adults, founded Odyssey House, a Bronx facility designed exclusively for the treatment of teenaged addicts.

Walter Vandermeer was the type of youngster that was expected to encounter problems. His mother had a third-grade education and produced several children by different fathers. Walter lived on the streets, panhandling and hanging out with criminals, and was well-known to social service agencies.

But 12-year-old Isabel Salazar was not an impoverished child of the streets; she was the daughter of Guillermo Salazar, a psychologist who'd been Fidel Castro's ambassador to Switzerland before coming to America. She attended the tony Miss Hewitt's School, whose alumnae include heiresses Barbara Hutton and Christina Onassis.

Dr. Salazar was involved in the treatment of drug addiction at Gracie Square Hospital, and often met with patients in his apartment. He was apparently somewhat lax in securing his medications, which gave Isabel access to Dexedrine and Thoracin. Her main source of drugs, however, was the streets of New York, particularly the Bethesda Fountain area of Central Park, where she could procure just about any illegal drug. "I take them," she said, "little blue pills, orange pills, green ones, pink and icy white ones—as often as I can, day and night. I take hash, pot, LSD, heroin, speed, anything I can get."

Isabel was a 98-pound waif who'd first tried drugs at 11 when a boyfriend gave her LSD in a glass of milk. She sometimes obtained money for drugs by telling her father she needed to buy clothes, and also earned drug money by selling to other teens. At about the same time Isabel was in the news, police arrested 39-year-old Victor Santiago, one of a number of wholesale pushers who enlisted youths in their early teens by promising them $50 per day. Police claimed the adults were clearing an average of $750 a day.

When Isabel's mother, Caroline, realized what her daughter was doing, she pulled her out of school, took her to Honduras and then to Miami in an attempt to keep her away from her drug sources. Once the two returned to New York on January 20, 1970, however, Isabel slipped back into her old habits.

Shortly after her return, Isabel disappeared. Three days later, she was found in the hallway of an Upper West Side apartment, tripping on hallucinogenic drugs. She was brought to the East 77th Street apartment of her parents where, still high, Isabel spoke with a *Times* reporter, describing what she saw. "Wherever I look," she said, "I see dots, and people look like pale ghosts." After what they'd been through, perhaps her parents really *did* look like pale ghosts. Her mother said she was taking Isabel out of the country again. "This is a jungle," she said, "this country. It's going down the drain faster than anybody realizes. We're moving to Hong Kong (probably not a good idea), maybe Africa. I'm just getting our visas and getting out of here."

Was Isabel's situation representative of a growing problem or was she merely a wealthy, privileged child looking for kicks? The *Times* noted that children were more open to experimentation than previous generations, and concluded by stating, "Some doctors say it is a fad and will pass; others feel it is a side-effect of the social revolution that is going on in this country; but some, like Dr. Denson-Gerber, feel that addiction is the by-product of a profound disillusionment the young feel toward their elders."

The heroin problem was new and thus frightening, particularly when it affected children believed to be immune from social dysfunction. John Cahill, son of the governor of New Jersey, was arrested for marijuana possession and Harvey Fleetwood, II, son of a prominent New York banker and a psychiatrist, was charged with being part of a $200,000 drug peddling ring. If youngsters like that could become ensnared in the drug culture, it could happen to anyone. It happened in New York and it happened in small towns. Illegal drugs, it seemed, were everywhere.

Other sources:
New York Times, February 1, 1970
Las Vegas Sun, February 16, 1970
New York Times, January 12, 1970

Ex-Staples Honor Student Nabbed in N.Y. Drug Haul

Bridgeport Post-Telegram, May 23, 1970

Connecticut is the wealthiest state in America, and Westport is one of its most affluent towns. Westport's high school graduates are often admitted to the country's most prestigious colleges, and Andrea Rosenberg was no exception. After graduating from Staples High in 1966 as one of the top ten in her class, Rosenberg was admitted to New York's Barnard College.

At Barnard, Rosenberg majored in anthropology, became a member of Phi Beta Kappa, and was a candidate for valedictorian of the Class of 1970. She accomplished this despite the fact that by her senior year, she had a very demanding part time job as one of the biggest drug dealers on campus. Barnard was the sister school of Columbia University, which had been at the epicenter of the violent student protests of 1968. The counter-culture atmosphere was also a drug atmosphere, and Rosenberg was one of the principal dealers serving the fertile Columbia market.

Such a sizable operation was bound to attract notice. After a three-week investigation utilizing undercover agents, the Narcotics Division of the New York City Police Department had enough evidence to obtain a search warrant for the apartment at 772 West End Avenue that Rosenberg shared with 24-year-old Harold Pezzano, a Columbia graduate student.

On the night of May 21, 1970, Lieutenant John Egan and five narcotics officers followed a customer into the apartment and found Rosenberg sitting at a table with drugs spread out in front of her, about to consummate a sale of hashish to a Columbia student. Rosenberg, described by Egan as a "very good-looking girl with long black hair," was quite composed and offered no resistance.

Egan's men found six pounds of high-quality black hashish, seven pounds of marijuana, LSD capsules in vials and tubes, amphetamines, and kif, a strain of hashish. They also found $4,300 in cash, a rather large amount for a Barnard student to have on hand, since it was roughly equal to the cost of one year's tuition and fees. The eventual disposition of the cash would have serious ramifications for Rosenberg and the arresting officers.

Rosenberg, Pezzano, and three customers, two from Columbia and one from Bernard Baruch College, were arrested. When the news hit the papers, Rosenberg's teachers were shocked. A statement from Barnard stated that the college was "saddened and stunned" but added that if she was guilty of the charges, Rosenberg was "old enough to face the consequences."

Rosenberg's fellow students were not as shocked. One coed, who'd dabbled in drug dealing, said, "I know people with that much stuff in their apartments right now." Others said they knew classmates who grossed as much as $3,000 per month from drug sales. They would front money to a buyer who would purchase the drugs in quantity, and then resold the drugs to their fellow students. One student flew to the West Coast to procure hallucinogens. There was not much trading in heroin or cocaine, as the students preferred marijuana and hashish. Most deals were consummated in off-campus apartments like the one shared by Rosenberg and Pezzano.

Ms. Rosenberg was released on $25,000 bail posted by her father, Seymour Rosenberg of Beverly Hills, California. Ironically, Seymour Rosenberg was a pharmaceutical executive. In a column in the *Anderson Herald*, Alice Widener speculated whether Rosenberg would ever appear in court. "Bail jumping is so fashionable for girls," she wrote. "Just take a look at the FBI's most wanted list." (See Chapter 4.)

Rosenberg, who had begun using the name Andrea Ross, did appear in court. In 1973, she pleaded guilty to a single count of drug selling and received five years' probation, a decidedly light sentence for a big-time drug dealer. Perhaps she was let off easy because she was a wealthy Barnard girl, or maybe there were other factors that made it difficult for prosecutors to obtain a tougher conviction.

Two years after Rosenberg's plea, three of the officers who arrested her were indicted and charged with violating her civil rights, illegally tapping her phone, obtaining a warrant with false information, and stealing the $4,300 found in the apartment. Two officers pleaded guilty to receiving stolen funds, saying that Officer William Roche had taken the money and given them a share. Amazingly, Roche was later found innocent.

The good girl gone bad was a common story in the late 1960s and early '70s. Perhaps good girls were infused with the idealism that permeated the era, or maybe, like Dr. Blaine suggested, they had relatively easy lives and were looking for adventure. In either event, it was a phenomenon that seemed to occur more frequently during the late 1960s than at any other time in American history.

Other sources:

Anderson Herald, May 29, 1970
Connellsville Daily Courier, May 23, 1970
Oswego Palladium Times, May 23, 1970
European Stars and Stripes, May 23 and May 25, 1970
New York Times, May 22, 1970
Columbia Spectator, March 6, 1975, and May 20, 1976
Bridgeport Post-Telegram, May 25, 1970

Gay Liberation

Hartford Courant, October 22, 1970

"Gay Liberation" was the caption under a photo of members of the Gay Liberation Front discussing their plan to take over California's Alpine County. Alpine, a rural county located in the Sierra Nevada Mountains, was sparsely populated and gay leaders believed they could take control of the political structure and transform the community into a supportive, gay-friendly environment.

The Stonewall riot of September 1969 had infused the gay movement with a new militancy, and gays emerged from the shadows of a culture that had been illegal in most jurisdictions. Homosexual activity was not legal everywhere in 1970, although there was little enthusiasm for enforcing the remaining "sodomy" laws. But it still wasn't easy for gays to live in a heterosexual environment. In December 1969, Don Jackson, a member of the Los Angeles chapter of the Gay Liberation Front, announced the plan to colonize Alpine County at a symposium in Berkeley. "Imagine a place," he said, "where ... there is no job discrimination, police harassment or prejudice ... a place where a gay government can build a base for a flourishing gay culture."

There were no incorporated cities in Alpine County and just 384 voters. Today, it has the fewest residents of any California county. Moreover, the county had recently changed its laws to enable new residents to become voters in 90 days. A thousand gays could easily take control of the government and elect gay officials to every post.

Most gays were not that excited about Jackson's plan. Alpine County is not Los Angeles, and living in a freezing, isolated mountain community in the midst of the resident Native Americans, mountaineers, and fishermen did not seem like paradise, no matter how gay-friendly it might be.

One of those who was not excited was Morris Kight, a showman who favored outrageous events like "kiss-ins" to agitate in favor of gay rights. But Kight's strategy was not succeeding, and in 1970 he said, "Alpine is freezing. It's no place where anyone gay would want to live. But we'll pretend to be serious."

To that point, few had taken notice of Jackson's plan, but when Kight cranked up his publicity machine, the media began to cover the story, which led to the photo and brief piece in the *Courant*. *Time* Magazine, *The New York Times*, and CBS News all reported on the plan to make Alpine County a gay haven. *Time* described the peaceful nature of the area and said, "Now that existence stands threatened, and by as unlikely a force as could be imagined—the militant homosexuals of the Gay Liberation Front."

The residents of Alpine County took notice. Herbert Bruns, Chairman of the County Board of Supervisors, said, "We're all very concerned. Naturally, we'll do everything we can to prevent anyone taking over our county."

Don Kilhefner of the Gay Liberation Front announced in October 1970 that 479 gays had already signed up for the coup, more than enough to take control of the local government. Alpine County was just the beginning, he said, for there were many similar communities around the United States that were ripe for gay takeover.

Jackson was serious, but few others were. Kight's goal was not to colonize Alpine County, but to gain attention and respect for the gay community—and in that regard he was successful. Thanks to the barrage of publicity, people started talking about gays—and calling them gay rather than homosexual or inverts—and throughout America citizens who'd thought of gays as perverts began to see them a little differently.

But they didn't want large numbers of them living in their communities and controlling the government. The residents of Alpine County met and formulated plans to make it more difficult to take over. Los Angeles gays, who were not that eager to move to an isolated community where they were unwanted, procrastinated. The launch date was postponed several times and, while no official announcement was made, the plan was eventually abandoned.

Alpine County may have resisted gay infiltration in 1970, but by 2008, attitudes had softened. The county was one of the few in California to vote against Proposition 8, which proposed a ban on gay marriage.

Other sources:
https://www.atlasobscura.com/articles/the-radical-plan-to-turn-one-california-town-into-a-gay-utopia
https://content.ucpress.edu/chapters/12618.ch01.pdf
https://en.wikipedia.org/wiki/Alpine_County,_California

Drill for GI Junkies: A Nauseating Shoot-Up
Hartford Courant, November 14, 1970

"Hey, everyone in the shootup rooms." That was the call signaling the start of the heroin addiction treatment session at Fort Bragg, North Carolina. Marines were accustomed to hearing commands like "Fall In," "Column Right," and "Present Arms," but being ordered to shoot up with drugs was a new one. Times were changing and the young men from the drug culture generation didn't miraculously reform when they were drafted or enlisted. They became the problem of the Army, Navy, Air Force, and Marines.

The Pentagon denied that there was a drug problem in the military,

5. Social Issues 145

pointing out that there were very few cases brought before disciplinary tribunals. They claimed that stories of widespread marijuana use in Vietnam were "grossly exaggerated" and there was "virtually no drug addiction" in the service. Those who knew better didn't believe the top brass was lying. "They aren't suppressing the information," one officer said. "They just don't know what's going on."

In June 1970, the *New York Times* published an article that began with an account of 18-year-old Marine John Little's death from a heroin overdose at Virginia's Quantico Marine Base. Master Chief Hospital Corpsman Marvin E. Reed, who spent a year in Vietnam as a drug abuse lecturer, said, "Marijuana is as available in Vietnam as chewing gum is here." He told a House of Representatives subcommittee that an estimated 17 percent of all military personnel had tried heroin.

The Pentagon claimed that it was impossible to maintain an expensive drug habit on a military salary, but what they didn't know or acknowledge was that many soldiers were supporting their habits by stealing and selling military supplies. In Vietnam, they sold equipment to the Vietnamese and, for all they knew, the Vietcong. "We gave the Charge of Quarters $100 for an hour in the supply room," said one veteran. "You could pay your way into or out of everything."

The innovative Fort Bragg program represented a dramatic change from punishment to treatment. Those who admitted to an addiction and agreed to participate were given decreasing doses of drugs in order to wean them from their habit. Once the patients arrived in the "shootup room," they lay down on mattresses in an environment more like Haight-Ashbury than Fort Bragg. There were fluorescent posters, including one of the Beatles and another of Peter Fonda from the movie *Easy Rider*. Rock music blared from a record player and a light shone through a rotating plastic circle of different colors, bathing the room in ever-changing hues.

Most of the patients were given a small dose of a barbiturate, plus medicine to make them violently ill once they came off their high. A few soldiers were given a harmless sugar-based solution that produced no effect at all. Each injected their medication and waited for ecstasy and nausea—or nothing.

The program was developed by Major Richard Cross, chief of psychiatry and neurology at the base's Womack Hospital and administered by 26-year-old Captain Richard Elmore, a pilot with a master's degree in psychological counseling. The man behind the experiment, however, was the base commander, 54-year-old Lieutenant General John J. Tolson, a 1937 West Point graduate and World War II veteran who'd spent 15 months in Vietnam and earned a Distinguished Service Cross for heroism at Hue.

Tolson estimated that 40 percent of the soldiers at Fort Bragg were "hard core drug users" and that about 75 percent had tried drugs. "We're a cross section of our society," he said, "and certainly drug abuse is the problem in the society of this country today." There had been two deaths from heroin overdoses at the fort on the same day and the instances of hepatitis (mostly from dirty needles) and AWOL soldiers were increasing. The military's existing policy, Tolson said, "hinged on fear, which to me is all wrong."

Tolson was an unusual military man, willing to ignore the rules in search of an innovative solution. "There were regulations we were violating technically," he admitted, "but nobody's stopped us." There were only 40 soldiers enrolled in the experimental program but Tolson was hopeful that a positive outcome would lead more men to volunteer.

The program was initially funded by contributions from the Fort Bragg Wives Club, but when Congress learned about it, they were intrigued. After listening to testimony about the pervasive military drug problem and the unique nature of the program, Representative Harold Hughes of Iowa said he would seek government funding.

Tolson continued the program and was never disciplined for violating military protocol. He retired in 1973 and in 1981 published a book called *Airmobility in Vietnam: Helicopter Warfare in Southeast Asia*. Tolson died in 1991, at the age of 76 from a heart attack.

Other sources:
New York Times, June 8, 1970
Fort Walton Beach Playground Daily News, November 18, 1970
Panama City News Herald, November 28, 1970
https://en.wikipedia.org/wiki/John_J._Tolson
New York Times, December 6, 1991

73-Year-Old Pot User Asks Legalization of Marijuana

Hartford Courant, October 15, 1971

It wasn't only young people who were smoking pot in the 1960s. Apparently, some Social Security checks were being used to buy nickel bags of marijuana, according to a correspondent to Ann Landers. "Buffalo Bill" told Ann he had been smoking pot since 1921 and it had never created any problems for him.

"Pot relaxes me and gives me a pleasant glow," he wrote. "The only thing wrong with it is that it's illegal. I think this ought to be changed." He bet Ann a $20 bag of pot that she would never print his letter.

Ann did print the letter and replied as follows:

"Apparently you can handle it, Dad, but don't assume everyone can. The psychiatrists with whom I consult are seeing increased numbers of potheads who have freaked and are now psychotic. Marijuana is NOT harmless for some people, and I am dead set against its legalization."

She didn't mention whether she had received the stakes and, if so, whether she had consumed them.

6

As Long as We Both Shall Love

The Evolution of Marriage

The concept of marriage means different things to different people. Ideally, marriages are love matches based upon admiration and mutual respect, but there are many other reasons couples have joined in matrimony. In 19th century monarchies, marriages were arranged to perpetuate political dynasties and forge advantageous alliances. For celebrities, marital unions can be business relationships designed to boost career prospects. For many, they are the means of creating and raising a family.

Institutions aren't particularly romantic, and the Catholic Church defines marriage as follows:

"The state of marriage implies four chief conditions: 1. There must be a union of opposite sexes; it is therefore opposed to all forms of unnatural, homosexual behavior; 2. It is a permanent union until the death of either spouse; 3. It is an exclusive union, so that extramarital acts are a violation of justice; and 4. Its permanence and exclusiveness are guaranteed by contract; mere living together, without mutually binding themselves to do so, is concubinage and not marriage."

By the 1960s, marriage was being defined in many different ways, most of which were antithetical to the teachings of the Catholic Church. While hardly anyone was talking about gay marriage, people were entering into open marriages, where each partner was free to pursue sexual pleasure with other people, and groups of heterosexual people considered themselves all married to each other. Marriage between people of different religions was becoming commonplace and that between people of different races was no longer a taboo subject.

Even the way in which heterosexual, monogamous couples of the same race and religion got married was changing; people were creating their own vows, some of which included a pledge to stay together only as long as the magic remained. Something that had once come only in vanilla now came in an array of flavors.

Other sources:
> The definition of marriage is taken from https://www.catholicculture.org/culture/library/dictionary/index.cfm?id=34750

Reno Ranches: Divorce Havens for Rich
New York Times, **October 28, 1963**

It was not easy to obtain a divorce in 1963. In New York, the only grounds for dissolving a marriage was adultery. California issued an interlocutory decree that did not become final for a year. But in Nevada, the process was relatively easy—for a Nevada resident, defined as anyone that lived in the state for six continuous weeks. Therefore, in order to get a quick divorce, unhappy couples, or at least half of the couple, often went to Nevada to establish a six-week residence.

For those with money, there were about a dozen luxury ranches where one could wait out those six long weeks. Mrs. Marshall Field, Jr., stayed at Glenbrook. Nelson Rockefeller's ex-wife Mary spent her time at Donner Trail, as did Saul Bellow, Arthur Miller, and Johnny Weissmuller of Tarzan fame. The majority of Donner Trail residents were women, and in most cases their husbands picked up the tab for six weeks of room and board, horseback riding, and social activities. Despite all of the activities, however, there wasn't a lot of excitement at the ranch. "It's a big thing if a couple of us go into town to the movies," said a woman from New Jersey. "Mostly we ride, write letters, play bridge, talk or put up our hair."

Donner Trail, located in Verdi, just outside Reno, was perhaps the most renowned divorce ranch. Since 1959, It had been owned and operated by Harry and Joan Drackert. Harry began his career as a rodeo rider and once won the title of Champion Cowboy of America in a competition at Madison Square Garden. He walked with a limp and liked to brag that he had broken every bone in his body. Harry quit the rodeo circuit in 1931 and moved to Reno, where he worked on dude ranches, eventually running the Pyramid Lakes Guest Ranch, another divorce way station.

In 1946, Harry met Joan Arby Deeley, a blond Maryland native who was working at the Mount Rose Lodge awaiting her divorce. Joan was a former model for New York's Power Agency, a champion skeet shooter, and an experienced rider. In 1950, she and Harry were married.

At Donner, Harry tended to the ranch while Joan ran the business operation and played house mother to the women. She could relate to the divorcees because she'd been one herself. Life at Donner was as pleasant as it could be; the meals were wonderful and Joan was a gracious hostess, picking up her charges at the airport and tending to all their needs. One graduate of Donner Trail sent her a letter that read, "Thank you again for a wonderful divorce."

Most of the women at Donner Ranch were attractive and well-dressed, for they were the wives of successful, relatively well-off men who could afford to send them to Reno in order to expedite getting rid of them. The total cost of the divorce, the stay at the ranch, and legal fees generally ran from $3–4,000. Since the men were paying, some of the women spared no expense. "He's admitted everything including adultery," said one, "why shouldn't he pay extra for riding."

In prior years, said Joan, it seemed as though more of the women had a man waiting in the wings for the divorce to become final. "Years ago," she said, "when more women seemed to have someone lined up, we'd celebrate when they got their decrees. The cook would bake a cake and we'd have wine with dinner." Now that wasn't the case, and the mood at Donner Trail was more somber and reflective.

"There are tears of course," said Mrs. Drackert, "but by the time most of them get here, they're resigned. The stress, strain and emotional upheaval have already taken place. They know there's no point in mooning or glooming." "They wish the men well," wrote author Charlotte Curtis, "feel sorry for them and wonder whether they're getting enough to eat."

Many of the women faced a future very different from the one they'd had as wealthy housewives. Some would have to go to work for the first time. Others had to return home and live with their families. Some had children with them, children they would now have to raise alone.

On their 43rd day at the ranch, the women, accompanied by Mrs. Drackert, went to the Reno courthouse for their hearing. Joan was there to testify that the women had been continuously in Nevada for the past 42 days. The hearings were quick, sometimes only 15 minutes, for the cases were uncontested and Nevada wasn't as particular as other states about why a couple wanted to split up.

In addition to offering expedited divorces, Nevada law kept most of the documents sealed. While some of the women may have been bitter, they understood the value of sparing their ex-husbands' reputations. "You don't have to go through all the grim details," said one divorcee. "If I got a divorce at home I'd have to. That could damage my husband's reputation. I certainly don't want to do that, even if he is a stinker. My financial position is only as good as his is."

A local myth said that many women went directly from the courthouse and threw their wedding rings into the Truckee River, but that was only a myth. Most rings were packed quietly into the luggage shortly after arrival.

After the Drackerts unexpectedly lost the lease on Donner Trail in 1970, they were forced to close the facility. By that time, divorce had become much easier in other states, and women no longer had to spend six weeks at Donner Ranch. An era had ended.

Other sources:
http://dewey.library.unr.edu/xtf/view?docId=ead/91-49-ead.xml
https://divorceseekers.files.wordpress.com/2012/05/vogue-june-2012-nostalgiatuck.pdf

Nude Newswoman Covers Wedding in Nudist Camp

Hartford Courant, May 11, 1964

Nineteen-sixty-four was a little early for hippies, and the wedding described in the article took place in an old-fashioned "nudist colony," "Sunny Acres Lodge Camp." The newswoman who reported on the event was Marian Dale of the *Fort Lauderdale News*, a perky 5-foot-6 brunette whose previous experience with such things was a clothed visit to a mostly uninhabited nude resort.

In retrospect, perhaps the most shocking aspect of the marriage was not that the bride and groom were naked, but that the bride, raven-haired Sissy Dawson, was only 16 years old. Her groom, a sailor named Charles Morrow, was 23 and had been a nudist since the age of 14.

Sissy was raised in the naturist lifestyle. She was the daughter of John Dawson, owner and operator of Sunny Acres, located in Delray Beach, Florida, and home of the Floritans. Sissy lived at the camp but attended public school, where she said everyone knew she was a nudist. Dawson, secretary-treasurer of the American Nudist Camp Association, served as best man for his son-in-law.

The couple met at Sunny Acres two years earlier and, as Charles said, it was love at first sight. That was unsurprising, for it took many sightings in conventional society to equal a first sight at Sunny Acres. Morrow's ship, which he would not identify, was in dry dock at Key West at the time of the wedding, and he had two years of active duty remaining, after which he planned a career in data processing.

Dawson said he wasn't worried about his daughter marrying at such a young age. "She's exceptionally mature and intelligent," he said. "Most parents rear their children in ignorance and hypocrisy. She has the judgment of an adult." The ceremony, Dawson claimed, was the largest nude wedding ever. And, he noted, he was saving a good deal of money by not having to buy a wedding gown.

John Dawson was very concerned about privacy. The entry to Sunny Acres was protected by an imposing metal gate and a sign warning of fierce dogs. During the ceremony, when a light plane dipped low over the camp, the bride's mother (one account said it was her father) brandished a shotgun to drive the intruder off. It was not unusual to see a shotgun at a wedding involving a 16-year-old, but running off a low-flying plane was a novel use of the weapon.

The bride was not actually nude; she wore a long, sheer veil and white patent leather pumps. The groom wore nothing at all, nor did the eight attendants, including three bridesmaids and Sissy's two younger sisters, who served as flower girls. Accompaniment was provided by a trio of musicians, who wore only a guitar, drum, and accordion, respectively. There were about 200 guests in attendance, and only one, attorney Paul K. Whitney, who performed the ceremony, was clothed.

Following the reception, Sissy donned a wedding gown (apparently Dawson had paid for one after all) and allowed photographers to take her picture. Then the bride and groom, fully clothed, left for a honeymoon trip to Miami Beach.

An event like the Morrow-Dawson wedding was newsworthy, but John Dawson wanted to avoid a media circus. At a recent anniversary celebration for the founding of the resort, there had been more reporters than guests, and he didn't want a repeat at the wedding. "A wedding is a sacred thing," he said, "and because we will not be garbed, is that any reason for jokes in poor taste?" Dawson prohibited cameras; the only photographs were those taken for an official nudist publication (although a brief filmed version of the ceremony is available on You Tube). Further, every male reporter had to be accompanied by a female reporter and both had to remove their clothes. That explained the presence of Marian Dale, who wrote the syndicated article that appeared in the *Courant*.

Dale's article was picked up by numerous papers, but it was mostly about her experience at the resort rather than the wedding itself. In fact, she got the bride's name wrong, referring to her as Sissy Sawson. Dale dutifully stripped down to her sunglasses and complained about a sunburn and annoying insects. When it was over, she dressed with a sense of relief. "I believe it," she said in closing. "Clothes are here to stay."

The Dawson-Morrow marriage was not here to stay. "I'm ecstatically happy," Sissy said on her wedding day, but apparently marriage was too much for the 16-year-old, no matter how mature her father thought she was. On December 1, 1964, Morrow was granted a divorce on the grounds of extreme cruelty. He said that after three weeks, Sissy had been cold and indifferent toward him. The marriage had lasted less slightly more than six months.

During the first week of January 1965, John Dawson announced his intention to hold a Lady Godiva beauty contest at Sunny Acres. He confirmed that his daughter and Morrow had divorced and that Sissy had remarried. She was 17 and on her second husband. Attire for the second wedding was not announced, but it had none of the fanfare of the first. Second weddings, clothed or not, never do.

Other sources:
  http://www.aparchive.com/metadata/youtube/51cdafa2b45a4e49d1c08b05a9e5e07d
  Butte, Montana Standard, May 9 and 11, 1964
  Cumberland Evening Times, January 7, 1965
  Eureka Humboldt Times, January 6, 1965
  Levittown Times, May 8, 1964
  Beckley Post-Herald and Raleigh Register, May 10, 1964

Andy Williams Tells How to Stay Married

Hartford Courant, **February 13, 1967**

Andy Williams, the crooner known for his renditions of *Moon River*, *Hawaiian Wedding Song*, and other pop classics, had been married to actress Claudine Longet since 1961. They met when Williams stopped one day to help Longet, the lead dancer in the Folies Bergere at the Tropicana, who was stranded on the roadside. Longet was 19 and Williams 33 when they married.

Longet had some minor acting roles and also performed as a singer, but Williams was a star, with best-selling records, steady concert appearances, and *The Andy Williams Show*, which ran from 1962 to 1971. The show won three Emmys and introduced America to the Osmond Family.

Williams told Marilyn Beck, author of the "That's Showbiz" column, that his marriage worked because "Claudine is smart enough to realize that performers are different than most people, more egocentric. The world caters to us, heaps attentions upon us—and lots of times it's difficult if the same kind of attentions aren't handed out at home. I'm the same as the rest. It's part of our natures to need attention, and, fortunately, Claudine gives it to me."

Andy and Claudine enjoyed a glamorous Hollywood lifestyle absent the debauchery that doomed so many Tinseltown relationships. They were friends with Robert and Ethel Kennedy and planned to go to The Factory, a private Hollywood club owned by Peter Lawford, Paul Newman, Anthony Newley, and others, the night Kennedy was assassinated. Williams sang at the funeral and remained friends with Ethel, sometimes serving as her escort in the 1970s.

Williams had given Beck his view of a successful marriage, but Claudine wasn't asked how she felt about having to stroke Williams' sizable ego. Apparently, she wasn't that wild about it, for within three years the couple was legally separated. After a long separation, they were divorced in 1975.

Williams remained single until 1991, when he married Debbie Haas, a union that lasted until Williams' death from bladder cancer in 2012. The same year he was married, Williams began a second career at his Moon River Theater in Branson, Missouri, the Mecca to which once-popular performers retreat when television is finished with them. For almost two decades, Williams packed senior citizens into Moon River Theater and performed as its headliner.

After her divorce from Williams, Longet began an affair with Olympic skier Vladimir "Spider" Sabich, which ended when she shot and killed him in 1976. Longet said the gun discharged accidentally while he was showing it to her and the police aided her defense by making several errors during the investigation, which prevented them from using much of their incriminating evidence at the trial.

Although they were divorced at the time, Williams was very supportive of his ex-wife, accompanying her to her court appearances, testifying to her character, and paying her legal bills. She was convicted of negligent homicide and sentenced to 30 days in jail, which she was allowed to serve on weekends.

The sentence was widely criticized as being too lenient, and when Longet quickly left for a vacation with her married defense attorney, Ron Austin, it did little to soften public opinion. She and Austin married in 1985.

Shortly after the shooting, *Saturday Night Live*, then in its first season, ran a sketch on its *Weekend Update* segment titled "The Claudine Longet Invitational Ski Championship" featuring a series of skiers descending the slopes and being "accidently shot" by Claudine Longet. After Longet's attorney obtained a cease and desist order, producer Lorne Michaels issued an apology.

Four years later, Mick Jagger wrote a song called "Claudine" about Longet's relationship with Sabich and the shooting. It was intended to be on the Stones' *Emotional Rescue* album but was pulled due to its controversial subject matter.

When Andy Williams spoke to Marilyn Beck in 1967, it is doubtful he foresaw any of those events in his and Claudine's future. Marriage wasn't as simple or one-sided as he thought, and perhaps Williams is lucky Longet didn't shoot him.

Other sources:
https://en.wikipedia.org/wiki/Claudine_Longet
https://en.wikipedia.org/wiki/Andy_Williams
https://www.biography.com/people/andy-williams-162966

Broker's Estranged Family Pickets Dad at Exchange
New York Daily News, **March 30, 1967**

People often married young prior in the early '60s, and sometimes the matches were poorly made. In one case, a poor match led to unusual consequences. As a Wall Street broker, 27-year-old Arthur H. Ross was accustomed to working under the pressures of market fluctuations, late hours, and demanding investors. But on March 29, 1967, Ross encountered a form of pressure he ever expected to see and hoped never to see again. His employer, Shearson, Hammill & Company, was known for its catchy advertising campaign, the tag line of which was "If you want to know what's going on on Wall Street, ask Shearson, Hammill." There was something unique going on on Wall Street the afternoon of March 29 and Arthur Ross was right in the middle of it.

Ross grew up in the securities business and spent the early part of his career with the family firm, Ross, Lyon and Company. On January 6, 1959, Ross, at the age of 19, married a petite, attractive brunette named Wende Levine, the daughter of a clothing manufacturer. Within a few years, Arthur and Wende had three children, Scott, Elliot, and Barton.

According to Wende's later testimony, "The early days of our marriage were wonderful and exciting. My husband spent a considerable amount of time with his family and he always enjoyed spending his free time with his children. As my husband became more successful, and his income began to appreciate, his main concern was not our happiness, but his own 'ego.'"

Soon after the Ross's were married, Arthur left his family firm for Shearson, Hammill and purchased a seat on the New York Stock Exchange. He made good money, about $75,000 per year, and the family lived well. They vacationed in Europe, Florida, and the Caribbean, and Arthur bought Wende a mink stole, a mink coat, and a Persian lamb coat, which were worth $10,000 in aggregate. In 1960, they purchased a split level home in a nice neighborhood in Woodmere, Long Island.

In 1965, Arthur began to stray. He went on a Bahamian vacation by himself, or at least without his wife. He began coming home late or not at all, and when he was home he was irritable. Ross said he planned to be a millionaire by the time he was 30, but his family was preventing him from achieving his goal.

Things began to get strange when Ross told his wife he was undergoing psychiatric treatment for a childhood disorder that caused twitching and constant sniffling. One night, he came home from the doctor's office and told Wende he wanted a divorce. As she later testified, "Dr. Schrier had advised him that he should not be married and he ought to be in a position where he could date." That seemed an odd diagnosis for sniffling, but Wende agreed to a separation in the hope that Arthur would find himself, come home, and be the loving husband he'd been during the first years of their marriage.

There was more to the situation than psychiatry. Arthur had become enamored of an attractive brunette model named Carolyn Patterson and was living with her in an apartment on East 55th Street. After buying Carolyn the requisite mink coat, however, he had a change of heart and decided to go back to his family. He wrote Carolyn a long letter on the stationary of Ross, Lyon and Company, in which he said, "I am sure you know, my darling, that there is or never will be anyone in my life except you. My love for you will forever be. You are the right girl, and I am the right guy, but our timing is wrong.... I have a wife who is sick [Wende suffered from arthritis and various other ailments] and even though there is no love between us, I must take care of her (for my children's sake).... Please forgive me for this attitude, but I must do what is morally right.... I love you 'till the end of time."

The reconciliation was unsuccessful. Wende found Carolyn's picture in Arthur's wallet, and Carolyn called the house and told Wende she and Arthur were in love. When Wende confronted her husband, he told her the affair was over. But it wasn't.

Arthur began seeing a marriage counselor, and Wende eventually joined him. Arthur seemed adept at finding professionals who told him what he wanted to hear, and this one told Wende that she should divorce Arthur. Wende became hysterical and told them they both needed to see psychiatrists.

Just before Thanksgiving 1965, Arthur again moved out of the family home, took an apartment on East 36th Street, and hired a woman named Evelyn Johnson as a maid. Mrs. Johnson was not happy working for Arthur Ross. She said she expected to do Mr. Ross's laundry and clean the apartment, but she did not like washing the clothes of Carolyn Patterson who, although her residence was listed as an apartment across the street from Ross's, was apparently living with him. Every morning when she arrived at the apartment, Mrs. Johnson testified, Miss Patterson was there "either nude or wearing one of Mr. Ross's bathrobes." The maid also didn't like having to answer the phone, which Carolyn did not do. She wanted Johnson to answer in case, as she told her, "the bitch may be acting up again."

In April 1966, Wende went to court to ask for a legal separation and obtained a ruling requiring her estranged husband to make temporary alimony payments of $300 per week. Wende was also granted custody of the children, occupancy of the family home (Ross had to pay the mortgage and all expenses) and use of the couple's Lincoln Continental. Ross also had to pay his children's tuition at Woodmere Academy. He was granted visitation privileges every other weekend, with the proviso that Ms. Patterson was not to be present when the children were there.

In March 1967, Wende was back in court again. The Ross's were still married and the order for temporary alimony had expired. Wende said she now needed $425 per week, in addition to the other payments Arthur was required to make. She presented a detailed list of her weekly expenses, and it was apparent that she was still living the life of a prosperous stockbroker' wife. Wende was spending $40 per week on clothes, $35 on entertainment, and $80 for groceries. At current prices, that would be $293 per week for clothes, $256 for entertainment, and $586 for groceries. Even accounting for the fact that she had three growing boys, that was a lot of groceries.

Arthur thought his estranged wife's spending was unreasonable. "The fact that the plaintiff and I are separated," he said in an affidavit, "does not constitute a hunting license for her to just go out as she has in the past and make tremendous and unnecessary purchases." While Wende said—and tax returns verified—that Arthur made $75,000 per year, he claimed that, after servicing over $90,000 in loans, he had only $13,000 for living expenses.

Wende said Ross had not made any payments since January, and she and her children were surviving only because her father was giving her money. When Ross continued to refuse to make the alimony payments, Wende decided to appeal to the court of public opinion.

On the morning of March 29, Wende and her three children boarded a train in Woodmere and headed for Manhattan. They stood on the sidewalk in front of the New York Stock Exchange and held up four signs that read, in sequence: "Our Daddy, Arthur H. Ross," "Vice President Shearson, Hammill & Co.," "Ignores Court Order," "Won't Support Us."

Six-year-old Elliot said, "Anyone who laughs at us gets socked." No one got socked, but the family provoked a lot of laughter from passersby. Elliot and his brothers didn't think it was funny, and flailed away with their signs at anyone who laughed. A few people threw pennies to them. After making their point, the family left for Penn Station and the return trip to Long Island. All of the boys cried on the way back. "We didn't see daddy," one of them wailed.

Daddy was glad not to have seen them, although he heard about the commotion taking place in front of his building. When reporters caught up with him later, he called his wife's claim that he was not making payments a "misstatement" but did not elaborate. He didn't mention Carolyn Patterson prancing nude around his apartment, his Bahamian vacation, or his sniffling. Like most stories in the *Daily News*, the saga of Arthur and Wende Ross was a one-shot proposition, and soon, much to Arthur's relief, their private lives became private again.

Other sources:
> Court documents regarding the divorce proceedings located at Records and Briefs, New York State Appellate Division: https://books.google.com/books?id=mYg0K-slz1hMC&pg=RA4-PA1&lpg=RA4-PA1&dq=Wende+ross+1967&source=bl&ots=c-Cvjtpv9Iz&sig=Bb09ABU2UVyyRxCBtD5rqz7oAms&hl=en&sa=X&ved=0ahUKEwjx-86vj3JDUAhVGLyYKHY_5BMAQ6AEIKjAB#v=onepage&q=Wende%20ross%201967&f=false

Five Women Protest the "Slavery" of Marriage
New York Times, September 24, 1969

On September 23, 1969, singer Tony Bennett was awarded a medal on the steps of New York's City Hall and celebrated the occasion by singing a ballad called *I Can't Give You Anything but Love*. Across the street, at the marriage license bureau in the Municipal Building, five women in their 20s who billed themselves as The Feminists confronted City Clerk Herman Katz with plans to give him everything but love. They were there to protest what they called the slavery of marriage and the complicit guilt of city administrators in facilitating the institution. Katz, the women said, was overseeing a system "in which women are being illegally made sex slaves in the unholy state of matrimony."

When Mayor John Lindsay arrived to honor Bennett, he was handed a list of "charges." Ti-Grace Atkinson, a doctoral student in philosophy at Columbia, told Lindsay that married women were "classic examples of slavery, bondage and rape victims." Atkinson (she was born Grace and added Ti, which means little or petite) was the former president of the New York chapter of the National Organization for Women who had split from NOW because she believed it was not radical enough.

Not many people were radical enough for Ti-Grace Atkinson. She'd defended Valerie Solanas (see Chapter 8), who had formed a group called S.C.U.M (Society for Cutting Up Men) and she thought NOW was not sufficiently aggressive on issues like abortion and marriage. Atkinson also believed that NOW President Betty Freidan was too concerned with moderating the organization's agenda in order to gain the support of less radical women.

Atkinson organized The New York Radical Feminists, commonly referred to as The Feminists, and it was they who were competing for attention with Tony Bennett at City Hall. They passed out pamphlets that read: "All the discriminatory practices against women are patterned and rationalized by this slavery-like practice. We can't destroy the inequities between men and women until we destroy marriage.... Do you know that rape is legal in marriage? Do you know that love and affection are not required in marriage? Do you know that you are your husband's prisoner? Do you know that, according to the United Nations, marriage is a 'slavery-like practice?' So, why aren't you getting paid? Do you resent this fraud?"

"Tony Bennett sings these songs of propaganda," said Atkinson. "Get married and everything will be all right. Marriage means rape and life-long slavery." "Love has to be destroyed," she said on another occasion. "It's an illusion that people care for each other." When asked about the prospects of continuing the human race without marriage, Atkinson said she advocated test tube babies. It would be less painful for women and result in fewer birth defects.

One can see why The Feminists thought NOW was too tame. NOW liked women, but The Feminists really *hated* men and were stolidly against the idea of marriage in any form. At first, no more than one-third of all members of The Feminists could be married, and in 1971 they completely excluded married women. "Sex is overrated," said Atkinson. "If someday we have to choose between sex and freedom, there's no question I'd take freedom."

Another New York radical group, which was not affiliated with The Feminists, was WITCH (Women's International Terrorist Conspiracy from Hell). WITCH was more street theater than terrorist; its members dressed up in costume and placed "hexes" on a number of institutions. They were entertaining but, despite their name, not quite as angry as The Feminists.

Sara Davidson wrote an article about The Feminists for *Life* magazine in 1969. She spent a lot of time with its members and found their opinions interesting but in some cases contradictory. And she felt that, despite the strident rhetoric, many of the women talked a tougher game than they played. "Even the most radical feminists..." Davidson wrote, "retain many female character traits: soft-spokenness; talkiness (interviews and phone calls are difficult to terminate); and a proclivity for handiwork. There was hardly a meeting I attended where someone was not knitting. While they condemn seductiveness, many want to look attractive. Pam Kearon [who was at the New York protest] said, 'People like to look nice for other people. It's a statement of respect. It's just not true that we want to look like ugly freaks.'"

As with any protest, there were hecklers at City Hall. "Are any of you girls married?" someone asked. "That's none of your business," replied Cronin. "We don't give out that information." When Katz invited the women into his office, Atkinson replied, "We don't want to go into any room alone. We've been in too many rooms alone." Katz should have thanked his good fortune, for being in a room alone with an aroused Ti-Grace Atkinson was no picnic.

Katz tried to be accommodating, but he was a civil servant, not a social change agent. Nor was he, he asserted, "an agent in any conspiracy against women." "It all started with Adam and Eve many years ago," Katz said to the backs of The Feminists as they walked out of his office. And Tony Bennett sang on.

Ti-Grace Atkinson sang on as well. She continued to speak and write on feminist issues; her best known book, *Amazon Odyssey*, was published in 1974, and she remains a leading voice in radical feminist circles. She was eventually ostracized by The Feminists, who felt that Atkinson was destroying the egalitarian nature of the organization for being seen as its leader.

Pam Kearon had a more difficult future ahead of her. After publishing two books: "Man Hating" and "Rape: An Act of Terror," she spent the last twenty-five years of her life dealing with mental illness.

Herman Katz kept on issuing marriage licenses, and even today couples vow to stay together through sickness and in health, until death do they part. The Feminists didn't succeed in eliminating marriage, although over the succeeding decades, relationships between husbands and wives changed dramatically. Contemporary women can marry or not marry as these choose, and those that choose marriage aren't often heard referring to it as slavery. If they feel enslaved, there's an easier solution than pestering the Herman Katz's of today. The entire country is like the Nevada of 1963, and slaves are easily emancipated.

Other sources:
ttps://en.wikipedia.org/wiki/The_Feminists
https://en.wikipedia.org/wiki/Ti-Grace_Atkinson
http://www.maryellenmark.com/text/magazines/life/905W-000-004.html
Radical Feminists: A Guide to an American Subculture by Paul D. Buchanan, Greenwood, Santa Barbara, Denver, and Oxford, 2011

Fired for Living Out of Wedlock, Clerk Sues
Middletown Press, **January 7, 1970**

Neil Mindel was a 23-year-old post office employee with an active love life that did not include marriage; he had lived with two different women without the benefit of matrimony. Shortly after Mindel went to work at the post office in April 1967, the FBI conducted a routine background check. A neighbor indicated she had seen a woman living with Mindel, information the FBI duly passed on to the postal service.

After receiving the results of the FBI investigation, the postal authorities requested Mindel's presence at a meeting on August 16, 1967. A month later, he received a letter informing him that he didn't meet the "suitability" requirements for federal employment and he was fired. His appeal to the Bureau of Personnel was denied, as was a subsequent appeal to the Board of Appeals and Review.

Mindel sued to get his job back and received the backing of the American Civil Liberties Union. ACLU attorney Paul Halvonik asked, "Is the FBI to be deployed to investigate the private sex lives of all government employees, including postal and file clerks?" He thought not, and pointed out that there was no evidence claiming that Mindel's sex life affected his job performance in any way.

A postal official said that cohabitation could be cause for dismissal depending on who was reviewing the application. He said the only reason it became an issue was because the neighbor had raised it during the investigation. "From the government's standpoint," he added, "it's just not good to have somebody living in such a relationship when everybody knows about it and looks on him as a federal employee. The commission is still bound by what we call the acceptable standards of the community ... and marriage is still considered the right thing to do in a case like that."

On March 30, 1970, the United States District Court granted Mindel's motion for summary judgment, on the grounds that his dismissal had been "arbitrary and capricious." The court saw no connection between Mindel's living arrangements and his ability to process the United States mail. They ordered the Postal Service to give him back his job.

Mindel is now living in Berkeley, California, and apparently has seen the light, for he co-habits with Kitty Goldsmit Mindel, who one can infer is his wife.

Other sources:
https://law.justia.com/cases/federal/district-courts/FSupp/312/485/1468870/

Couples Share Rent, Chores (and Sex)
Hartford Courant, **August 2, 1970**

If marriage was slavery, it would be difficult to figure out who were the slaves and who the masters in an eight-person family in Berkeley, California. If one were looking for unusual things, Berkeley was always a good place to start, and when he visited there in 1970, reporter Robert Strand found five adults and three children living together in a group marriage.

While the adults were clearly on the cutting edge, they were cautious enough not to allow Strand to use their last names. He identified them as

David and Louise, who had been legally married for 17 years and had three children, Becky, 33, Joseph, 59, and Warren, whose age was not given. Joseph was a former ballet dancer and Warren a former theology student and social worker. "People ask about sex," Becky said, "and the answer is yes. The whole family [presumably not the children] belongs to the Sexual Freedom League."

Unconventional marriages were not a new phenomenon. Mormons practiced polygamy in the nineteenth century and in 1848, John Humphrey Noyes founded the Oneida community in upstate New York. At its peak, the Oneida commune had over 300 members, and Noyes forbid monogamous marriage; sex between any consenting man and woman was permissible. The Oneida community was one of the longest-lived utopian experiments in the United States, surviving into the 1880s.

The modern concept of group marriage is commonly known as polyfidelity, as opposed to open marriages where two partners agree that each can have sexual relationships outside of the marriage. Under polyfidelity, all of the partners in the marriage are expected to be loyal to the others, but not to any one specific partner. In the 1970s and 1980s, polyfidelity was practiced by a number of groups at the Kerista commune in San Francisco. Strand reported that estimates of multiple person marriages ranged from the dozens to the hundreds.

It is difficult enough for two people to live together, and adding more personalities to the mix increases the probability of conflict. In 2012, counselor Kathy Labriola wrote of the pros and cons of polyfidelity.

> Polyfidelity can be a richly rewarding experience, creating an extended family and intentional community. Pooling resources is economical and ecological, and can reduce the stress of child rearing by spreading the work and the responsibility among several adults rather than just one or two parents. However, polyfidelity requires a very high level of compatibility and affinity between all partners. Everyone must agree on where to live, what to cook for dinner, how clean the house should be, how much money to spend and on what, whether to have children and how to raise them. Most people find it difficult enough to locate one partner they can successfully live with for the "long haul," much less two, three, four or more. And living together as a group decreases privacy and autonomy, often leading to interpersonal conflicts and stress. Living in a group requires excellent interpersonal skills, clear communication, assertiveness, co-operation, and flexibility in order to accommodate everyone's needs. Picking compatible partners and being accommodating are both key to successful polyfidelity.

That's a lot more cons than pros and it's safe to predict that most group marriages didn't last. Of course, on the positive side, if one of your spouses left you, you still had a few left. Since most people who were part of such marriages declined to use last names, it's hard to determine how many arrangements were successful over a long term.

6. As Long as We Both Shall Love

When Robert Strand interviewed the Berkeley family, things were going well. From the outside, if one could ignore the numbers, they were a lot like other families in their neighborhood. All of the adults were outwardly conventional and for eighteen months, they had been living in an eight-bedroom home in an upper-class neighborhood. None of the neighbors had complained about the unusual living situation.

Financial arrangements were like those of most conventional families. Resources were pooled to pay living expenses, with budget responsibility resting with the family treasurer. Household chore assignments were posted on a bulletin board. All of the adults shared childcare responsibilities. There were various sexual relationships between the men and women, with no permanent pairings. "When you like someone else," said Becky, "you don't get jealous of them." Warren added, "You can feel good about someone close enjoying himself with someone else." David said, "We have less jealousy and all its attendant evils than any conventional family." Still, a group marriage counselor made regular visits to the family to guide them in the relationship.

The primary advantage of group marriage, its practitioners said, was while it was difficult for one person to fill all of another person's needs, several people could each contribute to provide what that person needed. "[N]o human being can fill every need of another human being," said Becky. "That's what's wrong with so many marriages." On the other hand, Warren commented, "When you live on a one-to-one basis, you only get agitated once a week. If you live with five, you can get agitated every day." It wasn't easy, and virtually everyone living in group marriages agreed that professional counseling was a necessity. "Without counseling," Warren said, "no intentional family group will survive."

Failed group marriages ended for the same reasons that monogamous relationships fell apart, but since there was no legal marriage, there was no need for a formal divorce. Strand interviewed a 31-year-old female San Francisco theater personality whose group marriage of four women, three men, and two children ended badly. Everyone, she said, was "playing games" with the others. "Our marriage worked," she said, "but didn't endure. I would like to try it again with less neurotic people. It's really beautiful to have all that love."

Some trends from the 1960s and early '70s became part of mainstream life, but group marriage was not one of them. There are likely some group marriages today, but the concept never really caught on. Apparently, while two is company, eight is a crowd.

Other sources:

http://www.cat-and-dragon.com/stef/poly/Labriola/open.html

"Do Your Own Thing" Concept Starts Marriage "Vibrating"

Hartford Courant, February 12, 1971

No matter what form marriage took in the 1960s and early 1970s, there was a definite change in the ceremony that created the relationship. The traditional church wedding, the white bridal gown, and banquet hall reception were often replaced by non-religious ceremonies, free-form vows exchanged in pastoral fields, and couples wearing jeans and beads, followed by a barbeque or maybe an acid trip.

One reason fewer people were getting married in church was the growing number of couples who came from different religions; many churches did not perform marriages for mixed couples. Some ministers, however, like thirty-year-old Richard York of the Free Church of Berkeley, California (of course), were open to performing just about any type of ceremony. York had married members of the Black Panthers and those of the equally radical Students for a Democratic Society in decidedly non-traditional settings.

To York, it didn't matter who, it didn't matter where, and it didn't matter how. "The established church or the judge," he said, "just don't mean a thing to these kids. They want to control their own lives. They want to marry themselves in their own way." Marrying in their own way frequently involved writing their own vows, quoting people like Kahlil Gibran, Malcolm X, T.S. Eliot, or the Beatles.

The growing equality between men and women was reflected in the use of "husband and wife" rather than "man and wife" and fewer women were promising to honor and obey. Rather than pledge to remain together "until death do us part" some couples vowed to remain wedded "as long as we both shall love."

Part of the change in marriage customs sprung from the fact that many couples had already lived together and therefore had some idea what to expect. "The new wedding," said the Reverend William Glenesk of Brooklyn, "is more a ceremony to confirm what a couple has found by living together rather than to make promises about what they hope will happen." Glenesk's experience with modern weddings including officiating at the marriage of celebrity ukulele artist Tiny Tim and his bride Miss Vickie.

Many young people of the 1960s held radical political views, and their ceremonies often incorporated their beliefs. At one wedding, when asked who gave the bride in marriage, the guests responded in unison, "The Black Panther Party." One couple's vows read, "I, John, take thee, Mary, to be my woman, to work for the liberation of all people, for frustrated, lonely people, to commit ourselves to do battle through the journey which is the celebration of life."

The hippie lifestyle found its way into a number of ceremonies. One couple, from California, naturally, married in the nude. Another couple consummated the marriage in front of their friends immediately after the service, a natural extension of lifting the veil and kissing the bride. Traditional couples had taken honeymoon trips, but in the '60s, some brides and grooms took a trip of a different kind. One wedding cake was decorated with the flag of the National Liberation Front rather than a plastic bride and groom.

Marriages were different and wedding ceremonies were changing, but every couple, triple, or five-some faced the timeless challenge of finding a way to co-exist for the rest of their lives, or until it wasn't fun anymore. As in most articles about unusual lifestyles, none of the couples whose experiences were featured in the article gave their last names, so we don't know whether being given away by the Black Panthers, reciting vows taken from the writing of T.S. Eliot, or tripping on acid at the reception led to better and more lasting relationships than getting married in an Episcopal Church and having a reception at the Knights of Columbus Hall.

$1 Million in Dispute in Bigamist's Estate

Bridgeport Post-Telegram, December 5, 1971

Custom house broker Juan Abel Vargas, Jr., was good at many things. He had the ability to charm women, he was adept at making money, and he was extremely good at keeping secrets. For 24 years, Vargas maintained two families in close proximity to each other. Neither knew of the other and his wives and children all remembered him as a loving husband and doting father.

Vargas began his odyssey on August 10, 1929, when he married Mildred Schroeder of Missouri. Over the next several years, he and Mildred had three children. From 1929 through the early 1940s, Vargas was a married man who had affairs with other women, not an admirable habit but one he shared with many men. Then things began to get complicated. In 1942, he commenced an affair with a co-worker named Josephine. One day, Mildred appeared in his office unexpectedly and Vargas introduced the two women, but neither thought anything of it. Josephine knew Mildred was Vargas' wife and Mildred assumed Josephine was just a co-worker. It was nearly 30 years before they met again, under dramatically different circumstances.

In early 1945, Vargas confessed his affair to Mildred, without mentioning that it was the woman she had met in his office, and said that Josephine was pregnant with their child. Mildred asked Juan if he wanted a divorce, but he begged her not to leave him.

Josephine knew Vargas was married, but he told her he had obtained a divorce "in a little town in Mexico" and wanted to marry her. Juan and Josephine were actually married twice, once in Las Vegas on February 22, 1945, and again in Santa Ana on May 24, 1945, both times by a justice of the peace. The second wedding was made necessary by the fact that the couple had never received the promised marriage certificate from the Las Vegas ceremony. After Juan and Josephine were married, she continued to live with her parents because she was afraid to tell them she was married to a divorced man. Vargas never mentioned Josephine or the child to Mildred again.

Eventually, Josephine moved to Los Angeles and lived with Vargas in a residence at 6411 Lindenhurst Avenue. He also maintained a home with Mildred at 5925 Garth Avenue, approximately six miles from the home he shared with Josephine. Despite the proximity, neither woman knew of the other's existence, and Vargas's seven children had no idea they had step-siblings residing nearby. His son Juan Antonio said after Vargas's death that he had no idea his father was a "swinger." According to the testimony of both wives, Vargas was an attentive husband who sent cards when he was traveling and never forgot a birthday.

For 24 years, Vargas was able to keep both wives in the dark. Every evening other than Thursday and Sunday, he had dinner with Josephine, usually between six and seven and then, after telling Josephine he had to stay near his business, he went to Mildred's home, where he spent the rest of the evening, went to bed, and got up to leave for his office at 6:30. Vargas prepared joint tax returns with each wife, although it is not certain whether he filed both.

Apparently, two wives were not enough to satisfy Vargas, who although he stood just 5'2" and weighed 160 pounds, was quite successful with the ladies. The night clerk at the Cloud Hotel testified that between 1967 and 1969, Vargas registered 78 times, each time as Mr. and Mrs. At first she said there was a different woman each time, but then admitted that she had not been on duty all 78 nights and could not testify as to the nights she wasn't there.

Once, Vargas went on a business trip with his son Juan, and both brought girlfriends with them. The only thing the son remembered was that his father's girlfriend was named Blanca. While he condoned his son's affairs, Vargas was very strict with Juan's sisters. According to daughter Julie, he wouldn't allow them to wear eye shadow, nail polish, or short skirts.

On July 12, 1969, Vargas left Mildred's home, telling her he was going to work, but instead he accompanied Josephine to a family reunion. That night, to top off a very eventful day, he went to the Cloud Hotel with an unidentified woman. That was the last full day of Vargas's life.

As a later court decision put it, "This terrestrial paradise came to an end in 1969 when Juan died [on July 13] ... in an auto accident." Vargas, who did not have a will, left an estate of $1,063,165. Mildred made the funeral arrangements, and at the service on July 17, while Vargas lay peacefully in his casket, Mildred and Josephine met for the first time since 1942. After that, it didn't take long for the secret life of Juan Vargas to become public.

When the initial shock of their mutual husband's death and perfidy wore off, each woman began to think about practical things, namely the $1 million estate. Mildred believed she should inherit the money, and so did Josephine. And there were other women who thought they might have a right to a share. Vargas's lawyer said he'd received a call from a woman in Mexico who claimed she had married Vargas in Bogota, Columbia in 1927 and that the couple had five children together. That was the last, however, that the lawyer heard from the woman. A business associate said that in 1964 Vargas introduced him to a woman named Lucy, told her she was his wife and that they had two children together. Lucy never appeared to make a claim on the estate.

On September 15, 1969, Mildred, Josephine, and their attorneys went to court. The law stated that when a decedent had two marriages, the second spouse was presumed to be the legal spouse, with the burden on the first spouse to prove there had been no divorce or annulment.

The definitive way to determine that the first marriage had not been dissolved was to search the records of each jurisdiction in which the deceased had resided. Although Mildred had not done that, the Superior Court of Los Angeles County ruled on December 17, 1969, that Mildred was Juan's legal wife and entitled to inherit all his assets. Josephine appealed.

The California Court of Appeals upheld the lower court ruling, based upon the rationale that a search of court proceedings was not the only way in which a first wife could show that no divorce had been granted. There was significant circumstantial evidence that gave Mildred reason to believe that Vargas had never divorced her. First, when he told her of his affair with Josephine, Vargas begged Mildred not to leave him. He slept at her home most nights and prepared joint tax returns with her until he died. He was never away from home for more than a week or ten days. Further, in Los Angeles County, it was nearly impossible to obtain a divorce without notice to the spouse.

Josephine persisted and eventually obtained a ruling that the estate should be divided equally between the two spouses. Even though Vargas had never been divorced and could therefore not legally marry Josephine, she was deemed to be a "putative" spouse; she'd married him in good faith, believing him to be divorced. Since Vargas had accumulated virtually his entire net worth after he married Josephine, the court decided that it should be equally apportioned to each wife. Mildred appealed.

In ruling on Mildred's appeal in 1974, the court declared, "In practice, these sometimes conflicting theories have proved no more than convenient explanations to justify reasonable results, for when the theories do not fit the facts, courts have customarily resorted to general principles of equity to effect a just disposition of property rights.... The present case is complicated by the fact that the laws regarding succession and the disposition of marital property are not designed to cope with the extraordinary circumstance of purposeful bigamy at the expense of two innocent parties.... For this reason resort to equitable principles becomes particularly appropriate here." Juan Vargas was a unique case and principles of equity, otherwise known as common sense, would apply. Like King Solomon, the court cut the baby in half, affirming the 50/50 disposition of the estate.

"[T]he probate court," the Second District Court of Appeals concluded, "cut the Gordian knot of competing claims and divided the estate equally between the two wives, presumably on the theory that innocent wives of practicing bigamists are entitled to equal shares of property accumulated during the active phase of the bigamy." And nothing was more active than Juan Vargas's bigamy.

With the development of technology and surveillance, it is unlikely that Vargas could have pulled off his act today. Cell phones, GPS, and instant communication would almost certainly have thwarted his clever game. Vargas may have been the last of his kind, for which future Mildreds and Josephines might offer a hearty, "Thank God!"

Other sources:
http://caselaw.findlaw.com/ca-court-of-appeal/1848779.html
http://law.justia.com/cases/california/court-of-appeal/3d/36/714.html
Corona Daily Independent, December 1, 1971.
https://news.google.com/newspapers?id=kwkrAAAAIBAJ&sjid=z5kFAAAAIBAJ&pg=2270,1384814&hl=en

Jane Fonda, Tom Hayden Wed in Free-Form Rite

Bridgeport Telegram, January 22, 1973

On August 14, 1965, actress Jane Fonda married director Roger Vadim in her six-room suite at the Dunes Hotel in Las Vegas. It was Fonda's first marriage and the third for Vadim, a French director who had previously been married to Brigitte Bardot and been the lover of Catherine Deneuve.

The ceremony was private, with just a few invited guests, including Jane's brother Peter, who serenaded the wedding party on his guitar. Vadim forgot to get a ring and had to borrow one from the best man's wife.

Meanwhile, Fonda was thinking, "I honestly don't know why I'm doing this." After the judge performed the ceremony, the bride, groom, and their guests went downstairs and gambled.

Since Vadim had not bothered to register the marriage in France, the union was not legal in his native country. Therefore, in 1967, Vadim and Fonda went to a small town outside of Paris and had a civil ceremony. Even though they were legally married on two continents, Vadim let Fonda know that he did not believe in fidelity. He had affairs with numerous women, some of whom he brought home with the intention of initiating a threesome. Fonda was not as eager to experiment as her husband, but she didn't want him to think she was a repressed American, so she made an effort to be sexually unconventional.

The arrangement was too unusual and risky to last, and on January 16, 1973, the couple was divorced, although they remained friends. By that time, Fonda's life had become intensely political, and three days after she and Vadim officially split, Fonda married political activist Tom Hayden in a ceremony that was very different from the one at the Dunes Hotel.

The Fonda-Hayden wedding took place at Fonda's Laurel Canyon home in front of about 100 guests, including the bride's father Henry, her brother Peter, and Jane's four-year-old daughter Vanessa. The Reverend Richard York, the Episcopal minister mentioned in a previous article, performed the service, and asked the bride, "Will you, Jane, marry Tom and will you try in this marriage to grow together to be honest, to share responsibility for your children, and to maintain a sense of humor?" Fonda said she would, and the couple was proclaimed man and wife.

The wedding came very soon after the end of Fonda's first marriage, but she had told Hayden she wanted to have his child and thought that before they had children, they should get married, "rather than hassle with criticism that would drain our energies from our real work."

Their real work was the founding of a medical aid fund for Vietnam, a country that had become the focal point of Fonda's life. There were a number of Vietnamese students at the wedding and before the ceremony there were songs and poetry readings from students representing different areas of Vietnam.

About six months earlier, Fonda made her controversial visit to North Vietnam, speaking several times on Hanoi radio, where she denounced America's role in the war. On the final day of her visit, in an act that infuriated patriotic Americans, she was photographed seated on a North Vietnamese gun carriage. Fonda later referred to the pose as "a two minute lapse of sanity that will haunt me forever," but it was done, earning her the nickname "Hanoi Jane" and the undying enmity of many veterans.

Whether they failed to grow together, share responsibility for their children, or if they'd simply lost their sense of humor, the marriage of Fonda and Hayden didn't last. The couple divorced in 1990 and Fonda married media mogul Ted Turner in 1991, the year Turner's Atlanta Braves baseball team emerged from last place to appear in the World Series. During the postseason playoffs old radical Jane Fonda could be seen in the stands canoodling with her wealthy husband and enthusiastically performing the politically incorrect Braves' rally chant, the Tomahawk Chop.

The Fonda-Turner wedding (the third for each) was nothing like the Fonda-Vadim or Fonda-Hayden ceremonies. There was a celebrity-studded reception at L'Orangerie in Beverly Hills and for the wedding, which took place at Turner's Florida ranch, Fonda wore a high-necked, floor length Victorian designer dress. Ted Turner didn't forget a ring; for their engagement, he gave Fonda an opal stone 18-carat gold ring from Tiffany and Company, featuring two large diamonds. North Vietnamese President Ho Chi Minh would have found it materialistic, but by that time Fonda had come full circle.

When she and Turner divorced in 2001, Fonda announced yet another evolution, to born-again Christian. Roger Vadim married Catherine Schneider in 1975, but it lasted only about 18 months. After that, he stuck to mistresses. Hayden married Barbara Williams in 1993 and was still married to her when he died in 2016. Turner did not remarry. Fonda's three diverse weddings had resulted in three divorces, perhaps proof that the ceremony does not make the marriage.

Other sources:
  https://en.wikipedia.org/wiki/Jane_Fonda
  http://people.com/style/jane-fonda-auction-wedding-dress-engagement-ring/
  Vanity Fair, September 2011

7

You've Come a Long Way, Baby
Women in the 1960s

In July 1968, Phillip Morris introduced a new brand of cigarettes called Virginia Slims. Their target audience was young, professional women, and the slogan, which became a popular tag line, was "You've Come a Long Way, Baby." It was a catchy phrase, but while women achieved a number of victories during the 1960s, increasing their chances of getting lung cancer and heart disease was not one of them.

Cigarette smoking was not the only advance women made during the 1960s. The way in which they were perceived changed dramatically, spurred by what was commonly known as the women's liberation movement, or women's lib. At the beginning of the 1960s, women did what women had traditionally done, and for the most part they did not do what men did. They were supposed to look attractive, and any article about a woman, no matter what the context, generally commented favorably on her appearance, even if she was not all that beautiful. It would have been insulting not to do so.

By the end of the decade, women were doing things they hadn't done before, which was threatening to many men and some women. Women who'd thrived under the old system didn't like the new order. The granddaughter of former President Ulysses Grant didn't think much of women's lib and Sophia Loren had no problem with being a sex symbol.

One of the hottest topics on the political scene today, as it has been for over a century, is income inequality, and one of the contributors to today's inequality is the women's movement of the 1960s and 1970s. In the early 1960s, the best careers open to most women were teaching, nursing, and secretarial. The salaries in those professions were relatively low and quite compressed, and the income of women was very equal.

Today, the income of women varies greatly. We find them in high earning professions like medicine and law, and many are entrepreneurs. There is a much greater disparity in women's income than there was fifty years ago, which would seem to be a good thing. Since women now comprise about 47 percent of the workforce, the change in the distribution of their income has made a tremendous difference in the overall distribution. Do people who complain about income inequality want to go back to the good old days when women's income potential was so severely limited?

At the start of the 1960s, women's lib was still a few years away, and many thought their most desired goal should be marriage.

The Lonely Turn to Public Dances

New York Times, **November 19, 1963**

In the early '60s, most unmarried women over the age of 20 had one over-riding goal: get married. Careers were important, but career success was somewhat empty and meaningless without a husband.

In 1962, Helen Gurley Brown published the ground-breaking *Sex and the Single Girl* which, as Margalit Fox noted in Brown's obituary, "taught unmarried women how to look their best, have delicious affairs, and ultimately bag a man for keeps." The last phrase was important, for while the hip woman of the early '60s was more overtly interested in sex than her older sisters, the ultimate goal was marriage. Even Brown married, although she waited until the age of 37.

In a city the size of New York, there were numerous venues where one might meet a prospective mate. One of the most popular was Malochy's, a bar operated by writer Malochy McCourt, whose brother Frank wrote *Angela's Ashes*.

Malochy's was located on 3rd Avenue between 63rd and 64th Streets, in close proximity to the Barbizon Hotel, an all-women residence facility where attractive young ladies often stayed when they came to New York seeking fame and fortune. Among the famous residents of the Barbizon were Grace Kelly, Joan Crawford, and Ali McGraw.

For those not quite classy enough for bars like Malochy's, there were "public dances," which were the subject of the *Times* article. In one week in mid-November 1963, there were more than 150 such events held at various locations throughout New York City. "The goal," reporter Martin Tolchin wrote, "is matrimony. The directness of the goal embarrasses most dance-goers, who resent the auction block atmosphere. But they keep returning."

Diversity was not a prevalent concept in the early 1960s, and the object of most matchmaking events was to bring people of similar backgrounds together. Dances were targeted to specific age groups and nationalities, including Irish, German, Greek, and Polish-themed affairs. There were dances for those from 20 to 35, from 25 to 40, and those for older couples, generously described as "over 28."

On the assumption that educated people wanted to meet other educated people, there were dances limited to college graduates, with proof of degrees required for entrance. The more elite events required a graduate degree. "Some dances have so many requirements that you think you're looking for a job," said one young man. Dress tended to be rather formal, with suits for men and stylish dresses, elaborate hairdos, and jewelry for women.

As with most serious endeavors, there were strategies for singles dances. Friday events were generally more low-key, and Friday attendees didn't have to admit that they didn't have a date for Saturday night. One also needed a good excuse, other than desperation, for being there. "My friends dragged me," explained one woman at Jewish dance. "My parents won't let me just sit home," said a young teacher.

The teacher wound up meeting a third year medical student, who made the obligatory excuse. "I don't come to these things often—only when I've got nothing better to do [as if time hung heavy on the hands of a medical student]. I don't expect to meet my wife at one of these."

Both men and women usually went in groups so they'd have people to talk to in case they didn't find a partner. One member of the group often went inside first to scout the crowd for prospects. If they reported slim pickings, the entire entourage moved on in search of greener pastures.

Tolchin noticed that there was much more scouting than dancing. At a public dance at the Roosevelt Hotel, he estimated that roughly 100 couples were dancing, while about 800 others stood on the sidelines, chatting, drinking, and just listening to the music. That was no way to find a husband.

Even if they were never asked to dance, many women came back week after week. "Their mothers tell them before they leave the house that they have to keep on trying," said a friend of one regular. "All they need is one man." "Women hate going to these things," said a lumber company secretary. "The men look over the wares and select them on the basis of looks and other superficialities."

When a young lady was asked to dance, she generally posed what were known as "the four questions." "What's your name?" "Where do you live?" "Where do you work?" and "Do you have a car?" "IBM could take lessons from them," said a man at a dance at the Roger Smith Hotel. "They get right to the point without any wasted motion."

The public dance was something no one admitted to liking; it was merely an unpleasant part of the ritual of finding a marriage partner. But the singles returned week after week. As one man who was a regular said,

"Where else can you walk up to a total stranger and a moment later hold her in your arms."

Other sources:
https://www.theatlantic.com/international/archive/2012/08/sex-and-single-girl-legacy-helen-gurley-brown/322898/
New York Times, August 13, 2012

Women Made to Help Men
Hartford Courant, February 16, 1965

Even by the middle of the decade, many men had an attitude that might have been considered backwards even by Neanderthals, as shown by a letter to Ann Landers:

DEAR ANN LANDERS:
This letter is being written by three Marine lieutenants stationed on Okinawa. Ever since we came to this fascinating island we have been impressed by the hard-working women of the Far East. They toil in the fields 12 to 15 hours a day—often until they are 80 years of age. These women are pleasant and uncomplaining. They do not demand equal rights, recognition, or any such nonsense. They accept the fact that they were put on earth to work and cater to the whims and wishes of men. The pampered, parasitical American female would do well to take a lesson from her sister of the Far East.

A Trio of Leathernecks

Ann's answer was succinct. "Now that's what I call first-rate husband material! ... I have one sentence of advice. Stay right there on Okinawa and make three American girls very happy."

Teen Girls Ask Hints on How to Win Boys
New York Daily News,
Early 1960s, Date Unknown

Leathernecks were not the only ones who thought women were put on earth to please men. Many women and girls felt the same way. *Daily News* columnist Antoinette Donnelly received a letter from a reader who asked, "DEAR MISS D: We are a group of teen-agers and we would like you to decide for us what charm or beauty assets a girl should have to attract boys and hold them."

Miss D didn't talk about intelligence, career accomplishments, or an impressive knowledge of current events. She mentioned beautiful hair ("The teen-ager with lovely hair knows its asset value"), a "slim, trim figure," and charm. Charm consisted of "saying the right and tactful thing at the right time, not being too shy or too afraid to cheer a boy up with a nice word of praise and things like that."

There was no mention of working in the fields until the age of 80, but presumably girls with beautiful hair and a slim, trim figure could find a husband to support them and keep them out of the rice fields.

Dean of Women Handles Male Students' Problems

Hartford Courant, June 15, 1965

Dr. Bonnie Strickland, a 27-year-old "slim, trim brunette," was Dean of Women at Emory University in Atlanta, Georgia. She was a national news item because she was a young, attractive woman who held a responsible position at a coeducational institution. Strickland's job was to help students with their personal problems and, curiously, more male students than females came to the Dean with issues involving sex. The most prevalent question was whether an unwed father should continue in college or quit to support his family.

Strickland was a product of the Deep South; her ancestors served in the Confederate Army. "No child of my time," she later told an interviewer, "could have escaped the loathing southerners felt for the North, or the twisted, convoluted notions we held about segregation." Strickland attended graduate school at Ohio State, and always suspected she had been admitted and given a graduate assistant position under the mistaken impression that, since she was an alumna of Alabama College who came from a rural southern town, she was African American. When she arrived at Ohio State, she was assigned an African American roommate, which was a blessing in disguise, for Strickland learned that neither Northerners nor blacks were the ogres she'd been led to believe they were.

Ohio State may have been disappointed that they hadn't increased their minority population, but they were obliviously ahead of their time in the diversity game, for Strickland was, unknown to anyone, a lesbian. At 16, she realized that she was more attracted to women than men, but after consulting the Bible, Strickland decided that it was a "terrible thing" and remained outwardly heterosexual.

When she graduated with a doctorate in psychology in 1962, Strickland applied for several jobs. For years, she retained a letter from a

Midwestern school which stated that, while her qualifications were admirable, the school had decided to hire a man. She accepted a job as a psychology professor at Emory University and a year later was named Dean of Women. The Associated Press noted in the article that Strickland had enhanced Emory's staid image. "She is often seen driving her convertible with a German police dog draped over the back seat.... Wearing shorts, a gay blouse [if they only knew how gay] and a crash helmet, she recently took part in a campus soap box derby."

Colleagues wondered why such an attractive woman was unattached, and kept trying to fix her up with eligible young men. All of the men she brought to school functions, however, were gay and "dated" Strickland to help preserve her image.

In 1969, while still outwardly heterosexual, Strickland published a study that examined the psyches of gays and lesbians, and concluded that they were no more or less pathological than heterosexuals, a controversial finding a time when homosexuality was still considered a mental illness.

After more than ten years at Emory, Strickland took a job at the University of Massachusetts, which catapulted her into a liberal environment dramatically different from the one at Emory. She acknowledged her lesbianism, and during her more than 45 years at UMass, instituted the school's first course on lesbian psychology, which she noted proudly was very popular with black male basketball players, who identified with the lesbians as underdogs.

Strickland served as president of the American Psychological Association in 1987. She published extensively, and is best known for her work in the field of depression and gay and lesbian psychology. The Strickland-Daniel Mentoring Award is presented each year to a student who excels in feminist mentoring in psychology.

The Associated Press thought they had a cute story about the darling little woman who gave men advice about their love lives, and had no idea they were writing about a woman who would become one of the leading gay and lesbian psychologists in American academia. Strickland's journey personified the shift in the perception of women from the male stereotype of the mid–1960s to the increasingly diverse world of the 1970s and 1980s. Bonnie Strickland turned out to be much more than a "slim, trim brunette."

Other sources:
>https://books.google.com/books?id=6kLJeJ2SMxsC&pg=PA108&lpg=PA108&dq=bonnie+strickland+julian+rotter&source=bl&ots=P2JPKfnsvA&sig=kyXMMSira20I-R61TVj_TvclWck&hl=en&sa=X&ei=ymIpUrTsBYW48wSDwYHoDA&ved=0CDIQ6AEwAjgK#v=onepage&q=bonnie%20strickland%20julian%20rotter&f=false
>http://www.feministvoices.com/bonnie-strickland/

Meter Girls Have It Maid Again After New Shape-up

New York Daily News, September 9, 1965

Policing had always been a male province, but by the 1960s women had infiltrated the world of law enforcement, although in a distinctly feminine manner. Americans were not ready to have women chasing murderers or muggers, so they became "meter maids," entrusted with the responsibility of monitoring parked cars. The ideal meter maid was reliable, trustworthy, and trim.

In 1965, 90 women with aspirations of handing out parking tickets were hired on a probationary basis by the New York City Traffic Department. Eighty-four completed the program successfully and moved into permanent positions, while six did not. They were too fat. Since the maids had been walking their beats every day during the probationary period, Deputy Traffic Commissioner Stanley Posess wondered how so many of them could gain weight. "Maybe it's because they're out in the fresh air so much," he speculated.

Meter maids were represented by the Teamsters Union, never renowned for its progressive attitude toward women. The Teamsters' representative, Herbert Bauch, met with Posess but did not claim that it was unfair or discriminatory to dismiss the women because they weighed too much, for apparently he also liked his ladies trim. The chief of the Traffic Enforcement Bureau, Matthew Corey, hadn't alleged that the women's weight affected their work, only that the maids' excess poundage made them unattractive and poor representatives of the city.

"Corey has the job," explained the *Daily News*, "of judging whether a meter maid is too bulgy in a uniform to keep the job. He does not use scales or a tape measure. A spokesman explained yesterday, 'The weight is a flexible thing. Mr. Corey is looking at the weight in proportion to the height.'"

Bauch had one success, gaining the reinstatement of Rosemary Maleski, a 5'7" brunette who weighed 170 pounds. Maleski said that she was not fat, just "well-built." Bauch pointed out that her measurements were a seductive 38–28–36 (some accounts put an extra two inches on her hips—perhaps in the name of symmetry) and claimed she looked "like Miss Universe." "She does have the proper proportions," Corey admitted, and allowed her to keep her job. One of the other maids was allowed to resign and four others were given time to shape up.

Among the four who had to lose weight was Josta Granier of Jackson Heights, who'd come to the United States from Holland in 1950. Ms. Granier was five feet five inches tall and tipped the Toledos at 190 pounds, much more weight than Matthew Corey thought was appropriate for his maids. Larry Paskow, owner of the Harbor Island Spa in Miami Beach, heard about Josta's plight and offered a free stay at his facility in order to help her become shapely enough to monitor parking meters. After two weeks at Harbor Island, Granier was down to 174 pounds, a remarkable result for two weeks but not enough for the City of New York, which rejected her once more. Paskow owned another facility in Long Branch, New Jersey, and after her second rebuke Ms. Granier went there to try to shed a few more pounds.

While Josta was in Long Branch, Matthew Corey ran out of patience and terminated her employment.

She continued to work out at the spa and intended to re-apply when she thought she was thin enough to pass Corey's inspection. She said she received a number of sympathetic letters from people who said they'd also been fired for being too heavy. Apparently, none found it patently unfair and at least one asked for the diet secrets that had enabled her to shed 16 pounds. One letter writer, a policeman, was concerned. "I hope they cannot do this," he wrote, "because we'll all be next."

The story of blonde Patricia Lockner had a happier ending. Lockner, initially described as "an ample Kim Novak" had been given until September 1 to get down to fighting weight. By the deadline, she was no longer ample. "She looks more like Kim Novak now than Kim Novak," said a beaming department spokesman. And wouldn't Kim Novak look terrific in a meter maid's outfit?

While the process didn't work out well for Josta Granier, it was all for a good cause. The department spokesman said in summary, "We are very proud of our girls. They all put effort into this. We may have gotten slammed, but now we have a trim, uniform group of meter maids."

Other sources:
Amarillo Globe Times, August 3, 1965
The Middletown Journal, September 9, 1965
Fort Madison Evening Democrat, August 2, 1965

Most Beautiful By-Line

Newsday, September 25, 1965

Gloria Steinem is one of America's most influential feminists. She is intelligent and she is a powerful, talented writer, but what first got her noticed was what really counted for women in the early 1960s—her looks. Steinem's first big assignment, in 1963, was going undercover as a Playboy bunny for an article for *Show* magazine. She told people what it was really like to be a bunny and was critical of the sexual exploitation of women in the New York Playboy Club.

While the article was a great success, Steinem was not particularly happy about the fact that her good looks threatened to limit her writing to similar topics. She returned an advance for a book based on the article and was horrified when she was asked to pose as a call girl for a second expose.

Following the *Show* article, Steinem did freelance work for journals like the newly formed *New York* magazine and *Cosmopolitan* and was a writer for the satirical political television show *That Was the Week that Was* (also known as TW3). In September 1965, she was interviewed by *Newsday* reporter Harvey Aronson about her burgeoning career as a writer. Aronson was a serious journalist who wrote extensively on race relations and other heavy topics; he later became a respected journalism professor at Stony Brook. But in 1965, even a progressive, serious journalist like Aronson found himself focusing more on Steinem's looks than her writing ability. The title was telling—"Most Beautiful By-Line."

The article began, "The young woman who may well be the world's most beautiful by-line sits down for lunch in a small restaurant beneath her third-floor apartment in West 56th Street." "She is 30," Aronson continued, "but looks about four years younger. She has a five-foot-seven, 120-pound figure [Steinem would have made a great meter maid] of the sort that shows to great advantage getting out of taxicabs ... her face is a painting in an almost heart-shaped frame of shoulder length brown hair, and soft, straight features are dominated by wide, long-lashed brown eyes."

Aronson was not the only one who admired Steinem's beauty. A man who met her on the set of TW3 said, "I told her I would never figure her for a writer, but for somebody's mistress." In 1965, that was considered to be a compliment.

Aronson touched on Steinem's work, but most of the article focused on her appearance, and he asked Steinem if she thought her looks helped her in the world of journalism. "It helps in the short run," she said, "but not in the long run. People remember you, it's at least as good as being a Negro. In the long run? Well, it hinders your being taken seriously. Editors tend to assign you to stories on women." "She's fairly facile as a writer," said a male acquaintance, "but if it wasn't for her looks, she would be no better than a lot of other women who come to New York."

Aronson eventually got around to talking about Steinem's work and her financial success, noting that she had progressed from making $3,000 a year in 1961 to getting $3,000 per article by 1965. Still, anyone reading the article would be hard-pressed to learn how good a writer Steinem was or what she thought about any serious issues of the day. Aronson didn't go so far as to state her bust, waist, and hip measurements, as was frequently done in stories about women, but the reader was sure to remember the long lashes and the shoulder length brown hair, and they would certainly be on the *qui vive* when they saw her getting out of a cab.

Other sources:
http://www.gloriasteinem.com
https://journalism.cc.stonybrook.edu/?p=9106

Bill Allowing Women at Bars Gets Favorable Report from House

Hartford Courant, May 23, 1967

Most people in Connecticut that are more than 50 years old would not believe that during their lifetime, women of the Nutmeg State were not allowed to sit within three feet of a bar. They could work as barmaids and they could sit at tables *near* a bar, but unless they had really long arms, they could not enjoy a drink *at* the bar.

One might think the restriction was an antiquated law that had simply not been addressed, such as a prohibition on bringing one's horse into a courtroom, but it had been passed in 1937, not long after the end of prohibition. The primary reason for the law was a fear that tavern proprietors would hire attractive women (known as "b-girls") to sit at the bar and entice male customers.

By 1967, the law had become somewhat of an embarrassment, for most of the surrounding states allowed women to sit at bars. Bartenders turned a bit sheepish when they had to inform out-of-state customers that the women in their party had to keep their distance. They were concerned about losing business, especially if they were located near the state borders.

When a bill giving women the right to sit at a bar was introduced, however, it was hotly debated. "Women should be allowed to go anywhere men can go," said State Representative Mary Griswold of New Haven to loud applause. But many politicians were not applauding. Among them was Democratic governor John Dempsey, whose opposition to the bill was well-known. Another staunch opponent was State Representative William O'Neill of Colchester, a tavern owner who later served as governor from 1980–1991.

Leonard Frazier, an African American Democrat from Hartford who, it was noted, "usually speaks against discrimination of any kind" was an adamant opponent. "We're becoming a matriarchal society," he said. "We are losing our manlihood. A bar is the only place we can go and not be nagged."

Democrats position themselves as the party of liberalism and inclusion, and it is surprising in retrospect to see so many of them trying to deny equality to women in a seemingly innocuous context. The same people who were demanding equality for African Americans wanted to keep women away from the bar, their interest in male supremacy trumping equal rights and non-discrimination.

Even supporters were not that supportive. Albert Provenzano of Stratford, Chairman of the Liquor Committee that had recommended the bill, said the main reason he favored passage was that, since women, under the existing law, could be near a bar, they might still "entice" men from afar. Democrat Bruce Morris who was also in favor of the bill, noted that it only allowed women to sit at a bar, so that if a bar owner wanted to exclude women, he just had to remove all his bar stools.

The House approved the bill by a vote of 89–68. Of the 18 women in the body, 11 voted in favor, four voted against and three abstained. It was all for naught, however, as the measure did not pass the State Senate.

In 1969, the bill was introduced again, and this time the legislature had become sufficiently enlightened to pass it. Implementation took another three years, and by 1972, women were able to sit at bars and, if they chose, entice men to their heart's content. Coincidentally, 1972 was the first year I was able to legally go into a bar, and I don't recall being enticed by many females, b-girls or otherwise. In fact, most were downright resistant to our charm. Another barrier had tumbled without incident.

Other sources:

https://ctstatelibrary.org/the-long-road-to-barroom-equality/

Miss Shape

Hartford Courant, October 16, 1967

Miss Shape didn't rate a story—just a pair of photos and a caption. In October 1967, the men of Memphis State University decided to hold a contest to determine which of the MSU coeds had the best figure. In order to be certain that they weren't influenced by a pretty face, the women were judged with bags worn over their heads. The winner was 19-year-old Tricia Smith, who was pictured both with and without the bag.

If She's a Doctor or a Lawyer, Men Seem Wary

New York Times, June 13, 1969

Despite contests like Miss Shape, many barriers were being shattered by 1969. An increasing number of women were practicing medicine and law, which posed a threat to many men, both professionally and socially. Did men want to marry a woman whose professional standing was equal to or greater than theirs? If a man wanted someone to stay at home, prepare his meals, wash his clothes, and rub his back, Dr. Barbara Leibowitz, a "well-endowed redhead from Forest Hills" was probably not the girl for him.

Leibowitz graduated from the Albert Einstein College of Medicine at Yeshiva University in 1966. "Since then," she said, "some men have backed off because they don't want competition. Others over-react by talking only about their own business." Her father suggested she resolve her dilemma by going to "charm school." "He thinks I have to learn things like poise, hair, makeup, and all that stuff," Leibowitz said. Dad was a bit behind the times, for the charm school, also known as a "finishing school," was on its way out, replaced by medical school and law school.

Marilyn Goldstein ("a honey blond") was a corporate lawyer with Shapiro and Brown, a career her father had advised against. "Men will think you are too smart," he warned. "They won't want to marry you." Goldstein did her best to minimize her intelligence. "[A] lot of men take it for granted," she said, "that I'm a walking brain. As a matter of fact, I was a very poor student. I was more socially inclined."

"I like to go out with someone of the same intelligence level," said Dr. Jane Norman, "but sometimes these men are insecure and don't like to date women in their own category. In a sense, they date down. Men still like to go out with women they can overpower. But I probably wouldn't be interested in anyone that I would frighten."

Mixing intelligence and achievement with femininity was a tricky proposition. "They are young and single," the article began. "The skirts they swing are very often short and the eyelashes they flutter are often false." Twenty-nine-year-old lawyer Marsha Edelman had "no qualms about wearing false eyelashes and hairpieces to court (depending on my mood)" and preferred dating colleagues, since they had something in common.

Marilyn Goldstein said that if she were married, she would give up her career if her husband asked her to, but apparently he didn't. Her father's fears were groundless, for in 1981, Marilyn married Jack Malick and took the name Goldstein-Malick. Her obituary (she died of pancreatic cancer in

2008) stated that she had been an attorney in the General Counsel's Office of New York Life for 35 years.

Apparently Marsha Edelman, who later practiced immigration law, was guilty of more than wearing false eyelashes to court; her law license was suspended for nine months in 2011 for various violations regarding fees and retainers. Edelman's defense was a long record of service to the immigrant community (she was 69 at the time) and her diabetes, which made her forgetful.

Dr. Jane Norman was still practicing in 2017, specializing in internal medicine and geriatrics at Mount Sinai Beth Israel Brooklyn Medical Center. She'd been a physician for 53 years.

Shortly after she was interviewed for the *Times* article, Dr. Barbara Leibowitz accepted a cardiology fellowship at Tel Hashomer in Israel. She later became Associate Medical Director at Pfizer Corporation where she supervised drug testing. Leibowitz served as Director of Licensing and Development for the company before retiring to teach at Columbia. She attended the 50th reunion of the Einstein School, and, as verified by her photo in the program, she was still a redhead. Since the picture was cropped at the shoulders, her degree of endowment was unverifiable.

Other sources:
http://www.legacy.com/obituaries/nytimes/obituary.aspx?pid=119794970
https://www.avvo.com/attorneys/10022-ny-marsha-edelman-872062.html
http://caselaw.findlaw.com/ny-supreme-court-appellate-division/1568612.html
http://doctor.webmd.com/doctor/jane-norman-md-f2222421-5562-4193-8111-e49a09d50669-overview
http://www.einstein.yu.edu/uploadedFiles/alumni/Reunion%20Book.pdf

Svelte Blonde Is a Commercial Pilot

New York Times, February 16, 1970

It had been five years since Harvey Aronson drooled over Gloria Steinem, and supposedly women were being taken more seriously by 1970. Still, the *New York Times*, which considered itself a very serious newspaper, illustrated the story about pilot Turi Wideroe with a full length seated picture of her, wearing a short skirt that displayed her long, trim legs prominently in the foreground.

The *Times* described Wideroe as having the "height (just under six feet), the cheekbones, and the long, shapely legs of a fashion model." It translated her measurements from the metric 98–68–100 to 38½–26½–39 inches. The most frequent question she fielded about flying, Turi indicated, was not about keeping the plane in the air, but what she wore in the cockpit. For the record, Wideroe confided that she chose slacks because, she said, "skirts in the cockpit are too tough on the nylons."

The tone of the article cannot be solely attributed to male chauvinism, for the author was Judy Kelmesbud, who'd been given the assignment of profiling the first female commercial pilot in the "Western" world. The Norwegian Wideroe, a 32-year-old co-pilot for Scandinavian Air Services, was not the first woman to fly a plane. Amelia Earhart had been the most well-known aviatrix, and a woman named Helen Richey had been hired by Central Airlines in 1934. Although Richey was the first woman to pilot a commercial flight, she never had a regular schedule. Eastern bloc countries like Bulgaria and the Soviet Union had employed women pilots for a number of years, but during the Cold War era things that happened behind the Iron Curtain didn't count.

Wideroe came by her vocation naturally; she was the daughter of Viggo Wideroe, who founded a regional Norwegian airline in 1934. Turi initially intended to pursue a career as a book designer, and graduated from the Norwegian Academy of Arts and Crafts. After working in the publishing industry for a few years, she earned her pilot's license in 1962, got her commercial license in 1965, and soon began flying for her father's airline.

Wideroe first came to the attention of the *Times* in 1968 ("SAS to Train Woman Pilot") when she was hired by Scandinavian Air Services. After graduating third in her flight school class of 50, she was given a job as co-pilot on an SAS Convair 440 Metropolitan. Wideroe made history with her first flight on April 30, 1969, becoming the only one of SAS's 1,150 pilots who had measurements of 98–68–100, unless there were male pilots with unusual physiques.

Turi Wideroe was a pioneer, she was good-looking, and her 1970 appearance in New York on an SAS public relations tour generated a lot of attention. She appeared on *Today* and *To Tell the Truth*, and was the subject of a number of magazine and newspaper articles. "At least during this week," said an SAS spokesperson, "Ms. Wideroe is the most famous woman in New York. Maybe with the exception of Ms. Jackie Kennedy."

Not everyone, however, was excited about having a woman in the cockpit. A Danish pilot filed a protest, claiming that a woman didn't have the strength to handle a plane in an emergency. Wideroe said that was ridiculous and added, "There's no reason in the world why women on airlines have to be limited to coffee, tea, or milk jobs."

Wideroe flew for SAS for ten years. In 1970, the uniform in which she made her historic first flight was hung in the National Air and Space Museum in Washington, D.C. In May of the following year, Vice President Spiro Agnew presented her with the Harmon Trophy, awarded annually to an outstanding aviator, aviatrix, and astronaut. In 1972, Turi married Karl Erik Harr, a painter noted for his landscapes of the northern Norwegian coast. The couple had two children before divorcing in 1975.

In succeeding years, more women took to the air. Emily Warner was hired by Frontier Airlines in 1973 and on June 16, 1984, Warner and First Officer Barbara Cook flew Frontier flight 244 from Denver to Lexington, Kentucky, the first all-woman crew on an American commercial flight. In 1991, the United States Senate passed legislation allowing women to fly in military combat, an advance that ranks with women being allowed to smoke cigarettes.

After leaving the airline industry, Wideroe became a journalist and earned master's degrees in history from the University of Oslo in 1998 and the University of Tromso in 2008. She is 81 at the time of this writing and living in Norway.

Other sources:
  https://en.wikipedia.org/wiki/Turi_Wider%C3%B8e
  https://scandinaviantraveler.com/en/aviation/1970s-turi-wideroe-takes-the-world-by-storm
  https://www.thisdayinaviation.com/tag/turi-wideroe/
  https://airandspace.si.edu/explore-and-learn/topics/women-in-aviation/Wideroe.cfm
  https://en.wikipedia.org/wiki/Karl_Erik_Harr
  New York Times, August 1, 1991

Sophia Loren Kisses off WLM (Women's Liberation Movement)

The Bridgeport Post, September 25, 1970

"Being a sex symbol? What's wrong with it?" Sophia Loren asked. Not much, if you looked like Sophia Loren and were an international movie star. Loren said, "a woman shouldn't forget her duties and responsibilities as a woman" and that a woman "shows intelligence or does not show it if she has too much."

One can almost hear Betty Freidan's teeth grinding.

Descendant of Grant Scoffs Lib

Hartford Courant, October 11, 1970

There were others beside Sophia Loren who were not on board with the women's liberation movement. It represented change, and for some it represented too much change. For Julia Cantacuzene, the world of 1970 was very different than it had been when Julia Dent Grant was born in her grandfather's White House on June 6, 1876. In the year of the American Centennial, women couldn't vote and the only career to which they could realistically aspire was to marry well.

When Julia was less than a month old, Elizabeth Cady Stanton marked the hundredth anniversary of American independence by issuing a Declaration of Rights of the Women of the United States on behalf of the National Woman Suffrage Association. Stanton summarized the great advances made by the country in its first century, and then wrote, "...that while all men of every race, and clime, and condition, have been invested with the full rights of citizenship, under our hospitable flag, all women still suffer the degradation of disfranchisement."

Julia Grant would not obtain the right to vote until she was 44, but as the daughter of Frederick Dent Grant, son of President Ulysses S. Grant, she was in a position to pursue the career of marrying well. From 1891 through 1893, Julia traveled through Europe with her maternal aunt, Bertha Palmer, who was about as accomplished as a woman could be in the late 19th century. With her husband Potter Palmer, Bertha ran the Palmer House hotel in Chicago, and is perhaps best known as the inventor of the brownie, which she concocted in the hotel kitchen. Her mission in Europe was to represent the Board of Lady Managers of the Chicago World's Fair.

While traveling with Mrs. Palmer, Julia met Russian Prince Mikhail Cantacuzene, who was so enthralled with the young American that he followed her to Cannes. After a two-day courtship, Cantacuzene proposed and Julia accepted. They were married in 1899 at a Newport, Rhode Island, mansion leased by Aunt Bertha.

After their marriage, the couple lived in St. Petersburg, and when war came to Europe in 1914, Mikhail served as a general in the Russian army. The war ended for Russia in 1917, which was a very bad year to be a Russian prince. Michael and Julia fled the country in the wake of the Communist revolution, reached the United States via Finland, and after spending time in Washington, D.C., eventually settled in Sarasota, Florida.

The Cantacuzenes divorced in 1934 and Julia moved back to Washington, where she wrote a number of books, including a personal memoir of the Russian Revolution. Julia lost her eyesight at about the age of 80, but in 1970, when she was a spry but sightless 94, she spoke with the press at a small luncheon hosted by her friend, famous socialite Pearl Mesta.

Ms. Cantacuzene's opinions were pretty much what one might expect of a woman who was the granddaughter of a mid–19th century U.S. President and who had spent 18 years married to a Russian prince. She was asked what she thought of the youth revolution. "What youth revolt?" she replied.

"I believe most young people are busy studying. You just hear more about the others." And what about women's liberation? "A lot of nonsense."

Other sources:
http://ecssba.rutgers.edu/docs/decl.html
https://en.wikipedia.org/wiki/Julia_Dent_Cantacuz%C3%A8ne_Spiransky-Grant

Liberation Shunned by Women

Hartford Courant, February 11, 1971

On February 9, 1971, the Junior Women's Club of Ledyard invited Dr. Jane Torrey, a 45-year-old psychology professor at nearby Connecticut College and an organizer of the National Organization of Women, to speak at the Ledyard Town Hall.

The principal civil rights crusade of the 1960s was a quest to obtain equality for African Americans, and women's rights were a secondary consideration. When the 1964 Civil Rights Act was passed, a provision prohibiting discrimination against women in employment was added almost as an afterthought. There was a suggestion that it was included in order to alienate those who might otherwise support the bill.

The relationship between those fighting for the rights of African Americans and those fighting for the rights of women had always been tricky. Each group was hesitant to embrace the other's cause for fear of alienating potential supporters. In the 19th century, abolitionists declined to join forces with early feminists for that reason. Men who passionately favored freeing someone else's slaves were not quite ready to liberate their own wives.

Even after the Civil Rights Act forbade employment discrimination against women, employment ads remained segregated by Help Wanted/Male, Help Wanted/Female, and Help Wanted/Male or Female categories. Despite the inclusion of women in the Civil Rights Act, change was not coming quickly enough to suit many of them.

On June 28–30, 1966, there was a conference in Washington, D.C., to discuss the activities of the newly-formed Equal Employment Opportunity Commission. Among the attendees was Betty Friedan, a 1942 graduate of Smith College who had been a writer on labor issues during the 1940s and early 1950s. At her 15th college reunion in 1957, Friedan noted that many of her classmates had subordinated their own lives and careers to those of their husbands, and that for the many divorcees, the sacrifice had been in vain.

Friedan wrote a number of articles that were inspired by her classmates' situations and in 1963 she combined her work into the classic *The*

Feminine Mystique. At the conference, she became frustrated at the inaction of the EEOC and one evening invited a small group of 15–20 women to her hotel room.

There was a lot of animated conversation and the next day, at the conference's final luncheon, Friedan determined to convert the talk into action. She got a number of women to sign a sheet of paper pledging them to establish a group to fight for the rights of women. At the end of October, 30 women held an organizational meeting at which the National Organization for Women was founded. Friedan was elected its first president.

In February 1970, the same month Dr. Torrey spoke in Ledyard, 20 NOW members staged a protest on the floor of the U.S. Senate to demand hearings on the Equal Rights Amendment. There had been a number of encouraging signs, including NOW member Shirley Chisholm becoming the first African American woman elected to Congress, but the Equal Rights Amendment was languishing in committee.

For nearly an hour, Torrey described her ideal world, one where men and women were equals and women chose from a full array of career options. She argued that equality for women would benefit men, who "would be freed from the 'masculine mystique' that gave them more anxiety, ulcers and mental illnesses than their wives." In Dr. Torrey's world, anxiety, ulcers, and mental illness would be shared equally. The idea of women having equal job opportunities and receiving equal pay had the most appeal , but full-bodied equality with the sharing of all burdens had a downside, and therein lie the rub.

The audience was skeptical. "I resent being talked to as if we're a bunch of sheep," one woman said. Another was worried that one of Torrey's students might become her future daughter-in-law. A third thought that NOW needed to be more cognizant of biological differences between men and women. "The husband can't nurse the babies," she said, to which Torrey replied, "Your anatomy is not your destiny."

As with any discussion of women's liberation, the subject of marriage was a central topic. The *Courant* said that Torrey had chosen "the *often-lonely single life* (italics added) because she preferred a career to becoming a household 'drudge.'" That elicited a storm of protest from the drudges in the audience, who defended their decisions to marry and said they were happy with their choices. None of those who said they were happy with their marriages had full-time professional careers; they combined domestic activity with volunteer or part-time work.

Dr. Torrey hit some nerves, which she probably intended to do, and raised some defenses. The fact that the women were divided perhaps pointed out one of the key dilemmas of the movement for women's equality. Not every woman wanted to be a psychology professor and not all wanted to be housewives. The best world for women was one in which they had the choice to be either, but most women—and men—seemed to feel obligated to take one side or the other. That mindset creates an insistence that women be proportionally represented in all areas, whether they want to be or not. Freedom for women is freedom of choice and equal rights, not an obligation to be just like men. I think that's what Elizabeth Cady Stanton wanted back in 1876.

Other sources:
  http://now.org/about/history/founding-2/

Gals—Here's Check List; How Do You Measure Up?

Hartford Courant, October 19, 1969

The beginning of this chapter featured a letter to Ann Landers from three Marines who thought that women were born to serve men. After seeing the evolution in the perception of women over the next few years, let's check in with Ann at the end of 1969 to see what's changed.

DEAR ANN LANDERS:

Every now and then a chick lists the qualities she looks for in a date—or a future husband. So far as I can remember, no male has ever done so. May I be the first? I'll bet some of the unmarried girls out there might be interested in checking themselves against the list. Here it is:

1. She must be meticulous about hygiene, well-groomed and ladylike. A foul mouth turns off any decent guy immediately.
2. She must be a good listener. When she speaks it must reflect some thought. The girl who is constantly on stage, making with the small talk, dropping names and places is a bore.
3. The female who is physically aggressive deprives a man of his masculinity. Squeezing close when he is trying to drive, putting her lips up to be kissed, or reaching for his hand in a movie can kill a romance.
4. Live by this rule: Don't call him. Let him call you. If you have to telephone a guy or drop him a note to remind him that you're still alive—you're as good as dead. Sign me—

Still Looking

DEAR STILL:

Good list. Thanks for sending it. And now you gals out there who are also still looking, how did you stack up?

Perhaps things hadn't changed all that much. But it would be interesting to know how long Still Looking was still looking.

8

Mad Dogs and Skyjackers
Crime Keeps Up with the Times

The best thing about following crime on microfilm is that you don't have to wait for the following day to find out what happened next. You scroll merrily along following the crime, the chase, the capture, and the trial, all in a single afternoon.

Every era has its own special crime genre. In the late 1960s and early '70s, it was skyjacking. Most of the early skyjackers wanted to go to Cuba for political reasons, but it wasn't long before they began hijacking planes for ransom. There was a rash of incidents until airlines began to recognize the value of security, which had been almost non-existent.

Some crimes, like the alleged murder complicity of Stephen Bingham in the Soledad Brothers murders, were the result of the radical political environment of the 1960s. Others involved celebrities like Frank Sinatra, Jr., and Andy Warhol. Some were very serious while others, like that of the Dairy Barn bandit, were more humorous than grim. It was an unusual time and the criminals of the '60s and '70s were a varied lot.

Blackmailed for Love & 56G by Father of 8 Babies She Slew

New York Daily News, October 9, 1962

Sonia Wilson was an attractive, dark-haired 37-year-old English teacher with a secret past. Although Ms. Wilson was unmarried, she had a lover identified only as Mr. X, who she met when she was just 17 and freshly graduated from an exclusive girls' school. It was 1942, and with World War II in full swing, Wilson was working as a secretary at Stanton Ironworks in Ilkeston, Derbyshire, which produced military goods. Mr. X was a married executive with the company, and he and Sonia began an affair that would

8. Mad Dogs and Skyjackers 191

last 20 years. "I knew he was married," she said, "but I think I was infatuated with him. We used to go for long walks every night."

Soon, they were doing more than walking, and apparently condoms were in short supply in postwar Britain, for in 1946 Wilson became pregnant. She had the baby and, as instructed by Mr. X, killed it immediately after it was born. Mr. X helped her bury it in her garden.

Wilson left her secretarial job and went to work as a teacher in Ilkeston, but Mr. X continued to press his affections upon her. If she refused him, he said, he would reveal the fact that she had killed their baby. Soon, affection was not enough for Mr. X, and he began asking for money as well as sex as payment for his silence. Wilson began paying him more than 20 pounds per week.

Wilson's family owned a profitable contracting business, and in 1952, in order to satisfy Mr. X's increasing demands for money, she forged a company check for 56,000 pounds, resulting in the eventual bankruptcy of the business.

In the meantime, Sonia had Mr. X's baby approximately every two years, killing each as soon as it was born. She buried one in her garden and wrapped the other six bodies in newspaper and stacked them in a trunk in a storage room. Somehow, she managed to conceal her pregnancies and deliver the babies herself.

Wilson could tolerate delivering and killing babies, but she couldn't handle the continual requests for money. In 1962, she went to the police, told them everything that had happened, and was charged with two of the murders. She hired Lord Geoffrey Dawson Lane, who later served as Lord Chief Justice of England from 1980 to 1992, to defend her. Lane claimed the indictment was too vague and the judge agreed, dropping the murder charge. Wilson pleaded guilty to concealing the babies' birth and was immediately released from prison, credited with time served.

The prosecutors then set their sights on Mr. X, who turned out to be 55-year-old Ellis Bednall, an industrial security officer. Bednall was married, with six children of his own, and by the time he was arrested, he was a grandfather. He had been manager of the Stanton Ironworks field hockey team in the mid–1950s and appeared to be an upstanding member of the community.

Bednall was charged with 20 counts, including concealing the birth of the babies and blackmail. When he was arrested, he told police the birth of babies two through eight was a complete shock to him, as it undoubtedly was to Mrs. Harriet Bednall.

Sonia Wilson testified against Bednall and revealed all the sordid details of their affair—the births, the deaths, and the blackmail. Unfortunately, I was unable to find the results of the trial. Bednall passed away in 1974 at the age of 68.

Other sources:
Brandon (Manitoba) Sun, February 18, 1963
Fairbanks Daily News Miner, February 20, 1963
myheritage.com

Had Night Job: Burglary

New York Daily News, December 31, 1962

For more than a year, New York City Dairy Barns had been victimized by a thief who was given the nickname "The Ice Cream Bandit." Dairy Barn was a relatively new franchise; the first store opened in 1961, and almost as soon as the company started business, a serial burglar began robbing them. Somehow, the bandit managed to enter the stores without using any force, empty the safe, and escape unobserved.

Thomas Giery, a Dairy Barn relief manager for the Long Island region, was as puzzled as anyone, but he wasn't losing any sleep over it. In fact, Giery was an especially sound sleeper. "When I put my head down," he said, "I go to sleep. You could take every bit of furniture out of the house and I wouldn't hear a thing." Apparently, Giery was not sleeping *all* of the time he was in bed; he and his wife Betty Jane had eight children, ranging in age from three months to 12 years.

On Sunday, December 30, 1962, at about 3:30 a.m., Patrolman Joseph Stenson noticed a shadowy figure moving around inside the Dairy Barn store in Wantaugh, Long Island. He alerted Detective Arthur Golder, who was patrolling in the area. The two men entered the store and found, to their surprise, a woman, whom they immediately arrested.

The woman was 34-year-old Betty Jane Giery who, when taken to the police station, tearfully admitted that she was The Ice Cream Bandit. At night, when her husband fell into his deep sleep, Betty Jane went into his pockets and took out the keys to a Dairy Barn store; since he was a relief manager, he had keys to several stores. Thomas had also told his wife where the combination to the safes was hidden.

While Thomas slept, Betty Jane would take a cab from her West Islip home, get dropped off near a Dairy Barn store, and ask the driver to wait. Then she went inside, found the combination, and opened the safe. Sometimes there was no money in the main section, so she used a piece of wire and a pair of kitchen tongs to get to the part of the safe where employees made cash drops. Mrs. Giery had done this nine times.

When Thomas was awakened at 9:30 a.m. and told by police that his wife was in custody, he was astounded. He said he had no idea what his wife had been doing, and the police believed him. Betty Jane said she had spent all the money she stole on household expenses and that her youngest child needed a heart operation. Her husband said he hadn't noticed any unusual expenses and that there was no immediate need for his child to have surgery. Apparently, Betty Ann Giery was simply a bored housewife looking for excitement, who happened to have an unwitting, sound-sleeping husband with a lot of Dairy Barn keys.

Note: One of the interesting aspects of this article is that one of the co-authors was Robert A. Caro, who later wrote epic biographies of Robert Moses and Lyndon Johnson.

Slaying Ends a Happy Triangle
New York Daily News, October 1963

Most people associate promiscuous sex with the latter part of the 1960s, but life is never exactly as we remember it and some people, like Richard Richards and his friends, were ahead of their time. Richards, 38, was a prosperous Cleveland jeweler with four stores and a very active social life. On the morning of October 5, 1963, his adventurous life came to an end when his body was found in the trunk of his rented Cadillac behind a Howard Johnson's Motor Lodge. He had been killed by several blows to the head, leaving an estate of more than $1 million and no will.

What made Richard Richards' killing national news was the fact that police quickly established that the jeweler, who'd been divorced for six years, had a married girlfriend. That wasn't unique, but what was unusual was the fact that his girlfriend's husband was aware of the affair and approved of it.

The open-minded couple was Andrew Wasko, 35, and his wife June, an attractive, sexy 27-year-old blonde cocktail waitress from Parma Heights. The couple had a six-year-old child, and an 11-year-old from June's prior marriage who lived with them in their split-level home in suburban Brook Park. The third leg of the triangle was formed when June met Richards at a restaurant where she was having dinner with several co-workers. She gave the jeweler a hard time, telling him that a ring her husband bought her at one of Richards' store was over-priced. Two days later, she called him to apologize, and they began dating.

June and Andrew Wasko were an example of the adage that opposites attract. Andrew was a homebody, while June loved the fast life. "I like to go out and have a good time," she told reporters. When the two realized they preferred different lifestyles, they came up with a unique solution. "I have an arrangement with my husband," June said. "The main thing was to bring up the children properly. We didn't want a divorce."

Andrew, a mechanic at Republic Steel, sat next to his wife while she told her story to reporters. He had never met Richards, he said, but spoke to him occasionally when he called June. "I knew about it," he said of the affair between Richards and his wife. "We had an understanding [that] as long as she took care of the house and kids it was all right with me. She is a good mother." When June was out, Andrew did the housework and watched the children. His wife and Richards went out a lot, and June said, "I loved him very much. I love my husband, too, but in a different way from Richard."

When Richards' body was discovered, police investigated the connection with June Wasko. A jealous husband was normally a prime suspect, but Andrew Wasko wasn't jealous. His alibi on the night Richards was killed checked out, and June had been at work. She admitted to having a spat with her boyfriend the night before he died, but said it was minor, and the police believed her when she said she had nothing to do with the crime. Her story was too strange to be contrived.

What police thought was a love triangle turned out to be a more complex geometric shape, with more lines added as time went on. In January 1965, prosecutor John Corrigan received a call from a local businessman, who brought Corrigan a revolver he said was carried by Richards on the night he was killed. Richards often carried large amounts of jewelry and cash and wanted a weapon for protection. The man said the gun was given to him by Mary Kratovich, the sister-in-law of John Vanatta, who, in partnership with Richards, owned the Howard Johnson's Motor Lodge where Richards' body was found. Corrigan then found a Cleveland police officer who said he'd sold the gun to Richards in 1962 for $45.

A night clerk at the hotel said she heard Vanatta tell a number of people that he wanted to "take care of" Richards. She also said Vanatta had asked her to monitor phone calls between Richards and Vanatta's wife Helen, who he suspected were carrying on an affair.

Other clues began to emerge. Keys to Richards' Strongville hotel room were found in a field and traced to Vanatta. Then came the state's star witness, 31-year-old Donald Beatty, who had been dating the married Mary Kratovich for the past two years.

Beatty said that on the day Richards was killed, John and Helen Vanatta asked him to go with them and "scare someone." They got into a car and picked up Richards and brought him back to Vanatta's house. Vanatta gave Beatty a gun and told him to hold it on Richards and then took a baseball bat (a Little League model according to Beatty) and beat Richards with it. Richards fell to the ground and begged Vanatta not to hit him again but Vanatta continued beating him until Richards was dead. Vanatta and Beatty then put Richards' body into the trunk of his car and drove to the spot where it was found the next day. Perhaps the motive was jealousy over a suspected affair between Richards and his wife, or maybe it was a dispute Vanatta and Richards were having over the operation of the hotel.

In 1966, Vanatta was charged with first degree murder. His trial lasted seven weeks and several witnesses testified that Vanatta had asked them to kill Richards. Mrs. Kratovich said that Vanatta showed her a $1,500 watch he'd taken from Richards, plus $500 in cash he'd found in the car. Her boyfriend, Kratovich lamented, had only gotten "a lousy $3 from Richards' trouser pocket."

Corrigan was called as a witness, which required him to take a break from the Sam Sheppard trial, which was taking place at the same time. Sheppard was the physician who'd been convicted of murdering his wife in 1954 in a much-publicized case. The conviction was overturned by the Supreme Court and Corrigan was the lead prosecutor in the 1966 re-trial. Sheppard was acquitted, which was a better result than Vanatta achieved. After seven hours of deliberation, the jurors came back with a guilty verdict and Vanatta was sentenced to life in prison.

And people said not much happened in Cleveland.

Other sources:
    Willoughby News Herald, October 9, 1963
    Dover Daily Reporter, October 10, 1963
    Connellsville Daily Courier, October 10, 1963
    Sandusky Register, October 31, 1963
    Uniontown Morning Herald, October 25, 1966
    Uniontown Evening Standard, October 12, 1966
    Lima News, October 6, 1966
    Monessen Valley Independent, October 7, 1966
    https://www.encyclopedia.com/law/law-magazines/samuel-sheppard-trials-1954-and-1966

Public Flogging Seems Near an End in Delaware
New York Times, February 2, 1964

If you ask people when they think public flogging finally became illegal in the United States, most would say it was in the 18th century or, at the latest, the nineteenth. They would be very wrong, for in 1964, a time when many of us were alive, flogging was still legal in Delaware. America's first state had banned the pillory in 1905, but there were still 24 different offenses, including horse stealing and burning a courthouse, that could be punished with a flogging sentence of up to 60 lashes.

Delaware was the last holdout. Even the armed forces didn't use corporal punishment anymore. Flogging was banned on all U.S. Naval ships in 1850, and in August 1861, shortly after the start of the Civil War, it was abolished in the Army. Neighboring Maryland had eliminated the practice 11 years earlier and had not had a flogging since 1938. Indiana had a whipping as late as 1963, when a man received 20 strokes with a leather belt for setting fire to a stray dog.

One might assume that although flogging was technically legal in Delaware, it was an archaic law that remained on the books but was never imposed. That would also be incorrect, for Kent County had recently installed a new whipping post, and the reason the *Times* ran their story was because Delaware Superior Court Judge Stewart Lynch had recently imposed two whipping post sentences.

Flogging in Delaware had a long history, dating back to colonial times. The first reported incident occurred in 1654 when Marcus Jacobson was convicted of sedition and whipped, branded, and sold to a planter in Barbados. In 1679, a woman named Agnieta Hendricks received 27 lashes for bearing two children out of wedlock. Apparently, the punishment did not have the desired effect, for Hendricks had a third illegitimate child a year later, for which she received 37 lashes.

Whipping was officially incorporated into the Delaware penal code in 1717. In 1794, Governor Gunning Bedford succeeded in having it eliminated, but in 1819 a citizens' petition brought it back. In 1883, flogging for juveniles was eliminated and six years later, women were exempted from the lash. Although adult men could still be sent to the whipping post, few were. At the time Judge Lynch imposed his sentences, the last person who'd been flogged was John Barbieri, who took 20 lashes in 1952 for beating a woman after breaking into her house.

Red Hannah (or Hanna) and Old Susan were the nicknames, used since colonial times, for the red whipping post located in the yard of the Kent County Correctional Institute, and victims were described as "hugging Red Hannah." Anyone hugging Red Hannah was certain to draw a crowd, and the occasional whippings that took place during the first half of the 20th century generally attracted one to two thousand spectators. The more the better, for public humiliation was the main idea of flogging, and how could that occur without a healthy representation of the public?

Robert Caldwell, a professor of criminology at the University of Iowa, wrote a book called *Red Hanna: A Study of Whipping in Delaware*. He examined floggings from 1900–1942 and claimed that there was no reason to believe that being whipped reduced recidivism. He also noted that the majority of the whippees were poor black men. As part of his research, Caldwell attended a couple of lashings and reported that the whippers were not as brutal as they might have been. He said they generally used a stiff-arm technique, rather than really letting fly, and that while the skin of the victims had been reddened, there had been no blood.

8. Mad Dogs and Skyjackers

The two men sentenced by Judge Lynch were both habitual criminals. Forty-year-old Talmadge Balsar's most recent transgression was robbing a man named Robert Wilson of four dollars. Lynch's original sentence, issued in March 1963, was 20 lashes ("with a cat o' nine tails inflicted publicly on the bare back well laid on") and 25 years in prison. Lynch was ordered by the appellate court to amend the sentence, which he did—to 10 lashes and 15 years.

Nineteen-year-old Francis J. Cannon, Jr., was an eighth-grade dropout who had a juvenile record dating back to the time he was 12. He had been committed to the Ferris School for Boys in Wilmington in 1959 and psychiatrists branded him a sociopath. On December 4, 1961, Cannon was sentenced to 20 lashes and 3 years in prison, but the sentence was suspended. He had been arrested several times since, once just four days after being convicted of another crime.

Cannon's flogging sentence was the result of being arrested for stealing an automobile while on parole. Since automobiles weren't around when flogging was instituted, Judge Lynch apparently considered the crime the modern equivalent of horse theft. "This boy just doesn't seem to respond," he said. "I don't know if he's laughing up his sleeve at us."

Lynch thought that flogging was so humiliating that it might reform even the most hardened criminal. "I know just one thing," he said. "In my thirty years of practice, I learned that criminals feared the lash more than serving time." He said that those who wanted to eliminate the practice were "bleeding hearts and nice nellies."

Lynch was not a backwoods country jurist. He was a 63-year-old graduate of Harvard Law School who had been appointed to the bench by Governor Elbert N. Carvell in 1961. Despite the controversy created by his draconian sentencing habits, Lynch remained a judge until he retired in 1968.

Franklin Cannon appealed his case to the U.S. Supreme Court, which ruled that whipping was not unconstitutional under either state or federal law. The *Ironwood Daily Globe*, however, when reporting that flogging was not unconstitutional, felt obligated to point out that "There remains a considerable controversy in some states, however, over whipping in public schools."

The fact that flogging was legal did not mean that it was popular; Lynch was roundly criticized by civil libertarians, sociologists, and penologists. Governor Carvell said that the sentences were an embarrassment to the state and that he would do whatever he could to prevent them from being carried out.

Neither Cannon nor Balsar was ever flogged. Carvell, following a recommendation of the Board of Pardons, commuted Balsar's sentence. On August 28, 1964, Lynch withdrew his order to flog Cannon.

On July 6, 1972, Governor Russell Peterson signed a law removing the

Delaware flogging penalty, with one exception. Lashings were still permitted for anyone defacing a legislative bill. The legislature was prepared to be more lenient toward pedophiles, wife beaters, and murderers, but not toward anyone who would dare tamper with the dignity of the legislature. That lone exception was finally removed in 1986. In 1975, there was an attempt to reinstate flogging, but a petition did not gather enough signatures. In 1989, a Senate bill proposing whippings for drug crimes died in committee.

Apparently, nothing could stop the criminal career of Frederick Cannon. In August 1964, just as Judge Lynch dropped his whipping sentence, he was arrested on a charge of passing bad checks. It was discovered that he had done the same thing on three previous occasions.

Richard Nixon did a lot of bad things during his presidency, but it was during his administration, not the liberal administrations of Roosevelt, Kennedy, or Johnson, that public whippings were finally outlawed in the United States. Perhaps it was self-serving, for Delaware is not that far from Washington, and if many Americans had their way, Nixon might have been hugging Red Hannah. But Nixon was spared, as is any future President, horse thief, or defacer of legislative bills. There are no more whippings in Delaware.

Other sources:
    Hanover Evening Sun, January 9, 1964
    Boone News Republican, January 25, 1964
    Ironwood Daily Globe, January 22, 1964
    Salisbury Daily Times, December 30, 1964
    Lebanon Daily News, November 15, 1962
    Abilene Reporter News, December 7, 1962
    El Paso Herald Post, November 15, 1962
    Kittanning Simpson Leader, December 13, 1962
    High Tide News, February 2017

Sinatra Witness Tells of Plot Tip
New York Times, February 25, 1964

The kidnapping of Frank Sinatra, Jr., was one of the strangest crimes of the 1960s. Was it, as defense counsel claimed, a publicity stunt in which he participated? Was another famous singer in cahoots with the kidnappers? Since it involved Frank Sinatra, was the Mafia somehow part of the equation?

The kidnapping involved famous people but the perpetrators, although they were a peripheral part of the Hollywood "in" crowd, were quite common. The mastermind behind the abduction was 23-year-old Barry Keenan and his accomplices were his high school friend Joe Amsler and John Irwin, a 42-year-old house painter who was the ex-boyfriend of Keenan's mother.

Keenan and Amsler were graduates of University High School in West

8. Mad Dogs and Skyjackers

Los Angeles, where Nancy Sinatra was one of their classmates. Keenan had been invited to the Sinatra home on several occasions. He briefly attended UCLA but dropped out and become the youngest member of the Los Angeles Stock Exchange. After he was injured in a car accident, however, Keenan's promising business career collapsed. He became addicted to painkillers, lost his job, and was arrested for a couple of minor transgressions. His mind addled by his drug addiction, Keenan hatched a plan to generate the capital he believed he needed to revive his career.

Keenan's plan was to kidnap the son of a wealthy entertainer and use the ransom money for investments. He thought about kidnapping Bob Hope's son Tony or one of Bing Crosby's sons, but settled on Sinatra because he thought Frank, Jr., was tough enough to withstand the ordeal. In his twisted state of mind, he believed he was bringing the Sinatra family closer together, and intended to repay the money with interest after he was back on his feet.

Targeting the Sinatra family was probably not the smartest thing Kennan ever did. As the mobmuseum.com website pointed out in 2014, "Probably the last person in the world you would want on your bad side would be Frank Sinatra, the famous singer and actor with an equally infamous temper and a host of friends in the Mob, in politics and in entertainment. But that's exactly what a couple of young men in California set out to do 51 years ago."

Keenan created a 27-page plan for the kidnapping and wrote a rambling explanatory letter to his friends and family, which he placed in his safe deposit box. Since he had no funds to finance the caper, Keenan turned to his close friend Dean Torrance, half of the Jan and Dean singing group that had just had a #1 single called *Surf City*. He told Torrance of his plan, showed him the 27-page document, and asked to borrow $1,000.

Torrance thought the plan was crazy and that Keenan would never follow through, but he gave him the money, saying later that he thought he was just covering his friend's living expenses. Several of Keenan's friends heard of his plan, but they didn't take him seriously.

Keenan followed young Sinatra and made a few aborted attempts. He then asked Amsler, who like Keenan had a minor criminal record, to accompany him to Lake Tahoe, where the 19-year-old Sinatra was in the midst of a three-week engagement at Harrah's Club Lodge with the Tommy Dorsey Orchestra.

After the December 8th show, as Sinatra sat in his dressing room in his underwear munching on a leg of fried chicken, Keenan entered his room on the pretense of delivering a package. He pulled a gun, bound Sinatra's companion with tape, blindfolded the singer, and led him to a car, where Amsler was waiting.

Sinatra's companion quickly freed himself and called the police, who set up a series of roadblocks. Keenan and Amsler were stopped, but talked their way through and drove to a home Keenan had rented in Canoga Park. Keenan then drove back to Lake Tahoe, went skiing, and checked out of his room to establish an alibi.

Frank Sinatra, Sr., who was filming the movie *Robin and the 7 Hoods*, was contacted in Reno and told to go to a Chevron service station on December 10 and wait for a call on the pay phone. The drama unfolded like a prank call about having Prince Albert in a can. The phone rang, a mechanic answered and heard, "Is Frank Sinatra there?" He brusquely said that Sinatra was not there and hung up. A second call followed, and the man angrily said he was working on a car and that the caller should stop bothering him.

Suddenly, a black car came screeching into the parking lot. Sinatra jumped out and said, "I'm Frank Sinatra. Have I had any calls?" Irwin, whose job it was to make contact with the Sinatra family, called again and Sinatra answered. He said he would pay a million dollars to get his son released, but Irwin said they only wanted $240,000. He told Sinatra to leave the money in a suitcase between two school buses at a designated drop spot in Sepulveda. Irwin put Frank, Jr., on the phone and he assured his father that he was alive and unharmed.

Sinatra received offers of assistance from such diverse sources as Attorney General Robert Kennedy and mobster Sam Giancana, but took the advice of the FBI and agreed to pay the money, which the FBI photographed before placing it in a suitcase.

The money was delivered, but before it was picked up, Irwin panicked and released Sinatra at 2:30 a.m. on December 11. He'd been held captive for 54 hours, sometimes blindfolded, at other times placed in the trunk of Keenan's car. The young singer walked a few miles before encountering a security guard, who called the police. The FBI arrived and took Sinatra away, concealed in the trunk of their car to avoid publicity.

Irwin, who had a criminal record dating back to 1947, proved a less than trustworthy accomplice. He told his brother what had happened and his brother called the police. In the meantime, Keenan had gone to see Dean Torrance, who, despite being a famous entertainer, was a full-time student living with his parents. Keenan offered to repay the money Torrance had loaned him and left a bag containing $25,000 in the shower. Torrance returned the money to Keenan two days later.

All three conspirators were soon in custody. Keenan was arrested in Imperial Beach, near the Mexican border, with $47,938 of the ransom money in his possession. Another $168,927 was found in Amsler's apartment when he was arrested. A small amount was discovered in the safe deposit box Keenan shared with Torrance, where the FBI also found Keenan's letter confessing the crime.

The three men went on trial in February. One of the highlights of the proceedings was the testimony of Dean Torrance. Torrance first said he knew nothing of the kidnap plot, but then recanted his testimony and admitted that he was aware of it. The defense attorneys acknowledged that their clients had kidnapped Sinatra, but claimed that the entire episode was a plot by the Sinatra family to gain publicity for young Frank's career. Given the fact that all of the principals had grown up together and that Frank, Sr., was long rumored to be involved in organized crime, they felt the jury might believe them. "If this was a kidnapping," said defense counsel George A. Forde, "I'll be on the next moon-shot." The defense case was bolstered when Sinatra, Jr., testified that he had hoped his kidnappers would get away with it.

Irwin's defense, which was weak, was that he became involved only in order to talk Keenan out of his crazy idea. The jury believed neither Irwin nor the claim that the Sinatra's were complicit and found all three defendants guilty. Keenan was sentenced to life plus 75 years in prison. Amsler and Irwin received lesser sentences. Torrance was never charged, and the judge praised him for his honesty.

Amsler and Irwin were each released after serving three and a half years. Keenan was freed after four and a half years when it was determined that he was legally insane at the time he committed the crime. After Keenan was released, Torrance threw a fund raiser for him.

Keenan, who'd been a stockbroker before embarking on his kidnapping career, became a successful real estate developer. Married and divorced three times, he developed resort and casino properties and, after a few failures, finally found his footing. In addition to his resort properties, Keenan developed a number of drug and alcohol rehabilitation centers. Dean Torrance was his partner in a series of hamburger joints.

Although Jan and Dean had a few more hit records, notably *Dead Man's Curve* and *The Little Old Lady from Pasadena*, a TV pilot they made was not picked up and they were cut out of a beach movie. Agents were reluctant to incur Frank Sinatra's wrath, and Jan and Dean found bookings more difficult to come by. Jan Barry was seriously injured in an automobile accident, and the more suspicious conspiracy theorists believed that perhaps Sinatra's underworld connections had tampered with his car.

Two defense attorneys, Forde and the flamboyant Gladys Towles Root, were indicted on charges of inducing their clients to commit perjury. After a series of legal actions over several years, the charges were dismissed, but Root suffered serious damage to her professional reputation.

Frank Sinatra, Jr., died unexpectedly of cardiac arrest on March 16, 2016, while on tour. He was 72 years old.

Other sources:

https://www.fbi.gov/history/famous-cases/frank-sinatra-jr-kidnapping

https://en.wikipedia.org/wiki/Barry_Keenan
https://web.archive.org/web/20090227020354/http://www.history.com/this-day-in-history.do?action=Article&id=1214
https://themobmuseum.org/blog/fifty-one-years-later-frank-sinatra-jr-s-kidnapping-still-raises-questions/
http://people.com/celebrity/frank-sinatra-jr-s-kidnapping-barry-keenans-motive-details/
http://jananddean-janberry.com/blog/mysterious-financier-dean-torrence-and-the-kidnapping-of-frank-sinatra-jr/
Washington Post, March 17, 2016

Man Sets Up Guillotine to Kill Wife
The Morning Record (Meriden, CT), October 14, 1965

Twenty-five-year-old Leslie Bolin and his 21-year-old wife, Jeanette, were having marital problems. The Norton, Ohio, couple had separated, but when their year-old son was hospitalized, Leslie went to visit him. Jeanette was already there, and when her husband invited her to dinner, she accepted.

After dinner, things turned ugly. Leslie pulled out a gun and forced his wife into his car and drove her to an abandoned house in nearby Akron. He dragged her inside, gagged her with a stocking, tied her hands behind her back, and jabbed her in the legs with pins. He took Jeanette down to the basement where, to her horror, she saw a guillotine. The blade was raised, and there was a tub placed in position to catch her severed head.

Leslie forced Jeanette to place her head on the block, but as she knelt there in terror, waiting for the blade to drop, her husband changed his mind. He untied her, the two of them disassembled the guillotine, and Leslie drove Jeanette back to the hospital, where she had left her car.

As soon as Leslie was out of sight, Jeanette called the police. They arrested Leslie and drove to the Akron house, where they found the guillotine. "I was going to kill my wife," Bolin told the police, "but I couldn't go through with it. I love her too much." Bolin went to prison, unable to post a $100,000 bond, while a judge ordered a psychiatric evaluation, which was probably a good idea.

In December 1966, Bolin pleaded guilty to assault and was sentenced to one-to-five years in prison.

Other sources:
El Paso Herald Post, December 7, 1966
Twin Falls Times News, January 6, 1967
Idaho Free Press, August 4, 1966
Las Vegas Sun, July 11, 1966
Washington Court House Record, July 19, 1966
Bluefield Daily Telegraph, July 11, 1966

8. Mad Dogs and Skyjackers

Delaware County Daily Times, July 11, 1966
Oxnard Press Courier, July 11, 1966
El Paso Herald Post, July 11, 1966
Salt Lake Tribune, July 12, 1966
Butte Montana Standard, July 12, 1966

500G Bank Suspect Caught in Vegas

New York Daily News, April 1, 1967

On the morning of July 14, 1966, officials at the Fontana branch of California's Security National Bank found that they couldn't open the vault. It been jammed shut, and it wasn't until the next day that they were able to get inside. When they did, they discovered that $197,528 in cash and $377,528 in blank travelers' checks, money orders, and bank checks were missing.

Roger Lee Williams was also missing. The 27-year-old Williams had been an employee at the Fontana branch before becoming an assistant cashier and operations officer at Security National's Riverside headquarters. He had spent a month planning the caper and used a paper clip to prop the vault open the night before. After taking the funds, Williams left his 32-year-old wife Joanne behind and disappeared with his daughters Rochelle, 4, and Kelly, 3.

Nothing was heard from Williams or his daughters until Halloween, when Joanne answered the door at her Rialto home to find a woman and the two Williams girls, in costume. The woman said she was a babysitter who'd been hired by a man at a hotel and asked to take the girls trick-or-treating and leave them at the Rialto address. The woman also handed Joanne an envelope containing $4,000. Mrs. Williams was relieved to have her daughters back safely, and the money was welcome, for since her husband had disappeared, Joanne had been living on a $250 monthly check from the State of California.

Roger Williams continued to evade detection until March 31, 1967. Those were the days before what happened in Vegas stayed in Vegas, and it was in the gambling capital that Williams' luck ran out. He'd gone to see the movie *How to Succeed in Business Without Really Trying*, and whether it was the movie or something else, he had a premonition he was going to be caught that day.

He was right. After the movie, he went to a casino, where he had a stroke of incredibly bad luck. Williams found himself standing near an attractive 37-year-old former waitress named Doris Burton, who was sitting at a blackjack table with her husband Ed.

Burton had an excellent memory for faces. Even though Williams had grown a mustache and dyed his hair, she recognized him as a customer she had waited on in Rialto six years earlier. She also remembered that Williams was wanted for bank robbery. Burton approached a casino security officer and told him of her suspicions. The guard called the police, and soon Williams found himself in the Clark County jail.

Once he was in custody, Williams readily admitted his identity and said that since the previous December 9th he had been living in an upscale motel in Pinedale, California, under the name of Robert Moore. When reporters interviewed Mr. and Mrs. Frank Weddell, the owners of the motel, they said Williams was a wonderful guest, certainly not someone they would have suspected of being on the lam. He attended church, was friendly to everyone, and never caused any trouble. "I have never been around anyone with a sweeter disposition," said Mrs. Weddell.

When police searched Williams' room, they found $67,000 in cash in three suitcases. An additional $65,000 was in his car and another $15,000 in a Las Vegas hotel room. There was $250,000 secreted in various locations, which Williams identified to the police.

In total, the bank recovered all of the checks and all but about $40,000 of the cash, which Williams said he had lost gambling. Delighted to have gotten most of their money back, Security National paid Mrs. Burton a $5,000 reward. "Many people think I'm a rat fink for turning him in," Burton said. She didn't feel guilty, for she assumed Williams was going to get caught eventually and someone would get the reward. Why shouldn't it be her?

The other woman in the case, Joanne Williams, sued for divorce, but said she wanted to talk to her husband to see whether she had done anything that drove him to his criminal act. Williams' parents put up their house and $2,500 in cash to bail him out, and he lived with them until his trial.

On July 12, 1967, Williams pleaded guilty to one count of larceny, while three other counts were dismissed. "I took the money. That's basically it," he said after the hearing. "I would not call it a spree. It was more deeply rooted than that, but I cannot explain." "He was a very sick boy when he stole the money," his attorney added, and said he intended to present psychological evidence at the sentencing hearing.

Williams was sentenced in early August. His attorney said that during the summer of 1966, Williams had financial problems, his marriage was coming apart, and his job had changed. Those factors, he said, had produced "anxiety neurosis" that caused him to contemplate suicide. Instead, he decided to rob the bank. The judge imposed the maximum sentence of 10 years, subject to reduction after a final presentation of the psychological evidence. After hearing the evidence, the judge reduced the sentence to eight years.

Other sources:
Pasadena Independent, April 7, 1967, and April 11, 1967
Press Telegram (Long Beach, California), April 1, 1967

8. Mad Dogs and Skyjackers

Bakersfield Californian, April 5, 1967
Redlands Daily Facts, June 13, 1967, August 3, 1967, August 1, 1967, and November 10, 1967

Warhol Gravely Wounded in Studio; Actress is Held

New York Times, June 4, 1968

On the afternoon of June 3, 1968, artist Andy Warhol, clad in boots, trousers, and a brown leather jacket, was in his stark movie studio talking on the telephone to Viva, an actress who was Warhol's latest "superstar." Viva, a 25-year-old blond whose real name was Susan Hoffmann, was the daughter of a Syracuse attorney and had recently starred as The Waitress in one of Warhol's films, *The Nude Restaurant*. The *New York Times* described her as a "lanky, dreaming, extremely loquacious type who is quite nude throughout the formless proceedings."

Viva, who'd just signed to play in the movie *Midnight Cowboy* with Dustin Hoffman and Jon Voigt, was one of several actresses, including Marlo Montez, Ingrid Superstar, and National Velvet, that Warhol featured in his work. Warhol called them superstars but, as one journalist pointed out, they were women "whose thespian ineffectualities [are] the basis of their stardom."

Warhol was 39, a thin man of average height whose most notable characteristic was his lank, longish hair that was streaked with silver. He'd been born in Pittsburgh, attended the Carnegie Institute of Technology, and began his career as a fashion illustrator. After he moved to New York in 1960, Warhol began to create unique, unconventional works of art.

Warhol's work, branded "pop art," included paintings of everyday commercial objects, such as the iconic Campbell's Soup can and a Coca Cola bottle. He produced box sculptures—stacks of containers (such as Brillo boxes) that one might find on any supermarket shelf. Warhol was also renowned for photographic silk screen prints of celebrities like Marilyn Monroe, Elvis Presley, and Jackie Kennedy. He was an enigma to most Americans and a joke to many. "Andy Warhol could only have happened in the '60s," said one observer.

In the mid–1960s, Warhol turned to film, producing odd works like *Sleep*, a five-and-a-half-hour movie of poet John Giorno sleeping, *Eat*, which was four hours of a man eating a mushroom, and an eight-hour home movie of the Empire State Building. There were other equally strange films, taken with amateurish techniques on 16mm film. Warhol was quite productive, averaging one film a week; a movie about a sleeping man didn't require a complex script. Warhol's movies were characterized as underground film, starring women like Viva, Ultra Violet, and National Velvet and featuring non-descript plots. They were the precursor to Jerry Seinfeld's show about nothing, except they were not funny.

Warhol's most famous movie was *The Chelsea Girls*, a film about the lives of the occupants of New York's famous Chelsea Hotel. The *Chelsea Girls* had a lot of sex and it made a lot of money, grossing more than $500,000 with a production cost of less than $5,000. It was the first of Warhol's films to reach a popular audience.

Warhol's East 47th Street studio, known as the Silver Factory, became a social phenomenon where Warhol was the sun around which his worshipful stars revolved. Decorated with silver paint and aluminum foil, the Silver Factory, sometimes referred to simply as The Factory, was the scene of parties attended by a unique group of "celebrities" and friends. Musician Lou Reed was a regular, as were many of Warhol's home-grown stars. In 1967, Warhol moved from The Factory to a space at 33 Union Square West, which consisted of just two large rooms. One was a studio and the second was the room in which Warhol stood on June 3, 1968.

With Warhol in the studio were Mario Amayo, editor of a London publication called *Arts and Artists*, and Warhol's manager, Fred Hughes. About two hours earlier, a young woman had come to the studio and asked for Warhol. When told he was not there, she left. At about 4:20, while Warhol was on the phone with Viva, the elevator opened, and the same woman stepped into the studio. She argued briefly with Warhol's assistant, who left to go to the bathroom, leaving the woman with Warhol, Amayo, and Hughes. Seconds later, Viva heard "five shots and a lot of screaming." At first, she thought it was a joke, but then she heard the phone drop to the floor. While she held the open line to her ear, Warhol lay writhing on the floor with a bullet in his abdomen and two in his side.

Amayo was facing away from Warhol and thought the shots were coming from outside. "Then I noticed a revolver," he said, "like one of those guns you see in Dick Tracy in her hand." He heard Warhol call the woman by her name and shout "Oh, no," as he was hit. She fired again and hit Amayo but inflicted only a superficial flesh wound in his back. When she tried to shoot Hughes, her gun jammed.

The assailant backed calmly toward the elevator and stepped inside. The doors closed and she was gone, leaving behind a bag containing her address book. After unsuccessfully trying to jam the elevator apparatus, Amayo called for an ambulance and Warhol was rushed to Columbus Hospital. He spent more than four hours in surgery and doctors gave him a 50–50 chance of survival.

The shooter was Valerie Solanas, a 32-year-old writer whose play, *Up Your Ass*, had recently been rejected by Warhol, who found it so obscene

8. Mad Dogs and Skyjackers

that he told the *Times* he thought she was trying to entrap him. In order to placate her, Warhol paid her $25 to act in his film, *I, a Man*.

Solanas was a petite, 5'3" lesbian who dressed in masculine clothing and usually wore her hair tied up in order not to appear too feminine, although contemporary photos indicate there was not much danger of that. The previous year, she had founded an organization called the Society for Cutting Up Men, known by the acronym S.C.U.M. Her S.C.U.M manifesto, which she sold for a dollar to men and 25 cents to women, ran 21 pages and began:

"Life in this society being at best an utter bore and no aspect of society being at all relevant to women, there remains to civic-minded, responsible, thrill-seeking females only to overthrow the government, eliminate the money system, institute complete automation and eliminate the male sex."

Apparently, the first member of the male sex she wanted to eliminate was Andy Warhol, and it appeared that she had succeeded.

Amayo was able to describe Solanas to the police and they went looking for her. In the meantime, she came looking for them. At about 8 o'clock, Solanas walked up to Patrolman William Schemalix in Times Square and said, "The police are looking for me and want me."

Solanas was eclectically dressed, wearing torn sneakers, khaki jeans, a blue turtleneck sweater, a yellow knit sweatshirt, and a trench coat, seemingly more layers than were needed on a June afternoon when temperatures were in the 60s. She had two pistols in the pockets of her trench coat and when the police examined them, they found that one of them had recently been fired. Solanas was taken to the West 30th Street station and charged with felonious assault and possession of a deadly weapon.

Valerie Solanas was suddenly a public figure, and during the succeeding days, the public learned about her strange life. She'd been born into a dysfunctional family; her parents divorced when she was young and she rebelled against her mother and stepfather, eventually being sent to live with her grandparents. While just a teenager, Solanas had a son, who was put up for adoption. Despite her tribulations, she managed to graduate from high school, earn a degree in psychology from the University of Maryland, and take graduate courses at the University of Minnesota. After moving to New York City, she wrote, panhandled, and dabbled in prostitution. One of her published pieces was an article for *Cavalier* magazine in which Solanas described having sex with another woman while men paid $25 each to watch.

Warhol's studio was not Solanas's first stop on June 3. She visited a number of people, looking for someone to publish her play, and eventually wound up at the residence of producer Margo Eden in Crown Heights, Brooklyn. Solanas spent four hours with Eden, and when the producer said she wasn't interested, Solanas pulled out a gun. She said Eden should produce her play because she was going to shoot Andy Warhol, which would make her famous and draw attention to the play.

After Solanas left, Eden contacted multiple police departments and the offices of Mayor John Lindsay and Governor Nelson Rockefeller, telling them that Solanas intended to shoot Warhol. They told her they couldn't arrest Solanas for that and said they thought she was making it up.

She wasn't, and within hours, Warhol was in critical condition and Solanas was in custody, making a series of strange statements. First, she demanded that the *Times* retract its headline claim that she was an actress. She was a writer, Solanas insisted. "It's not every day that I shoot somebody," she told the judge. "I didn't do it for nothing." She said Warhol had too much control over her life. The judge sent her to Bellevue Hospital for analysis.

Solanas was declared unfit to stand trial and committed to Matteawan State Hospital for the Criminally Insane. In June 1969, she was declared fit, pleaded guilty to "reckless assault with intent to harm," and was sentenced to three years in prison.

Released in 1971, Solanas began stalking Warhol and was arrested again in November. She drifted, spending time in mental institutions, and was sometimes homeless. Solanas continued to promote her anti-male manifesto and was hailed as a hero by some of the more radical feminists, including Ti-Grace Atkinson. A leaflet distributed by one feminist group read: "ANDY WARHOL SHOT BY VALARIE SOLANAS—PLASTIC MAN VS. THE SWEET ASSASSIN ... NON-MAN SHOT BY THE REALITY OF HIS DREAM. A TOUGH CHICK WITH A BOP CAP AND A .38 [sic] ... VALARIE [sic] IS OURS." The Warhol shooting was the last most Americans heard of Solanas, however. She died of pneumonia in 1988 at the age of 52.

Although Warhol survived, he lived the rest of his life in fear that Solanas would attack him again. The shooting had caused permanent damage to eight of his organs and required him to wear a corset for the rest of his life. But Warhol continued to work. In the late 1960s, he added publishing to his repertoire, co-founding *Interview* magazine in 1969 and publishing *The Philosophy of Andy Warhol (From A to B and Back Again)* in 1975. His final work, *The Andy Warhol Diaries*, tracked his life from 1976 through 1987.

On February 22, 1987, Warhol died at the age of 58 from complications following surgery to remove his gall bladder.

Other sources:
>   http://time.com/3901488/andy-warhol-valerie-solanas/
>   https://en.wikipedia.org/wiki/Valerie_Solanas
>   https://www.warhol.org/andy-warhols-life/
>   https://www.biography.com/people/andy-warhol-9523875
>   *Independent Press Telegram*, April 18, 1971
>   *Wisconsin State Journal*, June 10, 1968

Eureka Times Standard, June 30, 1968
Lowell Sun, June 4, 1968
Kensosha News, June 26, 1968
Pasadena Independent, June 4, 1968
https://en.wikipedia.org/wiki/I_Shot_Andy_Warhol

Italian Factions Back Minchiello; Extradition Proceedings Started to Gain Custody of Minichiello

New York Times, November 3, 1969

Criminals keep up with technology. When rail travel was introduced, they began robbing trains. When the automobile made people more mobile, they became better at escaping after robbing banks. When air travel became commonplace, they began hijacking planes.

While criminals were on the cutting edge, law enforcement always seemed to be a step behind. It took railroads a while before they were able to safeguard their passengers and cargo. When the bank robbers of the 1930s began using fast cars to cross state borders and elude local police, it took a while before crime fighting became the job of the federal government.

When the airline industry began routinely flying civilians all over the country, little thought was given to security. Most safety concerns involved the possibility of a crash, and almost no one worried that a passenger might be dangerous. In the early days of air travel, passengers were important people; common folk stayed on the ground. When more and more people began to rely on airplanes to get around, the airlines did not adapt. Eastern Airlines began experimenting with metal detectors but never considered requiring every passenger to be screened. Airline personnel were asked to screen anyone they thought looked suspicious. That left it to the judgment of a few individuals, and it was very easy to board a commercial airliner carrying a gun, a knife, or a box of explosives.

In the late 1960s and early 1970s, there were nearly 300 hijackings. The most common destination was Cuba, where hijackers expected to be greeted with open arms, since relations between that country and the United States were hostile. Diverting planes to Cuba became so common that airlines established a protocol to deal with the situation. They cooperated with the hijackers in the interest of passenger safety and pilots were given maps of the Caribbean and taught a few phrases that allowed them to communicate in Spanish if necessary.

When hijackers landed in Havana, however, they were invariably disappointed, for Fidel Castro was highly suspicious of them, fearing they might be CIA operatives. Once they landed, they were put into prisons or work gangs, and it wasn't long before they wanted nothing more than to return to the United States, which didn't seem so bad after all. Other countries were likewise reluctant to grant asylum to hijackers, fearing it would lead to more hijackings.

Not all hijackers wanted to go to Cuba. Italy was the preferred destination of twenty-year-old Raffaele Minichiello, who had been born in Melito Urpino but moved to Seattle as a teenager. He served 13 months in Vietnam with the Marines, earning a Purple Heart. Like so many American youths, he was disillusioned by his experience in Southeast Asia, and when he was shipped back to Camp Pendleton in southern California, his troubles continued.

Minichiello believed that his pay had been $200 short and decided to use self-help to get it back. One night in May, after downing a six-pack of beer, he broke into the Post Exchange and stole exactly $200 worth of merchandise. He was caught and court-martialed but made up his mind to take flight before the sentence could be imposed.

The young Marine disassembled an M-1 rifle and packed it, along with 250 rounds of ammunition, in his bag before heading for Los Angeles International Airport, where he bought a ticket for a TWA flight to San Francisco. Once the plane was airborne, Minichiello went to the lavatory, assembled the rifle, came out and pointed it at a stewardess and demanded that the plane be diverted to New York. Since the Boeing 707 was anticipating a short flight, there wasn't enough fuel on board, and a stop had to be made in Denver.

In Denver, Minichiello released the 39 passengers, which included the pop band Harper's Bizarre, and three of the stewardesses. Once the plane and its four remaining crew members were airborne again, he told the crew that he really wanted to go to Rome, but that they should report the destination as Cairo in order to mislead authorities. Going overseas required another refueling stop, which was scheduled for JFK International in New York.

By that time, the FBI had been alerted and was waiting for the plane when it landed at Kennedy, much to the consternation of Captain Donald Cook. He had a man with an M-1 and plenty of ammunition on board and thought that the FBI was endangering the lives of the remaining crew members.

When the "refueling team" approached the aircraft, some of them were carrying guns, a most unusual piece of equipment for men who were supposedly going to dispense fuel into an airplane. Cook opened the window of the cockpit and screamed at them to get away from the plane. They continued moving forward and Minichiello fired a bullet into the roof of the cockpit.

Cook took off without his fuel and made another stop in Bangor, Maine, where there were no FBI agents, just a ground crew that pumped enough fuel into the plane to get it across the Atlantic. After they took off again, Minichiello was noticeably agitated. He was taking No-Doz tablets to stay awake, which did nothing to calm his jittery nerves. The crew thought that he was either going to kill them or kill himself.

The crew made one more stop in Shannon, Ireland, and finally arrived in Rome, where Minichiello took a police chief hostage and left the airport. Shortly afterward, he was discovered at Mass in the Sanctuary of Divine Love. It was All Saints Day, and apparently the devout young Catholic did not want to commit the sin of missing mass. When the priest noticed Minichiello wearing Bermuda shorts in church, he alerted police, who arrested the American hijacker. November 1 was not only All Saints Day; it was Minichiello's 20th birthday.

With Minichiello in custody, a multi-faceted drama began to play out. Captain Cook publicly blasted the FBI for endangering him and his crew. The United States began extradition proceeding in order to have the opportunity to try the Marine in American courts. Minichiello, who was a handsome young man, received numerous marriage proposals and an offer to appear in an Italian "spaghetti western" film. Producer Carlo Ponti, best known as Sophia Loren's husband, considered making a movie about his exploits.

The Italian government refused to extradite Minichiello. Anti-U.S. sentiment, attributable in part to the Vietnam War, ran high. Italy had no law against air piracy and Minichiello was only charged with weapons possession. He was convicted and sentenced to 18 months in prison, and upon his release he stayed in his former hometown, working as a waiter. When *Slate* wrote a story about him in 2013, he was still living there, a 64-year-old senior citizen with one very unusual story to tell.

Other sources:
New Yorker, February 17, 2014
Bangor Daily News, March 31, 2017
Slate, June 21, 2013

Hijacker Tells of Cuban Imprisonment
New York Times, **November 3, 1969**

In late 1969, six disillusioned American hijackers returned from Cuba to face trial. They'd risked their lives to get to the Communist nation, only to find that incarceration in the United States might be a better alternative. The hijacker identified in the *Times* headline was Robert Lee Sandlin, a 19-year-old from rural Texas who'd been in Cuban custody since he arrived in Havana in March. For the last two months, Sandlin had been housed in a mansion, where he was under guard but treated well and occasionally allowed to go into town.

Sandlin got back to the U.S. through Canada, where he'd arrived on a boat along with several other Americans. As soon as they crossed the U.S. border in Plattsburgh, New York, they were arrested. The other hijackers in Sandlin's group were Ronald Bohle, 22, Thomas Washington, 29, Joseph Crawford, 25, Thomas Boynton, 32, and Raymond Anthony, the oldest of the group at 55.

The six were the latest group of air pirates returning unsuccessfully from attempts to find happiness in a foreign land. The most famous of the previous hijackers was Alben Barkley Truitt, grandson of former Vice-President Alben Barkley, who diverted a chartered Cessna from Key West to Cuba in October 1968. Truitt was arrested when he landed and was eventually sent by sea to Canada. Like the six hijackers who surrendered in 1969, he crossed the border, was arrested, and sentenced to 20 years for air piracy and kidnapping.

Truitt's motive was more personal than political. He was in severe financial difficulty and, despite his privileged background, was unable to provide for his family. He chartered the plane on the pretense of taking photographs, but once airborne, he pulled out an explosive device and told the pilot to head for Havana. When they landed, Truitt told the Cubans he wanted to write a non-fiction book about their country. They were unimpressed and immediately put him in prison. After Truitt returned and told his sad tale, there was a noticeable decline in the number of hijackings, for virtually every person who diverted a plane to Cuba told a similar story on their return.

The six men who surrendered in Plattsburgh were brought before United States Commissioner Joseph W. Kelley, who added some levity to the proceedings. Kelley, who had been awakened at 4:00 a.m. for the hearing, said he was getting tired of being put to so much trouble for $4 per case. "For $24," he said, "I'm getting tired of being United States Commissioner."

When prisoner Raymond Anthony asked if he could smoke, Kelley replied, "Sure, but I hear that every cigarette takes 14 seconds off your life." Kelley's quip prompted a chuckle from the man facing a potential death sentence.

Sandlin, who was a communist who wanted to go to Cuba to be among kindred souls, had shown the pilot a shoebox filled with dynamite and told him to fly to Havana. Hijackings were so prevalent in 1968 that when Sandlin's plane landed, it parked next to a Peruvian jet than had been hijacked the same day. After his U.S. trial, Sandlin was committed to a psychiatric institution and released in 1973.

Anthony was a former used car dealer with serious financial problems. Many of the hijackers were inspired by dubious causes, but Anthony's was perhaps the strangest. He was sitting at home drinking when he received an unsolicited credit card application in the mail. For some reason, that

8. Mad Dogs and Skyjackers

enraged him and he drove to Baltimore and boarded an Eastern Airlines flight. With only a penknife, he convinced the crew to fly him to Havana. Anthony was not an ideologue with a Communist bent; he told the crew he was wearing Bermuda shorts and sandals because he planned to go to the beach. When he returned to the U.S., he was sentenced to 15 years in prison.

Crawford was another rebel without a cause who didn't seem to have any particular reason why he wanted to go to Cuba. He attracted the attention of one of the stewardesses with his repeated trips to the lavatory and when she asked him to remain seated, Crawford pulled out a knife and demanded that she take him up to the cockpit. He pointed his knife at the captain's ribs and said, "We're going to Cuba." He wound up in Plattsburgh with the rest, where he was sentenced to 50 years in prison. Crawford was paroled in 1990.

Thomas Washington was, like Anthony, a man with personal problems. He was an unemployed, divorced chemist with a three-year-old child. One day in December 1968, he snatched his daughter from his ex-wife and boarded an Eastern Airlines flight scheduled to go from Philadelphia to Miami. Once the plane was airborne, he handed a stewardess a note that read, "Dear Captain, this flight is going to Havana. I have a gun and nitroglycerine. I've studied chemistry."

Washington was highly emotional during the remainder of the flight. He cried and told the other passengers of the hatred and prejudice he faced as a black man, and how his mother-in-law was conspiring against him. When the plane landed in Havana, he apologized to the other passengers for having inconvenienced them and many of them shook his hand and wished him luck.

Washington's ex-wife flew to Havana to attempt to reclaim her daughter, but was unsuccessful. She finally obtained custody when her ex-husband arrived in Plattsburgh with the other prisoners. Washington was perhaps the most sympathetic of the six hijackers, and received the lightest sentence, two years for interfering with a flight crew.

Ronald Bohle was another young man with psychological problems who'd been discharged from the Navy after being diagnosed as a schizophrenic. Bohle enrolled in Purdue University North Central but left, deciding that he needed to find another society in which he could prosper. He thought Communism was the answer and told a stewardess, after pulling a knife on her, that he hated the United States and loved Russia. Bohle was convicted of air piracy and sentenced to 20 years in prison. He received a second trial in 1971, on the basis that his insanity defense was not sufficiently considered, but the result was the same—a 20-year sentence.

Thomas Boynton had started out well in life, as the son of a college chemistry professor, but Boynton's chemistry began to go astray when he entered his 30s. His wife, a go-go dancer, filed for divorce, and Boynton began drinking heavily. After he was fired from the Jobs Corps, his life completely unraveled. He decided that the capitalist system was the cause of his difficulties and that he would fare better under communism. After chartering a plane to fly him to Miami, he pulled a gun on the pilot and diverted it to Cuba. He wound up back in the United States with a 20-year sentence.

The crimes of the six men who surrendered in Plattsburgh did not result in any serious injuries, but occasionally the outcome of a hijacking was tragic. In 1973, a 35-year-old French woman named Daniele Cravenne, the wife of movie publicist and producer Georges Cravenne, took over an Air France flight bound for Nice. She was angry about her husband's film *The Mad Adventures of Rabbi Jacob*, which she thought was critical of Palestinians. Somehow, Cravenne believed that by hijacking the plane she could prevent the film's release.

Cravenne identified herself as a member of the Solidarity Movement for French-Israeli-Arab Reconciliation and made three demands. She wanted to stop the release of her husband's film, she wanted to be flown to Cairo, and she demanded that all motor traffic in France be stopped for 24 hours. The final demand seemed like something out of an old Woody Allen film, and it is unclear what it had to do with Palestine.

The pilot told Cravenne that the plane did not have sufficient fuel to reach Cairo and that he would need to make a refueling stop in Marseille. When they landed, Cravenne unwisely released the passengers and most of the crew. Several French policemen disguised as maintenance workers boarded the plane and shot her dead.

Three years earlier, another hijacking episode had a similarly tragic ending. On March 17, 1970, John DiVivo, a 27-year-old who'd put a bullet in his head in a failed suicide attempt eleven years earlier, took over an Eastern Airlines flight bound from Boston's Logan Airport to Newark.

DiVivo didn't seem to have a plan. He told the pilot to fly east until he ran out of fuel, seemingly oblivious to the fact that running out of fuel over the Atlantic Ocean would lead to no good. The captain convinced him that they needed to return to Boston and DiVivo agreed to let him turn the plane around. But as soon as the plane reversed course, he shot both the pilot and co-pilot. The co-pilot died, but before he did, he and the pilot managed to wrestle the gun away from DiVivo and shoot him.

DiVivo and the pilot survived, and somehow the latter landed the plane safely at Logan. DiVivo was arrested and charged with air piracy. In October 1970, while awaiting trial, he hung himself in his cell.

Perhaps the most unusual skyjacker, even though he wasn't successful, was 73-year-old John McReery, a World War I veteran. On August 5, 1969, McReery left for a fishing trip. When his Eastern Airlines flight took off from a scheduled stop in Charlotte en route to Tampa, McReery walked up to the cockpit and told the pilot he had a knife and wanted to go to Cuba.

When the pilot told him there wasn't enough fuel to get to Cuba, McReery returned to his seat.

When the plane landed, McReery was taken into custody. He said he merely wanted to simulate a hijacking, and after hearing his story, a judge declared him incompetent to stand trial.

Other sources:
http://skyjackeroftheday.tumblr.com
Life Magazine. April 18, 1969

Cockpit Gun Battle Climaxes $100 Million Skyjack Thriller

Bridgeport Post-Telegram, June 5, 1970

Arthur Barkley didn't want to go to Cuba. He had a grievance with the United States government and wanted money. Barkley was a 49-year-old truck driver and World War II veteran who believed that he had overpaid $471.78 in taxes. He waged a long legal battle to recover the money, attempting to take it all the way to the Supreme Court. His plea began, "I am being held a slave by the United States."

The Supreme Court denied Barkley's request for a hearing, and as he left home on June 4, 1970, he kissed his wife, told her, "I'm going to settle the tax case today," and went to the Phoenix airport and boarded a TWA flight headed for Washington's National Airport (now known as Reagan Airport). When the plane was over Albuquerque, Barkley walked into the cockpit with a .22-caliber pistol, a razor, and a can of gasoline (and to think people are now denied boarding rights if they have an oversized bottle of shampoo).

Barkley told the pilot he would incinerate everyone on board if he did not receive $100 million from the Supreme Court. The passengers were told that a scheduled stop in St. Louis had to be skipped because of weather problems, and the plane continued east toward Washington. Barkley forced the pilot to land at Dulles Airport, which was approximately 28 miles from National. TWA decided that they would meet Barkley's demand and withdrew $100,750 from two Washington banks. TWA Pilot Billy Williams, who'd previously volunteered to take over a plane hijacked to Rome, brought the money on board.

While $100,750 was far more than the $471.78 Barkley believed he had been overcharged, it was considerably less than $100 million, and the hijacker was incensed. He threw the money on the floor of the cockpit and ordered pilot Dale Hupe to get the plane back into the air. He told Hupe to send a radio message to President Nixon saying, "You don't know how to count money, and you don't even know the rules of law."

The plane circled Dulles for two hours. Passengers had been drinking during the ordeal, and several appeared to be inebriated. "The atmosphere was not tense," said passenger Christopher Smith, a college student. "You could call it a subdued cocktail party."

It was anything but a cocktail party in the cockpit, where Hupe and co-pilot Donald Salmonson dealt with the agitated Barkley, who spoke of suicide and rambled almost incoherently at times. In addition to sending messages to Nixon, he had Hupe contact the Supreme Court and various government agencies. He told the pilots he would give the airline one more chance to deliver the $100 million, a request they dutifully relayed by radio.

By this time, TWA had gotten the FBI involved and agents arrived at Dulles with one hundred mail sacks stuffed with newspaper scraps. They lined them up on the runway so that Barkley could see them and the hijacker told Hume to land.

As soon as the plane hit the ground, all hell broke loose. Two sharpshooters riding on the back of a fire truck shot out the landing gear. When he heard the gunfire, one of the passengers kicked out an emergency exit and climbed out on the wing. Other passengers followed. Barkley stuck his head out the cockpit window and shouted something.

The deplaning passengers scrambled on the grass as two FBI agents jumped onto a wing and climbed into the plane. Hupe tackled Barkley, who shot him in the stomach. Salmonson wrestled the gun away. The FBI agents then burst into the cockpit and shot Barkley in the hand. He was dragged off the plane and charged with air piracy.

Barkley's wife, who'd kissed him goodbye that morning without an inkling of the adventure that was about to unfold, stood by her husband. She said he "believes in the country and the constitution." In November 1971, Barkley was declared incompetent to stand trial and committed to a psychiatric institution.

Barkley's actions marked the beginning of a new era of skyjacking. Previous culprits had wanted to go to Cuba to live under Communism. Barkley and his successors wanted money. The famous D.B. Cooper parachuted from a hijacked plane in 1971 with $200,000 in ransom money and was never seen again.

Today, we don't have many skyjackings. There are some, most notably the September 2011 terrorist plot that destroyed the World Trade Center, but they are carefully planned operations, not the half-baked schemes perpetrated by the people profiled above. The numerous security measures implemented in reaction to the rash of hijackings of the late 1960s and early

1970s make it impossible to simply walk onto a plane with a pistol or a box of explosives. But during its heyday, skyjacking was all the rage.

Other sources:
> skyjackeroftheday.tumblr. skyjackeroftheday is a terrific collection of profiles of many hijackers, and is a teaser for a book called *The Skies Belong to Us—Love and Terror in the Golden Age of Hijacking* by Brendan I. Koerner

Oldest Convict

Hartford Courant, October 30, 1970

Prisoner O. John Weber was not a likely candidate to escape from Ohio's Chillicothe Correctional Institute. At 95 years of age and nearly blind, Weber was quite content to live out the remainder of his days at Chillicothe. He had spent 44 years in prison, was the oldest prisoner in the Ohio system, and was probably the oldest prisoner in the United States. "The world outside the walls is too strange and terrifying" a reporter wrote after talking to Weber, "and he is too old and feeble to cope with it."

Weber immigrated to the United States from Hungary in 1921 and five years later, while intoxicated, he grabbed a shotgun and threatened to kill his wife. Mrs. Weber was holding the couple's 18-month-old daughter, and when she tried to grab the gun, it went off and killed the little girl. Weber was convicted of first-degree murder and sentenced to life in prison, spared the electric chair only because the jury recommended mercy. He'd been in jail ever since.

Under Ohio law, those convicted of first-degree murder were not eligible for parole. In 1972, after Weber achieved a modicum of fame, Governor John J. Gilligan commuted his sentence to second degree murder, which opened up the possibility of parole. Weber was denied eight times, primarily because he didn't want to leave. Not only was the prospect of living outside the walls frightening; if he was released, Weber faced possible deportation to Hungary, which he'd last seen in 1921.

Weber stayed where he was and died in early 1976, at the age of 100, believed at the time to be the oldest prisoner in the world. Since he had little surviving family, St. Stephen the Martyr Catholic School provided him with a funeral and six junior high school boys served as pallbearers. A few nieces and nephews attended the service, but the majority of the congregation consisted of the 85 children from St. Stephen's. During his eulogy, the priest couldn't resist a slam at the prison system. "What does society want?" he demanded, "the last drop of blood for one mistake?"

It was only one mistake, but it was a big one, for which Weber spent the last 50 years of his life in prison. While he was the oldest person in prison at the time of his death, he was not the oldest to have been incarcerated, nor the oldest to die in prison. In his book, *A Century in Captivity*, Dennis Caron told the story of Prince Mortimer, captured and enslaved as a child in his native Guinea during the 18th century. Mortimer was a slave for 80 years before being sentenced to life imprisonment at the age of 87 for attempting to poison his master by lacing his chocolate drink with arsenic. He spent 16 years in the horrific Newgate Prison before passing away in 1827 at the age of 103.

Other sources:
    Central Ohio's Historic Prisons, by David and Elise Meyers, Arcadia Publishing, Charleston, SC, Chicago, IL, Portsmouth, NH, and San Francisco, CA, 2009
    Burlington Hawk Eye, November 4, 1970
    Gastonia Gazette, February 4, 1976
    A Century in Captivity, The Life and Trials of Prince Mortimer, a Connecticut Slave, by Denis Caron, New Hampshire Revisiting New England Series, 2006

Police Kill TV Assailant in Toronto
Hartford Courant, December 15, 1970

Brian "Spinner" Spencer played left wing in the National Hockey League from 1969 through 1979. Like many professional hockey players, he was a Canadian, and grew up in rural British Columbia. Spencer's family lived in primitive conditions, with few amenities, but his father, who ran a gravel pit, spared no expense or effort in his attempt to make his twin sons, Brian and Byron, into professional hockey players. He managed to buy them equipment and always found time to drive them to practice. Brian shared his father's dream and as a youngster his world revolved around hockey. He never finished high school, but in 1969 his dream was realized when Spencer was selected by the Toronto Maple Leafs in the NHL amateur draft.

Spencer spent most of the 1969–70 season with Tulsa of the Central Hockey League, but was called up late in the year and got into nine games with Toronto. He began the following season with Tulsa, but was summoned by Toronto in mid–December. The Maple Leafs were saddled with a losing record and thought Spencer, who had a reputation as a tough guy, might provide a spark.

Toronto had an 8–18–1 record when they took the ice for Spencer's first game of the season on Saturday, December 12, 1970, against the Black Hawks in Chicago. Brian had called his father to make sure he tuned in to the game on television, for he was scheduled to be an interview guest between periods. When Roy Spencer turned on his set, however, he found that the

8. Mad Dogs and Skyjackers

Canadian Broadcasting Corporation's Vancouver affiliate was carrying the game between the Vancouver Canucks and the Oakland Golden Seals.

Roy was a sick man at that point, suffering from emphysema and serious kidney disease. He'd been drinking that night and when he saw the Canucks and Golden Seals on his screen rather than his son, he became incensed. Spencer grabbed a 9mm pistol, jumped in his car, and drove 85 miles to the studio. Outside, he confronted newsman Tom Haertel and demanded to know why the Maple Leaf game was not on. When Haertel said the station had no discretion over which game they could carry, Spencer pulled his gun and dragged the newsman into the foyer.

Once the men were inside the studio, Spencer forced a technician to take the station off the air. He lined up seven employees against a table, began a rant against the CBC and said, "There's going to be a revolution soon in Canada."

"I was a commando," Spencer told his hostages. "I've killed before. But no one will get hurt if everyone's quiet." He said that the station had better remain off the air, and that if the broadcast resumed, he would hold them personally responsible. Then he left.

The police had been called, and by the time Spencer walked out the door, several members of the Canadian Mounted Police were waiting for him. One of them, Roger Post, told him to stop. Spencer fired at Post, striking his holster, and a second shot wounded a Mountie in the foot. The Mounties returned fire and Horton fell, mortally wounded in the shoulder, armpit, and mouth. He was dead when he arrived at Prince George Regional Hospital.

Brian Spencer learned of his father's death in the Maple Leaf locker room following the game, but he insisted on playing the next day. He played one more season for Toronto before being traded to the New York Islanders. The stocky, curly-haired wing was not terribly talented, but his tough play and aggressive style endeared him to the fans. After the 1972–73 season, he was voted the Most Popular Islander. The next year, however, Spencer was sent to the Buffalo Sabres and he finished his NHL career with the Pittsburgh Penguins in 1979. After a brief stint in the minors, he retired in 1980.

Spencer's entire life had been hockey and when his playing career ended, he had a difficult adjustment. Shortly after he retired, his second marriage ended and he moved to Florida to work as a mechanic. Spencer had a knack for fixing things, but being a mechanic was nothing like playing in the NHL. He liked reminding people he'd been a hockey star and he liked to drink. Spencer had no ability to manage money and was perpetually strapped for cash. For a former athlete, heavy drinking and financial problems were a recipe for disaster, and it came soon enough.

In February 1982, Spencer was living in a trailer with a prostitute named Diane DeLena. One night, DeLena, who worked under the name of Crystal, went on a call placed by Michael Dalfo, the 29-year-old son of a wealthy realtor. Dalfo, who had been using cocaine, was unable to perform and sent DeLena away. He'd made her feel uncomfortable, however, and when she found Spencer at the Banana Boat Bar, she told him about it.

In the meantime, Dalfo had sent away two more hookers because he thought they weren't attractive enough, and put in a call for a fourth. Since he lived in a condominium complex in which the units were all similar, he stood outside his unit, clad only in a black bikini bathing suit, so the woman would be able to find him.

Spencer, upset that Dalfo had disrespected his woman, put DeLena in a car and went looking for Dalfo. DeLena wanted to forget the entire matter, but she was afraid of Spencer, who had a history of violence against women. She went along but planned to tell Spencer she couldn't remember which unit was Dalco's. That plan was foiled when they found him standing outside.

Spencer told Dalfo to get in his car and the three drove to an isolated area. The two men began arguing, and DeLena, frightened, ran away. The following morning, a truck driver found Dalfo lying under a tree, suffering from two bullet wounds but still alive. He called the police, who rushed Dalfo to the hospital, but it was too late. Although Dalfo had clearly been murdered, and Spencer was the prime suspect, there were no witnesses and no hard evidence; therefore there were no arrests.

DeLena left Spencer a few months later and eventually married a man named Leslie Falco, who didn't know that his wife had been a prostitute. They had two children together and life seemed to be going well until early 1987, when Diane was called in for questioning about the Dalfo murder.

Diane Falco saw her life unraveling if she was implicated in the killing of Dalfo, so she pointed the finger at Spencer and agreed to testify against him in return for immunity. Since they now had a witness, the police were able to charge Spencer with murder.

The hockey community rallied behind Spinner Spencer. Pete Axthelm, the well-known sports journalist, wrote an article about the case in *Sports Illustrated*, questioning whether there was sufficient evidence for a conviction. Spencer wrote a letter to the magazine asserting his innocence and former teammates supplied his bail.

The jury agreed with Axthelm and Spencer was acquitted. The only evidence was Diane Falco's testimony, and she admitted that she had not seen anything nor heard any gunshots. On the other side of the ledger was her assertion that she had left the two men together, Spencer had a gun, and the next morning Dalfo was found dying of two gunshot wounds. That was circumstantial, however, and with no forensic evidence and no eyewitnesses to the shooting, the jury determined that there was a reasonable doubt.

Spencer's freedom didn't last long. He continued drinking, and had been arrested five times for driving while intoxicated between 1982 and 1985. On June 2, 1988, after a night of heavy drinking and alleged cocaine use, Spencer was in his pickup truck with a friend when a stranger pulled alongside them and pointed a gun into the cab, demanding money.

Spencer had stood up to the toughest goons in hockey and wasn't about to give in to a Florida punk. He refused to turn over his money, which was supposedly only a few dollars, and the man shot him dead. It was only three months after he'd been cleared of the murder charge. Spencer, just 38, left two ex-wives and five children.

Spinner Spencer packed a lot of living and dying into his 38 years. He was involved, directly or indirectly, in three murders. A book about his life, titled *Gross Misconduct*, by Martin McNally, was made into a television movie. The dream of Roy Horton had turned into a nightmare.

Other sources:
  http://www.hhof.com/LegendsOfHockey/jsp/SearchPlayer.jsp?player=14405
  http://dennis-kane.com/the-sad-story-of-roy-spencer-and-his-son-brian/
  Sports Illustrated, May 11, 1987
  New York Times, February 14, 1987
  Los Angeles Times, June 1, 2010

Hijacker Gives Up at Argentine Field

Hartford Courant, August 5, 1971

As hijacking became more prevalent, it became more difficult to get away with it, but that didn't prevent people like Robert Lee Jackson from trying. Like Arthur Barkley, Jackson wanted money—not $100 million, just a mere $100,000. And while he got it momentarily, Jackson wasn't able to keep it.

Jackson was a 36-year-old high school dropout and Navy deserter who was divorced and had three children. At the end of June 1971, he met a 23-year-old woman named Ligia Lucrecia Sanchez Archilia in Mexico. Sanchez was a Guatemalan artist whose fiancé had recently died, and she was depressed. Somehow, the two came up with the idea to hijack a plane.

Jackson and Sanchez boarded a flight in Acapulco that was headed for San Antonio. Soon after they were in the air, Jackson pulled a pistol on one stewardess and sent another with a message to the pilot that he wanted him to fly to Monterey. When the plane landed in the Mexican city, Jackson allowed 101 passengers to deplane, keeping just one Mexican woman and the crew as a hostage. He demanded a $100,000 ransom, which was quickly provided by Braniff Airlines. After releasing the remaining passenger and giving her $1,000 of his ransom money, Jackson had the pilot fly to Lima, Peru, with the eventual goal of gaining political asylum in Algeria.

At Lima, the crew was exchanged for six volunteers, including two stewardesses. They convinced Jackson that in order to reach Algeria, they would have to stop for fuel in Rio de Janeiro. When the plane touched down in Rio, it was surrounded by police and, without taking on fuel, Jackson had the pilot put the plane back in the air just ten minutes after it landed.

The problem was that the plane had just four hours' worth of fuel. There were only three cities within four hours of Rio that had both a Braniff presence and Algerian diplomatic personnel. The crew convinced Jackson to let them land in Buenos Aires, Argentina. By that time, Jackson had gone without sleep for two days, fueled by amphetamines provided by the airport doctor in Lima. Sanchez spent most of her time sleeping. In Buenos Aires, Jackson let most of the crew de-plane, leaving him and Sanchez on the plane with a pilot, $100,000, and no plan. The 7,500 miles they'd flown thus far had set a distance record for hijacking, eclipsing the 6,900 miles logged by Minichiello.

The CIA was contacted and sent agent Thomas Polgar to Buenos Aires, where the battle evolved from one between Jackson and the authorities to one between the Argentine police and the United States. Braniff wanted to get Jackson to Algiers to avoid violence, and the United States was prepared to support them. The Argentine police wanted to storm the plane and remove Jackson by force.

The police refused to allow maintenance workers to refuel the plane and moved into position on the runway. They planned to tell Jackson that if he did not surrender, he would be put to death by slow torture. Polgar convinced the police to be patient, while Braniff Flight Supervisor Jose Alvarez Tovar talked to Jackson by radio and managed to establish a rapport with him. Tovar distracted Jackson by talking about details of the flight and various aviation minutiae.

While Tovar kept the hijacker busy, diplomatic negotiations continued. The Argentines said that rather than dealing with Polgar, they wanted a formal request from the U.S. Government not to storm the plane. While the CIA tried to get a government request to Argentina, the Argentines decided they would not agree to the request if it was made.

Captain Schroeder offered to de-plane and negotiate on Jackson's behalf, and the latter, nearly exhausted by this time, agreed to let Schroeder leave as long as he promised to come back. The captain told the Argentines that Jackson was discouraged and that they could talk him into giving up. They stuck to their idea of taking him by force. Schroeder prepared to go back to give the news to Jackson, but Braniff headquarters told him not to go. The captain was adamant, saying he had given Jackson his word.

8. Mad Dogs and Skyjackers 223

Finally, Braniff relented and told Jackson by radio that Schoeder would return with a U.S. Embassy official, who would in fact be Polgar. Jackson was wary, and said that Schroeder had to come aboard first, and that if he was satisfied there was no trap, Polgar could follow five minutes later. Jackson also requested that the captain bring some beer, which he did, since the police thought that the combination of beer with the uppers Jackson had been taking would induce depression, which might cause him to surrender.

On the morning of July 4, at about 4:00 a.m., Polgar went aboard the aircraft in a driving rainstorm. Schroeder was in the pilot's seat, Jackson in the co-pilot position, and Polgar sat behind Schroeder. He said that the Argentine police were not going to let the plane take off and that Jackson did not have a lot of options. He reminded him that he had not committed any serious crimes on Argentine soil and assured him that his life would be spared if he surrendered.

That led to a long discussion, during which Polgar described Jackson as follows: "He was coherent enough but with an astonishing lack of logic and an obvious failure to realize the gravity of his deeds or the consequences thereof. He did show great susceptibility to flattery—a certain warmth of personality and a sense of humor, perhaps exaggerated by his many hours of wakefulness and the effect of pep pills."

Jackson wrote down a number of conditions for his surrender. They concerned such diverse topics as his children, Sanchez, who he wanted to be guaranteed safe conduct wherever she wished to go, clarification of the charges he would face, and the disposal of the remaining amount of the ransom money. He wanted part of it to go to his legal defense, part to support his children and transport them to Argentina, and the rest to establish a children's home in Algeria.

One of Jackson's concerns was the extradition treaty between Argentina and the United States. Polgar explained that it didn't cover air piracy, since there were no airplanes when the treaty was signed in 1898, but agreed to provide Jackson with a copy. Jackson then said he knew the plane wasn't going to take off, and therefore wouldn't need a crew, but he wanted Schroeder to remain as a hostage for protection against the police.

At 4:50, Polgar left the plane and met with General Caceres Monie. He told the general that Jackson was ready to surrender if they showed a little patience, and fortunately the general agreed. At 7:00, Polgar went back on board with a copy of the treaty and convinced Jackson to let Schroeder leave the plane. Sanchez took her two suitcases and departed at the same time, leaving just Polgar and Jackson on board. At that point, it was just a matter of waiting until Jackson wore down. He asked Polgar to leave so he could drink his last can of beer in private.

Polgar, who had managed to mollify the Argentines, now had to deal with the Braniff Security Officer who, with his personnel safe, wanted to rush the plane and take Jackson by force. Polgar managed to dissuade him, and shortly after 9:00, convinced Jackson to surrender to General Monie.

Jackson walked off the plane with his fingers raised in a peace sign, carrying a suitcase with the ransom money, which was later found to be $14,000 short, and an unloaded pistol, which the police quickly confiscated. Sanchez's only weapon had been a toy gun. "He was rather benevolent in the end," said John Wachter, legal counsel for the U.S. Embassy. "He didn't want to do anyone any harm." Wachter also said the United States would attempt to have Jackson extradited to face charges in the U.S., but the Argentine government refused and insisted on trying him in their own country.

Jackson told the Argentine court that he became angry at the U.S. justice system after his wife was awarded custody of their children in the divorce proceedings. There was no romantic connection, he insisted, between him and Sanchez. She had simply gone along for support and the prospect of starting a new life in Algeria. Jackson said that $3,000 of the missing ransom money had been given to one of the stewardesses so that she could buy an Arabian horse. The court was unimpressed by Jackson's benevolence, and sentenced him to five years in prison. Sanchez received a three-year sentence.

A year later, a reporter caught up with Jackson, who was working in the prison bakery and writing a book titled *Where Goest Thou*. The book must have been a short one because Jackson was going nowhere.

Other sources:
New York Times, July 5, 1971
Desert Sun, July 4, 1972
https://www.cia.gov/library/center-for-the-study-of-intelligence/kent-csi/vol16no3/html/v16i3a02p_0001.htm

Bingham's Mother Waiting for Word
Hartford Courant, August 24, 1971

Stephen Bingham's family had been prominent in Connecticut for generations. "The Binghams of Connecticut," wrote the *Courant*, "are a noted family in the state: noted for quiet money, noted for their forebears, noted for a sympathy for the underdog and a willingness to help."

Stephen's grandfather, Hiram Bingham II, was born in Hawaii in 1875 and married a member of the Tiffany family. He was a Yale professor and World War I veteran who served as lieutenant governor of Connecticut for two years and was elected governor in 1924. After just one day as governor, Bingham was selected to finish out the Senate term of Frank Brandagee, who had committed suicide. In 1926, he was elected to a full term in the Senate, but was swept out of office in the 1932 Democratic landslide.

Jonathan Bingham, Stephen's uncle, was a liberal Democrat who represented New York in the House of Representatives. Stephen's father, Judge Alfred Bingham, published a journal called "Common Sense" which advocated replacing capitalism with a socialistic system that guaranteed every family a minimum annual income of $5,000. Detractors called it "Commie Sense." "We were very idealistic," said Stephen's mother Sylvia. Although the Binghams had an income well above $5,000, Sylvia said, "I do not think it is correct to describe us as wealthy. I would say perhaps well-to-do."

While the Binghams might not consider themselves wealthy, they were rich enough to allow them to live in a large 18th century farmhouse in rural Salem, Connecticut and devote their time to social causes without worrying about earning a living. The Binghams had followed a common path for successful families, with the older generation, the one that earned the money, being conservative, while subsequent generations, that didn't, turning to liberalism.

After graduating from Milford Academy, where he excelled in track and cross country, Stephen Bingham went to Yale. By his sophomore year, he lost interest in track and became immersed in politics and social issues. He worked in the presidential campaign of John F. Kennedy, joined the Yale Young Democrats, worked as an intern in the office of U.S. Representative Robert Giaimo, and served as editor of the *Yale Daily News*. Influenced by Allard Lowenstein, Stephen became involved in the anti-segregation movement in the South and spent two months in Mississippi working for the Freedom Summer civil rights project. Many of those who became involved in radical causes during the 1960s believed that the solution was to destroy the system, but Stephen Bingham wanted to work within the system; he decided to become an attorney.

Six months into his law school career at the University of California, Bingham married Gretchen Spreckels, whose family had founded Spreckels Sugar in the 19th century. That didn't mean, Gretchen said, that they were rich. "We were on the side of the family," she claimed, "which had so many to divide it up that there wasn't really very much for anyone."

Gretchen was as committed to liberal causes as her husband, and the two joined the Peace Corps and were assigned to Sierra Leone. No one as intelligent and sensitive as Stephen Bingham could go through such an experience without reflecting on serious issues. Bingham began to question the common logic that it was good to try to impose "civilizing" American standards on Africans. Were we really destroying their pride and trying to turn them into the little Americans we thought they should be?

In the fall of 1967, Stephen and Gretchen returned to California and

Stephen resumed his study of law. After working for Robert Kennedy's presidential campaign in 1968, he graduated from law school in 1969. Stephen became interested in the cause of Cesar Chavez and migrant workers and envisioned his life's mission as bringing legal services to the poor. Meanwhile, the marriage that survived Africa could not survive California, and the couple divorced.

Stephen Bingham was an idealist who wanted to make the world fairer, but as a man who knew three generations of Binghams said, "There is a certain naivete about all the Binghams. They can't seem to believe that there are some really bad and evil people in the world." Stephen's own father said that his son was a young man, "who often takes an overly romantic approach to political problems."

Stephen Bingham could not see any evil in George Jackson, an inmate at San Quentin Prison, and Jackson would enmesh Bingham in the great adventure of his life. George Jackson was the type of character who appealed to Bingham's sense of romanticism; he was a black man who had received a sentence out of proportion to his crime, which was stealing $70 from a gas station, and who had been treated poorly while in prison. Jackson also appealed to Bingham's intellect, for he was self-educated, having read extensively during his lengthy incarceration. While in prison, Jackson became enamored of Marxism. In 1970, he published a book called *Soledad Brother: The Prison Letters of George Jackson*. Additional letters were compiled into books called *Soledad Brother* and *Blood in My Eye*.

In 1970, Jackson was charged with the murder of a prison guard. Bingham worked for the law firm of Franck, Hill, Stender, Ziegler and Hendon, which represented Jackson, Fleeta Drumgo, and John Cluchette, known as the Soledad Brothers, after the prison in which the murder had occurred. A Soledad Brothers Defense Committee was formed, with supporters including Jane Fonda, Tom Hayden, Allen Ginsburg, and Julian Bond.

While celebrities rallied to his defense, Jackson had been making elaborate plans to escape from prison. On August 1, 1971, when five of his relatives visited him, his 12-year-old nephew set off a metal detector with a cap pistol attached to the inside of his thigh. Two other children had toy guns, and prison officials thought the incident was an attempt to test their security in preparation for the delivery of real weapons. Later they found Jackson's escape plan, which involved his sisters smuggling derringers to him in the hollowed-out heels of their shoes. On August 7, Jackson's brother Jonathan took over a Marin County courtroom and freed three prisoners, taking the judge hostage, which put the prison system on high alert.

At 10:15 on the morning of August 21, Bingham arrived at San Quentin, accompanying Vanita Anderson, a member of Jackson's defense team. Anderson had met with Jackson earlier in the week and, under San

8. Mad Dogs and Skyjackers

Quentin's rules, one visit per week was the limit. Bingham was there to take her place if she was denied access. Anderson, as feared, was not allowed to go in, so Bingham went instead. He carried a briefcase and an expanding folder, which contained the galley proofs for Jackson's book. When Bingham went through the metal detector, it registered. Guards inspected his briefcase and found that it contained a tape recorder with metal batteries.

Bingham was admitted to the prison but told he could not visit Jackson at that time. He waited, and called his uncle, a professor at the University of California, to tell him he was delayed and would not be able to come for lunch. Finally, at 1:15 p.m., he was told he could meet with Jackson in Visiting Room A. He entered and the two men sat across from each other, separated by a heavy mesh screen with an opening so that papers could be exchanged. Jackson had undergone a thorough search before entering the room.

After conversing for a while, Bingham asked to be excused in order to get some cigarettes. Prison officials were not certain if he took his briefcase with him or left it on the table. He returned and at 2:25 the visit ended. After Bingham left, guards prepared to search Jackson before he was returned to his cell.

At about the time Bingham was exiting through the prison gate, Jackson, just as the guards began to search him, pulled an Afro wig from his head and extracted a 9mm automatic pistol and ammunition clips. He took the guards hostage, released 29 prisoners from their cells, and a riot ensued. Jackson was shot and killed, while three prison guards lie dead and two inmate trusties had their throats slashed.

Shortly after 4:00, Bingham arrived at his uncle's house. No one noticed anything unusual, and he was invited to stay for dinner. He declined, saying that he had to attend a political meeting, and after chatting for a while, Bingham left about 5:30. He went to his meeting, with no knowledge of what had happened earlier at San Quentin. He learned of the killings when he returned home and found about 30 people waiting on his porch. They told Bingham what had happened and that he was a suspect. "My first feeling," he said years later, "was just horror that Jackson and five other people had been killed, but when they mentioned the news reports linking me to it, my horror turned fairly quickly to terror."

Bingham stayed with friends in Berkeley for two days and became convinced that he should leave the country. Lawyers told him he wouldn't be safe in prison, since he was believed to be an accessory to the killing of three guards. He was sent to a woman in Las Vegas, who shaved his beard and mustache, dyed and straightened his hair, and furnished him with false identification in the name of Robert Dale Boarts.

With funds supplied by friends, Bingham flew from Las Vegas to Philadelphia, where he obtained a passport in 24 hours by claiming a family emergency. He got on a plane to Prague, which was then in Czechoslovakia. The

Eastern Bloc counties were not part of the international police organization, and he believed his chances of avoiding extradition were better there.

On August 31, Bingham was charged with five counts of murder. Marin County District Attorney Bruce Bales said he was convinced that the only way Jackson could have procured a gun was if Bingham had given it to him. Under California law, an accomplice to a crime was as culpable as the actual perpetrator.

Although Bingham was a wanted criminal, he learned later from FBI files that they weren't looking very hard for him. But he didn't know that at the time, and assumed that any false move would give him away. He moved around frequently and didn't contact his family for more than a year. For his first couple of years in hiding, he didn't work, worried that getting the necessary permits would expose his identity.

After living on the charity of friends for two years, Bingham took a series of jobs, including receptionist in an Italian hotel and waiter at an Austrian resort. In 1974, having lived safely underground for three years, he decided to move to Paris. He took film and photography classes and met 19-year-old fellow student Francoise Blusseau. The two became lovers and remained in Paris for ten years. On four occasions, Bingham traveled to North America, three times to Canada and once to the United States, where he saw his parents for the first time in seven years.

By 1984, times had changed, and Bingham thought it was safe to surrender and put his fate in the hands of the legal system. The radical days of the 1960s were long gone, and the violent emotions of the era had cooled. Under the changed conditions, Bingham thought he would get a fair trial. He returned to the United States and hid in San Jose for six months while former Attorney General Ramsey Clark negotiated his surrender to authorities. Bingham spent eight days in prison before his friends raised bail. A week later, he and Francoise were married.

In 1986, Bingham was acquitted after a ten-week trial. No one ever learned how or from whom George Jackson got his weapon. Bingham resumed his practice of law, working in San Francisco for Bay Area Legal Aid, where he advocated for welfare rights. In 2009, his 22-year-old daughter Sylvia was killed while riding a bicycle to work in Cleveland. The man driving the truck that killed her was sentenced to three years in prison for aggravated vehicular homicide.

As a young man, Stephen Bingham was looking for excitement, and he found it. He was naive, he was idealistic, and he was sincere. And he was probably not the man who gave George Jackson his lethal weapon. His story was a result of the unique world of the 1960s. Bingham wasn't a good kid gone bad, he was a wealthy idealist who lived much more dangerously than his ancestors. He was a rich child of the 1960s.

Other sources:
https://en.wikipedia.org/wiki/Soledad_Brothers
https://en.wikipedia.org/wiki/George_Jackson_(activist)
http://yale64.org/news/bingham1.htm
People, July 28, 1986

Texas Ranger Kills Gangster from Bonnie and Clyde Era
Bridgeport Post-Telegram, October 15, 1971

Huron "Ted" Walters didn't realize that times had changed. Known as Terrible Ted, he was a man who didn't change, his mind frozen in the Depression-wracked 1930s when a national crime wave terrorized America. There were a number of well-known criminals during the '30s, of which Bonnie Parker and Clyde Barrow were perhaps the most famous. Among Clyde Barrows' associates were brothers Ray and Floyd Hamilton. Walters was part of the Hamilton gang, whose members robbed banks, killed people, and were eventually captured and imprisoned. The headline in the *Post-Telegram* article used the names of Bonnie and Clyde, but the infamous pair never knew Walters, who hooked up with the Hamiltons after Barrow and Parker had been killed.

Raymond Hamilton was executed in 1935 and Floyd Hamilton and Ted Walters were sent to prison in 1938. Walters, who was sentenced for bank robbery, auto theft, and assault, had been caught earlier, but he escaped from Texas State Prison in 1936. In 1943, he tried it again, attempting to break out of escape-proof Alcatraz Prison. Walters scaled the prison wall but injured his spine jumping to the ground. Two days later, he was found hiding in a waterfront cave.

After serving a total of nearly 30 years in prison, Walters was released on parole in May 1971. He'd had a lot of time to reflect since his attempted escape in 1943, and many prisoners mature and leave as changed men. Willie Sutton is a prime example, becoming an elder statesman after his release in 1969. Walters' former gang leader Floyd Hamilton also changed his life after leaving prison. He found religion, and some of the lawmen who'd put him in jail helped him find employment as a night watchman at a Texas car dealership. On at least two occasions, Hamilton could have easily resumed his criminal ways. Once, he found the company's vault inadvertently left wide open, with a substantial amount of money inside. He closed it. On another occasion, a salesman left a briefcase with money inside. Hamilton returned it.

Walters chose a different path when he was released. He had no job skills other than as a criminal and as soon as he was out of prison, Walters returned to a life of crime. On October 13, his 1962 Plymouth Valiant was stopped by a police officer in Euless, Texas, which precipitated a shootout in which Walters suffered a slight wound.

Two days later, Hoyt Houston of Bedford went out to his shed to put his kitten back in its box and found a strange pair of shoes on the floor. Looking around, he found Walters lying in his boat. Walters pointed a shotgun at Houston and forced the farmer to go back into the house with him. When they went inside, Mrs. Houston noticed that Walters was injured and offered to treat his wound. While she ministered to Walters, the couple's 15-year-old daughter escaped from the house and by chance ran into police officer Dave Eudy, who was looking for Walters. Eudy called for help and a cordon of police came out and surrounded the Houston home.

One of the officers knocked on the door and Mrs. Houston, under orders from Walters, told him everything was fine. They didn't believe her and as they maintained their watch from afar, Walters forced the family into their car. Mary Houston was driving and Walters sat in the back seat training his shotgun on her husband's head. The couple's second daughter sat between them.

It wasn't long before the car reached a roadblock at a bridge just outside Grapevine, roughly 300 feet from the spot where Bonnie and Clyde had gunned down two police officers in 1934. The police spent about 20 minutes trying to convince Walters to surrender. He wouldn't, which wasn't surprising, for in the 1940s he'd told an interviewer, "I'd rather be shot down like a mad dog than have the cops take me."

While the officers distracted Walters, Texas Ranger Tom Arnold maneuvered into position and fired a shot into the car, hitting Walters in the head. The other officers moved in and fired several shots into his body. He was dead, putting an end, at the age of 58, to Walters' life of crime. "I've been around guns all my life," Walters once said, "and the damned things have always got me into trouble." That was a fitting epitaph.

Other sources:
http://texashideout.tripod.com/ted.html
http://texashideout.tripod.com/hamwalters.html
http://texashideout.tripod.com/walters.html

Tax Agents Walk Nude in Memphis
Bridgeport Post-Telegram, June 16, 1972

Racial tension, anti-government sentiment, and public exposure came together to produce a very strange episode in Memphis, Tennessee, in 1972. Notable incidents often arise from seemingly insignificant beginnings, and

8. Mad Dogs and Skyjackers

this was no exception. The spark in this case was $194.77 in unpaid sales taxes owed by 29-year-old African American LaSaunders Hudson, owner of BH&K Cleaners. Hudson said he hadn't paid his taxes because if he did, he wouldn't have enough money to support his family. He and his business partner sent a letter to the state indicating their intention not to pay and claiming, "it is impossible for black citizens of the state of Tennessee and of America to be on a par with other citizens of America."

The State of Tennessee was unmoved and sent Don Duncan, chief of field operations for the Collection Division of the Department of Revenue, plus eleven agents, to Hudson's store on Park Avenue to collect the tax. It seemed like a rather large force to collect less than $200, but Duncan took unpaid taxes seriously. If Hudson didn't pay, Duncan told him, the state would place a lien on his property, and if he didn't satisfy the lien, they would shut down his business. Suitably cowed, Hudson gave agent John Mabile a check for the full amount of the tax and, while the other agents waited at the store, Mabile went to the bank to make the deposit.

The check bounced. When Mabile returned to BH&K and told Duncan the check was worthless, the latter went into the store to confront Hudson. When he got inside, Hudson pulled a gun and told him to call the other agents back in. Three of the eleven came inside.

Hudson didn't shoot them. He didn't tell them to leave and never come back. He told them to take off their clothes. Since Hudson had a gun, the three agents (Duncan was exempted) stripped. One of the three, Lee Mullins, was black, knew Hudson, and tried to reason with him. "Get 'em off, Mullins or I'll kill you," Hudson replied. After the men removed their clothing, Hudson ordered them to go back outside. Duncan was held hostage and Hudson said he would not be released until Hudson had an audience with Governor Winfield Dunn.

The cleaning establishment was located in the Orange Mound section of Memphis, a predominately black neighborhood and, when they heard of the confrontation, many people from the area gathered to support Hudson. The crowd eventually swelled to about 2,000 people and when the three agents emerged from the building naked, hiding their genitals with their hands, the crowd began to cheer and applaud. "I certainly hated to walk out the door without any clothes on," said Mabile. "I was embarrassed."

Fortunately, there was a moving van nearby, and the men were able to grab some furniture pads to cover themselves. Finally, a pastor came along and gave them trousers, in obedience to the Lord's command to clothe the naked. The police arrived and singer Isaac Hayes joined them at the Black Panthers headquarters next door. The police began sending notes to Hudson, who still held Duncan hostage. A college student who was a friend of

Hudson's dropped them through the building's mail slot and returned with Hudson's replies.

When Hudson refused to back down, Governor Dunn flew to Memphis to meet with him at a hotel far from the potentially volatile site of the standoff. A car driven by a black city official pulled up to the back door of the cleaners, Hudson ducked out the door and into the car, and was on his way to his meeting with Dunn. The agents had their pants, Duncan had his freedom (after spending eight hours bound with electrical wires), and Hudson had his meeting with the governor.

Hudson and Dunn met for an hour and discussed the legacy of slavery and the problems faced by black Americans, and Hudson admitted that he had transgressed and knew he was in trouble. He was taken into custody and held overnight in the Memphis jail. At his hearing the next day, the judge asked Duncan about his threat to shut down Hudson's business. "Pretty high-handed tactics, wouldn't you say?" "Well," Duncan replied, "Perhaps I used the wrong terminology." Hudson was charged with assault with intent to murder, but a kidnapping charge was dropped. Apparently Tennessee statutes didn't address the crime of forcing revenue agents to disrobe.

Postscript: The National Directory of Registered Tax Preparers and Professionals lists a LaSaunders Hudson as employed by the Jackson Hewitt Tax Service in Memphis. Assuming it is the same man who stripped Department of Revenue agents to protest paying taxes, that is a remarkable irony.

Other sources:
Cumberland News, June 17, 1972
National Directory of Registered Tax Return Preparers and Professionals

9

It's All About the War

Politics in the Vietnam Era

Americans refer to the Donald Trump presidency as an era of unprecedented division, but the politics of the 1960s and early 1970s were just as polarized. The Vietnam War forced one president from office and dirty politics eventually resulted in the resignation of his successor. If Spiro Agnew had access to Twitter, he would have made Trump seem restrained. (And with Pat Buchanan as his speech writer, Agnew would have seemed more literate.) Put on your helmets, buckle your seat belts, and get ready for the politics of the 1960s.

The Klansman
Unknown New York Newspaper, October 16, 1960

Politicians are not known as a particularly principled lot. Money talks and candidates generally accept the backing of just about anyone who provides financial support or the promise of a large bloc of votes. But politicians have limits, and even ethically challenged office seekers draw the line somewhere. In 1960, when Republican presidential candidate Richard Nixon received the endorsement of W.J. Griffin, Grand Wizard of the Florida Ku Klux Klan, Nixon had to draw that line. Even a few million votes, if they existed, were not enough to tempt Nixon to accept the endorsement of probably the most reviled organization in America.

Griffin's endorsement may have been the result of an internal Klan feud, for his rival, Bill Hendrix, had endorsed notoriously racist Arkansas governor Orval Faubus. When asked who he supported, Griffin didn't want to jump on Hendrix's bandwagon, and therefore said he backed Nixon.

While Nixon cringed, Democrats leapt at the opportunity to link the Republican candidate to the KKK.

"The Ku Klux Klan is riding again in this campaign," shouted New York Democrat Adam Clayton Powell. "If it doesn't stop, all bigots will vote for Nixon and all right-thinking Christians and Jews will vote for Kennedy rather than be found in the ranks of the Klan-minded."

During the third Nixon-Kennedy debate, Kennedy pointed out that Nixon had been endorsed by the Florida Grand Wizard, and while he quickly said that of course Nixon neither solicited nor accepted the endorsement, he'd made his point. The Klan liked Nixon, and if you liked Nixon, you were one with the Klan.

"In an election," wrote David Marx Chalmers, "in which Kennedy's narrow victory depended on the overwhelming margins piled up in Negro precincts in cities such as Chicago, perhaps Griffin's words helped make the difference."

As a Roman Catholic, Kennedy was classified with African Americans and Jews on the Klan blacklist, but apparently there weren't enough Klansmen to elect Nixon in 1960. He would have to wait eight years to become President.

Other sources:
   Backlash: How the Ku Klux Klan Helped the Civil Rights Movement, David Marx Chalmers, Rowman & Littlefield, Lanham, Boulder, New York, Toronto, and Oxford, 2003

Sen. Goldwater Asks: Must Public Subsidize Shirkers, Illegitimacy?

New York Herald Tribune, Date Unknown

The subject of Senator Goldwater's column was a law passed by the city of Newburgh, New York, that required any able-bodied person on the relief rolls to work for the city in order to receive their money. A second provision of the ordinance declared: "All mothers of illegitimate children are to be advised that should they have any more children out of wedlock, the mothers shall be denied relief."

"Is it wrong to deny continued support from public funds" Goldwater asked, "to an able-bodied individual who refuses to take a job and provide for himself? Is it wrong to discourage illegitimacy? Is it wrong to say that public funds will not be used to subsidize and encourage illegitimate births?"

Political correctness was far in the future, and most people in America considered childbirth out of wedlock to be shameful in addition to bad financial planning. The mores of the era are also evidenced by Goldwater's closing comments. "Are we not the guilty ones," he posited, "we who have created the dishonest chiselers who exist on relief by our lax attitude and our acceptance and approval of programs which encourage indolence?"

Apparently, many offended dishonest chiselers went to their polling places in November 1964, for Goldwater was badly beaten by Lyndon Johnson, carrying just six states and 36 percent of the popular vote. In the history of American electoral politics, only four major party candidates have ever gotten a lower percentage of the popular vote in a two-man race.

Johnson, a masterful politician, successfully portrayed Goldwater as a dangerous war-mongering racist who would decimate Democratic social welfare programs. Goldwater helped him along, partly by writing columns like the one cited above. "By the time the convention opened," Goldwater said later, "I had been branded as a fascist, a racist, a trigger-happy warmonger, a nuclear madman and the candidate who couldn't win."

Johnson did a skillful job of capitalizing on Goldwater's propensity to shoot from the hip, often putting the bullet in his own foot. "Barry," Dwight Eisenhower once told him, "you speak too quick and too loud." Goldwater agreed. "There are words of mine floating around in the air," he once said, "that I would like to reach up and eat." Included in that category was a 1961 quote in which he said, "Sometimes I think this country would be better off if we could just saw off the Eastern Seaboard and let it float out to sea." That was not a strategic comment from a man who would run for president three years later, and Johnson made sure that no one forgot it. He carried the Eastern Seaboard from Maine through North Carolina.

After the election debacle, many Americans believed the Republican Party was in danger of extinction. Goldwater and his conservative philosophy were given the blame and he was relegated to the political wilderness for several years. By 1980, however, conservatism was in vogue once more and Ronald Reagan, whose first major appearance on the national political stage was a speech endorsing Goldwater in 1964, was elected President. Goldwater, who'd returned to the Senate in 1969, became the grand old man of the conservative movement.

Although many disagreed with Goldwater's philosophy, few questioned his sincerity and integrity. He believed in limiting the power of government, even when, in cases like school prayer, government would have enforced a practice he supported. Although he personally believed in racial integration and desegregated his family's department stores, Goldwater voted against the 1964 Civil Rights Act.

By the summer of 1974, as the Watergate crisis reached its final stages, Goldwater was held in such high regard by his colleagues that they selected him to tell Nixon that the jig was up and he no longer had the support of the Republicans in the Senate. The next day, Nixon resigned.

Goldwater lived until 1998 and was destined to see the massive expansion of the social welfare programs he had warned against in the early 1960s. Forty percent of all American births now occur out of wedlock. As most people do, Goldwater mellowed as he aged, or at least he appeared to. He became a strong advocate for a woman's right to obtain an abortion, claiming that it was up to the individual, not the government, to decide. In the 1990s, he championed the rights of gays to serve in the military, something liberal president Bill Clinton was unwilling to do. Goldwater also became honorary chairman of a group working to end job discrimination against gays. "You don't have to agree with it," he said, "but they have a constitutional right to be gay."

How did the conservative railing against welfare recipients become an advocate for abortion and gay rights? It seems inconsistent, but in fact there was a rigid consistency to Goldwater's western belief in rugged individualism, self-sufficiency, and self-determination. A person who believes in self-determination and self-sufficiency will support a women's right to obtain an abortion while insisting that a man had an obligation to work for his keep. Goldwater never strayed from his basic values; their application merely placed him on different points along the traditional conservative/liberal spectrum on various issues.

Barry Goldwater was a complex man, reviled and revered by various groups and at various times. In today's social media environment, with its ubiquitous cameras and microphones, his loose tongue would place him in perpetual hot water. It's doubtful he could run for president, for principle doesn't sell in today's environment. Of course, it didn't sell in 1964, either.

Other sources:
https://www.washingtonpost.com/wp-srv/politics/daily/may98/goldwater30.htm?noredirect=on
https://en.wikipedia.org/wiki/List_of_United_States_presidential_elections_by_popular_vote_margin

Poverty Program Now Faces Big Test
New York Times, August 16, 1964

In March 1964, President Lyndon Johnson shepherded his $947 million anti-poverty bill through the United States Congress. He called it a "war on poverty" and described the world created by his vision as "The Great Society," a label borrowed from a 1914 socialist tract of that name published by Graham Wallas. Johnson predicted "a society where no children will go unfed and no youngster will go unschooled," with "abundance and liberty for all."

The Great Society programs were the culmination of initiatives begun during the Kennedy administration under the influence of economic advisor Walter Heller. As with so many programs that were initiated by Kennedy, it was Johnson who had the political acumen to craft the philosophy into a workable program and get it passed by Congress.

Johnson's formative years were during the Roosevelt administration, and although he was greatly influenced by The New Deal, his program had a very different approach. Most New Deal initiatives were ad hoc stabs at tackling the problem of the moment, while The Great Society was an ambitious, comprehensive attempt to attack the root causes of poverty rather than treat the symptoms. "You tell [Sargent] Shriver no doles," Johnson instructed his aide Bill Moyers. The goal was to increase opportunity and allow the poor to participate in what was at that point a thriving economy, rather than merely transferring income from the rich to the poor.

It was now August, less than three months from Election Day, and Johnson was eager to show the voters some tangible results. There was no way poverty could be eliminated or even reduced in five months, but he wanted programs in place and people in them. Johnson's Republican opponent, Barry Goldwater, had been hitting Johnson hard for pandering for votes from the poor. He claimed that the program was infeasible and would "constitute a curious combination of the techniques made famous by the phrases 'Madison Avenue' and 'The Wizard of Oz.'"

Opposing poverty programs is a tricky business. As Republican Senator John Tower from Texas explained, "What we Republicans must do is point out we're not shooting Santa Claus. We're shooting down a balloon of hot air."

In keeping with Johnson's goal of getting to the root causes of poverty, most of the programs were aimed at creating increased opportunity to break the cycle of poverty. One of the major initiatives was employment programs for poor teenagers. The goal was threefold: stop youngsters from dropping out of school, keep them from getting in trouble, and teach them skills that would enable them to permanently break out of poverty.

Despite the differences, some programs mirrored those of the New Deal. There were camps reminiscent of the Civilian Conservation Corps. The Jobs Corp was designed to make heretofore unemployable youths suitable for the job market. Volunteers in Service to America (VISTA) was a domestic replication of Kennedy's Peace Corps, with its volunteers deployed in inner cities and impoverished rural areas.

If he was pandering for votes, as Goldwater had claimed, Johnson was successful, swamping Goldwater in one of the most lopsided presidential elections in American history. With four more years in the Presidency, Johnson was in a position to nurture his Great Society programs to fruition and was able to put the massive resources of the federal government behind them.

We are now more than 50 years removed from the start of the program and able to assess the effectiveness of Johnson's ambitious plan, piece by piece. One of the goals of the Great Society was to better the condition of African Americans by using the lure of federal funds to increase racial integration, particularly in the South. Along with integration, Johnson believed, would come greater political power and increased opportunity. In 1965, only 6.7 percent of blacks in Alabama and just 10 percent of those in Mississippi were registered voters. Blacks who weren't intimidated by threats of violence were rejected by rigged "literacy" tests. By 1970, two-thirds of the eligible black voters in Alabama and Mississippi were registered.

In 1965, only 2.3 percent of southern blacks attended majority white schools. By 1968 the percentage had increased to 23.4 percent and by 1988 it was 43 percent. In addition, the segregation laws of southern states were eliminated, again through the incentive of federal largesse. Give Johnson an excellent grade in the area of integration. The process had begun under Kennedy, and perhaps change was inevitable, but the major gains occurred during the Johnson administration.

A second plank of the program was increased access to higher education. In 1964, just 11.7 percent of males and 6.8 percent of females held college degrees. By 2016, the percentages had increased to 33.7 percent and 34.6 percent, respectively. Not only were there more graduates, but women actually graduated at a higher rate than men, a dramatic change from 1964. One can debate the role of the Great Society programs in the result, but there is no question that today's population has far greater access to educational opportunities than their parents and grandparents.

Another key aspect of the Great Society was increasing access to health care, with the principal vehicles being the Medicare and Medicaid programs. The Medicare rolls increased from 19 million in 1966 to 57 million in 2016, while the number of enrollees in Medicaid rose from 4 million to 70 million. The increase in Medicare coverage, however, is due in large part to a significant growth in the elderly population, and the continuing battle over Obamacare indicates that The Great Society did not solve America's health care problem. The biggest downside of Medicare is that it costs approximately ten times as much, in inflation-adjusted dollars, than projected.

The "Model Cities" program was designed to rejuvenate American cities and improve the economic status of their residents. The program was discontinued in 1974 and, given the current depressed condition of so many inner cities, must be regarded as a failure. But Johnson was fighting a difficult battle in this arena, for the goal of most inner city residents in the 1960s was not to better their lives within the cities, but to move to the more affluent suburbs. Give Johnson a failing grade in a very difficult course.

But the main goal of the Great Society was ultimately to reduce poverty, and by that standard, the results are mixed. Ronald Reagan once said, "In the '60s, we waged a war on poverty, and poverty won." While that is a clever turn of phrase, it's not that simple. The War on Poverty was more like the War of 1812 than the Second World War. Poverty didn't surrender, but neither did the other side, and each could plausibly claim victory. Poverty among the elderly clearly dropped, partly due to Medicare. Poverty rates increased in large metropolitan areas, but as stated earlier, that is in part because many people escaped poverty by moving out of the deteriorating cities.

As far as overall poverty, it depends on what measurements are used. If government transfer payments are counted as income, it would appear that poverty has declined somewhat since the mid–1960s. But since the aim of the Great Society was to make the poor self-sufficient, making them less poor by subsidy doesn't count.

James Pethokoukis, writing for the American Enterprise Institute, claimed that the 2016 poverty rate was slightly higher than that of 1966. On the other hand, the *Washington Post* claimed that the poverty rate declined from 22 percent in 1960 to 16 percent in 2012. As noted earlier, each writer seemed to have their own method of calculating economic well-being.

One of the essential assumptions behind Johnson's programs was that the economic boom of the mid–'60s was a permanent condition, and that economic cycles would be controlled or eliminated through enlightened fiscal policy. However, those stubborn cycles manage to thwart the economic geniuses of the 1960s, and it can be safely said that when we fought a war on economic cycles, economic cycles emerged victorious. The declining economy in the years following the launch of the Great Society knocked one of the legs from under Johnson's plan, while the escalating war in Vietnam siphoned funding from social programs.

Perhaps "The Great Society" was too lofty an aim. If Johnson had called his program "A Better Society" he would have been on the mark. Americans are more integrated and more educated, which is what opportunity is all about. There were no miracles, but the society that is without poverty has yet to be discovered. The Great Society programs were costly, but progress isn't cheap.

Lyndon Johnson died in 1973, before subsequent generations would realize many of the benefits of his ambitious efforts. Many of his initiatives, such as the Model Cities Program, died as well, but the Great Society imprint in still with us for, much to the ire of many conservatives, it firmly established the federal government as the instrument to fight social problems. That is perhaps the most lasting achievement of The Great Society.

Other sources:
   Orlando Sentinel, April 19, 1985.
   Politico, January 28, 2018.

The Weekly Standard: A Not So Good Society by James Piereson, September 30, 2016.
Washington Post, May 17, 2014.
American Enterprise institute, April 4, 2016.
https://www.statista.com/statistics/184272/educational-attainment-of-college-diploma-or-higher-by-gender/

The U.S. in Vietnam: Why It Is There
New York Times, February 12, 1965

The United States got involved in Vietnam by baby steps, and few Americans realized what was happening. There was no "shot heard round the world" as in Lexington nor was there a Pearl Harbor. It all happened gradually, but by 1965, U.S. involvement in Vietnam was increasing, and many Americans wanted an answer to the question the *Times* posed in its opening paragraph: "What are we doing out there anyway?" "There is no easy answer" writer Max Frankel said, "because the involvement embraces not only Vietnam but also all of Southeast Asia, and because it cannot be traced to any specific decision or time. It is the result of a gradual, often uncharted, evolution of American policy throughout Asia, dating at least to World War II."

Frankel began his story of Southeast Asia at the end of the colonial era precipitated by World War II and the emergence of Communist China shortly after the war. The withdrawal of European nations left a political void in the region and the United States, in its role as the guardian of democracy, wanted to ensure that the newly-independent countries remained independent and had the ability to determine their own fate. Unless, of course, they chose Communism or socialism. Although America's stated goal was self-determination, the true objective during the Cold War years was to prevent the spread of Communism to unstable regions.

On the same pages as Frankel's article appeared, there were a number of complementary pieces setting forth the opinions of several world leaders. One of them, titled "Lodge Says Action in Vietnam is Wise," indicated that Henry Cabot Lodge, former Ambassador to South Vietnam, believed that President Johnson's decision to escalate attacks on North Vietnam was the correct one. "Americans," Lodge said, "had a right to be in South Vietnam and 'a right to be protected.'" "We don't need a negotiation. What we need is dependable evidence that this brutal and murderous intrusion into South Vietnam will stop."

In another article, eighty-year-old American Socialist Norman Thomas disagreed. "We are saving our face," Thomas said, "at the cost of our soul."

A third opinion came from former Vice President Richard Nixon, who agreed with Johnson that the North should be attacked in strength, even though many in the U.S. opposed escalation of the war. "This is no time for consensus government," he said. "It's a time for leadership. The average citizen doesn't know what the stakes are in Vietnam."

The Catholic Church had its own opinion, set forth in a piece titled, "Pontiff Appeals for Peace Effort." Addressing a group of pilgrims in Rome, Pope Paul VI made a plea for peace that was generally interpreted as a desire for the United Nations to pursue a negotiated settlement. He expressed his concern that the availability of nuclear weapons could result in mass destruction.

"Mao is Said to Bar War Unless China is Attacked by U.S." headed a piece summarizing an article in the West German magazine *Stern*. Chinese Communist leader Mao Tse Tung told American journalist Edgar Snow that China had no troops in foreign lands and would not fight the United States unless it attacked his country.

Also on the front page was an article about the bombing of the U.S. Army barracks at Quinhon, which resulted in 21 deaths, the greatest number of American deaths in any single battle to date. Communist guerrillas had apparently entered the barracks carrying three suitcases loaded with TNT, and the GIs vowed revenge. "I hope we blast the hell out of them," said a sergeant.

While U.S. soldiers were looking to blast the hell out of the North Vietnamese, an article to the left of the one on the Quinhon bombing bore the headline "Limit on Conflict Stressed by U.S." The first sentence read, "Administration officials insisted today that there remained in their own minds a distinction between outright war against North Vietnam and retaliatory air strikes of the kind they ordered three times in five days this week." That was the essence of the dilemma. Strike back, but not too hard.

Limited war is an oxymoron and almost impossible to execute successfully. That was the crux of the dilemma that four presidents, and especially the last two, faced in Vietnam. The American people didn't want all-out war, but they wanted victory, at least at first. Then they didn't want defeat. Richard Nixon had no one but himself to blame for Watergate, but the Vietnam situation he inherited from Lyndon Johnson in January 1969 was an almost impossible situation.

The main article explained how the U.S. became involved in Vietnam; the two principal reasons were the unrest created by the change of borders after World War II and the emergence of Communist China in 1949. There was conflict between the stated goal of self-determination and the quest to contain Communism. Wars of national liberation, if led by Communists, were not what the U.S. had in mind when they spoke of self-determination.

The new nations faced a dilemma. They were courted on one hand by the United States, which had seemingly unlimited resources but was half a world away and by China, which was struggling economically but perched on their doorstep with an immense army. Most new countries skirted cautiously, and some leaders, like Indonesia's Sukarno, played each power against the other, trying to get the most from each by threatening to enter the camp of the other.

When the French signed a peace treaty in Geneva in 1954 abandoning their claims to what was then called Indochina, the county was split into two sections, North and South Vietnam. The United States had provided assistance to the losing French effort but was not a signatory to the treaty.

After the French left, the U.S. formed the Southeast Asia Treaty Organization (SEATO) to protect its interests in the region. The majority of the nations in SEATO, however, were not from Southeast Asia, and the organization, viewed with distrust in Asia and eventually with skepticism in America, was never really effective.

As in Korea a decade earlier, it was intended that the eventual fate of Vietnam would be reunification under a single government, but neither side was eager to give up the power it held under the divided arrangement. The U.S. backed South Vietnam dictator Ngo Dinh Diem, whose reign was so despotic and ineffective that the U.S. eventually aided in his overthrow. Diem's reign underscored one of the weaknesses of U.S. Cold War policy— the nearly unqualified support of any ruler, no matter how incompetent and/or corrupt, who declared himself anti–Communist.

The essence of Cold War politics was that the Communist world and the "free" world were competing to control every country in the world. When the Russian Revolution occurred in 1917, the revolutionaries and their international allies assumed that the events in Russia were the start of a worldwide upheaval. A decade later, when that hadn't happened, a rift developed between those Soviets who believed that Communism could only be effective if spread throughout the world and those who believed "Communism in one country" was a viable concept.

The United States operated on the assumption that world conquest was the goal of Communism, despite the fact that the two largest powers, China and the Soviet Union, faced serious economic difficulties and were most concerned with maintaining order at home and satisfying their population's many economic wants. They had little surplus with which to finance revolutions in other countries.

Before Diem was removed in a coup, his subjects in the south began to rise against him and were soon aided by factions from the north. Under President Eisenhower, U.S. physical presence in Vietnam had been nominal, with less than 1,000 "military advisors" in the country. When the revolt against Diem began gaining momentum, President Kennedy increased the number of "advisors" to 23,000.

Meanwhile, there was a revolution in adjacent Laos, also backed by North Vietnam. By that time Lyndon Johnson had succeeded Kennedy, and

Johnson authorized air strikes in Laos. While Vietnam was the main theater, the U.S. was also meddling, mostly financially and diplomatically, in almost every Southeastern Asian country. Enemy troops were moving through Laos and Cambodia to reach South Vietnam, and American military leaders insisted that in order to stop infiltration into the South, they had to pacify neighboring countries. That was the situation in February 1965.

It was a big Vietnam day for the *Times*, for the war in Southeast Asia was fast becoming the most important topic in America. Soon, the question "Why are we here?" would be replaced by "How do we get out?" which was the subject of Richard Nixon's speech of November 1969.

Agnew Says "Effete Snobs" Incited War Moratorium

New York Times, October 20, 1969

Reaction to the October 1969 national moratorium against the Vietnam War was mixed. Craig Badiali and Joan Fox sacrificed their lives (see Chapter 4). Many people who had not considered themselves "anti-war" turned against the conflict for the first time. The one man who could most directly impact the situation, President Richard Nixon, said his policy and actions would not be affected in any way by the protest. The most spirited response came from Vice President Spiro T. Agnew, the designated attack dog of the Nixon Administration.

On October 19, four days after the protests, Agnew gave an address to a group of Republicans assembled in New Orleans. He spoke about Nixon's program of Vietnamization (the shift of military responsibility to the South Vietnamese Army) and of the peace offers that had been floated to North Vietnam. Agnew admitted that many complaints about the military draft were justified and said Nixon was proposing to adopt a lottery selection system.

But what everyone remembered about the speech were Agnew's comments about the participants in Moratorium Day. "A spirit of national masochism prevails," he said, "encouraged by an effete corps of impudent snobs who characterize themselves as intellectuals." He said that the typical college student "now goes to college to proclaim rather than to learn." "The young, at the zenith of physical power and sensitivity, overwhelm themselves with drugs and artificial stimulants." The Moratorium, Agnew concluded, "served as an emotional purgative for those who feel the need to cleanse themselves of their lack of ability to offer a constructive solution to the problem." He called politicians who supported the protestors "ideological eunuchs."

Agnew said what Nixon thought but could not say in public. Phrases like "impudent snobs" and "ideological eunuchs" were memorable, polarizing, and visceral, galvanizing both left and right to even greater extremes. The attack dog had done his job.

President Proud to Have Agnew in Administration

New York Times, October 31, 1969

Spiro Agnew had been handling the bulk of the dirty work for the Nixon Administration, which was a worthy distinction in a presidency most memorable for its dirty work. Nixon tried to remain presidential, and when harsh words were needed, Agnew stepped to the microphone. The Vice President favored melodic, multi-syllabic denunciations, like the famous "nattering nabobs of negativism," "pusillanimous pussyfooters," "vicars of vacillation," and "intolerant clamor and cacophony." His insults were literate and vicious but not his original thoughts; most of his memorable expressions were created by presidential speech writer Pat Buchanan.

Agnew was somewhat of a joke when he was nominated for the Vice Presidency in 1968, for the Maryland governor was a relative unknown, chosen over nationally prominent figures like Nelson Rockefeller and Ronald Reagan. Agnew was initially seen as relatively innocuous, and his strong stance on law and order appealed to Nixon, who knew Americans were frightened by the domestic violence of 1967 and 1968.

People soon learned who Spiro Agnew was, as he displayed an unfortunate propensity for the offensive remark. During the campaign, he referred to Polish-Americans as "Polacks" and to a Japanese reporter as a "fat Jap." Perhaps his most infamous comment, after a tour of an inner-city ghetto, was "If you've seen one slum, you've seen them all." The man who was supposed to be an asset had become a liability. The Humphrey campaign ran an ad that had the words "Spiro Agnew for Vice President" on the screen, accompanied by a soundtrack of a man laughing so hysterically that he finally began wheezing.

When Nixon and Agnew were elected, Agnew continued his tough talk. Nixon sent Agnew to the barricades while remaining in the background, and many wanted him to go on record as to whether he agreed with his Vice President. Shortly after Agnew's remarks on Moratorium Day, Nixon said, "I am very proud to have the Vice President with his Greek background in our administration, and he has done a great job for this administration." Privately, however, Nixon was speaking much less favorably, denigrating Agnew's intelligence and joking that no one would ever assassinate him, for fear of getting Agnew as president.

With Nixon's public support, Agnew continued as spokesman for the Administration, saying the things that Nixon was thinking but didn't want to say in public, like Agnew's comment about what should be done with young radicals. "We can...," the Vice President said, "afford to separate them from our society—with no more regret than we should feel over discarding rotten apples from a barrel."

Agnew turned out to be a rotten apple himself. He had begun accepting bribes when he was governor of Maryland and apparently continued to do so as Vice President. When accusations began to surface in 1973, he steadfastly denied them. Finally, faced with insurmountable evidence, Agnew pleaded no contest to the same charge on which the Feds finally nailed Al Capone. He had of course not declared his bribes as taxable income, and was allowed to plead to charges of tax evasion on October 10, 1973, receiving the relatively light sentence of probation and a $10,000 fine. Although in a fiery speech just a few days earlier Agnew had declared that he would not resign even if he was indicted, he immediately stepped down as Vice President and was replaced by Gerald Ford.

Agnew was unrepentant, claiming that he had been pressured into resigning by the Nixon Administration. He never spoke to Nixon again, although he did attend his funeral in 1994. When Agnew wrote his autobiography in 1980, he denied his guilt, but in 1981 a taxpayers' suit resulted in a judgment against him for accepting nearly $150,000 in bribes and kickbacks. He paid the judgment, with interest, but was denied when he tried to take the payment as a tax deduction.

In his post-political career, Agnew became a broker of international transactions, using the contacts he'd made during his years in politics. He died of leukemia in 1996 at the age of 77.

Personal Note: While researching *Crash of the Titans*, a history of the New York Titans American Football League team, I met and became friends with Roger Ellis, who played offensive line for the Titans for three years. After he retired from professional football, Ellis joined the Secret Service, where he served in Agnew's guard. In the wire service photo of Agnew's courtroom plea, Ellis can be seen standing behind him. From Roger, I received a much different impression of the former Vice President than the one I'd gotten from the media. Ellis found Agnew to be a very gracious man, considerate of his Secret Service escort, and always careful to see that they didn't have to work unnecessarily long hours.

Roger maintained a correspondence with Agnew until the latter's death, and occasionally shared some of it with me. The letters were chatty and pleasant, like those of any older man writing to a friend. Agnew talked about grandchildren and the problems of aging, with no reference to nattering nabobs or vicars of vacillation. Roger was well aware of what Agnew had done, but the Spiro Agnew he knew was his friend.

Other sources:
   https://en.wikipedia.org/wiki/Spiro_Agnew
   https://www.senate.gov/artandhistory/history/common/generic/VP_Spiro_Agnew.htm
   Washington Post, October 4, 2016
   New York Times, October 11, 1973
   New York Times, September 19, 1996

Text of President Nixon's Address to Nation on U.S. Policy in the War in Vietnam
New York Times, **November 4, 1969**

Richard Nixon ran for the Presidency in 1968 on the promise that he had a plan, which he could not divulge, for terminating the seemingly endless war in Vietnam. Once he took office, it was apparent that if Nixon had a plan, it wasn't a miraculous one, and it wasn't going to bring the war to a rapid close.

During the first week in November 1969, just two days short of a year from his election, Nixon addressed the American people about the situation in Vietnam. If one can divorce themselves from his legacy, and momentarily set aside the venom that infused the anti war movement, Nixon's speech wasn't that bad, and one can almost sympathize with his dilemma.

Notable in the President's words was the absence of the word "victory." Presidents Eisenhower and Kennedy rarely spoke of Vietnam, and when Lyndon Johnson talked about the war, it was in terms of winning. But by November 1969, not even the President was talking about winning the war—only ending it in a way that didn't appear to be abject failure.

Nixon never revealed exactly what his secret plan was, but the previous July he had addressed a personal letter to North Vietnamese President Ho Chi Minh outlining a potential framework for peace. The reply, received by Nixon just three days before Ho's death, was that there was only one way to achieve peace, a complete and immediate withdrawal of all United States troops.

That was the crux of Nixon's problem. The North Vietnamese knew that Nixon had to end the war, and needed only to wait him out. Nixon was desperate to negotiate, while his adversaries had no reason to come to an agreement. They had been fighting foreign invaders for centuries, and while plucking young Americans off college campuses and sending them to the

Vietnamese jungle was horrible, the life of a Vietnamese peasant might have been a cut below that of a Viet Cong soldier. And it was their home game.

The North Vietnamese went to the Paris peace talks and began an endless argument about the shape of the table. Every week of delay made Nixon's position more untenable, as he came under increasing pressure to get American troops out of Southeast Asia.

Nixon began his speech by attributing the country's violent division over the war to the fact that "many Americans have lost confidence in what their government has told them about our policy." He briefly sketched the war situation and then laid out the alternatives. The first was complete and immediate withdrawal, which Nixon said would have been easy for him and would have prevented "Johnson's War" from becoming "Nixon's War."

Vietnam had become Nixon's War because, he said, immediate withdrawal was out of the question. It would mean abandoning our South Vietnamese ally to a totalitarian conquest by the North and cause American allies around the world to lose confidence in the United States. "We had a prelude of what would happen in South Vietnam when the Communists entered the city of Hue last year," Nixon said. "During their brief rule there, there was a bloody reign of terror in which 3,000 civilians were clubbed, shot to death and buried in mass graves…. For the United States this first defeat in our nation's history would result in a collapse of confidence in American leadership not only in Asia but throughout the world."

Anyone egotistical enough to run for the Presidency has their eye focused clearly on their historical legacy, and Nixon was no exception. Vietnam had driven Lyndon Johnson from office and Nixon believed it would be the defining issue of his administration. Regardless of what withdrawal would mean to the South Vietnamese and other allies, it was unacceptable because of what it would mean to the legacy of Richard Nixon.

A bigger concern than allies was the domestic political situation. Complete withdrawal under severe pressure from the left reeked of surrender and weakness, and would alienate a large part of Nixon's Republican base. Nixon always claimed that while vocal protestors received all the publicity, there was a "Silent Majority" that supported his agenda. He was correct, for much of the country was quietly conservative and would be deeply upset by an American military defeat brought about because Nixon had yielded to long-haired protestors. Further, many people still believed in the "domino theory" which stated that if one country fell under the Communist yoke, the others would fall in succession like a row of dominoes. Abandon Vietnam and the Chinese would be landing on Australia's north shore. If liberal Democrat Lyndon Johnson couldn't end the war without political fallout, certainly Nixon could not.

If Nixon couldn't withdraw American troops immediately, if North

Vietnam wouldn't negotiate seriously, and the American public wouldn't tolerate a continuance of the war, what were his options? There weren't many, but Nixon outlined some of the attempts he had made to negotiate peace through third parties and the efforts made by Secretary of State William Rogers, former Ambassador to South Vietnam Henry Cabot Lodge, and Nixon's assistant for national security affairs who the *Times* erroneously identified as Dr. "Keisinger." (Henry Kissinger had not achieved the fame he would have within a couple of years.) After describing his unsuccessful efforts for a negotiated peace, Nixon set forth his plan. The American military would gradually turn over responsibility for the war to the South Vietnamese and, during the transition, American troops would be systematically withdrawn.

The President called his plan the "Nixon Doctrine." "In Korea," he said, "and again in Vietnam, the United States furnished most of the money, most of the armament and most of the men to help the people of those countries defend their freedom against Communist aggression." Under the Nixon Doctrine, "we shall furnish military and economic assistance when requested in accordance with our treaty commitments. But we shall look to the nation directly threatened to assume the primary responsibility of providing the manpower for its defense."

If Nixon wanted to get American boys out of South Vietnam, the policy that became known as "Vietnamization" was about his only option. But it ignored the fact that if the Vietnamese had been capable of fending off the Viet Cong, the United States wouldn't have been there in the first place. "It was, after all" said the *New York Times*, "the inability of the South Vietnamese Army to fight effectively, even after more than ten years of training and equipment by the United States, that prompted the dispatch of combat troops in 1965." President Eisenhower's initial plan of supporting the Vietnamese had been to supply and equip them and let them do the fighting. When Kennedy began sending advisors to Southeast Asia, he said, "It is their war. They are the ones who have to win it or lose it."

After Kennedy came Lyndon Johnson, who the *Times* said, "promised [during the 1964 campaign] that he would not send American boys to do the job that Asian boys should be doing." But by the time Johnson left office, there were more than a half million American boys doing what the Asian boys could or would not. The Vietnamese required more and more aid, and by 1966 the money sent to Vietnam was shifted from the foreign aid budget to that of the Department of Defense. By that time $1.6 billion had been expended, which was a lot of money in the late 1950s and early 1960s.

Vietnamization was not a new concept; it dated back to the French colonial forces of the early 1950s. A few months after Nixon's plan was announced, General Henri Navarre, who had commanded the French forces in Vietnam, said, "Vietnamization is an old idea. It was the basis of

9. It's All About the War 249

my own plan when I was sent to Indochina in 1952." In that less sensitive era, the French plan was referred to as "yellowing" the war. (An American general later referred to the American plan as "changing the color of the corpse.") The French plan was unsuccessful, but perhaps it wasn't necessary for Vietnamization to succeed as long as it provided cover for Nixon to withdraw American troops and end the war.

After Nixon announced his plan, the United States embarked on the nearly impossible task of making the Army of the Republic of South Vietnam self-sufficient by providing longer officer training programs and more weaponry. In addition to military training, the U.S. provided assistance in the areas of conducting elections, social reforms, and economic development so that the country could more effectively govern itself after it fended off the North Vietnamese. By March 1971, the ARVN had more than a million men under arms and the most modern weapons United States dollars could buy. The South Vietnamese Air Force was the fourth largest in the world.

In mid–1970, the South Vietnamese had their first major test when Nixon authorized the invasion of Cambodia to attempt to stop Viet Cong infiltration to the south. Initial reports indicated that the South Vietnamese troops performed well, and it appeared that Vietnamization was off to a good start. A later study by Major Jeff Hacket, however, found that "ARVN (the South Vietnamese Army) had used their best-trained units to face an enemy who was more concerned about their self-preservation rather than fighting. Moreover, they relied heavily on U.S. air and artillery support."

The invasion of Cambodia signaled an expansion of the war, which sparked more protests and led to the passage of the Cooper-Church amendment, which cut off funding for Cambodian operations. With U.S. forces prohibited from operating outside of Vietnam, the Vietnamese were left on their own during an initiative in southern Laos called Operation Lam Son 719.

Lam Son was a disaster, as Vietnamese officers proved incapable of managing a large battle and coordinating air and artillery support for the infantry. The South lost 5,000 killed and wounded and none of the operational objectives was achieved.

In late March 1972, the North Vietnamese launched a major battle which became known as the Easter Offensive. The aim was to inflict a crushing defeat on the South prior to the U.S. presidential election and thereby improve the North's negotiating position. With only about 40,000 U.S. troops still in Vietnam, the ARVN had limited support and was routed. It didn't affect Nixon; he was bringing the troops home anyway; there was nothing else he could do.

In August 1970, after several months of Vietnamization, the *New York Times* published an article critical of the President's policy. It reviewed prior unsuccessful efforts at Vietnamization and said that no matter who did the fighting, America was to blame for the outcome. "Asians would be killing Asians with American arms," the *Times* said. "Defoliation and destruction of crops would continue; villages be destroyed; refugees be generated; casualties continue ... the United States would still have moral responsibility for the war." The *Times* concluded by asking how many times a policy should be attempted "before we acknowledge failure and attempt a genuine political settlement by negotiating an end to the war in Vietnam."

What the *Times* didn't acknowledge was that North Vietnam had no incentive to negotiate anything as long as Nixon was under political pressure to end the war. He had tried to negotiate and was told that complete American withdrawal was the only option, and that option was not politically viable.

In 1973, after nearly all U.S. soldiers had left Southeast Asia, a truce was finally negotiated. Secretary of Defense Melvin Laird said, "As a consequence of the success of the military aspects of Vietnamization, the South Vietnamese people today, in my view, are fully capable of providing for their own in-country security against the North Vietnamese."

Everyone knew that wasn't true, and Laird probably knew it wasn't true, but it had to be said, a false epitaph to one of the lowest episodes in American history. Without U.S. support the regime in the south quickly collapsed. Fifty thousand American soldiers had died in the steaming jungles for the belief that the collapse of South Vietnam would cause the rest of Southeast Asia to fall like dominoes, which they didn't. For a time in the late '60s, it seemed that the United States would be the first domino to tumble, for the war so deeply divided the country the revolution seemed possible.

There was no evil bogeyman behind the creation of the Vietnam War—not Lyndon Johnson and not Richard Nixon, although they shouldered most of the blame. It developed tiny step by tiny step, inch by inch, military advisor by military advisor, country by country during the administrations of Eisenhower, Kennedy, Johnson, and Nixon, through the actions of mostly well-intentioned men who always believed that another 50,000 troops was the answer. Books like David Halberstam's *The Best and the Brightest* and the memoirs of Johnson's Secretary of Defense Robert McNamara shed bright light on how the tragedy of Vietnam unfolded and how, in November 1969, Richard Nixon found himself in a nearly impossible situation. The face-saving plan of Vietnamization, which Nixon had to know was bound to fail, was his only way out.

Other sources:
/www.history.com/topics/vietnam-war/vietnamization
https://millercenter.org/the-presidency/educational-resources/vietnamization
ttps://thevietnamwar.info/vietnamization-theory-reality/
New York Times, August 1, 1970

Agnew Says TV Networks Are Distorting the News

New York Times, November 14, 1969

Spiro Agnew wasn't right about much during his tenure as Vice President, but five decades of perspective have shown that Agnew hit the nail squarely on the head during his talk to the Mid-West Regional Republican Committee in Des Moines, Iowa. The Vice President wasn't really talking about the current issue of "fake news" but was pointing out a growing trend of the television networks to pass off opinion as fact and claimed that a very small group of men controlled the most influential news medium in America. That group, he pointed out, was centered in what Agnew called "the geographical and intellectual confines of Washington, D.C. or New York City."

Agnew's speech was the brainchild of Pat Buchanan, in response to the television coverage of Nixon's address to the nation on Vietnam. Nixon believed that the public had reacted favorably to his speech, but the reporting of all three major television networks was uniformly negative.

"Are we demanding enough of our television news presentations?" the Vice President asked. "The audience of 70 million Americans gathered to hear the President of the United States was inherited by a small band of network commentators and self-appointed analysts, the majority of whom expressed, in one way or another their hostility to what he had to say."

He pointed to criticism of Nixon's talk by specific commentators and added, "Others, by the expression on their faces, the tone of their questions and the sarcasm of their responses, made clear their sharp disapproval."

Agnew contended that television networks should not have the same degree of editorial freedom allowed newspapers for, while there were numerous newspapers, there were only three networks. That brought the obligatory comparison to the censorship of Adolf Hitler and Nazi Germany, which Buchanan anticipated by having Agnew reference the nearly unqualified support for Winston Churchill when he opposed Hitler, support that was denied to Nixon in his war against Communism.

"They can make or break by their coverage and commentary a moratorium on the war," Agnew said. "It was also the networks that elevated Stokely Carmichael and George Lincoln Rockwell from obscurity to national prominence."

It was not just Nixon who was victimized, Agnew said, and used the example of how Hubert Humphrey's campaign had been destroyed by television coverage of the 1968 Democratic Convention. He claimed that selective use of footage of the violence in Chicago gave the impression that the police were totally at fault, since the provocations of the protestors were not shown.

Agnew's biggest complaint was that a handful of men, elected by no one but themselves, held a monopoly on what news the public was allowed to see. In that instance, he was barking up the wrong tree, for today we have a plethora of cable news networks plus on-line sources, yet newscasts are more opinionated than ever. It's hard to believe that MSNBC and Fox News are basing their stories on the same facts.

Some of the Vice President's concerns, however, were timeless. "Normality has become the nemesis of the network news," he said. "Bad news drives out good news. The irrational is more controversial than the rational.... One minute of Eldridge Cleaver is worth 10 minutes of Roy Wilkins [the moderate leader of the NAACP]. The labor crisis settled at the negotiating table is nothing compared to the confrontation that results in a strike—or better yet, violence along the picket lines.

"And the American who relies upon television for his news might conclude that the majority of American students are embittered radicals. That the majority of black Americans have no regard for their country. That violence and lawlessness are the rule rather than the exception on the American campus."

Fifty years later, nothing has changed. Most news broadcasts are a succession of angry people shouting at each other, potential health scares (If you've eaten a raisin at any time prior to 2004, you may have an increased risk of cancer of the earlobe), people with a gripe, and wall-to-wall coverage of any natural disaster, shooting, or dysfunction. If we want to stem illegal immigration, perhaps we should require potential immigrants to watch American news broadcasts. They might become so frightened or disgusted that they would choose to stay home.

The speech closed by pointing out the good the networks had done by focusing the country's attention on important issues and then challenged them to bring more objectivity and fairness to their broadcasts. Agnew told the American people to "let the networks know that they want their news straight and objective" and encouraged the public to write to the networks and express that opinion.

3 Networks Reply to Agnew Attack
New York Times, November 14, 1969

The response of the networks to Agnew's remarks was predictably defensive and self-righteous. Leonard Goldenson of ABC said, "In our judgment, the performance of A.B.C. News has always been and will continue to be fair and objective."

Dr. Frank Stanton of CBS conceded that the media was not immune from criticism. "We do not believe, however, that this unprecedented attempt by the Vice President of the United States to intimidate a news medium which depends for its existence upon Government licenses represents legitimate criticism.... Whatever [the] deficiencies [of the media], they are minor compared to those of a press which would be subservient to the executive power of Government."

Julian Goodman of NBC struck a similar chord, saying, "Vice President Agnew's attack on television news is an appeal to prejudice.... It is regrettable that the Vice President of the United States would deny to television freedom of the press."

Reaction to the speech seemed to reinforce Agnew's contention that the opinion of the networks was not reflective of the opinions of the general public. While all three networks accused him of censorship and fascism, the opinions of those who contacted the media were split almost down the middle, about half in favor of Agnew's speech and half against.

But the Vice President was fighting a losing battle, for all the reasons he stated. The media controlled the news and, to a great extent, public opinion. Ironically, it was not television but the print media, in the persons of Carl Bernstein and Bob Woodward, that helped uncover the rampant corruption and obstruction of justice that would result in Nixon's resignation less than five years later.

Agnew Becomes Duffer for a Day

New York Times, February 8, 1970

When Vice President Spiro Agnew teed off in the Bob Hope Desert Classic, he became the highest level elected official ever to play in a PGA Tour pro-am. Agnew was not a great golfer, laboring under an 18 handicap, but when the Vice President wants to play in a tournament, ability is no obstacle.

The Desert Classic, offering a $125,000 total purse, was held at the La Quinta Country Club in Palm Springs. It consisted of 90 holes for professionals (18 more than most tour events) and 72 holes for amateurs. Foursomes were comprised of three amateurs and one professional, and for the first three days of the tournament, one of the foursomes consisted of pro Doug Sanders and three unknowns. On Saturday, Agnew, host Bob Hope, and California Senator George Murphy took the place of the amateurs in Sanders' foursome.

Sanders was a 36-year-old veteran who never won a major title but came close on several occasions. His best chance would come a few months later, when he lost the British Open to Lee Trevino in a playoff. Sanders was known for his flamboyant attire and always wore brightly colored ensembles, in an era when bright, clashing colors were considered stylish.

When Agnew's foursome appeared on the first tee, they were surrounded by about 75 media people, far more attention than was given to any other foursome. Agnew, with the world watching, hooked his first drive well over the fairway ropes and into the gallery.

Hope parked his cart in the fairway and waited for the Vice President to hit his second shot from the rough. Sanders, dressed in orange shoes and shirt, green slacks, and a green and orange sweater, stood next to the cart. Perhaps he should have been wearing something less conspicuous, for Agnew's wild slice hit Sanders in the forehead and drew blood.

Agnew rushed up and apologized to Sanders and his wife and a doctor friend of the golfer's applied Novocaine to the wound. Someone asked Sanders what club Agnew had hit. "I don't know," he replied, "but he hit it solid."

Sanders regrouped and parred the hole, but Agnew's round was memorable only for the skulling of his partner. He picked his ball up several times, played the wrong ball once and, as Hope pointed out, kept the gallery on their toes. On the fourth hole, when his second shot went into the crowd, he said, "I'm going to kill somebody." On the final hole, where the largest group, estimated at 3,000, was gathered, he hit his second shot beyond the ropes. Rather than risk hitting back over the assemblage, he picked his ball up and called it a day.

Despite his tribulations at the 1970 Classic, Agnew was back to try again the following year. Sanders even agreed to play in his foursome, perhaps figuring that lightning couldn't strike twice in the same place.

Sanders emerged unscathed, but Agnew sliced his first tee shot into the gallery, where it hit a 66-year-old man from Oregon, bounced off him, and hit his wife in the arm. Agnew went over and apologized, then teed up a second shot. That turned out a little better, for Agnew hit only one person, a woman who had to be taken to the hospital for x-rays of her ankle. Despite encouragement from the gallery, Agnew decided not to tee up a third ball. Three casualties on two shots were enough. The remainder of the round was uneventful and Hope quipped, "He did play the last 15 holes in great shape and on the back nine he got a birdie, an eagle, an elk, a moose and a mason."

When Gerald Ford was selected to replace Agnew after the latter's resignation, he proved a worthy successor in at least one regard. In June 1974, Ford, a 17-handicapper, was playing in a celebrity tournament in Minneapolis when one of his errant shots hit 17-year-old Tom Gerard in the head. Gerard was not seriously injured.

It wasn't that long after his harrowing appearances in the Desert Classic that Spiro Agnew had much bigger problems than golf shots bouncing off the skull of his partner. But Agnew's tribulations on the course made him more likeable, for most people who play golf are more like Spiro Agnew than Jack Nicklaus. And what made a man who had many abrasive characteristics a bit less offensive was the fact that, unlike his boss, Agnew could laugh at himself. And when Spiro Agnew played golf, there was a lot to laugh about.

Other sources:
https://en.wikipedia.org/wiki/Doug_Sanders
https://www.golfchannel.com/article/grill-room/feb-13-history-vp-strikes-multiple-fans-drives/
https://sports.vice.com/en_us/article/9apw73/throwback-thursday-spiro-agnew-shanks-golf-balls-the-vice-presidency
New York Times, June 25, 1974

Brother Takes Role in War

Bridgeport Post-Telegram, May 18, 1971

Glenn Stohrer was tired of fighting in Vietnam. After five months in Southeast Asia, the 21-year-old Army radio operator-rifleman came home to Yarmouth, Maine, on April 8, 1971, for a two-week leave, and wanted to stay home. "Glenn didn't want to go back," his father Carleton said. "He told us it's all pointless over there and that they were playing games with his life." He said his son had never been against the war before he joined the Army, "but he was embittered when he came back.... He was a wreck when he came home." "Try to imagine the worst thing in your mind," Glenn told his family, "and it's twice as bad as that ... it's unbelievable and unreal."

While Glenn was home on leave, his 22-year-old brother Wesley came to visit. Wesley, who was classified 4-F due to a knee injury suffered while skiing, had just finished a winter teaching at Sugar Loaf Mountain. When his brother told him how unhappy he was, and how he didn't think he could stand to go back, Wesley decided to do something about it.

He and Glenn talked about the possibility of him going to Vietnam in Glenn's place. The plan was for Wesley to do one tour, and when he got his first leave, Glenn would go back in his place. Wesley said later that he knew Glenn wouldn't go back and if he didn't do something his brother would go AWOL and be in serious trouble. Their father, a local contractor and a World War II submarine veteran, heard them talking about it and said he wanted nothing to do with the scheme. He assumed it was just talk.

It was much more. Glenn showed Wesley photos of his friends and told him about them. Wesley memorized procedures and phrases. "Walk straight," Glenn told him, "look stupid, and salute anything with brass."

When Wesley shaved his sideburns and cut his hair, he bore a passable resemblance to his brother.

When the time came for Glenn to ship out, he and Wesley told their father they were going to Connecticut to visit friends and that Glenn would leave from there. Wesley, they said, was going on a cruise to the Bahamas. Rather than set sail for the Caribbean, however, Wesley donned Glenn's uniform, took his identification, and boarded a flight that eventually got him to Vietnam on April 21. He was sent to Chu Lai and then by truck to Hawk Hill, where Glenn's unit, the Reconnaissance Platoon, Company C, Second Battalion, First Infantry, 196th Infantry Brigade, was stationed.

When Wesley arrived on Hawk Hill, Glenn's close friends knew immediately that it wasn't him, but decided not to turn Wesley in. "The guys were hysterical," Wesley said later, "and thought it would be interesting to see what happened."

For a while, Wesley was able to escape detection. "I didn't have any trouble playing the role of soldier," he said. "I just saluted when everyone else did, ended every sentence with sir, and just acted stupid the rest of the time." Eventually, however, it became clear to just about everyone in the unit that the soldier wearing Glenn Stohrer's uniform was not Glenn Stohrer. For one thing, Glenn had always carried a pack of cards with him, which Wesley didn't. Second, Wesley didn't have Glenn's notoriously voracious appetite. Someone noticed that Wesley didn't know the difference between a Specialist 4, which was Glenn's rank, and a PFC. When he saluted a First Sergeant, others became suspicious.

When the unit was ordered into the field for a possible offensive action, one of the soldiers pulled the plug; he didn't want the unit jeopardized due to Wesley's lack of training. The man told his sergeant and the sergeant brought Wesley to Captain Francis G. Downey.

When confronted, Wesley immediately admitted his identity and was sent to Chu Lai and placed in a five foot by ten-foot cell that was just six feet high. After nine days, the army verified that Wesley was a civilian, and he was allowed to move into Military Police barracks. The Army placed a call to Carleton Storer and told him what had happened. Carleton contacted Glenn's girlfriend, 19-year-old Gail Crane, and she passed the word along to Glenn, who was in Virginia. He immediately went back to Maine to turn himself in, arriving in Portland May 25.

Both brothers were in trouble. Glenn was AWOL and Wesley faced up to five years in prison on charges of illegal entry into South Vietnam. But the army was in a benevolent mood. After verifying Wesley's identity with the FBI, they decided not to charge him with any crimes and put him on a plane back to the United States. His short stint in Vietnam turned Wesley against the war and he was not impressed with military efficiency. "Talk about a slow process," he said. "It took them two weeks to find out who I was after I told them."

The boys' parents defended them. "He's not a coward," Carleton said of Glenn. "If they invaded Casco Bay, he'd be the first one down there." Mrs. Storer said, "It was a brotherly gesture. Wesley told me he was willing to give his life for his brother and was willing to come home with a leg blown off for his brother."

Glenn was sent back to Vietnam, busted two grades to private, and fined $146. Apparently, he survived the remainder of his tour, for when Carleton died in 2008, both Wesley and Glenn were listed as survivors. Wesley parlayed his unusual experience into an appearance on the television quiz show *To Tell the Truth* during the 1971–72 season.

Soldiers who fall in combat are often described as making the ultimate sacrifice. But perhaps Wesley Storer made the ultimate sacrifice, voluntarily putting his life on the line to spare his brother. Neither forfeited their life, but it was one of the most unique stories in one of the most unusual wars in the history of the United States.

Other sources:
http://americal4ofthe3.com/images/6471.pdf
http://www.fosters.com/article/20100308/NEWS0104/100309635
http://www.ttttontheweb.com/tttt69s3guide.html
Fort Pierce News-Tribune, June 15, 1971
European Stars and Stripes, May 21, 1971
Bennington Banner, May 18, 1971
Oxnard Press Courier, May 18, 1971
Daily Kennebec Journal, May 26, 1971
Lincoln Star, May 18, 1971
Press Telegram, Long Beach, California, May 25, 1971

President's Cousin Seeks Help

Hartford Courant, June 4, 1971

Every American president seems to have had at least one relative who was a source of embarrassment. Beer-guzzling Billy Carter became a national celebrity during his brother's administration and even had a brand of beer named for him. Richard Nixon's brother Donald became involved in some shady business dealings and Franklin's Roosevelt's sons always seemed to be in trouble (see Chapter 2).

Nixon prided himself on coming from humble origins, and in early June 1971 he received an air-mailed letter marked "Personal—Family" from a member of his humble family, 24-year-old second cousin Kathy Timberlake. Timberlake said she was in desperate straits and her $27 per month welfare payment wasn't enough to sustain her. She'd been collecting unemployment compensation and disability payments, but they ran out about three months before she wrote the letter. "And I just freaked out," she said.

The President was not the only one who received Timberlake's letter. She sent copies to the *San Francisco Chronicle* and other media outlets, and soon the story appeared in newspapers around the country. The President, a conservative Republican whose Vice President railed against welfare shirkers, had a relative on the dole.

Kathy was the daughter of Nixon's first cousin, Dr. P.F. Timberlake, but she had not lived with her family for about five years and had not seen them in several months. After graduating from high school in Newport Beach, California, Timberlake briefly attended Orange Coast College in Costa Mesa before embarking on a journey typical of many lost young souls of the late 1960s. She got married, but after two months her husband left her to follow a rock band on tour. The problem with their marriage, Kathy said, was that her husband was doing acid but she wasn't. At one point, she was so upset by her failing relationship that she tried to kill herself. A couple of years earlier, in 1966, her brother Phillip had committed suicide at the age of 20.

After her divorce, Kathy continued to have problems with men. She was attractive and thought that men always tried to take advantage of her. By 1971, Kathy was living in Cotati, California, a small town about 65 miles north of San Francisco, in a tiny apartment behind a bar named The Eight Ball. Most of the $90 per month rent was paid by her roommate, Kathleen Walsh, a student who hadn't known Timberlake until the two moved in together.

Kathy had worked at a series of jobs, including electronics assembler and a dancer in a bar, but was not employed at the time of her letter to Nixon. "I don't feel as though I can work at all in this society," she wrote. "I've either been fired from every job I've held or have had an emotional breakdown.... I just want to live peacefully, some way. Maybe after awhile I'll get myself together enough to do something worthwhile, to help other people."

Her letter to Nixon began, "I don't know if you remember me..." and told the President of her depression and despair. "I am writing to tell you my life's existence has become too unbearable.... I can't work or do anything because of my emotional state ... no one cares if I should fade away." She said she was going to the Mental Health Services clinic in Santa Rosa, but it didn't seem to be doing her much good. "She didn't expect to be helped," her roommate said. "She just kept going to be amused."

Kathy had thought it was a good idea to send her letter to the media, but when reporters began descending on her Cotati apartment, she had second thoughts and took refuge at the Sonoma County Community

Mental Health Center. Her roommate told reporters that Kathy was "emotionally disturbed," but she too become spooked by the barrage of media and left town. Kathy's 19-year-old sister Kerry moved into the vacant apartment with her boyfriend, which didn't sit well with landlord Simon Jaffe, who tried to evict them.

The media blitz also hit Timberlake's parents. Kathy had told reporters that although many people thought her parents were well off, they were barely scraping by. Dr. Timberlake wouldn't address his own financial situation, but said he hadn't seen his daughter in several months and had not known of her now famous letter. "I think she created her own problems," he said, "and she's going to have to solve them."

The *Lompoc Record* voiced a similar opinion. "Like thousands of other young people today, she has been scarred by five years of aimless wanderings from pad to pad in Northern California, sampling psychedelic drugs, soured love experiences, and psychiatric problems."

President Nixon wrote to Timberlake's mother, telling her that he had a lawyer looking into the matter and would see if he could help. In the meantime, Kathy applied for full disability and made an appointment with a psychiatrist.

In late June, Timberlake was in the news again. At a meeting of the Philadelphia Welfare Rights Organization, a woman stood up and announced that she was Kathy Timberlake. A reporter, who suspected the woman was not Timberlake, asked her for identification. The woman could not produce it and admitted she was an imposter.

Timberlake's letter led reporters to find another Nixon relative living on public assistance, although the circumstances were completely different. Cousin Philip Milhouse, 57, of Grass Valley, California, and his 47-year-old wife Anna had been living on welfare and disability payments since 1966. Both Milhouses, however, were physically disabled. Philip had suffered a heart attack and his wife had a number of ailments.

Nixon had been expected to roll back some of the Great Society programs, out of concern for the deficit or fear of creating a system of dependence. Uncovering Nixon relatives on the dole complicated the issue.

Philip and Anna Milhouse were a non-story, for there weren't many people who wanted to deny assistance to the disabled. Kathy Timberlake presented another facet of the debate, an able-bodied person who'd made a shambles of her life and expected other people to pick up the pieces. If her parents weren't willing to help her, should the American taxpayer be forced to do so?

The debate still rages, but Kathy Timberlake disappeared from the news with the same rapidity that she had suddenly appeared. There were other human-interest stories and the press moved on to cover them. The crisis had passed, but it wasn't long before Richard Nixon had far greater troubles than a destitute cousin.

Other sources:
San Rafael Daily Independent Journal, June 3, 1971
Des Moines Register, June 5, 1971
Racine Journal-Times, June 4, 1971
Lompoc Record, June 16, 1971
Hanover Evening Sun, July 1, 1971
Daily Review, Hayward, California, June 28, 1971

10

From Panty Raids to Anti-War Protests

Student Unrest

Youth rebellion was one of the defining characteristics of the late 1960s. There were some high school protests, but most media attention was focused on college campuses. The most frequently protested issues were racism and the war in Vietnam. The majority of the racial incidents, unsurprisingly, were instigated by African American students while the overwhelming majority of anti-war activity was initiated by whites.

College administrations were slowly evolving, and some presidents were sympathetic to student aims. Others resented the idea of students dictating to the administration. While anarchy never took root permanently, the structure of many universities and high schools changed to allow the students greater freedom and more control over their lives. The process was never smooth, and campuses saw more upheaval during this period than at any other time in the history of academia.

Negro Students Killed in Riots

Hartford Courant, February 9, 1968

The seed for the deadly Orangeburg massacre was planted in a bowling alley. During the fall of 1967, a group of African Americans tried to convince Harry Floyd, owner of the segregated All Star Bowling Lane (the only one in Orangeburg) to allow black men and women to rack up strikes and spares with their white neighbors. Floyd refused, and on the night of February 5, 1968, 40 students from nearby South Carolina State College, a predominately black school, showed up at the alley. They were asked to leave and departed peacefully. The following night an even larger delegation appeared, and this time the police arrested several people, including John Stroman, the group's leader. In the process of making the arrests, police roughed up some of the protestors and school officials said they saw young women being held by one officer while being clubbed by another.

The incidents at the bowling alley led to protests on the SCSC campus, which caused South Carolina governor Robert McNair to call out the National Guard, which intensified the already incendiary atmosphere in Orangeburg. On the night of February 8, a group of 50–75 students gathered on a hilly area and started a bonfire. Firemen and state policemen were dispatched to the scene and from that point accounts differ.

The most plausible story is that someone threw a wooden banister at the first responders, injuring one of them. Initial news reports stated that the students fired on the police, but it was later ascertained that no shots were fired from the hill. When National Guardsmen and police officers, who were waiting across the street, heard that shots had been fired, they charged up the hill and at 10:33 p.m. began raining buckshot into the retreating crowd. When the shooting ended, two South Carolina State students and one high school student were dead. The latter had been sitting on the steps of a campus building waiting for his mother to get off work. Twenty-seven people were injured, most shot in the back or the back of their legs as they attempted to run away.

At a press conference the next day, McNair called the shooting "one of the saddest days in the history of South Carolina." He placed the blame on black power advocates and worried that the state's reputation for racial harmony had been stained.

One of the wounded was Cleveland Sellers of the Student Non-Violent Coordinating Committee, a national civil rights organization. While he was being treated in the hospital, Sellers was arrested for inciting a riot, conspiracy to riot, and riot, for the protest at the bowling alley. He was convicted of the latter charge in 1970 (the first two were dismissed) and served seven months in prison. Nine officers were arrested, but all nine were acquitted after the jury deliberated for just two hours.

The incident in Orangeburg was the first time college students had been killed during a protest, preceding the Kent State shootings by two years. It was the first time police officers had been arrested in connection with a college protest. Yet, reaction around the country was muted. In an article in *Southern Patriot* in 1970, Dave Nolan speculated on the reasons for the modest reaction. One factor was that the Kent State victims were white while those in Orangeburg were black. Had the incident happened a few years earlier, Nolan speculated, there might have been outrage, such as with the violence at Selma in 1963, but recent violence and the rise of the Black Power movement had frightened many who were formerly sympathetic. When the passive resistance of Martin Luther King was supplanted by violent resistance, people were more willing to accept the police claim that the battle had been an "exchange of gunfire."

In subsequent years, the incident became the subject of great controversy. After Jack Bass co-authored a book called *The Orangeburg Massacre*, he received an angry letter from FBI Director J. Edgar Hoover, which he said was filled with inaccuracies. Bass replied and made both letters public, generating a great deal of press coverage.

After his release from prison, Cleveland Sellers earned a master's degree from Harvard and a doctorate from the University of South Carolina. He was granted a full pardon in 1995 and subsequently hired by the latter school.

In 1968, in the aftermath of the shooting, the gymnasium at South Carolina State was named for the three victims. In 2001, 33 years after the incident, there was a ceremony acknowledging the shootings at the school's Martin Luther King Auditorium. Governor Jim Hodges spoke and expressed his deep regret over the incident. Two years later, Hodges's successor, Mark Sanford, issued a formal apology for the actions of the South Carolina government. It was too late to save the lives of the three victims, but at least it was an acknowledgment of how wrong things had gone during the 1960s.

Other sources:
https://blackpast.org/aah/orangeburg-massacre-1968
https://en.wikipedia.org/wiki/Orangeburg_massacre
Neiman Reports, The Neiman Foundation for Journalism at Harvard University, Volume 57, Number 3, Fall 2003: *Documenting the Orangeburg Massacre* by Jack Bass

Trinity Trustees Captive

Hartford Courant, April 23, 1968

Trinity College, located in Hartford, Connecticut, is a small liberal arts school with approximately 2,300 students. Connecticut's second oldest college, it was founded in 1823 by a combination of Episcopal clergy and laymen as a non-denominational institution for men. Among its prominent graduates are writer George Will, television commentator Tucker Carlson, and playwright Edward Albee.

In 1968, Trinity was all-male, and the student body was small enough to allow for the photos of all freshmen to be published in the student handbook. Many of the mores of the 1950s remained in place, including limits on the hours during which women could visit dormitories and fraternity houses and the requirement that "At least one mature, responsible couple who are not married students or recent graduates must chaperone any planned party."

Yet, some of the radicalism that was beginning to permeate even staid eastern campuses was creeping into Trinity. While the list of the school's organizations featured traditional clubs like The Balloonists Society, it also included the radical Students for a Democratic Society, whose Trinity chapter had been established in 1966, as well as the Trinity Coalition of Blacks. The newest organization was the Revitalization Corps, organized to work with the Hartford community and improve the living conditions of its citizens. In another sign of the times, the student handbook provided information on where the students could obtain forms to apply for a student deferment from the military draft.

The section of the handbook titled "The Campus" stated, "If you enter the campus from the parking area through the main arch in Downes Memorial Clock Tower, you will pass beneath the Trustees room." If you happened to pass through the Downes Memorial Clock Tower arch on the late afternoon of April 22, 1968, you would have come upon a most remarkable sight, one that couldn't have been imagined a year or two earlier.

The trustees were meeting in the Williams Memorial Building to consider a proposal to provide scholarships for black students, which had been recommended by the student body by a vote of 608 to 96. A group of 168 students, led by the Trinity Association of Negro Students (TAN) had gathered outside the building and announced that the trustees would not be allowed to leave until they approved the measure. They also wanted the trustees to agree to support courses in Negro history, urban affairs, poverty, psychology of the ghettoes, and community development.

The trustees meeting was chaired by 68-year-old Trinity president Albert C. Jacobs, who'd led the institution since 1953. Jacobs was from an older generation, a veteran of both world wars and a Republican who'd worked at Columbia University when Dwight Eisenhower was president of the college. Jacobs was not in the best of health and was planning to retire in just a few months. His replacement, Theodore Davidge Lockwood, was a trustee and therefore also in the meeting.

The trustees became aware of their dilemma when William Gwinn tried to leave to go to another meeting and was told to get back inside. Once they realized they were being held prisoner, the trustees discussed their options. Some thought they should refuse to make a decision under coercion, while others recommended that the proposal be approved. A third faction wanted to summon the police. Jacobs offered to resign and let Lockwood take his place immediately, but his offer was not accepted.

One trustee suggested that they encourage students to counter-demonstrate, but that proposal was wisely shelved, as another trustee pointed out that the last thing they wanted was to pit groups of students against each other, with the possibility of violence.

The trustees' other concerns were practical. The students had cut off the telephone switchboard and there was no way to call out. They had neither food nor bathroom facilities, problems that were resolved when the wife of Dean Dorowitz brought food and empty milk cartons.

Meanwhile, outside the building, Terry Jones, the leader of TAN, addressed the media and set forth his group's grievances. He pointed out that there were only 16 blacks among Trinity's 1,160 students, and that nearly all were from outside Connecticut. Only one was from Hartford. Jones wanted students from Hartford and New Haven to be given priority for the proposed scholarships.

The battle lines had been drawn. The students appeared ready for a lengthy siege, as many had books with them and were studying on the steps. The trustees had been supplied with food and empty milk cartons and were trying to figure out how to respond. These were unique times and they were in uncharted waters.

Trinity Strike Ends in Accord
Hartford Courant, April 25, 1968

After being detained for just three hours, the trustees were allowed to leave the Williams Memorial Building. As soon as they left, the students occupied the facility, secured the doors with ropes and prevented anyone from entering, other than newsmen, who were given prepared statements.

Thirty-two hours after it began, the demonstration ended, and the students evacuated the building. Jacobs stated that the scholarship proposal was being given favorable consideration, but emphasized that no concessions had been made to the demonstrators. "Trinity has welcomed well-qualified Negros and given them financial assistance for some time," he said. When asked why there were only 16 blacks at the school, he replied, "We have had trouble getting qualified Negroes."

The reaction of the student body was mixed. A petition signed by 14 percent of them recommended that no disciplinary action be taken against the protestors. Many, however, while agreeing with the aims of the protest, did not think the trustees should have been forced to make the decision under pressure.

Trinity eventually provided the scholarships, and over the next few years, the school began to change. In 1969, women were admitted for the first time. The previous October, Lockwood, who at 43 was significantly younger than Jacobs, had taken the helm. During his inaugural speech, he said that the "duty of the college was to permit and tolerate student expression."

Lockwood served as president of Trinity until 1981, and at the time of his departure, granted a long exit interview, during which he spoke at length about the 1968 incident.

"I think it is difficult," he said, "when you're trying to recreate these events historically, it's so difficult to recapture the feeling of dismay because now when we look at the demands themselves, we wonder how we got so hung up. But, of course, it was a new experience I think for the East, which had never experienced Berkeley. We only read about it. We had no notion of what it was to live in that atmosphere or to have activist students of that ilk, and we were just not ready for it.... I think they discovered on that occasion how easy it was to play politics on campus, that we were very vulnerable to political action if it was at all organized." "[The incident] crushed Al Jacobs," he added.

It was indeed a new experience for Trinity, but similar incidents were taking place on campuses across the country. The day after the trustees were held captive, the massive uprising at Columbia made the Trinity incident seem insignificant. "It took us off the front pages," Lockwood said.

Trinity may have been off the front page, but it was never the same as it was before 1968. The restrictions on women visiting the men's dorms are long gone and the student population today mirrors the racial and ethnic diversity found on virtually all campuses. Although there are more than 140 clubs and organizations at Trinity, it does not appear that the Balloonists Society is among them. A new day has dawned.

Other sources:
> https://commons.trincoll.edu/edreform/2012/05/the-effect-of-student-social-movements-on-trinity-college-policy
> The Trinity College Handbook 1968–69
> Exit Interview with Theodore Lockwood, May 1981: https://digitalrepository.trincoll.edu/w_books/13/

Student Anti-War Strike Urged

Hartford Courant, April 25, 1968

The last week in April was a tumultuous one on college campuses throughout the United States. At Columbia, buildings were occupied and administrators held captive. The trustees at Trinity College were trapped in their meeting room, and two organizations, the International Student-Faculty Strike for Peace and the Student Mobilization Committee to End the War, urged students at all colleges throughout the United States to go on strike on Friday, April 26 to protest the war in Vietnam, racism, and the military draft. In addition to the activities in the United States, there were to be peace demonstrations in Europe, Latin America, Asia, and Africa.

The *Courant*, based in Hartford, Connecticut, focused its reporting on state schools. The strike at Yale was led by the Yale Anti-War Coalition, the one at the University of Connecticut by the "April 26 Movement," and that at the University of Hartford by the Martin Luther King Society. Wesleyan would not strike, instead holding its "Day of Concern" on Thursday (see below).

Each Connecticut school planned an assortment of activities. UConn students could attend a "teach-in" on the shores of Mirror Lake, where they could reflect on war and racism. At the University of Hartford, there would be a memorial service to honor those who had died in Vietnam and those Hartford students who were expected to be killed in Vietnam if the war continued. The school's SDS chapter planned to plant a row of white crosses stretching from Dana Hall to the Gengras Campus Center. Yale would hold a demonstration at the New Haven Army induction center and a number of seminars conducted by Yale faculty and graduate students.

The strike was not against the faculty, most of whom were in sympathy with the students. Many instructors cancelled classes or excused those who chose to boycott them. University of Pennsylvania President Gaylord Harnwell gave all of the school's students permission to strike and the American Association of University Professors overwhelmingly approved a motion to create a bill of rights for students, granting them freedom of expression and participation in the management of their schools.

While other colleges made plans, the students at Columbia created the most memorable events of the week, when the Student Afro-American Society (SAS) and the SDS took over five buildings in protest of the university's plan to construct a new gymnasium in the predominantly black Morningside Heights area. Students also demanded that the college end its affiliation with the Institute for Defense Analyses.

The demonstration was intended to encompass the Vietnam War, but the antiwar aspect was eclipsed by the racial protest, as radicals H. Rap Brown and Stokley Carmichael joined the protestors and announced a plan to have the residents of Harlem demonstrate in concert. Once Brown and Carmichael arrived, the black protestors demanded that white students leave the occupied buildings because they were not sufficiently committed to radical action.

The white students took over the office of Columbia President Grayson Kirk, scattering books and papers and smashing bathroom fixtures. Kirk, hoping to avoid an escalation of the violence, evacuated quietly and kept the police away.

Liberal New York mayor John Lindsay stepped in and persuaded

Columbia to stop construction on the gym, hoping that would quell the protests. Ninety of Columbia's 125 faculty members passed a resolution demanding an end to the Morningside Heights project and said they would strike if the students would leave the occupied buildings.

While Columbia students succeeded in scaring the bejesus out of America, the overall national strike fell short of the organizers' expectations. Response was strongest at the eastern schools, while the rest of the country was lukewarm at best. Most students were more concerned with their own lives than in making a statement on race or the war. Temple decided to strike on Wednesday because exams were scheduled for Friday. At the four major colleges in Chicago, classes were held on Friday pretty much as usual. At Yale, just 32 students marched to the induction center. At the University of Illinois, just 200 of the 11,000 students attended a rally. At the normally radical University of California at Berkeley only 1,500 of the 28,000 students protested, and at Rutgers there were just 40 protestors. The best turnout was 5,000 at San Francisco State, but that was mainly because the protest was followed by a Miles Davis concert. Even at Columbia, only about a thousand of the 28,500 students were involved, and many Columbia students protested the protestors. At Wayne State, a Viet Cong flag was hoisted to the top of a flagpole, but firemen quickly took it down and anti-protestors burned it. An American flag was raised in its place.

In some cases, the failure to act was a blessing. A group at the University of Pennsylvania called Ameri-Cong had announced plans to burn a dog with napalm in order to demonstrate its horrific effects. On strike day, several veterinary students and members of the Women's Society for the Prevention of Cruelty to Animals showed up and Ameri-Cong, assuming their intentions were serious, wisely decided not to napalm the dog.

Although high school students had been urged to strike, their response was limited. At the tony Choate School in Connecticut, 100 of 560 students attended a vigil. Three hundred pickets marching at Stuyvesant High School were attacked by counter demonstrators.

There was some activity in foreign cities, including Paris, where students flew the Viet Cong flag from the Eiffel Tower, the Arch de Triomphe, and Notre Dame. There was a sit-in in Rome and a modest protest in Tokyo.

All in all, strike day was a mixed bag. The very radical students, like the group at Columbia who seized buildings, got the headlines. But the protestors represented a rather small percentage of the overall student population. Two years later, as the war in Vietnam still raged and students became more radicalized, a strike ended the school year at many colleges. But in 1968 student revolt was a relatively new concept, and the national strike was somewhat of a dud.

Other sources:
Wichita Falls Times, April 26, 1968
Philadelphia Daily Pennsylvanian, April 26, 1968
Bennington Banner, April 27, 1968
Nashua Telegraph, April 25, 1968
Chicago Tribune, April 27, 1968

Wesleyan Thinks Things Over
Hartford Courant, **April 26, 1968**

On April 25, 1968, there were no classes at Middletown, Connecticut's Wesleyan University. There were no athletic practices and virtually everything that would generally take place on a mid-weekday in the middle of a semester was cancelled so that students could participate in a "Day of Concern."

At noon, Wesleyan president Edwin Etherington, former president of the American Stock Exchange, addressed a group of students and faculty to communicate his vision for the Day of Concern. It was, Etherington said, "an unprecedented day during which we are examining ... the role of a university at a time when society is or ought to be conscience-stricken." He said that if the "men and women in our universities, busy at their work preserving, disseminating and advancing knowledge, fail to concern themselves with matters of conscience, mankind is surely confronted with dismal and unacceptable prospects."

There were about 1,300 students enrolled in Wesleyan, and an estimated 300 took part in at least one event during the day. Etherington, Professor David Swift (chairman of the Day of Concern committee) and Academic Vice President Robert Rosenbaum were among those who fasted. Apparently the remaining 1,000 students were not conscience-stricken, as many played football and a few fraternity boys took advantage of their day off to make some home improvements.

The committee planned a number of events, including speeches, panel discussions, movies, and a presentation of theatrical satire. One of the more interesting discussions concerned the underground press, and was led by 1967 Wesleyan graduate Arthur Gingrande, who worked for a Boston paper called *Le Chronic*. A number of underground papers had sprung up, and Gingrande talked about topics like financing (getting "bread" he called it), the advantage of steering clear of profanity, and how to relate to mainstream readers.

On April 26, the students went back to class, Etherington had a meal, and Gingrande went back to Boston. Campus life went back to normal, and many students became more concerned with day-to-day issues like classes and exams than with world peace. After graduation, some of them cut their hair, shaved their beards, and went to work on Wall Street. But there are also a number of Wesleyan graduates who have pursued liberal causes throughout their lives, and perhaps they were infused by the spirit of the Day of Caring.

Arthur Gingrande, the underground journalist, went to law school and wound up concentrating in IT and intellectual property law. As of 2018, he was "of counsel" to a law firm that specialized in personal injury and insurance claims. There's a lot of bread to be made in those fields.

The Negro Student at an Integrated College: His Problems, Attitudes and Goals

New York Times, June 3, 1968

By 1968, the sight of a black student on a formerly white campus was no longer a novelty. With African American students becoming more numerous, the *Times* sent a reporter to investigate conditions at seven eastern colleges where blacks comprised approximately 5 percent of the student body. Perhaps the most surprising thing they learned was that the old goal of integration had in many cases been replaced by a black militancy that wanted to segregate the races.

"White America has no compassion," read a statement from the Vassar Students African American Society, "love, or peaceful notions in its heart for suffering blacks. It has plainly demonstrated that the only tactics that can move its violent heart are those of violence.... Force only responds to force and power to power. Pretty soon this nation will be shuddering in a paroxysm of black power."

Blacks at several colleges wanted segregated housing, which alienated many white liberals who had fought for integration. When Northwestern University promised segregated dormitories for blacks, the Federal Government informed them that they had violated the 1964 Civil Rights Act, which prohibited housing discrimination based on race. When Cornell announced plans to form a black women's cooperative, they were threatened with a suit by the New York Civil Liberties Union. The concept of segregation was baffling to liberals, who saw blacks doing what Hoss Manucy had wanted to do in 1964 in St. Augustine (see Chapter 4).

The few black students in the late 1950s and early 1960s had attempted to imitate white culture in their dress and habits, but now that blacks were more numerous, they wanted to maintain their own culture. The more radical (who were extensively covered by the media, since they made for a better story) wanted nothing to do with the white world, including courses geared to whites, white foods, or white people.

10. From Panty Raids to Anti-War Protests

"After I'd been here for a while," said a Yale senior, "I realized that the whites here were much more ignorant than I ever could have believed." Cornell junior Charisse Cannady had a white roommate who helped her with French essays, but once her French class ended, she wanted nothing more to do with her. "The only whites I can have a meaningful relationship with," she said, "are those who have something I can use." "I never really understood whites until I came here," added a Yale freshman. "You have to live with them to hate them."

That kind of attitude was not what whites who'd fought for integration had in mind, and they were upset. They thought that after suffering from discriminatory treatment all their lives, blacks had come to expect it, and saw it even when it wasn't there. A black student said that during his first day at Yale, three whites asked him what room he was looking for. He assumed they were hoping he wouldn't be their roommate. "Or else you get the great big grin," he said, "and smile—'Nice to see you'—and you know that it's not nice to see you at all." And you know that the white youngster who greeted him with a friendly grin and a smile wasn't happy to be called a racist.

Less than a year after the *Times* article appeared, Charisse Cannady found herself smack in the middle of the Cornell riots of 1969. She was the head resident at Wari House, a black woman's cooperative, and at 3:00 a.m. on April 19, Cannady heard a brick come flying through her window. When she saw a burning cross on her porch, she called the police.

The police had a lot to do that day. False alarms were being pulled repeatedly, and when they responded to Cannady's call they were skeptical. She became upset when she thought they left without much of an investigation, but their preliminary observations, including the structure of the cross and the way it had been ignited, led the police to believe that the burning cross had been an inside job, placed there by black radicals.

The reason for the false alarms and chaos was that the Afro-American Society, with the backing of the SDS, was planning to take over Willard Straight Hall and wanted to create a diversion. The students stormed into the hall in the middle of the night, rousing and evicting parents who were sleeping there for Parents' Weekend. After a 35-hour occupation, AAS leaders emerged from the building carrying rifles with ammunition slung across their shoulders. The scene was captured in photographs that outraged many Americans and scared others.

Cornell President James Perkins was more saddened than outraged. When he assumed his post in 1963 one of his main goals had been to increase the number of African Americans at the school. By 1969, black enrollment had increased from 20 to 250, but Perkins was to learn that just admitting blacks was not enough. Figuring out how to manage an integrated campus was much more difficult than he had imagined.

America had come a long way in race relations, but it was clear from what was taking place on college campuses that it had a long way to go. A system with two separate societies was unworkable, and over the succeeding decades the pendulum swung back toward the middle. There is still a long way to go, but the experiences of the late 1960s teach us how far we have come.

Other sources:
Cornell Daily Sun, May 14, 1970, and April 17, 2014
Cornell '69: Liberalism and the Crisis of the American Union, Donald A. Downs, Cornell University Press, Ithaca and London, 1999

Student Protest Flares in Europe

New York Times, **June 4, 1968**

When U.S. college students planned their nationwide strike in April, they anticipated that European students would rise in concert. That hadn't happened, but it wasn't long before the flame of revolution was burning on European campuses. The *Times* covered three protests, each reflecting the unique national culture of its students.

The British protest at Oxford consisted of 300 students demanding an end to the proctors' rule prohibiting the distribution of certain literature. Proctors were the principal enforcers of discipline at Oxford, and the circulation of political pamphlets had come to their attention when a group called the Committee of 90 led excursions to a number of factories, where they distributed flyers supporting a student uprising in Paris and expressing criticism of the British government. The proctors told the students they had broken the rules, but when they offered to forego punishment if the students admitted guilt, they learned about the new rules of student engagement. Rather than being grateful for being spared punishment, the students demanded an end to the restriction.

Led by the Committee of 90, the protestors went to Clarendon Hall (an ancient edifice designed by Christopher Wren), stood outside the iron gates that surrounded the school's administrative offices and chanted, "End Proctorial Tyranny." The proctors had their own bowler-clad police force that the students referred to as "bulldogs." The bulldogs swung the gate open in order to come out and urge the students to leave. Once the gate opened, however, the students rushed in and sat down outside the proctors' offices.

Two of the proctors, Charles Smith and Dr. Robert Gasser, came out to discuss the issue. Later that day, when the tension was abated, the proctors announced that the restriction on pamphlet distribution would be lifted. That would have been unheard of just a few years earlier, but it was a changed world at the venerable British universities. Earlier, Cambridge had announced the formation of a committee consisting of seven undergraduates and two graduates to present grievances to the administration.

Smith, speaking on behalf of the Oxford proctors, said he did not like making decisions under duress, but added that the proctors were planning to institute the changes even before the Committee of 90 had come bursting through their gates. Trevor Munroe, one of the leaders of the Committee, thought differently. He said the students had previously attempted to discuss their concerns but "the proctors respond to no other method than the organized numbers of our committee."

There were a few other student demonstrations in England, and all were conducted with proper British civility. In Edinburgh, students attempting to enter the French consulate to show their solidarity with the uprisings in France were stopped by the police, and settled for passing a note inside. There was a sit-in at the Hornsey College of Art demanding changes in the way the school operated. Unlike the students who trashed the President's office at Columbia, Hornsey students spent their time "in meetings and cleaning up the school."

Another student riot took place in Yugoslavia, a place that was a mystery to many people in the United States. The Southeastern European country, led by President Josip Broz Tito, was the sole Communist nation not aligned with either the Soviet Union or China. On color-coded political maps, Yugoslavia was the only country of its color.

The riots at Belgrade University were not polite affairs like those at Oxford. Yugoslavian students attacked the police, shouting "We want action—enough with words." Sixty were injured in two bloody encounters. One evening, a large mass of students attempting to enter a song and dance event hurled bricks and stones, set trucks and cars afire, and attacked firemen who arrived to extinguish the blaze. The next morning, 3,000 students announced a march from Old Belgrade to the capital area and demanded the resignation of the head of the city's security department.

The issues at Belgrade University were the same as those at schools in other countries: living conditions and demands that the students have a greater voice in the administration of the college. Other complaints, although similar to those in United States colleges, were unique to Communism. American students protested the limited educational access of groups like African Americans, while those in Belgrade argued that proletarians were under-represented on Yugoslavian campuses. Even though tuition was free and admission was open to all who passed the entrance exams, the cost of housing, food, and other living expenses rendered college unaffordable for many students. A greater voice in school administration, the protestors claimed, would allow for "[the] decreasing of social inequities in society and true democracy in all walks of life." Democracy, however, was not what the autocratic Tito had in mind. If there was to be equality, it would be created by his edict.

Italy was known for disorganization and anarchist tendencies, and its student riots were perhaps the most violent in Europe. Students not only fought with the police, they battled with each other, as 300 moderate students, upset at the disruption of their education, attacked extremist factions that were blocking the gates of Rome University. The two groups threw stones, burning rags, and sticks at each other before 150 police waded in and demanded that the extremist students unlock the gates. When they refused, the police cut the chains with large clippers and arrested 53 students. Nine were injured and the rest dispersed.

The police had become involved at the request of Professor Pietro d'Avack, the "Magnificent Rector" of the University. D'Avack had been remarkably patient despite months of unrest, concerned because the police had been accused of brutality in earlier incidents. His patience was finally exhausted when the students barricaded the gates and his resolve stiffened when the moderate students attacked the radicals.

The demands of the Italian radicals were familiar ones. They called for an end to examinations and grades, which they said were devices of the ruling class to determine the "suitability of the student for filling the role the class society assigns to him." That sounded a lot like the Communists in Belgrade.

The United States was not the only country with rebellious students. European youngsters were just as angry, and although each group expressed its displeasure in its own nationalistic fashion, most of the issues were similar. Eliminate tests, do away with grades, let the students manage the schools, and everyone would be happy. And free tuition would also be nice. It didn't happen then and hasn't happened yet. Grades are still with us and a degree costs more than students of the '60s could have imagined. And students continue to protest.

Teen-Age Revolt: Is It Deeper Today Than in Past Generations?

New York Times, October 7, 1968

Rebellious teenagers are nothing new. In the early years of the 20th century, teens were just beginning to be considered a separate class, for prior to that, youngsters had been miniature adults. They went to work at very young ages, married young, and by the time they were out of their teens often had families and adult responsibilities. When youngsters began attending school longer, they had more free time and less responsibility. No longer just extensions of their parents, they began to forge their own identities.

In the 1920s, youngsters began to create their own dances and forms of music and started dressing a little differently than their parents. By the 1940s, sexual attitudes were beginning to open up just a bit, and with many fathers away at war, teens had greater independence and less supervision.

In the 1950s, with the proliferation of new forms of communication, particularly television, young people became exposed to life beyond their neighborhoods, and one result was a rise in behavior known as "juvenile delinquency." During the '50s many adults thought juvenile delinquency was a major threat to society, but by the '60s rebellion took on a different tone.

Teenagers of the '60s seemed more aggressive and assertive than their predecessors and the issue was not just individual lifestyle; many youngsters wanted the entire world to change. Perhaps it was the level of creature comforts that the World War II generation had been able to give their children. Maslow's well-known hierarchy of needs states that once basic material wants are satisfied, humans strive for self-actualization. With homes in the suburbs, two cars in the garage, and college on the horizon, many middle-class youths were looking for something more than just material goods. Parents wanted their children to have better lives than they did, but many teenaged students complained that their parents put too much pressure on them to become materially successful. There was more to life, they believed, than money.

The *Times* opened its article with brief stories of two teens, one a male who smoked marijuana on the weekends and sold pot to his friends to finance a trip to India to meet "God, a guru or just a really good man."

A girl the *Times* identified by the pseudonym Joan McWilliams was more interested in sex than drugs. She was a junior at a Manhattan private school who had had three affairs during the past four months, trysts she referred to as "marriage tryouts." She said the experience was helping her grow up and prepare for marriage. "Joan" gave two reasons for her actions. The first was that "Life's too short to wait for anything as important as sex," and the second was the availability of birth control. She said her parents didn't know what she was doing and would disapprove if they did.

Sociologist Harry Silverstein said that there had been a gradual shift in attitudes toward sex but that, until recently, behavior had not caught up with attitudes; sex was something teens thought about but did not practice more often than their parents' generation. By 1968, he believed that teens were practicing what they preached.

Dr. William Lewit, professor of pediatrics and Psychiatry at the Albert Einstein College of Medicine, said that puberty had been accelerated a year or two, which was causing teens to become more sexually active. In addition, he thought parents pushed their children to mature sooner, sending them to boy-girl parties at 11, where they danced and held hands. Another scholar believed that since people were marrying later, they didn't want to wait for marriage to experiment with sex.

Teenagers appeared less concerned with consequences than previous generations. The headmaster of New York's Dalton School, an upper class preparatory institution, said, "In my generation, most of the kids couldn't afford to go to jail, and if they got thrown out of school it was a disaster. Education was their way out of poverty."

Poverty wasn't looming in the future of most Dalton students, and their headmaster thought they were less respectful of laws and rules than their elders had been. "They think they can cheat on tests, steal from one another's lockers and exploit each other emotionally," he said, "as long as they have the right opinions about the war or civil rights or something else. That is not morality."

He also saw a marked generational divide, recalling that he and his peers might have been anti–Fascist, anti–Communist, or perhaps Communist, but "we didn't make sharp distinctions between ourselves and our elders. We did not feel, as today's activists do, that we had made some new discoveries in morality or that we had a copyright on virtue."

A sociologist from the New School commented on what was generally referred to as the "generation gap." "The more rapidly a society is changing," he said, "the more it will be true that parents and children will have been raised in different and, in increasing respects, uncompatible (sic) realities."

One of the different realities was the commonplace use of marijuana among the young. Although marijuana use was illegal, most students saw it as no worse than underage drinking. Previous generations had been scared about trying drugs, but this one was not. A New York student newspaper survey indicated that 35 percent of students had used marijuana at least once. Principals and administrators thought drug use was much less than reported, and they may have been right. Some conservative students who wanted to appear cool didn't want to admit they hadn't tried pot.

That was certainly true when sex was the subject. While the common notion was that teens were having promiscuous sex at the drop of a hat, a student at Lincoln High School who was asked to produce an essay titled, "Movies I'd Like to Make," wrote about the difficulty of making a movie about sex. "The guys I know can't even talk to girls," he said, "much less have sexual relationships with girls…. Don't believe everything you hear."

Regardless of what they were actually doing, teens wanted to rebel against their elders and assert their independence. Some, however, were revolting in a very orderly way. Seventeen-year-old Howie Swerdloff, a student at John Browne High School in Queens, was leading a movement to form a union for students. Swerdloff collaborated with two females at the

10. From Panty Raids to Anti-War Protests

High School of Music and Art to organize a conference at the Ethical Culture Society that was attended by more than 200 students.

The students made several demands: "An end to all military assemblies; abolition of dress codes and haircut regulations; hiring of more Negro and Puerto Rican teachers; placement of draft resistance guides in school libraries; student-run assemblies on political topics chosen by the students; free distribution of birth control literature and devices, and; publication of the first names of all teachers so students will not have to address them as Mr. or Miss." Who did they think they were, priests? (See Chapter 4.)

That was a lot of demands and other than perhaps one or two, they were likely to be non-starters with the administration. While schools might agree to end military assemblies, it was hard to imagine that teachers and parents would be enthusiastic about passing out free birth control devices to teenaged students. Of course, if our erstwhile movie maker was correct, the availability of birth control devices was a matter of wishful thinking. Swerdloff admitted that most of the demands would be rejected, but told the reporter his biggest concern was that the main goal of education seemed to be forcing students to conform.

More than 40 years later, Swerdloff reflected on the student experience of the 1960s. "The way they dealt with us," he said in 2011, "was they repressed us. So of course that just encouraged us further. They were totalitarian institutions.... It was more about being young, in some ways ... than it was about anything else.... It was really a generational conflict with authority.... I was in trouble with the authorities constantly." Swerdloff said he was referred to as "Little Lenin."

Students were successful in forcing school administrators to acknowledge that they had some of the same rights as adults. Prior to that time, it was presumed that they were children subject to any rules authorities saw fit to impose. In 1965, the Supreme Court heard a case involving students in Des Moines, Iowa who wore black armbands to protest the war in Vietnam and ruled that the armbands were a form of free speech guaranteed under the constitution. In the majority opinion, Justice Abe Fortas wrote, "First Amendment rights, applied in light of the special characteristics of the school environment, are available to teachers and students. It can hardly be argued that either students or teachers shed their constitutional rights at the schoolhouse gate."

Were the teenagers of the 1960s more rebellious than any other generation of teens or was rebellion a condition inherent to youth? Dr. Lewit answered that question by explaining the development of the human mind. At about 13, he said, children shift their thinking from merely concrete to abstract, but since they are as yet unable to synthesize the real and ideal, they must develop a consistent ideology that explains everything.

"Only when young people move into their 20s," Dr. Lewit said, "do they begin to accommodate their ideologies to the way things really are. Only then are they able to accept what they could not as teenagers, that there may be two inconsistent ways of seeing something, both with claims to validity. That is an adult attitude." That may be an ideal adult attitude, but it does not seem to be one that informs the adult politicians of today.

Prosperity made the teens of the 1960s more economically secure and more interested in idealistic issues. Increasing mobility made them more independent. The big issues of their parents' generation, the Depression and World War II, caused people to pull together. The issues of the 1960s, such as civil rights and the war in Vietnam, tore people apart.

Many historians have written about youth rebellion of the '60s, and most of the emphasis has been on antiwar protests, unrest on college campuses, and the civil rights movement. The activities of younger people were not as widely publicized, but as Gael Graham wrote, "[H]igh schools were pulled into the cultural and political maelstrom," for many national issues involved issues like school desegregation, busing, and school prayer. Graham cited a study of 21 colleges and 15 high schools in 1968 and 1969 and concluded, "By the end of the 1960s, there is more trouble in American secondary schools than in American colleges." During the 1968–69 academic year, 70 percent of urban and suburban schools and 53 percent of rural schools had experienced protests.

One of the reasons for the lack of publicity for high school unrest may have been the fact that most of their protests involved situations peculiar to their individual schools, like discipline, hairstyles, curriculum, etc., rather than broader causes such as racism and the war.

Neil Phillip Buffett, in his doctoral thesis at Stony Brook University, argued that insufficient attention was paid to high school activism. He examined civil rights and environmental activism in high schools in Brooklyn and Bellport, Long Island, and drew some interesting conclusions.

In the Fall of 1969, Zoilo Torres and Paulette Samuels organized the Black and Puerto Rican Student Union (BPRSU) in Bellport, while the following year Ronald Rozsa formed an organization called Students for Environmental Quality (SEQ). Buffett claimed that SEQ was supported by the middle-class community while BPRSU was viewed as a threat. He also learned that each form of activism was determined by the race, ethnicity and background of the participants.

Buffett found that high school activists tended to focus on events in their own neighborhoods rather than national issues. Brooklyn and Bellport conservation groups dealt with ecology and development in their hometowns rather than global environmental issues. He also concluded that adolescents, with their limited life experience, tended to view issues in a vacuum, unconscious of other aspects of the problem. When they wanted to stop development for environmental reasons, they were oblivious to related issues like the economy and the availability of jobs or affordable housing. "It is these somewhat naive perspectives," Buffett wrote, "which grounded civil rights and environmental activist campaigns, and these most basic philosophies which often times led to their success."

The environment and racism were generally viewed as distinct, unrelated issues, and the current concept of environmental racism was rarely broached; there was little crossover between the civil rights and environmental groups. Students at John Dewey High School who fought waterfront developers didn't focus on racism or social justice. They were solely concerned with protecting the environment.

One issue that was not in the mainstream of the student movement was feminism. Perhaps women's issues such as career choice and adult gender roles did not directly influence high school girls, or maybe they were just consumed by issues such as race and the war.

Teenage unrest did not end with the 1960s. Adolescents who rebelled by growing long hair and beards bore children who rebelled by shaving their heads and sticking safety pins through their cheeks. Some old hippies who intended to show their tolerance by smoking pot with their children saw them turn into conservative Republicans. Teens continued to do whatever their parents didn't want them to do, because they needed, as always, to forge their own unique generational identity.

Other sources:
https://www.huffingtonpost.com/matt-wolf/10-youth-movements-that-c_b_4958409.html
https://en.wikipedia.org/wiki/Juvenile_delinquency_in_the_United_States
On the Ground: An Illustrated Anecdotal History of the Sixties Underground Press in the United States, Sean Stewart, editor, PM Press, 2011
Expressions of Student Outrage from the High School Free Press, Diane Divoky, editor, Avon Books, New York, 1968
Black, White and Green, High School Student Civil Rights and Environmental Activism in New York City and on Long Island, Doctoral Thesis of Neil Phillip Buffett, Stony Brook University, 2011

Student Protest 1969: Less Concerned with War Than with Other Issues
New York Times, **January 14, 1970**

This piece from the *Times* was not really an article; it was a summary of a study by Chicago's Urban Research Corporation of 232 United States college campuses. The company spent a year analyzing the student unrest that exploded beginning in 1968 and found some interesting facts. The highlights were as follows:

- At least 215,000 students directly participated in a protest.
- 3,652 students were arrested.
- 956 students were suspended or expelled.
- 76 percent of protests resulted in no violence or destruction of property.
- 60 percent of protests did not interrupt college routine.
- Non-negotiable demands were made in just 6 percent of protests and ultimatums in 13 percent.

The second part of the findings involved the causes supported by the protestors. Allowing for the fact that some protests were undertaken for multiple reasons, URC assigned the following causes:

Racial	59%
Student Power Issues	42%
Anti-War	25%

The study found no geographic tendencies; protests could arise in any part of the country, but it did find that protests were much more likely to occur in schools whose student bodies had "high scholastic aptitude." Thirty seven percent of the protests were at schools whose entering freshman had average SAT scores of 1156 or higher, although they comprised just 20 percent of schools.

Given the high percentage of protests that involved racial issues, it is not surprising that black students participated in protests at a level much higher than the overall percentage of black students. The authors of the study believed that the media had misrepresented black protests in three areas. They found that such actions were (i) not as violent as represented; (ii) not led by white students, and; (iii) not generally about black separatism. Photos such as those taken during the Cornell riots showing blacks holding guns had created an image the authors thought untrue. Apparently, black protestors had common cause with Spiro Agnew in claiming that the media was biased (see Chapter 9). Likewise, the media's focus on extreme radicals overemphasized their role. Most protesters were not wildly radical.

Black protests at predominately white schools involved the following demands:

10. From Panty Raids to Anti-War Protests

Demand for black studies courses	61%
More black teachers or staff	48%
More black students	47%
End to discrimination/honoring black leaders	28%
Desire for segregated facilities	13%

There was significant support of these issues from white students, who believed that change would make everyone's college experience more relevant.

The biggest concern of white protestors was "student power," which did not usually mean student control of the institution, but greater responsiveness to student input and more representation on decision-making bodies. Only 8 percent of protests demanded student control of the college; the rest just wanted their opinions to be heard and considered.

"Generally speaking," the report concluded, "protests did not achieve their stated aims." At the time of the study, 69 percent of student demands raised in their protests remained unsatisfied. Protests of greater duration and which had more violence were more likely to succeed. As the author stated, "[I]t would seem from the statistics that the radical point of view that institutions are unyielding unless threats of disruption are levied turn out to be accurate."

Although the study concluded that most demands were not met, the fact that 31 percent were represented progress. Asking for a lot and taking less is a time-honored negotiating technique, and many of the concessions involved issues that never would have been discussed without protests.

The URC study is an interesting one in that it attempted to remove bias by reporting cold facts, which often contradicted the picture presented by the media. Perhaps the most interesting finding is the one set forth in the headline: most protests did not involve the Vietnam War. That conclusion flies in the face of one of the most enduring memories of the era, but it makes eminent sense. Students are most concerned with what is occurring in their world. If they were drafted, their world would change, but until then their focus was on the campus. And in 1968 and 1969, there was a lot happening on campus.

11

It's All About Me

Part of my fascination with the 1960s and 1970s is that I experienced some of the history personally. I wasn't an actor in world or national events, but occasionally I was in the vicinity when something important was happening. During my research, I found two such incidents.

1,000 Antiwar Demonstrators Block Traffic;
6 Held in Sit-in

Hartford Courant, May 13, 1972

On May 8, 1972, in response to a North Vietnamese invasion of the South, President Richard Nixon announced that the United States would begin mining North Vietnamese harbors. He gave all foreign ships three days to leave and said the mining would continue until all U.S. POWs were released and a general cease fire was agreed to.

By 1972, the people of the United States were tired of the Vietnam War. Not even the fiercest "hawk" thought it was going to end victoriously and the best they could hope for was "peace with honor." Young men had a personal interest in the continuation of the war and in 1970, when the draft deferment for full-time students was eliminated, campus anti-war activism accelerated. It was no longer a matter of principle; it was one of self-preservation. Nobody wanted to be the last one shot while the Nixon administration tried to figure out how to end the war gracefully.

In the spring of 1970, Nixon's announcement of the expansion of the war into Cambodia precipitated a nationwide student strike. In early May, National Guardsmen killed four students and wounded nine more at Kent State University during a confrontation following the torching of an ROTC building by students.

The day after the Kent State shootings, the University of Connecticut School of Liberal Arts and Sciences made the following announcement:

11. It's All About Me

"In view of the atmosphere of fear and violence which currently permeates many university campuses in this country, it has become increasingly difficult to maintain normal academic procedures. Recognizing this, the faculty of the College of Liberal Arts and Sciences of the University of Connecticut finds it necessary to take the following steps:

"Normal academic programs may be suspended for the remainder of the semester, so that students and faculty will not be denied the opportunity to respond in a constructive way to this ominous situation, and so that they will be free to engage in non-violent activities aimed at the ending of the United States military intervention in Southeast Asia and the systematic suppression of dissent which has already led to five deaths [sic] at Kent State University."

The university senate, which held an emergency meeting for the first time in 30 years, adopted the following grading standards for the spring semester: "[I]nstructors could not in any way penalize students for absenting themselves from classes between May 5 and May 15, 1970; that, while any student who so desired could take a regularly scheduled final examination, it would be based only on course work covered before May 5, 1970; and that students who had a passing grade on May 5, 1970, could, by electing not to take a final examination, take instead a course grade of 'S.' (Satisfactory)."

Many students, whether or not they were passionate about the Vietnam War, simply went home, and the semester effectively came to an end. Two years later, when I was finishing my freshman year and the mining of the harbors was announced, there was no strike, but the UConn community rose in protest. My reasons were not personal, for I was not at risk of being drafted. The draft was conducted on a lottery system based upon birth date, and anyone with a number under 100 was liable to be called to active duty. I was eligible for the lottery held on February 3, 1972, and received the number 235, meaning I was safe.

On the evening of May 11, we marched in the streets and one of my dorm mates, who had kneeled in the road in protest, was struck by a car and suffered a broken leg. After the march, there was a mass meeting in McMahon Hall, at which plans were announced for a protest in Hartford the following day, with a bus available to transport students the 28 miles from campus.

On Friday, May 12, approximately 1,000 people marched in Hartford, spilling onto the southbound lanes of Interstate 91 and stopping traffic for approximately 20 minutes. They pulled down the American flag from in front of the Federal Building on Main Street and hoisted in its place the blue and yellow standard of the Viet Cong. A number of white crosses were driven into the lawn of the Governor's Mansion.

Several speakers addressed the crowd, including Hillary Putnam, professor of philosophy at Harvard and a member of the Progressive

Labor Party. It was time, she said, to begin the "project of revolution in the United States." "We've got one power," she said, "and that's the power of numbers. Every week until this crisis stops, we have to shut more and more of this country down."

It was heady stuff, but the day came to an end and we climbed on the buses to return to Storrs and day-to-day student life. I was on the track team, which was scheduled to compete in the Yankee Conference championship meet in Kingston, Rhode Island, the next day. Apparently, spending a day marching through the streets of Hartford was not the best way to prepare, and I did not do very well.

The Yankee Conference meet paled in importance to what was going on in the world. Just three days after we marched in Hartford, presidential candidate George Wallace was shot by Arthur Bremer during a Maryland campaign appearance. A month later, the Watergate office complex was burglarized by Republican operatives.

Most people believe that the time when they are coming of age is one of tremendous importance in the history of the world, and my generation is no exception. There was a lot going on in the late '60s and early '70s, but it was the war in Vietnam that created the most conflict. Nixon knew he had to do something before the 1972 election and in October, just weeks before Election Day, he announced that an agreement had been reached with North Vietnam.

The peace announcement took the legs out from under Democratic challenger George McGovern, whose opposition to the war was the most credible plank of his platform. I was a volunteer in the McGovern campaign, and spent Election Day in Bridgeport, Connecticut, working the phones trying to get voters to the polls. Political campaigns are notoriously disorganized and the scene on Election Day is the worst of all, but even given that qualification, the McGovern headquarters in Bridgeport was probably the most inept, chaotic operation I have ever witnessed in person. Twenty-somethings with a taste of power ranted and raged and volunteers were frantically dispatched thither and yon with little purpose.

After the polls closed, we climbed aboard the bus (politics was conducted by bus that year) and listened on the radio as state after state came in for Nixon. By the time we pulled away from the curb, the election was over. I got back to campus just in time to turn on the television and watch Sammy Davis, Jr., hug a clearly uncomfortable Nixon and call him his "main man." The perfect ending to a perfect day.

After the election, the war entered a strange stage. It was not over, but there was little fighting. Everyone wanted to avoid being drafted, for it seemed as though the Army was just biding time. Finally, in 1973, hostilities officially ceased and in 1975 the final Americans ignominiously left Saigon.

By that time, the President we had fought so hard to remove from office had removed himself by his own arrogance and blundering. The military draft effectively ended in December 1972 and in the future, anti-war activity would be based on general principles rather than self-interest.

The rally in Hartford didn't end the war, and it was probably inevitable that it would have ended anyway, for by 1972 it was opposed by even moderate politicians. But regardless of its overall importance, the march was significant to those of us who were there. We were young, inexperienced, and susceptible to radical polemic that often proved completely unworkable. Much of what we espoused in those days was arrant nonsense, which became evident when we matured and learned more about how the world works. There was no revolution, the capitalist system survived, and most of us are part of it. In the matter of ending the war, however, I think we were on target, although we may have been more influenced by group dynamics and emotion than cold logic. But we were right.

Other sources:
   http://blogs.lib.uconn.edu/archives/2015/05/04/kent-state-and-student-strike-at-uconn/
   http://law.justia.com/cases/connecticut/supreme-court/1973/165-conn-507-2.html

Watkin's Glen: "The Ultimate Bummer"

Bridgeport Post-Telegram, July 30, 1973

It wasn't all a bummer—only when it started raining. While the Watkins Glen Music Festival might not have been a weekend that an adult newspaper reporter enjoyed covering, it was an entirely different experience for a 19-year-old. There was great music, performed by The Grateful Dead, The Allman Brothers, and The Band. There was an endless supply of drugs and alcohol, and while the solidarity and bonding may not have equaled Woodstock standards, there was only one Woodstock.

The *Post-Telegram* article began, "There was no mistaking this for Woodstock. The sense of community, the 'togetherness' and 'good vibes' that four years earlier transformed a wet and hungry crowd into Woodstock Nation, never seemed to materialize in this town of farm folk and race cars."

While the quality of the Watkins Glen gathering may not have equaled Woodstock, it surpassed the iconic concert in quantity. The 600,000 people that went to Watkins Glen were far more than the estimated 400,000 at Woodstock. In 1969, the tiny town of Woodstock had been overrun and 600,000 people were a lot to handle for Watkins Glen, New York, which had a population of less than 3,000. It would be equivalent to the entire population of China, plus half of India, descending on New York City.

It was not that the small village, located in southwestern New York State, was unaccustomed to crowds; Watkins Glen International Speedway attracts large numbers of race fans all summer. But the town had never seen anything like the youthful horde that descended upon it the last week of July 1973.

I was working at the University of Connecticut that summer, painting dormitory rooms, and although I don't remember how it came about, somehow we decided to go. On Thursday about noon, I skipped out with one of my co-workers, a tall, lanky fellow who stood about 6'4" and had a beard and long straight hair, which he usually wore in a ponytail. His name was Dave but we all called him Handsome Harry, which was what our boss, who couldn't remember anyone's name, had christened him. In those days, hitchhiking was the way to get around if you didn't have a car, and that was how Handsome Harry and I got to a friend's house in Stamford, where about six of us piled into a station wagon and headed for Watkins Glen, without benefit of a GPS. None of us had ever been there before, but we had a map, and once we got close, all we had to do was follow the long line of cars.

The concert was scheduled to take place on Saturday, but it turned out to be a good idea to get there Thursday night, since by Friday, traffic was backed up for about 150 miles. Four people were killed in accidents. Logistics have never been the long suit of large concerts, from Woodstock, where everything evolved spontaneously, to Altamont, where a Hell's Angels security guard fatally stabbed a young man who attempted to charge the stage. Even the aborted concert at Powder Ridge in 1970, where there was no music due to an injunction, was a logistical nightmare. People who attend rock concerts, however, are not looking for efficiency. They want to have an "experience," and what better way to create an unforgettable experience than complete chaos?

Traffic wasn't nearly as bad on Thursday night; it was backed up just 20 miles. The promoters had said they would only sell 150,000 tickets (at $10 each) in order to avoid the crowds that had choked Woodstock, but the lack of a ticket didn't stop people from coming. There was precious little of the promised security and the concert was in a wide-open field with easy access. At one point, a young man told a reporter, "It's a free concert."

No music was scheduled for Friday, but when Robbie Robertson of The Band started to do a sound check, he decided that since so many people were already there, they might as well play a few numbers. The Grateful Dead followed and played two long sets.

Those who arrived early got some bonus music and those who got there late were so far from the stage they were at a different event. "It's like camping in a garbage dump and listening to a transistor radio," said one disappointed youth. Trash was everywhere except in the few receptacles and the lines to the inadequate number of porta-johns were endless.

Before the music began on Saturday, a sky diver, 35-year-old Willard Smith, jumped from a plane and descended to earth carrying lit flares. To someone sitting in the audience who had taken hallucinogens, the sight of a man dropping from the sky spewing flames must have seemed part of the trip. The crowd cheered, but up in the sky the flares had ignited Smith's clothing and he was on fire, and by the time he landed, he was a charred corpse.

I didn't find out that Smith had died until I read about it afterwards. We assumed he had landed safely and we awaited the start of the music, which commenced with the Dead, who kicked off their set with *Bertha*. The main act was on the stage, but with 600,000 people clustered in a field, there were mini-dramas everywhere. One of my lasting memories of the weekend was a group of New Yorkers (their accents gave them away) standing near us yelling loudly and repeatedly for their lost friend, who was apparently nicknamed "Psycho." I remember it because they shouted his name with the volume that only New Yorkers can muster and with the repetition that comes from the ingestion of large amounts of drugs. The mass nudity of Woodstock was missing, but there was one attractive bare-breasted girl standing nearby engaged in casual conversation with friends.

People were hawking drugs of all varieties and often passing out free samples, but many became so dehydrated by the sun that the substance they wanted most was water. The combination of sun, alcohol, and drugs caused some people to sleep through much of the concert. It was intensely hot and dry on Friday, but on Saturday water was plentiful, pouring from the sky onto the open field where 600,000 people, or at least all that were left, sat there and took it. The Band, which followed the Dead, had their set interrupted by the storm, but after the rain stopped they started up again, and then the Allman Brothers finished off the concert with a three-hour performance. Each band, especially the Dead, was known for long instrumentals, which was helpful when playing for people who expected an entire day of music from just three groups.

Butch Trucks, the drummer for the Allman Brothers Band, wasn't a big fan of the Dead. "Pretty much when we played with them," he said, "it bored me stiff. They would just mill around on stage, and half the time tried songs they didn't know. They would fall apart in the middle, quit playing and stand there and just look at the audience. But still, they'd draw these massive crowds!"

After the Allman Brothers finished their set, all three bands returned to the stage for a jam, lasting from 60 to 90 minutes, depending upon the source. "Here's the funny part," Trucks said. "I think a lot of those people came to hear the greatest jam of the three best jam bands in the country. So after we finished playing, we all came out for the jam and all I can say—I've heard the tapes—is it was an absolute disaster. I kept listening and listening, then thought about that night. It was a jam that couldn't possibly have worked because of the mixture of drugs. The Band was all drunk as skunks, The Dead was all tripping and we were full of coke."

I didn't think it was that bad and neither did Rick Danko of The Band. When asked years later about the highlights of the group's existence, Danko said their three most memorable appearances were Woodstock, the Isle of Wight, and Watkins Glen.

The return portion of any trip always seems the longest, and the sojourn from Watkins Glen back to UConn was no exception. We packed up our gear, slogged through the mud, and piled into the station wagon for the long ride home—or at least part of the way home. After driving for a while, my friend Dan said, "This is as far as I can go," and pulled over to the side of the road somewhere near Binghamton. We stretched out in the wagon and tried to sleep with cars whizzing by on the highway every couple of minutes.

Harry and I thumbed back to campus from Stamford, but had a slight delay when the police chased us off the road in Meriden. One didn't bring luggage to a concert, and we basically had the clothes we'd worn all weekend, which were damp, clinging, and smelly. My feet were itching from the dampness in my shoes, and the dormitory shower felt as good as a European health spa.

When we were walking through the rain from the concert ground to the car, I was soaked and my feet were squishing in the mud. I distinctly remember thinking, "I'm never going to do this again." And I didn't. That was the last massive rock concert I attended and at this point in my life I don't expect to be going to any more. But I'm glad I did it once. It was the largest music festival in history and I was there.

I've been in the banking and finance business for several decades. A few years ago, I was at a business social event with a female banking executive who is about my age. We got to talking and found that we were both at the Watkins Glen concert in 1973. I looked at the woman and tried to picture her as a teenager at a rock concert, and I was able to do it. She is energetic and bubbly, and when I visualized long, straight hair in place of the short-styled look she wore in the 21st century, I could see the young girl she had been forty years earlier. She was probably going through the same exercise with me, and I wonder if she was able to reach the same conclusion, or if she couldn't get past the gray-haired, sixty-year-old financier she saw in front of her. Casey Stengel once said to a young player who was astonished to learn that he had actually played baseball, "I wasn't born old, you know." None of us were.

Other sources:
http://www.glenphotos.com/summerjam/
https://en.wikipedia.org/wiki/Summer_Jam_at_Watkins_Glen
https://www.theguardian.com/theguardian/from-the-archive-blog/2013/jul/26/summer-jam-woodstock-music-rock
https://www.forbes.com/sites/jimclash/2016/04/06/butch-trucks-on-watkins-glen-the-band-was-drunk-dead-tripping-and-allman-brothers-band-coked-out/#68b0b2111c78

Bibliography

Newspapers

Abilene Reporter News
Alamogordo Daily News
Albuquerque Journal
Altoona Mirror
Amarillo Globe Times
Ames Daily Tribune
Anderson Herald
The Argus
The Arizona Republic
Bakersfield Californian
Bangor Daily News
Beckley Post-Herald and Raleigh Register
Bennington Banner
Billings Gazette
Bluefield Daily Telegraph
Boone News Republican
Bradford Era
Brandon (Manitoba) Sun
Bridgeport Post-Telegram
Bridgeport Telegram
Burlington Hawk Eye
Butte Standard
Cedar Rapids Gazette
Charleston Gazette
Charlotte Herald News
Chicago Tribune
Columbia Spectator
Connellsville Daily Courier
Cornell Daily Sun
Corona Daily Independent
Cumberland News
Daily Kennebec Journal
Daily Mail
The Daily Register
Daily Review (Hayward, CA)
Danville Bee
Des Moines Register
Desert Sun
Dover Daily Reporter
Dover Times Reporter
Doylestown Intelligencer
Dunkirk Evening Observer
El Paso Herald Post
Eureka Humboldt Times
Eureka Times Standard
European Stars and Stripes
Fairbanks Daily News Miner
Fort Madison Evening Democrat
Fort Pierce News-Tribune
Fort Walton Beach Playground Daily News
Gastonia Gazette
Glens Falls Post Star
Hanover Evening Sun
Hartford Courant
The Harvard Crimson
High Point Enterprise
High Tide News
Hutchinson News
Idaho Free Press
The Independent
Independent Press Telegram
Independent Record
Ironwood Daily Globe
Kenosha News
Kingston Daily Freeman
Kittanning Simpson Leader
Las Vegas Sun
Lawrence Daily Journal-World
Lebanon Daily News
Levittown Times
Lima News
Lincoln Star
Lompoc Record
Los Angeles Times
Lowell Sun
Medicine Hat News
The Middletown Journal
Middletown Press
Monnesson Valley Independent
Nashua Telegraph

Bibliography

New York Daily News
New York Herald Tribune
New York Times
Newark Advocate
News Herald (Panama City, FL)
Oakland Tribune
Ogden Standard Examiner
Ogdensburg Journal
Orlando Sentinel
Oswego Palladium Times
Oxnard Press Courier
Pasadena Independent
Philadelphia Daily Pennsylvanian
Portland Press Herald
Press-Telegram (Long Beach, CA)
Provo Daily Herald
Racine Journal-Times
Redlands Daily Facts
Salisbury Daily Times
Salt Lake Tribune
San Antonio Light
San Rafael Daily Independent Journal
Sandusky Register
The Stanford Daily
Star-News
Syracuse Post Standard
Twin Falls Time News
Tyrone Daily Herald
Uniontown Evening Standard
Uniontown Morning Herald
Washington Post
Wichita Falls Times
Willoughby News Herald
Wisconsin State Journal

Periodicals

American Enterprise Institute
The Atlantic Harper's
Jet
Life
Neiman Reports
New Yorker
People
Playboy
Politico
Rolling Stone
Slate
Sports Illustrated
Texas Monthly
Vanity Fair
The Weekly Standard

Books

Alpert, Jane. *Growing Up Underground*, New York: William Morrow & Co., 1981.

Asinof, Eliot. *Craig & Joan: Two Lives for Peace*. New York: Dell Publishing Company, 1971.

Atkins, Gary. *Gay Seattle: Stories of Exile and Belonging*, Seattle: revised edition. University of Washington Press, 2013.

Ball, Edward. *Peninsula of Lies: A True Story of Mysterious Birth and Taboo Love*. New York, London, Toronto, Sydney: Simon & Schuster, 2004.

Buchanan, Paul B., *Radical Feminists: A Guide to an American Subculture*. Santa Barbara, Denver, and Oxford: Greenwood, 2011.

Caron, Denis, *A Century in Captivity: The Life and Trials of Prince Mortimer, a Connecticut Slave*, New Hampshire Revisiting New England Series, 2006.

Chalmers, David Marx, *Backlash: How the Ku Klux Klan Helped the Civil Rights Movement*. Lanham, Boulder, New York, Toronto, and Oxford: Rowman & Littlefield, 2003.

Cook, Kevin, *Kitty Genovese: The Murder, the Bystanders, the Crime That Changed America*. New York, and London: W.W. Norton & Co., 2014.

Cryer, Dan, *Being Alive and Having to Die: The Spiritual Odyssey of Forrest Church*. New York: St. Martin's Press, 2011.

Divoky, Diane, editor. *Expressions of Student Outrage from the High School Free Press*. New York: Avon Books, 1968.

Downs, Donald A., *Cornell '69: Liberalism and the Crisis of the American Union*. Ithaca, and London: Cornell University Press, 1999.

Hagan, Joe, *Sticky Fingers: The Life and Times of Jann Wenner and Rolling Stone*. New York: Knopf & Doubleday Publishing Group, 2017.

Harrington, Dale, *Mystery Man: William Rhodes Davis: American Nazi Agent of Influence*. Washington, D.C.: Brassey's, 1999.

Matela, Elizabeth M., *Reducing Bodies: Mass Culture and the Female Figure in Postwar America*. New York and London: Routledge, a division of Taylor and Francis, 2017.

Meyers, David, and Elise Meyers, *Central Ohio's Historic Prisons*. Charleston, SC, Chicago, Portsmouth, NH, and San Francisco, CA: Arcadia Publishing, 2009.

Moldea, Dan E., *Interference: How Organized Crime Influences Professional Football*, Open Road Media, 2014.

Norwood, Stephen, editor. *New York Sports: Glamour and Grit in the Empire City.* Fayetteville: University of Arkansas Press, 2018.

Post, Steve. *Playing in the FM Band.* New York: Viking Press, 1974.

Ryczek, William, *The Amazin' Mets, 1962–1969,* Jefferson, NC: McFarland, 2006.

Simmons, Sylvie, *I'm Your Man: The Life of Leonard Cohen.* New York: HarperCollins, 2012.

Stewart, Sean, editor. *On the Ground: An Illustrated Anecdotal History of the Sixties Underground Press in the United States.* PM Press, 2011.

Articles

Graham, Gael. "Flaunting the Freak Flag: Karr v. Schmidt and the Great Hair Debate in American High Schools, 1965–1975." *Journal of American History,* 91 (September 2004).

Kirillova, Liana. "When Affirmative Action Is White: Italian-Americans in the City University of New York, 1976–Present." Southern Illinois University at Carbondale, 2016.

Websites

abm-enterprises.net
afflictor.com
airandspace.si.edu
alanfreed.com
alliancetoendhunger.org
althouse3.blogspot.com
america14ofthe3.com
americamagazine.com
americanheritage.com
aparchive.com
archive.boston.com
artsy.net
atlasobscura.com
awo.com
bahamianology.com
barnardarchives.wordpress.com
billkilleen.blogspot.com
biography.com
blackpast.org
blogs.lib.uconn.edu
bls.gov
books.google.com
brittanica.com
broadway.showtickets.com
caselaw.findlaw.com
cat-and-dragon.com
catholicculture.org
christianitytoday.com
cia.gov
civilwarhome.com
commons.trincoll.edu
conspiracy-café.com
content.ucpress.edu
ctstatelibrary.org
dennis-kane.com
dewey.library.unr.edu
divorceseekersfiles.wordpress.com
doctor.webmd.com
ecssba.rutgers.edu
ed.psu.edu
einstein.yu.edu
encyclopedia.com
encyclopediaofarkansas.net
ep.tc
episcopalchurch.org
ers.usda.gov
fbi.gov
feedingamerica.org
feministvoices.com
forbes.com
fosters.com
futurechurch.org
glenphotos.com
gloriasteinem.com
golfchannel.com
gracedobush.com
heraldscotland.com
hhof.com/LegendsofHockey
history.com
historynewsnetwork.org
homohistory.com
huffingtonpost.com
imdb.com
inflation.edu
instagram.com
itsgila.com
jananddean-janberry.com
jfk.hood.com
journalism.cc.stonybrook.edu
jtonzelli.com
law.justicia.com
leagle.com
legacy.com
leonardcohenfiles.com
Linkedin.com.
maryellenmark.com
mausoleums.com
mentalfloss.com
michaeljbrodyjr.org
millercenter.org
mitpress.mit.edu
niddk.nih.gov

now.org
obesitytimebomb.blogspot.com
ojjdp.gov
oleoheir.com
pbs.org
people.com
prabook.com
psychology.ucdavis.edu
qc.cuny.edu
queensofvintage.com
revolvy.com
ripopmusic.com
rogerebert.com
sammelville.org
scandanaviantraveler.com
senate.gov
singlemotherguide.com
skyjackeroftheday.tumblr.com
snopes.com
sports.vice.com
statista.com
telegraph.com.uk
texashideout.tripod.com
theatlantic.com
theguardian.com
themobmuseum.org
thespeaker.com
thestar.com
thevietnamwar.info
thisdayinnavigation.com
thoughtco.com
time.com
touchstonemag.com
trivisoma.com
ttttontheweb.com
ugly.org
units.miamioh.edu

vanityfair.com
virginiamemory.com
warhol.org
washingtonpost.com
wbai.org
web.archive.org
wikipedia.com
yale64.org
yesteryeargallery.wordpress.com
youtube.com

Other

Black, White and Green, High School Student Civil Rights and Environmental Activism in New York City and on Long Island, Doctoral Thesis of Neil Phillip Buffett, Stony Brook University, 2011.

Cato's Letter, published by the Cato Institute, Washington, D.C.

Exit Interview with Theodore Lockwood (digitalrepository.trincoll.edu).

Father Divine, A study in Charisma—a film by Leo Levy.

The FBI, COINTELPRO-WHITE HATE and the Ku Klux Klan in Florida 1964–1971.

Federal Reserve Economic Data.

Interview with Hoss Manucy by Edward Kallal, Jr., February 21, 1976.

National Directory of Registered Tax Return Preparers and Professionals.

Observation Post.

Records and Briefs, New York State Appellate Division.

Trinity College Handbook 1968–69.

Washington Court House Record.

Index

Adams, John Quincy 39
Agnew, Spiro 12, 184, 233, 243-46, 251-55, 280
Ainsworth, Macie Marie 36
Alabama College 175
Albee, Edward 263
Allen, Woody 214
Allman Brothers 285, 287-88
Almazan, Juan Andreu 49
Alpert, Jane 99-106
Alpert, John 99
Alves, Jane 90
Amayo, Mario 206
American Motors 58
Amsler, Joe 198-201
Anastasia, Albert 43
Anderson, Vanita 226-27
Anthony, Raymond 212-13
Arnall, James 60
Arnold, Henry (Hap) 50
Arnold, Martin 120-22
Arnold, Tom 230
Aronson, Harvey 179-80, 183
Arrick, Larry 136
Asinof, Eliot 98-99
Atkinson, Ti-Grace 158-160, 208
Atlanta Braves 170
Attica Prison 45, 104
Attleboro High School 72
Austin, Ron 154
Austin High School 74
Axthelm, Pete 220

Babson College 14
Badiali, Bernard, Jr. 95-98
Badiali, Bernard, Sr. 95, 98
Badiali, Mrs. Bernard, Sr. 98
Badiali, Craig 95-99, 243
Baez, Joan 54, 58
Bailey, Jim 58
Bales, Bruce 228
Ball, Edward 85-86, 88
Balsar, Talmadge 197
Baltimore Orioles 94
Bancroft, Anne 57

The Band 285-88
Barbieri, Jack 196
Bardot, Brigitte 168
Barkley, Alben 212
Barkley, Arthur 215-16
Barnard College 82-83, 100, 141
Barrow, Clyde 41, 64, 229-30
Barry, Jan 201
Bass, Jack 263
Bauch, Herbert 177
Bean, Betty Lou (Mrs. Alan Freed) 28
The Beatles 69-70, 72-73, 164
Beatty, Donald 194-95
Beaumont, Florence 95
Beck, Marilyn 153-54
Bedford, Gov. Gunning 196
Bednall, Ellis 191
Bednall, Harriet 191
Behr, Peter 82-84
Belgrade University 273
Bellaire, Rick 73
Bellow, Saul 149
Bender, Marilyn 129
Benjamin. Dr. Harry 84
Bennett, Tony 158-60
Bergrud, Maren 92
Berklee School of Music 72
Berkow, Ira 41, 44
Bernard Baruch College 141
Bernstein, Carl 253
Berra, Yogi 42
Bieber, Dr. Irving 118
Bingham, Alfred 225
Bingham, Hiram II 224
Bingham, Jonathan 225
Bingham, Stephen 190, 224-28
Bingham, Sylvia 225
Bitsis, Katherine 43
Blaine, Dr. Graham D., Jr. 121, 142
Blake, Robert 44
Bloom, Jonathan 10
Blusseau, Francoise 228
Bohle, Ronald 212-13
Bolin, Jeanette 202

Index

Bolin, Leslie 202
Boling, Inga 28-29
Bond, James 90, 127
Bond, Julian 226
Boynton, Thomas 212-13
Boze, Wilhelmina 36
Brandagee, Frank 224
Brando, Marlon 79
Brazee, Ronald 95
Breker, Arno 21
Bremer, Arthur 284
Brewer, Pamme 124-27
Brezhnev, Leonid 108
Bridwell, Lowell 18
Brigham Young University 59
Brock, Jimmy 69
Brody, Michael James, Jr. 106-10
Brody, Michael James III 108
Brody, Renee 106-10
Brooks, Mel 57
Brown, Craig 113
Brown, H. Rap 267
Brown, Helen Gurley 172
Brown, Sam 94
Browning, Norma Lee 38
Bruce, Lenny 80
Bruns, Herbert 143
Bryant, Farris 66
Buchanan, Pat 233, 251
Buckles, Frank 47
Buckley, William F. 12, 83
Buffett, Neil Phillip 278-79
Burton, Doris 203-4
Burton, Richard 33
Bush, George W. 39, 47, 57
Butler University 108

Cage, John 135
Cahill, John 140
Caldwell, Robert 196
Calloway, Bo 60
Cambridge University 273
Camp Pendleton 210
Campbell, Georgina 36
Cannady, Charisse 271
Cannon, Francis J., Jr. 197-98
Cantacuzene, Julia (aka Julia Dent Grant) 186
Cantacuzene, Mikhail 186
Capote, Truman 63, 138
Carewe, Marian 37
Carlson, Tucker 263
Carmichael, Stokely 251, 267
Carnegie Institute of Technology 205
Carney, Art 135
Caro, Robert 193
Caron, Dennis 218
Carpenter, Beth 71
Carter, Billy 257
Carter, Jimmy 52, 60-62, 67

Carvel, Gov. Elbert N. 197
Casals, Pablo 134
Cash, Johnny 54
Castiglione, Dr. Lawrence 65
Castro, Fidel 50, 139, 209
Cavell, Edith 19
Cerdan, Marcel 20
Chalmers, David Marx 234
Chanfray, Richard 123
Chapman College 40
Charles, Prince 3, 52-54
Chavez, Cesar 113, 226
Cheam School 53
Chew, F.R.G. 53
Chisholm, Shirley 188
Choate School 268
Christie, Agatha 85
Church, Frank Forrester 132-34
Churchill, Winston 2, 251
Civil War 16-19, 47, 196
Claridge, John 89
Clark, Dick 23, 27-28
Clark, Ramsey 228
Cleaver, Eldridge 252
Clein, Haiman 71
Clinton, Anson (Buzz) 71
Clinton, Bill 57, 236
Cluchette, John 226
Cocker, Joe 54
Cocteau, Jean 19-21
Cohen, Leonard 3, 54-56, 63
Cole, Edward 60
Cole, William 71
Collins, Judy 54-55
Columbia University 64, 82-83, 91, 100-1, 141, 183, 264, 266-68, 273
Como, Perry 123
Connecticut Bank and Trust 44
Connecticut College 187
Consumnes River Junior College 113
Cook, Barbara 185
Cook, Donald 210-11
Cooper, Dr. Charlotte 81
Cooper, D.B. 216
Copper, Jack 85, 86, 88
Corey, Matthew 177-78
Corman, Roger 127
Cornell University 270, 271, 280
Coronado High School 73-74
Corrigan, John 194-95
Craig, Phyllis 130-31
Cranbrook School 58
Crane, Gail 256
Cravenne, Daniele 214
Cravenne, Georges 214
Crawford, Jim 13
Crawford, Joan 172
Crawford, Joseph 212-13
Cronkite, Walter 110
Crosby, Bing 199

Index

Cross, Richard 145
Crown Hotel 53–54
Crump, Pleasant Riggs 19
Cunning, Daniel 23
Cunningham, Hugh 126
Curtis, Charlotte 150
Cushing, Betsey 40
Custin, Mildred 129, 130

Dale, Marian 151–52
Daley, Thomas 97
Dalfo, Michael 220
Dalida (aka Yolanda Cristina Gigliotti) 123–24
Dalton School 276
Daniel, Price 17
Danko, Rick 288
Daughters of Bilitis 119
d'Avack, Pietro 274
Davidson, Sara 159
Davies, Mr. and Mrs. Edward 59
Davis, James Rhodes 49
Davis, L.O. 66–67
Davis, Miles 268
Davis, Sammy, Jr. 79, 284
Davis, Stringer 85
Dawson, John 151–53
Dawson, Sissy 151–53
DeLena, Diane (aka Diana Falco) 219–220
Demmerle, George 102–3
Dempsey, John 180
Deneuve, Catherine 168
Denson-Gerber, Dr. Judianne 139–140
Depres, Christopher 71
Depres, Mark 71
Dern, Bruce 128
Diem, Ngo Dinh 242
Dillinger, John 64
Disney, Walt 137
Divine, Father 30–32, 41
Divine, Mother (Penninah) 31–32
DiVivo, John 214
Donnelly, Antoinette 174
Douglas, William O. 74, 133
Downey, Capt. Francis G. 256
Drackert, Harry 149, 151
Drackert, Joan 149–51
Drake, Vicki (aka Victoria Bowles) 131–34
Drumgo, Fleeta 226
DuBay, William 75–78, 90, 111–12
Dubois, Robert 109
Duke, David 80
Duke University 101
Duncan, Don 231
Dunn, Gov. Winfield 231–32
Durocher, Leo 67
Durston, Edward 137–38
Dutto, Monique 129
Duvalier, Papa Doc 50
Dylan, Bob 54, 63, 108

Earhart, Amelia 184
Ebert, Roger 127
Edelman, Marsha 182–83
Eden, Margo 207–8
Edward VII, King 86
Edwards, Bonita 36
Edwards, Marcelle 35–37
Egan, John 141
Eisenhower, David 59
Eisenhower, Dwight 235, 242, 246, 248, 250, 264
Eisenhower, Julie Nixon 59
Eliot, T.S. 164–65
Ellis, Michael 136
Ellis, Roger 245–46
Elmore, Richard 145
Emerson, Faye 50
Emory University 175–76
Enright, Dan 110
Erdlen, Christiana 38
Etherington, Edwin 269
Eudy, Dave 230
Evans, Monica 135–36

Falco, Leslie 220
Farrakhan, Louis 84
Faubus, Orval 233
Felix V, Pope 112
Fernald, Louanne 126
Field, Mrs. Marshall, Jr. 149
Finberg, Bonnie 131
Fiske, Edward 91
Fleetwood, Harvey II 140
Floyd, Charles (Pretty Boy) 41, 43
Floyd, Harry 261
Flynn, Errol 119
Fonda, Henry 169
Fonda, Jane 2, 168–70, 226
Fonda, Peter 128–29, 168–69
Ford, the Rev. Arthur A. 92–93
Ford, Gerald 62, 245, 254
Forde, George A. 201
Foreron, Virginia 97
Forest Hills High School 99
Forsythe, Max 89
Fort Bragg 144–46
Fortas, Abe 277
Fox, Joan 95–99, 243
Fox, Margalit 172
Francis, Collette 37
Francis, Connie 26
Francis, Pope 112
Frankel, Max 240
Frazier, Leonard 180
Freed, Alan 23–29
Freed, Marjorie 28
Freidan, Betty 158, 185, 187–88
Freidman, Jerry 81
French, Marc 89–90
French, Valerie 136

Index

Funkie, Lewis 136
Furrer, Albert 46–47

Gabor, Eva 34
Gabor, Magda 33–34
Gabor, Zsa Zsa 33, 38
Galbraith, John Kenneth 133
Garland, Judy 118
Garner, James 44
Gasser, Dr. Robert 272
Gaston, Patricia 36
Gehr, Richard 54
Gerard, Tom 254
Gernreich, Rudy 119
Giamo, Robert 225
Giancana, Sam 200
Gibran, Kahlil 164
Giery, Betty Jane 192–93
Giery, Thomas 192–93
Gilligan, Gov. John J. 217
Gingrande, Arthur 269–70
Ginsburg, Allen 121, 226
Giorno, John 205
Glassboro State College 95, 96, 98
Glenesk, the Rev. William 164
Goldenson, Leonard 252
Golder, Arthur 192
Goldin, Selig 125
Goldman, Susan 81
Goldstein, Marilyn 182
Goldwater, Barry 234–37
Goodman, Julian 253
Gordonstoun 53
Graham, Billy 30, 90, 108
Graham, Gael 278
Granier, Josta 177
Grant, Frederick Dent 186
Grant, Ulysses 186
Grant, Ulysses III 17
Grateful Dead 285–88
Gray, Linda 57
Green, David 53
Gregory, Dick 79
Griffin, W.J. 233, 234
Griswold, Mary 180
Gwinn, William 264

Haas, Debbie 154
Hacket, Jeff 249
Haertel, Tom 219
Halberstam, David 250
Haley, Bill 26
Hall, Gordon Langley (aka Dawn Simmons) 84–89
Halvonik, Paul 161
Hamilton, Floyd 229
Hamilton, Roy 229
Hard, James Albert 19
Hardin, Louis (Moondog) 25
Harnwell, Gaylord 267

Harper's Bizarre 210
Harr, Karl Erik 185
Harriman, Averill 102
Harris, David 58
Harvard College 39, 263, 283
Harvard Law School 197
Harvey, Mason 77
Hawk, David 94
Hay, Harry 119
Hayak, F.A. 5, 8
Hayden, Tom 2, 169–70, 226
Hayes, Dennis 132–33
Hayes, Isaac 231
Hayling, Dr. Robert 68
Heller, Walter 237
Helms, Jesse 79
Hendricks, Agnieta 196
Hendrix, Bill 233
Hendrix, Jimi 1
Hepburn, Audrey 119
Herbers, John 66
Hickerson, John 30
Highland Regional High School 95, 97, 99
Hill House School 53
Hilton, Paris 34
Hitler, Adolf 2, 67, 251
Hodges, Jim 263
Hoffman, Abbie 1, 102
Hoffman, Dustin 3, 52, 56–57, 205
Hoffman, Susan (aka Viva) 205
Hood, John 17
Hoover, J. Edgar 263
Hope, Bob 199, 253, 254
Hope, Tony 199
Hopper, Dennis 128
Hornsby, Leslie (Twiggy) 81, 89
Hornsey College of Art 273
Houston, Hoyt 230
Houston, Mary 230
Huber, Florence 34–35
Hudson, LaSaunders 231–32
Hughes, Fred 206
Hughes, Harold 146
Hughey, John D. 101, 103–6
Hughey, Dr. John David 101
Humphrey, Hubert 89, 102, 244, 251
Hunt, Florence B. 131
Hunt, John 32
Hunter, Ian 90
Hunter College 120, 122
Hupe, Dale 215–16
Hutton, Barbara 22, 139
Hynes, John 26

Irwin, John 198, 200–1

Jackson, Don 143–44
Jackson, George 226–28
Jackson, James 69
Jackson, Robert Lee 221–24

Index 299

Jackson State College 78
Jacobs, Albert C. 264–65
Jacobson, Marcus 196
Jagger, Mick 55, 154
Jelke, John J. 106
Joel, Billy 54
John Brown High School 276
John Dewey High School 279
Johns, H.W. 34
Johns Hopkins University 85, 87
Johnson, Claudia (Lady Bird) 84, 86
Johnson, Evelyn 156
Johnson, Lyndon 1, 3, 17, 19, 79, 193, 235–42, 246–48, 250
Jones, Edwin 59
Jones, James Earl 30
Jones, Jim 29, 30, 32
Jones, Terry 265
Jorgenson, Christine 84–85
Joyce, Joseph 72
Julliard School of Music 120, 134

Kallal, Edward, Jr. 67
Karr, Chesley 73–74
Katz, Herman 158–60
Katzenbach, Nicholas 79
Kay, Sibylla 136
Kearon, Pam 159–60
Keenan, Barry 198–201
Keister, Douglas 34
Kelly, George (Machine Gun) 41
Kelly, Grace 172
Kelly, Joseph W. 212
Kelmesbud, Judy 184
Kennedy, Diane (Mrs. James A. Pike) 92–93
Kennedy, Ethel 153
Kennedy, Jackie 84, 86, 119, 184, 205
Kennedy, John F. 119, 225, 234, 237–38, 242, 246, 248, 250
Kennedy, Joseph P. II 40
Kennedy, Joseph P., Sr. 39
Kennedy, Robert 153, 200, 225
Kent State University 262, 282
Keppell, Alice 86
Kerouac, Jack 63
Kight, Morris 143–44
Kilhefner, Don 144
Killeen, Bill 124, 126–27
King, Martin Luther, Jr. 30, 67–68, 79, 91, 262
Kingswood School 58
Kirk, Grayson 267
Kirkland, Sally 136
Kissinger, Henry 248
Kling, Thomas 44
Knudson, Semon E. 59
Kores, Beatrice 70
Kores, Edward, Jr. 69–72, 110
Kores, Edward, Sr. 70
Kores, Jeanne 70
Kosen, Sultan 90

Kratovich, Mary 194–95
Ku Klux Klan 60, 66–69, 79–80, 233–34
Kubrick, Stanley 133
Kuhn, Bowie 94
Kuznicki, Jason 5

Labriola, Kathy 162
Laird, Melvin 250
Landers, Ann 146–47, 174, 189
Lane, Lord Geoffrey Dawson 191
Lansky, Meyer 48
Lawford, Peter 153
Leary, Timothy 76, 138
LeClair, Linda 82–84
Leibowitz, Dr. Barbara 182–83
Leonard, George 72–73, 110
Leonard, Judy 73
Leonard, Robert Z. 22
Lepera, Patsy 49
Lewit, Dr. William 275, 277–78
Lincoln, Mary Todd 84
Lincoln High School 276
Linda and the Loveletters 71
Lindsay, John 94, 158, 208, 267
Linkletter, Art 137–38
Linkletter, Diane 137–38
Lipson, Eden Ross 105
Little, John 145
Little Richard 25–26
Lockner, Patricia 178
Lockwood, Theodore Davidge 264–66
Lodge, Henry Cabot 240, 248
Lombardo, Josef 64–65
Longet, Claudine 153–54
Loren, Sophia 185, 211
Louderback, Lew 81
Lowenstein, Allard 225
Luther, Martin 112
Lymon, Frankie 26
Lynch, Stewart 196–98
Lynn, Neva 35–38

Mabile, John 231
MacRae, Gordon 136
MacRae, Heather 136
MacRae, Sheila 136
Maddox, Lester 60–62
Major, Capt. Fred 23
Malcolm X 164
Maleski, Rosemary 177
Malick, Jack 182
Manucy, Halstead (Hoss) 66–69, 270
Manufacturers Trust 42–43
Manville, C.B. 34
Manville, Thomas, Sr. 34
Manville, Tommy 33–38, 41, 60
Mao Tse Tung 241
Marais, Jean 21
Margaret, Princess 84, 86
Marine Midland Bank 103

Index

Marriott, J. Willard 58
Mars, Kenneth 57
Marshall, Thurman 46–47
Martinelli, Elsa 57
Marvel, William 18–19
Mastriana, Louis Pasquale 48–50
Mattachine Society 119
Matthau, Walter 135
Maudlin, Michael 90
Mayer, Jean 9–11
Mayer, John 49
Mayer, Louis B. 22
McCoin Lois 35–36
McCourt, Frank 172
McCourt, Malachi 172
McGovern, George 284
McGraw, Ali 172
McIntyre, Cardinal James Francis 75–76
McKee, "Holy Joe" 130
McLaney, Michael 48–50
McMurray, Joseph 65
McNair, Robert 262
McNally, Martin 221
McNamara, Robert 250
McReery, John 214
Mdivani, Alexei 22
Mdivani, David 22
Mdivani, Serge 22
Meekley, Phyllis 126
Melville, Herman 101
Melville, Sam (aka Samuel Grossman) 101–5
Meredith, James 78–80
Mesta, Pearl 186
Meyers, Russ 127
Miami University (Ohio) 98
Michaels, Lorne 154
Milford Academy 225
Milhouse, Anna 259
Milhouse, Phillip 259
Miller, Arthur 149
Miller, Timothy 89
Mindel, Kitty Goldman 161
Mindel, Neil 160–61
Minh, Ho Chi 2, 170, 246
Minichiello, Raffaele 210–12, 222
Miss Hewitt's School 139
Mitchell, John 133
Monie, Gen. Caceres 223–24
Monroe, Marilyn 205
Moore, James W. 17
Moorman, Charlotte 134–35
Morgan, Robin 104
Morgenstern, Joseph 116–17, 131
Morisse, Lucien 123
Morris, Bruce 181
Morris, Samuel 30
Morrow, Charles 151–53
Mortimer, Prince 218
Mott the Hoople 73
Mottola, Helen 44–45

Moyers, Bill 237
Mullally, Joseph 64–65
Mullins, Lee 231
Munroe, Trevor 273
Murphy, George 253
Murphy, Michael J. 117–18
Murray, Mae (aka Marie Adrienne Koenig) 16, 21–23
Mussolini, Benito 2

National Velvet 206
Navarre, Henri 248
Neale, J. Henry 107
Negri, Pola 22
Nelson, Lester (Baby Face) 41
New School 276
New York Islanders 219
New York Mets 94, 96
New York University 64
Newley, Anthony 153
Newman, Paul 153
Nichols, Mike 57
Nicholson, Jack 127–29
Nicklaus, Jack 255
Nitschke, Margot 10
Nixon, Donald 257
Nixon, Richard 3, 9, 107–9, 198, 216, 233–35, 240–41, 243–47, 249–51, 257–60, 282, 284
Nolan, Dave 262
Norman, Dr. Jane 182–83
Norris, Dr. Haygood 66
Northshore Junior High School 114
Northwestern University 270
Norvell, James 79
Nostradamus 5
Notre Dame University 64
Novak, Kim 178
Noyes, John Humphrey 162

Oakland Golden Seals 219
Obama, Barack 57–58
Ohio State University 24, 175
O'Horgan, Tom 130
Oliver, Arnold 70–71
Onassis, Christina 139
O'Neill, William 180
Ono, Yoko 134–35
Orange Coast College 258
Owens, Gladys Irene (Mrs. James Roosevelt, Sr.) 40
Oxford University 272–73

Palmer, Bertha 186
Palmer House 186
Parachini, Victor 47
Parker, Bonnie 41, 64, 229–30
Paskow, Larry 178
Patterson, Carolyn 156–57
Paul VI, Pope 75, 111, 241
Paxton, Tom 55

Index

Peabody, Mary 68
Peale, Dr. Norman Vincent 30
Peebles, Catherine 52
Peevler, Charles 46–47
Penn State University 98
Percy, Charles 48
Perkins, James 271
Peterson, Martha 82–83
Peterson, Gov. Russell 197
Pethokoukis, James 239
Pezzano, Harold 141–42
Phillip, Prince 52
Piaf, Edith 19–21, 118
Piel, Gerald 6–7
Pierson, Nina 37
Pike, James A. 90–93
Pike, James A., Jr. 92
Pindling, Cyril 48, 50
Pink, Sidney 57
Polgar, Thomas 222–24
Ponti, Carlo 211
Poore, Charles 56
Posess, Stanley 177
Post, Roger 219
Post, Steve 80–81
Potter, Harry 90
Powell, Adam Clayton 234
Powers, David Guy 65
Presley, Elvis 205
Provenzano, Albert 181
Purdue University North Central 213
Putnam, Hillary 283

Queens College 64–65

Rand, Ayn 100
Ray, James Earl 67
Reagan, Ronald 89, 137, 235, 238, 244
Rebozo, Charles (Bebe) 49–50
Redford, Robert 57
Reed, Lou 206
Reed, Marvin E. 145
Reich, Joe 132
Reichert, Joseph 97
Reitz, J. Wayne 126
Reston, James 86
Reynolds, Quentin 42
Richards, Renee 138
Richards, Richard 193–95
Richey, Helen 184
Riddle, Thomas 17
Rigot, Victor 46–47
Ritchings, Edna Rose 32–33
Rivera, Geraldo 109
Robertson, Robbie 286
Roche, James 59
Roche, William 142
Rock and Roll Hall of Fame 29
Rockefeller, Mary 149
Rockefeller, Nelson 121, 149, 208, 244

Rockwell, George Lincoln 251
Roddy-Eden, Anita 36
Roger Smith Hotel 173
Rogers, William 248
Rome University 274
Romero, Cesar 57
Romney, Ann (Davies) 57–60
Romney, George 58–59
Romney, Milton (Mitt) 58
Romney, Mitt 3, 52, 57–60
Roosevelt, Anna 39
Roosevelt, Eleanor 39
Roosevelt, Elliot 39, 47–50
Roosevelt, Franklin D., Jr. 39
Roosevelt, Franklin D., Sr. 39, 47, 50, 257
Roosevelt, James, Jr. 40
Roosevelt, James, Sr. 39, 40–41, 47
Roosevelt, John 39
Roosevelt, Teddy 19
Roosevelt Hotel 173
Root, Gladys Towles 201
Rosen, Ron 81
Rosenbaum, Robert 269
Rosenberg, Andrea 141–42
Rosenberg, Seymour 142
Rosencrans, Williams 68
Ross, Arthur 155–58
Ross, Barton 155, 157
Ross, Elliot 155, 157
Ross, Scott 155, 157
Ross, Wendy Levine 155–57
Rubin, Jerry 102
Rudd, Mark 104
Russell, George 60
Russian Revolution 186, 242
Rutgers University 268
Rutherford, Dame Margaret 85, 88
Ryan, Dick 44–45
Ryan, Leo 29–30

Sabich, Vladimir "Spider" 154
Sachse, Salli 128
Sackville-West, Vita 85–86
St. Laurent, Yves 129
St. Stephen the Martyr Catholic School 217
Salazar, Caroline 140
Salazar, Guillermo 139
Salazar, Isabel 139–40
Salling, John 18
Salmonson, Donald 216
Samuels, Paulette 278
San Diego State College 137
San Francisco State University 268
Sanchez, Ligia Lucrecia (Archiila) 221–24
Sanders, Carl 61
Sanders, Doug 253–54
Sanders, Dr. William 70
Sandlin, Robert Lee 211–12
Sanford, Mark 263
Santiago, Victor 140

Index

Sarah Lawrence University 81
Sark, Bank of 50
Sarvary, Irene 43
Schemalix, William 207
Schenmeker, William 46–47
Schneider, Catherine 170
Schneider, Romelle 40
Schroeder, Captain 222–23
Schuster, Arnold 43
Seaver, Tom 94
Security National Bank 203–4
Seeger, Pete 55
Seinfeld, Jerry 206
Sellers, Cleveland 262–63
Severinson, Doc 73
Sexton, Steve 95
Sharpe, Theo 20
Sheen, Bishop Fulton 90
Shelley, Joseph 66
Sheppard, Sam 195
Shriver, Sargent 237
Siegal, Stanley 138
Silverstein, Harry 275
Simmons, John Paul 85, 87–88
Simmons, Natasha 85–86, 88
Simpson, Judge Bryan 68
Simpson, Tony 114–15
Sinatra, Frank 198–201
Sinatra, Frank, Jr. 190, 198–201
Sinatra, Nancy 198
Smith, Anna Nicole 33
Smith, Charles 272
Smith, Christopher 216
Smith, Joe 26
Smith, Joel 131–32
Smith, Judge Lewis 31
Smith, Tricia 181
Smith, Willard 287
Smothers Brothers 2
Snow, Edgar 241
Solanas, Valerie 158, 206–8
South Carolina State College 261–63
Southern Virginia University 60
Spencer, Brian 218–21
Spencer, Byron 219
Spencer, Roy 218–19
Spock, Dr. Benjamin 94
Spreckels, Gretchen 225
Springer, Jerry 138
Stanford University 58–59, 131–32
Stanton, Elizabeth Cady 186
Stanton, Dr. Frank 253
Staples High School 141
Starkman, Rosalind 129
Starr, Ringo 89
Steinem, Gloria 2, 178–80, 183
Stengel, Casey 5, 32, 288
Stenson, Joseph 192
Stohrer, Carleton 255, 257
Stohrer, Glenn 255–57

Stohrer, Wesley 255–57
Stoke, Harold 65
Stoner, Jess (J.B.) 60, 67
Stonewall Bar 119, 143
Stony Brook University 179
Strand, Robert 161, 163
Strasberg, Susan 128
Strauch, Harold 110–11
Strickland, Bonnie 175–76
Stroman, John 261
Stuyvesant High School 268
Suit, Hal 61
Sukarno (Kusno Sosrodihardjo) 242
Sullivan, Ed 69, 72, 108
Sutton, Willie 3, 16, 41–45
Swanson, Gloria 22
Swarthmore College 100
Swerdloff, Howie 276–77
Swinton, Patricia 101, 105–6

Tate, Doc 41
Taylor, Avonne 35
Taylor, Elizabeth 33
The Temptations 73
Tenco, Luigi 122–24
Tenuto, Frederick 43
Termpapers Unlimited 14
Thomas, Marlo 138
Thomas, Norman 240
Ticehurst, Marjorie Hall 86
Timberlake, Kathy 257–59
Timberlake, Kerry 259
Timberlake, Dr. P.F. 258–59
Timberlake, Phillip 258
Tiny Tim (Herbert Khaury) 164
Tito, Josip Broz 273–74
Tolchin, Martin 172
Tolson, Gen. John J. 145–46
Toronto Maple Leafs 218–19
Torrance, Dean 199–201
Torres, Zoilo 278
Torrey, Dr. Jane 187–88
Tovar, Jose Alvarez 222
Tower, John 237
Trevino, Lee 253
Trinity College 263–66
Troy, Elinor 37
Trucks, Butch 287
Truitt, Alben Barkley 212
Truman, Harry 10
Trump, Donald 138, 233
Turner, Ted 2, 170
Tyler, Steven 55

Ugly (ad agency) 89–90
Ultra Violet 206
United States Naval Academy 61
University High School 198
University of California at Berkeley 58, 227, 268

Index 303

University of California at Davis 120
University of California at Irvine 40
University of Colorado 108
University of Connecticut 12, 13, 267, 282–83
University of Florence 64
University of Florida 124–26
University of Illinois 268
University of Maryland 207
University of Massachusetts 176
University of Minnesota 207
University of Mississippi 78
University of Oslo 185
University of Pennsylvania 267–68
University of South Carolina 263
University of Texas 134
University of Tromso 185
University of Wisconsin 124

Vadim, Roger 2, 168–70
Vadim, Vanessa 169
Valentino, Rudolph 22
Vanatta, Helen 194
Vanatta, John 194–95
Vancouver Canucks 219
Vandermeer, Walter 139
Van Vooren, Monique 129
Varese, Edgard 135
Vargas, Josephine 165–68
Vargas, Juan Abel, Jr. 165–68
Vargas, Juan Antonio 166
Vargas, Julie 166
Vargas, Mildred Schroeder 165–68
Vassar College 270
Verushka 89
Vesco, Robert 40
Vietnam War 1–3, 59, 94–96, 98–99, 107–9, 130, 145–46, 169, 233, 240–43, 246–47, 249–51, 255–56, 266–68, 277–78, 281–83, 285
Vishno, Vincent 70
Viva (aka Susan Hoffmann) 205–6
Voigt, Jon 57, 205
Von Anhalt, Frederic Prince 33
Vonnegut, Kurt, Jr. 133

Wachter, John 224
Wall, Mary Ellen (Mrs. William DuBay) 76–77
Wallace, George 62, 134, 284
Wallace, Henry 119
Wallas, Graham 236
Walsh, Kathleen 258–59
Walter, Barbara 97
Walters, Huron "Ted" 229–30
Ward, Burt 57
Warhol, Andy 190, 205–8
Warner, Emily 185
Warren, Kenneth 14

Warren, Ward 3, 13–15
Washington, Thomas 212–13
Wasko, Andrew 193–94
Wasko, June 193–94
Watkins Glen Music Festival 285–88
Wayne, Carol 138
Wayne, John 127
Wayne State University 268
Weber, O. John 217
Wedell, Mr. and Mrs. Frank 204
Weissmuller, Johnny 149
Weld, Tuesday 26
Wesleyan University 267, 269–70
West, Mae 130, 136
Westbrook High School 69–70
Wheeler, Gen. Earle 94
Whitaker, Patrick 131
Whitney, Isabel 85–87
Whitney, Paul K. 152
Wideroe, Turi 183–85
Wideroe, Viggo 184
Wilder, Billy 22
Wilhelm II, Kaiser 33
Wilkins, Roy 252
Will, George 263
William, Prince 54
Williams, Andy 153–54
Williams, Barbara 170
Williams, Billy 215
Williams, Joanne 203–4
Williams, Kelly 203
Williams, Rochelle 203
Williams, Roger Lee 203–4
Williams, Walter Washington 17–19
Wilson, Robert 197
Wilson, Sonia 190–91
Windsor, Claire 37
Winskill, Mary (Mrs. James Roosevelt, Sr.) 40–41
Wolfe, H.E. 66
Woodmere Academy 157
Woodruff, Rosemary 76
Woodward, Bob 253
Woolf, Virginia 86
Woolson, Albert 19
World War I 46–47, 214
World War II 39, 47, 90, 190, 278
Wren, Christopher 272
Wright, Robin 89

Yale University 224, 267–68, 271
Yanovsky, Esther 90–91
Yarrow, Peter 96
Yeshiva University 182–83
York, Richard 164, 169
Young, Neil 55

Zweger, John 137

www.ingramcontent.com/pod-product-compliance
Lightning Source LLC
Chambersburg PA
CBHW021346300426
44114CB00012B/1103